Squatter Citizen

Life in the Urban Third World

Jorge E. Hardoy and David Satterthwaite

EARTHSCAN PUBLICATIONS LTD   LONDON

First published 1989 by
Earthscan Publications Limited
3 Endsleigh Street, London WC1H 0DD

Reprinted 1995

British Library Cataloguing in Publication Data

Hardoy, Jorge E. (Jorge Enrique)
 Squatter citizen: life in the urban third world
 1. Developing countries. Social conditions
 I. Title   II. Satterthwaite, David
 909′.097240828

ISBN 1-85383-020-8

Production by David Williams Associates
Typeset by Rapid Communications, London WC1
Printed and bound in Great Britain by
Biddles Limited, Guildford and King's Lynn

Earthscan Publications Limited is an editorially independent susidiary of Kogan Page Limited and publishes in association with the International Institute for Environment and Development and the World Wide Fund for Nature.

Dr Jorge E. Hardoy is President of The Instituto Internacional de Medio Ambiente y Desarrollo (IIED-AL), Buenos Aires.

David Satterthwaite is Senior Researcher at the Human Settlements Programme of the International Institute for Environment and Development (IIED), London.

Both were advisers to *The World Commission on Environment and Development* and this book will include some of the background material presented to this Commission.

Contents

TABLES

BOXES

Preface

We have many people to thank for their help in preparing and publishing this book. We are particularly grateful to Neil Middleton and Richard Sandbrook for encouraging us to write it, and to Diana Mitlin for the care with which she read and commented on the draft manuscript. Special thanks also to Bob Buckley and Julio Davila for comments on parts of the text and to Sara Dunn, Lavinia Greenlaw and, again, Neil Middleton for making the book more readable, and Radhika Holmstrom and Kate Griffin for its promotion.

Squatter Citizen is based on various papers, articles and briefing documents that we wrote between 1983 and early 1989. The works on which each chapter is based are listed along with other sources and references (see pp. 314-51). Some have not been published, including briefing documents prepared for the World Commission on Environment and Development (the Brundtland Commission) at the request of its Secretariat. Others were commissioned by institutions who then published their own versions; where these are used (as in Chapter 8) we return to our original version as the basis for the text.

Much of this book is based on previously published work which has been much expanded and updated and many more examples have been introduced. The text has been organized in eleven relatively short sections (nine chapters, an introduction and an epilogue) so that what had previously been published as one paper may now be divided between two or more chapters.

We have tried to make the text more readable for a general audience. With the help of Earthscan's editors, "jargon" and specialist terminology have been cut to a minimum. Boxes are included in each chapter to provide more and more detailed examples. When writing on subjects as broad as "life in the urban Third World" examples are needed to illustrate points and to stress the diversity of circumstances, but too many can make a text rather heavy to read and the line of its argument difficult to follow. Since 1979, we have experimented with the use of boxes to allow the inclusion of many detailed examples without making the text too long.

In writing this book, we drew on the research and writings of dozens of friends and colleagues. Special mention should be made of the teams in India, Nigeria, the Sudan and Argentina with whom we have collaborated since 1977 as part of the International Institute for Environment and Development's (IIED) Human Settlements Programme: the Centre for Urban and Regional Research (Centro de Estudios Urbanos y Regionales) in Buenos Aires, the Lagos Group for the Study of Human Settlements, the International Institute for Development Research in Allahabad, and the Sudanese Group for Assessment of Human Settlements (University of Khartoum).

Since 1977, we have worked together on four topics. The first was "popular settlements" and the problems faced by their inhabitants. Different kinds of popular settlement were studied: some formed by squatter invasions, others by gradual illegal encroachment, others by becoming incorporated into an expanding city after first developing as rural settlements. One study also concentrated on inner-city tenements and cheap boarding houses (in Buenos Aires) while another in Khartoum looked at the development of rental housing sub-markets. In each study, researchers established contacts with community organizations and provided technical and professional advice on upgrading and legal issues relating to tenure. Most of the funding came from the International NGO Division of the Canadian International Development Agency with supplementary funds from the United Nations Centre for Human Settlements (Habitat).

The second topic for collaborative research was the links between housing and health. We examined the health problems faced by the inhabitants of selected illegal settlements and the extent to which such problems are linked to housing and environment. This research also had action aspects as the researchers worked with the inhabitants of these settlements to tackle some of their more serious health problems. This was funded by the Ministry of Housing, Physical Planning and the Environment in the Netherlands, with additional support from the World Health Organization (WHO).

The third topic was a series of national assessments in which teams visited different nations to assess housing, land and settlement policies to gauge the extent to which governments were implementing the recommendations they had officially endorsed at the United Nations Conference on Human Settlements (Habitat) in 1976.

Thirty-one national assessments were completed in three phases: the first on the larger market-oriented Third World nations, the second on small-population nations, the third on nations which had recently undergone rapid social change. This work was funded by the International NGO Division of the Canadian International Development Agency and by the United Nations Centre for Human Settlements.

The fourth topic was the present and potential role of small and intermediate sized urban centres in national, regional and rural development. Each team studied the development of urban systems within a region in their nation over 70 or more years, to provide a more detailed understanding of the forces and factors which influence the development of different urban centres. IIED staff undertook a review of existing empirical and theoretical literature on this subject. This work was funded by the Swedish Agency for Research Cooperation with Developing Countries, the Swedish Council for Building Research and the United Nations Centre for Human Settlements (Habitat).

Squatter Citizen also draws on research undertaken by IIED-America Latina, IIED's independent Latin American office in Buenos Aires. The work noted above on small and intermediate urban centres has been developed in Latin America, working with the Latin American Office of the United Nations Development Programme and the United Nations Fund for Population Activities. This has developed policy guidelines for governments and international agencies and has included a series of national- and city-level case studies. IIED-America Latina is also part of a network of institutions investigating the constraints faced by local governments in improving shelter conditions and providing basic infrastructure and services. New research programmes have also been developed on themes such as the causes and consequences of natural disasters, especially the effects on poorer groups, and the extent to which aid agencies fund projects for meeting basic needs and for supporting urban development.

There is also a larger network of individuals and research groups on whose work this book has drawn or with whom we collaborate in research, publications and the organization of seminars. These institutions and their publications can be found in "Sources and References" and in the section on "Suggested Further Reading". We believe that our effectiveness as researchers, writers and activists depends on constantly building and reinforcing a large network of people who work along complementary lines and whose collective efforts will have more impact on the policies of governments and agencies than the work of any single institution.

Special thanks are due to all those institutions who fund our work, especially Ron Leger and his colleagues at the International NGO Programme of the Canadian International Development Agency. This Programme has long recognized the need to enlarge the network of people and institutions concerned about critical human settlements issues and has long supported our efforts to reach a larger audience with such concerns.

Jorge E. Hardoy, IIED-America Latina, Buenos Aires
David Satterthwaite, IIED, London
1 May 1989

Introduction

An urbanizing world

Virtually all Third World nations are becoming increasingly urban – so much so that the United Nations suggests that 80 per cent of the growth in population in the next few decades will be urban not rural. In the last few decades, nearly all nations have experienced a rapid growth in their urban populations and now the large, sprawling conurbation with millions of inhabitants is a worldwide phenomenon. Cities of half a million or more inhabitants are found in regions which until relatively recently were sparsely populated.

Over the last 30 to 40 years, growth in many Third World cities has been so rapid that it is equivalent to an entire new city built on the periphery or over the old city every 10 to 15 years. Architecture and land use, and the choices made by governments as to which city-dwellers are awarded public jobs and basic infrastructure and services, all maintain and segregate the privileged few from the poverty of the many.

Many of the cities which have experienced the most rapid growth in population are products of changes brought about by the breakdown of colonial empires and the formation of independent governments since World War II. Such growth reflected the need to build the institutions for new nations practically from scratch, including not only government but financial institutions, and legal and educational systems. Virtually all Third World cities, in one way or another, also reveal the national and international constraints that their societies face in their aspirations to improve living standards. These cities are also reminders of governments' unwillingness or inability to implement essential reforms in rural areas, the underlying cause of the movement of so many rural people to cities in the last 40 years.

This book seeks to describe the vast, rapid and complex process of urban change in the Third World and to consider its impact on the lives of its citizens. Chapter 1 provides the context for the whole book, describing the development of Third World cities in the colonial and post colonial periods and the gap that continues to grow between the "legal" and the "illegal" city. Chapter 2 reviews the inappropriate and ineffective ways in which governments have intervened to influence this development. Chapter 3 considers the ways in which poorer people find housing in cities while Chapters 4 and 5 describes the failure of most governments' policies to improve housing conditions for poorer groups. Chapters 6 and 7 examine the environmental problems of Third World cities – in people's homes and workplaces and in the wider neighbourhood, city and regional environments. Chapter 8 considers recent and current trends in urbanization and what these imply for 'the urban future'. Chapter 9, 'Outside the large cities' outlines developments and problems in smaller urban centres and the rural areas that usually surround them.

Chapters 7, 8 and 9 also show just how arbitrary and misleading it is to divide a nation into "rural" and "urban" – whether in terms of rural and urban population, settlements, resources or economic activities. None the less the distinction between 'rural' and 'urban' areas is widely used by governments and aid agencies in the allocation of resources and it has become conventional wisdom that there is "urban bias", that urban areas receive more than rural areas. This book is not a plea for a diversion of funds and attention from rural to urban areas, but it does try to highlight the very serious housing, health and environmental problems faced by hundreds of millions of urban dwellers in the Third World. It also questions whether these people have been favoured by urban bias in the policies and expenditures of governments and aid agencies – have urban residents been favoured over rural residents? (see pp. 282–5 and 308–11).

The last 15 years have brought a considerable growth in our knowledge and understanding of rural poverty and its causes; some governments and aid agencies have acted on this knowledge. But there has been less interest in urban poverty. In perhaps a quarter of all Third World nations, people suffering from poverty in urban areas now outnumber those suffering from poverty in rural areas. In most other Third World nations, there are large numbers of poor urban citizens whose needs should not be ignored, even if there are more rural poor.

Basic human needs are the same for urban and rural dwellers – adequate means of livelihood, a secure shelter, access to clean water, health care and education, protection against natural disasters and contamination from wastes – as well as basic political and civil rights. The means by which these are provided in urban rather than rural areas may differ; for instance, once the size and density of a settlement reaches a certain point, sewers rather than pit latrines are often needed to dispose of human wastes safely. In choosing to concentrate on the needs of urban inhabitants and the failure of government to work with these people in meeting their needs, we do not mean to imply that the needs of rural dwellers are less pressing. Indeed, why should the needs of a rural landless labourer forced to migrate to an urban area be any more or less valid before or after they have migrated – or their needs be any more or less valid than a household which has spent its entire life in an urban centre?

Coming to terms with the problems which accompany urban growth is part of coming to terms with the knowledge that most nations in the Third World will continue to become more urbanized, even if we believe that this urban process is slower and more complex than that suggested in other books (see Chapter 8). This urbanization process is part of a fundamental economic change both within nations and within the world economy; recognition of this fact, and attention to the accompanying housing, health and environmental problems faced by most urban inhabitants is long overdue. This process of urbanization is not itself "the problem"; indeed, in many instances, it has arisen from the development of stronger and more diversified economies. In many nations, it also reflects their increasing incorporation into a global economy. The main causes of the problems which accompany it are inadequate and inappropriate responses, both from governments and from aid agencies. Central to the message of this book is that many Western precedents and models should not be followed; the ways that governments in Europe or North America responded to rapid urbanization and its accompanying problems are totally inappropriate to current problems in most Third World nations.

Homogenizing the Third World

First, we need to justify the need for another book on this subject. There is no shortage of books, chapters, papers, articles and, more recently, films and television programmes which summarize the so-called problems of Third World cities – their rapid and "uncontrolled" growth, the millions living in "slums" and the very high rates of "unemployment". An urban future dominated by "mega-cities" of 10, 20 or 30 million or more inhabitants is commonly referred to. The various reports now regularly published on global problems often include a chapter or section on city or human settlement problems.

Most of these works include suggestions by the authors for solutions to the general problems that they identify. Nearly all these works are by Western authors; it is very rare to find a general work about Third World cities by someone from the Third World. One obvious reason is that very few people in the Third World have either the resources to undertake research outside their own nation, or access to libraries with sufficient information about cities outside their own nation or region to allow them to write general works.

We also find that we receive an ever growing number of requests to write short articles on this subject – for instance to describe "housing problems in Third World cities" or "Urban Change in the Third World" in 1,500–3,000 words. These requests often require a short section on "what governments and aid agencies must do". Sometimes, these sections have to be kept to one or two pages – the justification being that busy and important people have no time to read more lengthy pieces.

But this trend towards an ever greater number of summaries generalizing about Third World cities (or any other aspect of the Third World) carries with it considerable dangers. Perhaps the most worrying is that each short summary contains generalizations which are at best only partially true and at worst both inaccurate and misleading. Perhaps it will surprise the reader to learn that most urban centres in the Third World are *not* growing rapidly and that only a very small proportion of the Third World's population lives in mega-cities (see Chapter 8). It is also possible to argue – as we do in Chapter 8 – that the mega-city will remain the exception rather than the rule, even if we consider what is likely to happen up to 40 years from now.

In addition, as we argue in the first five chapters, rapid growth of illegal settlements in and around cities can be viewed not as the growth of slums but, in a very real sense, as the development of cities which are more appropriate to the local culture, climate and conditions than the plans produced by the governments of these same cities. It is undeniable that the growth of cities and the growth of illegal settlements has been accompanied by growing poverty and environmental degradation – as described in Chapters 6 and 7. But it is possible to argue that one of the main causes of this poverty and environmental degradation is neither the growth of the cities, nor the growth of these illegal settlements, but the unrealistic attitudes and actions of governments and aid agencies to such growth. Changes in the attitudes and approaches of both governments and aid agencies can greatly reduce this poverty and environmental degradation in most Third World nations.

The fact that so many generalizations are made about the problems of Third World cities and how to solve them, together with the trend towards publishing an increasing number of readable and well presented overviews, means that the generalizations become conventional wisdom. This book will question the validity of much of this conventional wisdom. It is not so much about what governments should do about the problems of Third World cities; the diversity of national and regional societies, the differences in the scale and nature of urbanization and of accompanying environmental problems and the political structures which have developed within them make nonsense of most general recommendations. Rather it is an attempt to consider what is actually happening in Third World cities in all their diversity and how inaccurate generalizations and conceptions inhibit our understanding of the problems and their causes. Some important common threads do emerge, and we try to identify these. The ways in which the poor are excluded from legal housing markets and from receiving public services like water supply and health care are unique to each city and neighbourhood – but in nearly all cities, the poor are excluded. The ways in which the poor find some form of accommodation – even if it is simply sleeping in a public place – are also unique to each city since they are much influenced by, among other things, the power of the government, the attitude of government to the poor, the level of prosperity of the city, the distribution of income among its inhabitants and the structure of land ownership. But the dangers to the health of poor people arising from the myriad ways in which they find accommodation are often very similar from city to city.

The context for this book

It is very difficult to generalize about the 120 or so Third World nations which today include more than three-quarter's of the world's population; each has its own culture (or cultures), resource base and locational advantages and disadvantages in regard to the world market. The size, population and economic structure of each also differ greatly. But there are some broad generalizations which are valid and which have a bearing on urban problems. Many Third World nations have such a shortage of resources and so little chance of developing a stable and prosperous role within the world market that it is possible to question seriously their viability as nation-states. One can hardly castigate a government for failing to address the needs of its citizens when the entire nation has such an inadequacy of resources that, under current conditions, there are insufficient resources to allow basic needs to be met.

There are around 70 independent Third World nations with less than 7 million inhabitants of which around 30 have less than a million. Only a few have the resources (such as oil) or the locational advantages (like Singapore) which provide a basis for prosperity. Many of these nations can never, under current conditions, achieve a level of development which allows the elimination of poverty. This is also true for some of the more populous countries. Many of the poorer nations lack a stable, viable economic base to allow them to function as nation-states. They still lack people with the professional and technical skills needed for government and the development of national economies, even if substantial progress has been made in recent years. They lack the information about their population, economy and natural resource base needed to allow basic choices to be made about the use of scarce resources. These deficiencies were disguised during the 1950s, 1960s and early 1970s, as most nations managed to survive – pulled along in the wake of a rapidly expanding world economy. Now their fundamental problems are all too evident. Such nations are concentrated in Central America, sub-Saharan Africa and Southeast Asia and the Pacific. Most only gained independence in recent decades. Their national boundaries were defined by the colonial powers (sometimes with the connivance of local élites) but this definition was neither based on the economic viability of the new nation state nor on existing economic and cultural links. New national boundaries often cut across the territories of cultures with long histories and so severed important economic, social and cultural links. They often cut across important trade routes so that those using them now have to negotiate boundary officials and customs posts where previously there had been free movement. When considering the problems faced by governments in the poorer nations, one should also not forget that those countries which did try to implement basic reforms, had their institutional, political and economic life threatened by foreign governments or interests.

There are other Third World nations which do have better long term prospects but even their development strategies seem to have lost any impetus, for reasons which have defied the interpretation of national and international élites. Perhaps one explanation is that these élites discuss development with little knowledge of culture and history. They ignore the role that free people, democratic institutions and laws guaranteeing equal rights can play in development. Even most of the more scientifically and technologically advanced Third World nations are ruled by small minorities from a handful of cities with little knowledge of the diversity of societies, cultures, resources and potentials which exist within their national boundaries. Yet only on this knowledge can relevant and effective development strategies be based. The growing gap between rich and poor nations is mirrored by a growing gap between the small élites (usually concentrated in national capitals) and the majority of poor citizens.

This is the context for some basic problems which must be solved if homelessness and the number of people living in very poor conditions are to be reduced significantly. Why are Third World cities still so poorly understood, despite so many reports, conferences and learned publications? Why are city problems and the problems facing the majority of their inhabitants, so low amongst the priorities of governments and the élites in power? What makes cities grow – both in size and in population – in ways which increasingly reflect, by the multiplication of unhealthy and degraded human environments, unequal national and global development, development which blocks the establishment of efficient democratic institutions? How can we change these processes, and help the inhabitants of these cities to earn sufficient income? How can we promote community participation, which is at the root of effective participatory democracy, and facilitate social exchanges in order to develop cities which are not too costly in terms of time and energy to build and which make basic services accessible to all citizens?

1. The Legal and the Illegal City

Building cities from the bottom up

Most new housing and most new neighbourhoods in Third World cities are organized, planned and built outside the law. Most urban citizens have no choice but to build, buy or rent an "illegal dwelling" since they cannot afford the cheapest "legal" house or apartment. It is now common for 30 to 60 per cent of an entire city's population to live in houses and neighbourhoods which have been developed illegally. In most cities, 70 to 95 per cent of all new housing is built illegally.

This chapter is about the gap between the legal city and the illegal city – how it developed and how and why it is sustained. A series of Boxes intersperse the text of this and the next two chapters, telling the stories of how low income people organized and developed their own houses and neighbourhoods in different cities. These stories present a more accurate picture of how the cities of the Third World are being built than the official view presented in countless government documents, which list the number of housing starts and units completed, or the number of schools or kilometres of paved road constructed.

Box 1.1: The development of San Martin, Buenos Aires, Argentina

In late 1981, some 20,000 people invaded 211 hectares of abandoned private land in two outer districts of Buenos Aires. These invasions began in September when an initial, relatively small and well organized squatter invasion prompted many other people to join in. Towards the end of November 1981, as word spread about the invasion, some 3,000 people entered the settlements, with their belongings, in the course of just five days. The government tried to bulldoze them but was successfully resisted – largely by women and children who stood in front of the bulldozers. Support for the squatters soon grew – especially from priests and church groups and certain lawyers.

The police then tried to isolate the new settlements by forming a cordon with 300 vehicles and 3,000 men. One of the squatters described how they got around this:

> We worked at night. On the houses too. We knew that the police did not have the authorization to tear down houses; their function was to keep us from building them. The people who were going to enter the settlement waited outside the police circle; when it loosened up, because they were asleep and there were less of them, we lined up behind the first opening, we brought in the material, the wood. All the neighbours helped. In two hours, we built one house; later the neighbour who just arrived helped to raise others. By morning, when the police entered, five or six houses had been built.

In the Autumn of 1982, the security forces gave up their attempt to maintain the cordon. One reason was the Malvinas war and the consequent weakening of the confidence and power of the military government. As one squatter commented in October 1982:

> 20,000 people, driven by hunger, driven by high rental costs and unemployment, searched for abandoned lands . . . and that is why, today, thank God, we are here, we're organized, we're united . . . the only thing the authorities gave us was a police cordon which frightened our children and jeopardized our progress. And we had to fight, clandestinely, any way we were able and had to suffer and that suffering, though the law says differently, is what gives us the right to be here.

San Martin was one of six new settlements (*barrios*) formed by this invasion. Despite the illegality, the new settlers were determined not to live in a *villa miseria* (the name given to squatter settlements in Buenos Aires; literally translated it means "misery settlement"). To avoid this, they organized the lay-out of the site so that space was left for access roads and for community facilities. A democratic system of planning and organizing the settlement soon developed. At the lowest level – the level of the block – "block delegates" were elected (one representative and two deputy representatives) who served for six months on the "Board of Delegates". Committees were also elected to supervise and co-ordinate activities and petitions. Each neighbourhood had a Co-ordinating Committee which was represented on what came to be called "the Co-ordinating Committee of Neighbours of the West Quilmes Settlement".

This organization developed soon after the invasions. As one settler remarked:

> the organization did not come already planned . . . the need was there for a filter against all those people who tried to infiltrate, against the criminals, against the dictatorship, against the police . . . the only way to get rid of that is to be well organized . . . that is why meetings were held here at four or five in the morning during the first days. The local parish priest was an important supporter right from the initial invasion and he helped in the organization.

The Co-ordinating Committee published a newsletter *Nuestra Esperanza* ("Our Hope") and quickly took charge of negotiations with public agencies for electricity, health care and public works. Initially, they had little success. Illegal connections were made to the electricity grid and to the mains water supply; the electricity company had agreed to supply the settlement but the police kept the company out. The need for piped water was particularly pressing, since the nearby stream, a possible alternative source was contaminated with wastes from local paper, weaving and meat packing plants.

Conditions in San Martin and the other *barrios* remained very poor, since the local government refused to pave the streets, install sewers or drains, or provide health care. Diarrhoea epidemics, which were especially serious in the summer months, led to the community organizing a campaign to demand health care. When this failed, the inhabitants organized for themselves a basic level of health care and built a health centre with help from the local Catholic parish. They also built their first school.

In the run-up to democratic elections in 1984, each political party made promises to the inhabitants of San Martin; offers such as the services of a physician or the supply of medicine were made by both the main political parties, while a former military junta member promised a totally equipped dispensary. The Co-ordinator's response was:

> To the political party that came to tell us, "We have four physicians", "we have milk and medicine to distribute", we answered, "fine, bring them, leave them at the parish, we will take them to the *barrio*."

With the election of a democratic government in 1984, the municipal authorities became more sympathetic to the squatters' needs and there are no longer fears of eviction. Some medicines have been provided and vaccinations made available; on occasion, garbage has been collected – although the longer term problems of no drains and sewers, or paved roads and pathways, remain.

Source: Beatriz Cuenya, Hector Almada, Diego Armus, Julia Castells, Maria di Loreto and Susana Penalva, *Habitat and health conditions of the popular sectors: a pilot project of participative investigation in the San Martin settlement, Greater Buenos Aires* (Buenos Aires: CEUR), see note 1.

It could be said that the unnamed millions who build, organize and plan illegally are the most important organizers, builders and planners of Third World cities. But governments do not recognize this, they do not see these people as city-builders; indeed, they usually refuse to recognize that they are citizens with legitimate rights and needs for government services. It is very rare for infrastructure and services essential to health and well-being – piped water, sewers, storm drainage, all-weather roads, public transport, electricity, health care – to be supplied for these settlement by government. Where they are, the provision takes place years or even decades after the settlement first developed and usually only after the inhabitants have mounted a long and well organized campaign for such provision.

This illegal process, by which most new city houses and neighbourhoods are developed, has been evident for many decades and yet very few governments are prepared to acknowledge it. Most governments mix indifference with repression; some illegal settlements are tolerated while others are bulldozed. A few governments have become more tolerant and have tried to provide basic infrastructure and services. Very few governments have taken action to ensure that poorer households can find legal alternatives to these settlements. None have acknowledged that these people and their community organizations are the most potent force that Third World nations have for a more efficient, healthy, resource-conserving and democratic process of city construction.

Poor people demonstrate great ingenuity in developing these new residential neighbourhoods and in organizing the construction of housing – even if government regards them as illegal. Their ways, their plans, their designs and their building materials are often far better suited to local needs, local incomes, local climatic conditions and local resources than the official, legal standards demanded by governments. As will be discussed later, this is usually because official standards are derived from western models which have little relevance to local circumstances and take no account of local climate, local preferences and availability of local building materials.

Government rules and regulations in regard to building, planning, environmental protection and employment regulations ensure that even the most basic aspects of the lives of these citizens – obtaining shelter, earning an income, obtaining food, water and health services – are illegal. Because so many aspects of their lives are illegal, poorer groups are open to exploitation from landowners, businesses and the police or military personnel. As one lawyer has pointed out, the vast majority of city dwellers see the law as a tool which the wealthy and well-connected can use against them.[2]

Thus there is an enormous gap between what is actually happening and the official government view of what should happen. We maintain that the fault lies with unrealistic and inappropriate government views. Most of these are imported from the West and thus from completely different cultures and contexts. Many current government programmes are still based on legislation passed under colonial rule, whose main purpose was to keep the colonized out of the cities or the city districts, in order to guarantee the quality of the environment for the colonial rulers and other foreigners, and to keep down costs.

All nations are characterized by a number of values, life-styles, customs, traditions and institutions – in other words by their culture or cultures. These are specific and unique to themselves. Culture implies knowledge – that is to say, experiences accummulated and refined over long periods. People's culture has always been reflected in the houses, neighbourhoods and settlements that they develop for themselves; one can learn much about a culture and its economy from its house designs, the materials used and the ways that settlements are planned.[3] But most governments have long ignored both history and culture as essential inputs into their "planning for development". They see no legitimacy in the actions of their citizens who are the true builders and planners of large areas of their cities. They cannot see in the many illegal settlements the seed of what could develop as a more accurate and appropriate reflection of the nation's culture. They cannot grasp that the house designs, the materials used and the plans for these settlements are more realistic and often more appropriate than their own unfulfilled plans for "low cost housing". Governments do not seem to see the problems of building and managing cities in the same way as most of their citizens.

The priorities of city and national governments are often almost entirely unrelated to their citizens' most pressing needs. City mayors and the vested interests who support them may want highways, metro systems, improved parking facilities, civic buildings and water supply systems which start from the more central districts. But when the people living in the poorer neighbourhoods are questioned, their priorities are usually cheap and regular public transport, garbage collection, health centres and schools, protection against floods (for those living in flood prone areas) and, of course, water supply and drains, jobs and the possibility of obtaining small credits. Big projects have little or no appeal for them. The city where they live and work is unrelated to the city that the mayors and technocrats want to build. The neighbourhoods of the poor form a city of pragmatists. Every square metre, every scrap of material and every unit of currency is usually put to good use. In many cities, community associations or clubs formed by these people become involved in the construction or improvement of these neighbourhoods – or in their defence against the threat of bulldozing. The committees formed by the inhabitants of San Martin are just one among many possible examples (see Box 1.1). Community organizations are rational in their aims and actions. Yet the ideas, actions and resources which might eventually improve the urban environment are not in their hands but in the hands of small groups of technocrats with little power to make independent decisions and often with little sensibility as to the kinds of programmes which can benefit poorer groups.

Of course, this reflects the fact that most governments are not elected and cannot claim to have the support of their citizens – but it is also true of many elected governments. The failure of governments and aid agencies to understand peoples' culture and needs means they become isolated and attract sharp criticism from community organizations all round the world. The majority of citizens, forced by circumstances beyond their control to live in overcrowded, degraded environments with no basic services, are less passive in the face of such injustice. They increasingly demand that their rights should be acknowledged. They – many of them "squatter citizens" – constitute the greatest and most dynamic resource in building and managing the Third World city.

Each city is unique because the culture of which that city is a product is unique. Each illegal settlement will have its own history, shaped by the circumstances in that city. In some cities, under certain governments, poorer groups have found it possible to invade land and remain there; under others, government repression of such invasions has been too strong to permit this. In some cities, at certain times, poorer groups have been able quietly to develop houses in certain areas with little harrassment from the authorities, even if organized land invasions were not permitted. In others, the government has repressed squatter invasions but has tolerated the development of illegal subdivisions where land-owners illegally divide their land into house plots and sell them to poorer households. It is very difficult to generalize about how an illegal settlement is formed and developed, since it depends on many factors which differ from city to city. The possibilities for poorer groups to invade a land site or quietly encroach on some small unoccupied site depend greatly on the structure of land ownership, the legislation in force which defines the balance between landowners' rights and the rights of government to acquire and use land "in the public interest", and the way that the courts interpret this legislation. Of course, it also depends on the attitude of the government in power at any particular time to illegal settlements. This chapter and those following try to identify and describe some common threads in the process by which cities develop and how this affects their poorer citizens – but care should be taken not to assume that what is described for one city is necessarily true for another.

The colonial legacy

Most of the Third World's largest cities owe their foundation and early development to colonial rule. This is especially so in Latin America where virtually all cities with more than a million inhabitants were founded by the Spaniards or Portuguese. Latin America's ten largest cities were all founded before 1580.

In sub-Saharan Africa, nearly all national capitals and many other contemporary cities were established by European colonial powers – Britain, France, Portugal, Germany, Belgium. Almost every urban centre in East Africa with more than 20,000 inhabitants in the 1970s had been an established colonial administrative station by 1910.[4] The British, French, Dutch, Spanish and Portuguese also founded many settlements in South-East Asia and the Pacific, and many of the region's larger cities first grew as colonial centres of administration, trade and industry. For instance, Jakarta, Manila, Yangon (Rangoon), Ho Chi Minh City (Saigon), Singapore, Calcutta and Hong Kong were all created by European powers in locations where only villages had existed previously.[5]

An understanding of the origin and early development of Third World cities and of the institutions which arose to control and administer them is vital since these institutions and the laws and regulations they administered have helped shape the contemporary city, its institutions, legal systems and the attitudes of those who govern it. The colonial legacy has contributed much to what seem today to be intractable problems.

This can be seen in the planning of cities, their location and the attitudes of their governments to the poor. Let us take first the question of city planning. In most large cities and many smaller ones too, the theory and practice of urban planning under the colonial powers, both when the cities were founded and during the decades or centuries of domination, can still be seen. The colonial imprint is easily visible in and around the city centre – the central districts, the layout of streets, the location and form of squares and public spaces, the design of avenues (often built over destroyed city walls), the architecture and land uses. The values of the colonial powers are still symbolized in the architecture which housed their institutions and senior representatives – the palaces of governors, archbishops, the churches and city halls, the houses of the wealthy traders, colonial administrators and land and mine owners. They may also still be evident in names; for instance, many Indian cities still have a district known as the "Civil Lines", which was once the residential area reserved for Europeans. Many colonial cities were imposed within or alongside a pre-colonial city. In territories controlled by European colonial powers but previously occupied by advanced indigenous cultures, such as in Mexico, Guatemala and Peru, in many Arab nations, and in much of India or Nigeria, the location of settlements shows an often surprising continuity; many of the major colonial cities in these areas were built around or over urban centres which pre-date the colonial city by centuries.

Since all colonial economies were dependent on serfs or slaves (or at least cheap labour), colonial rulers often chose the more densely occupied areas for the construction or reconstruction of the new sites of government. In such cities, colonial governments imposed cultural and social segregation. Most of the worst aspects of apartheid in South Africa were present – strict controls on "native" population movements into the city (often with women and children not allowed to live with their husbands who were working there); strict segregation between the residential areas of "natives" and the white élite; little or no provision of infrastructure and services to the native townships while the residential areas of the whites were well served; and, of course, little or no political rights for the natives. Most Third World cities today retain this segregation of the city – the city of the rich and the city of the poor as developed by colonial rule. But today, this segregation relies more on income than race – the nation's own élite and rich foreigners inhabit the areas once reserved for colonial staff and other Europeans, as well as the new garden suburbs developed since colonial rule.

Today, most urban planning and government investment in water supply, sanitation, drains and roads takes place in middle and upper income areas which house only a minority of the total population. This is very similar to what happened under colonial rule. In much of colonial Africa and Asia, while there was little or no planning for the native townships, the Europeans often lived in a "garden city" type of lay-out with the residential areas of the colonial staff developed with very low densities. The European quarters were often surrounded by a *cordon sanitaire* (a green belt of open space) where no native was allowed to live. In this green belt were often found parks, race courses and sports clubs – for the exclusive use of the Europeans – and military camps. The *cordon sanitaire* was meant to safeguard the Europeans from the epidemics and diseases of poverty which ravaged the indigenous population; in certain Nigerian towns, the green zone was to be at least 440 yards (402.3 metres) wide since it was then believed that this was further than a malarial mosquito could fly.[6] It is for reasons such as these that settlements built for European settlers in the cities of Fez and Marrakesh in Morocco or Tunis in Tunisia were built at some distance from the old Arab cities.[7] The frequently used term for the European quarters was "the sanitary district"; this was usually the only part of the city in which there was water piped to each house, drains, and provision for sanitation and the removal of household wastes.

For example, in Delhi (India) around 1930, there were some 200 "natives" per hectare in the old city and its suburbs, and just 8 persons per hectare in New Delhi, the new capital of India developed by the British for the British. The proportion of children who die before the age of five is always a good indication of housing and health conditions; infants in the old walled city in Delhi (where the Indians lived) were more than six times more likely to die before the age of one than infants born in New Delhi.[8] In Zambia, after a Town Planning Ordinance introduced in 1929 and a Public Health Ordinance introduced in 1930, local governments applied stringent building regulations based on British models to the European residential areas but ignored conditions in the zones in which the "native" populations were allowed to live. In one such zone, 4,000 people lived in 1,700 mud huts 12 feet apart, infested with vermin and provided with only 50 communal pit latrines for sanitation.[9] At this time, a plan was being developed for a new capital – Lusaka – and the government centre and civil servants' housing were given a well-drained, wooded area with low population density while the land allocated for African housing was subject to flooding.[10] Nairobi, capital of Kenya, which originally grew to serve the construction and servicing of a railway, was conceived as a European city to serve the white settlers. The only Africans tolerated were those whose labour the colonial class needed; Nairobi was systematically racially zoned in the plans of 1905, 1927 and 1948.[11]

Hospitals and health services in colonial Africa and Asia were also primarily for the colonial élite. The fact that many nations today have a high concentration of hospitals and medical facilities in the capital city usually owes its origin to colonial rule. Medical research during colonial rule also served the rulers' interests; far more attention was paid to the diseases which threatened the rulers (such as malaria and sleeping sickness) than to the diseases which ravaged the native population.[12]

While there are examples of legislation and of town plans introduced in the late Colonial period in Africa and Asia which sought to improve living conditions for the indigenous population, these were based on European models designed for economies, societies and cultures completely distinct from those in which they came to be applied. For instance, in British colonies in Africa, as new Town and Country Planning laws were passed in Britain, so too did colonial administrators begin to adopt the English planning system with its structure and procedures. Even in poor African nations, these often made assumptions about levels of private car ownership in designing road widths and parking provision, based on criteria in use in Europe. And the plans gave little thought to the inhabitants' preferred divisions between public and private space or to the obvious fact that most inhabitants would walk or cycle to work or to shops or to visit friends. [13] The problem is well summed up by Carole Rakodi when she describes how town-planning notions such as that of the "garden city" became debased as they were taken from Britain and the original concept of Ebenezer Howard (the founder of the garden city movement) and put into a very different economy and society:

> The original concept of a "garden city" envisaged the creation of a balanced community, providing jobs, houses and facilities for its whole population within walking or cycling distance. In the case of Lusaka (Zambia), one or two components of Howard's idea (generous planting, organic rather than grid layouts) were lifted out of one context and utilized in another, to influence the planning of residential areas for only one section of the urban population: the Europeans. [14]

Many colonial governments also put in place a range of laws, norms and codes governing housing, building and planning which still remain today, largely unchanged. The explicit objective of much of this legislation was to reinforce the political and economic control of the foreign power or to guarantee its colonial officers and other Europeans a high standard of living and security. Many of the norms and codes governing building and planning were never intended for anything but the residential areas of the Europeans. The colonial governments also developed them at a time when the nation's economy was predominantly agricultural and rural based, and people's right to move to urban centres was often severely restricted. Not surprisingly, they are very poorly suited to an independent nation where rapid urban growth and increasingly urban societies have become the norm. But it is not only that the context today is different; it is also the fact that these were laws, norms and codes developed by an alien culture.

Inappropriate Western concepts still underpin the norms and codes in force in Third World nations. For instance, many assume that most people will live in "nuclear families" with one or two children who will go to school, and with the house and place of employment separated. This has led to many house designs and site plans at odds with family size and structure, community needs, cultural preferences and the pattern of employment.[15]

Take the case of zoning regulations which usually set standards for the number of persons or houses allowed per unit of area and the kinds of activities which can take place within specific zones. Zoning regulations then – as today – often forbid a mix of houses and businesses, while house designs make no provision for the workshop or retail store which many households want to include in their houses since these provide vital income. Caroline Moser has documented the many ways in which western norms and codes have ignored or misunderstood women's needs. For instance, Western style grid-iron site lay-outs have been imposed in many cities – but these do not allow women to work in their house and still keep an eye on their children and their neighbour's children. Culturally specific needs become forgotten. For instance, women's needs in Islamic societies for private open space within the house and relatively sheltered pathways to get to shops and clinics are rarely (if ever) considered.[16]

In Latin America, the colonial legacy is not so strong. Most nations achieved independence in the first half of the nineteenth century which is well before most of the laws, codes and practices governing the built environment in Europe had been developed. Much of the building and planning legislation currently in force in Latin America, however, is largely derived from European models or practices of the late nineteenth or early twentieth centuries. This, like legislation in Africa and Asia, is based on models developed in very different economies, climates and, for most of the continent, cultures. It did not evolve, as it had originally in Europe, based on local custom, precedent and circumstance, and influenced by local demands.

Clearly, inappropriate planning norms and codes still in force today cannot be blamed only on the colonial past or on the import of inappropriate models several decades ago. Most independent governments have done little or nothing to change them, often because they are so embedded in the legislative structure and so difficult to change. More fundamental revisions of laws must precede the revision of planning law – but lawyers tend to protect the rights of property owners – including protecting them against the claims for house sites made by poorer groups. This was brought out in a comment made by the Secretary to the Ministry of Justice under the government of Allende in Chile when new approaches to solving housing problems were being tried. He pointed to the contradiction between government programmes which aim to improve the living conditions of poorer groups but which must operate within a legislative structure designed to serve the interests of middle and upper income groups.

Two additional colonial legacies are worth noting: land ownership concepts and the location of cities. Colonial governments needed to legitimize the occupation of the land they needed – often the best agricultural land. This meant the imposition of Western concepts of land ownership and transfer (for instance the right to sell land) which were usually at odds with the patterns of land use and control developed by the original society and completely at odds with deeply held customs and beliefs. Colonial land legislation promoted individual rights over communal rights. Traditional concepts of public or community ownership or control and community responsibility which were so widespread in much of Africa, Asia and Latin America prior to colonial rule, may have provided a sounder, more egalitarian tradition on which to build the new laws; but with the imposition or adoption of Western models and concepts, this was never possible.[17]

City locations also reveal colonial priorities. Most of the Third World's larger cities are the main seaports or on natural crossroads. This reflects the importance given by colonial governments to trade and communications and the need to exercise political and administrative control. For example – the five largest cities in India in the 1981 census (Calcutta, Bombay, Madras, Delhi and Bangalore) largely owe their pre-eminence to developments under colonial rule. Trading ports founded by the British East India Trading Company in the seventeenth century provided the initial stimulus for the development of Calcutta, Bombay and Madras. While several ancient cities have at some time flourished within or close to present day Delhi, it was the movement of India's capital by the British to New Delhi which initiated rapid development there and this has continued ever since. Much of the impetus for the early development of Bangalore derives from the preference of colonial rulers in the State of Mysore for Bangalore over Mysore, the official state capital.[18]

Thus the colonial heritage is still very real in many Third World nations – in the separation between the cities of the rich and the cities of the poor, in the imposition of laws and institutions based on Western models which deny the value and validity of cultural traditions, and in the location of cities. The colonial heritage goes yet deeper than this and is still visible in many current patterns of economic activity and their inter-connections. For instance, it can be seen in the large disparities between regions and between the cities and rural areas in basic service provision and in connections to road and railway networks; in the location of ports and industrial centres; in the use of the best lands for cash crops with land ownership frequently heavily concentrated in the hands of a small élite; in the shortage of technical and administrative skills; in the destruction or suppression of ancient community organizations and systems and, finally, even in the writing of each culture's history. These provide some critical clues as to how today's problems developed.

The illegal city

Throughout history, the poor usually had to build their own houses and neighbourhoods and they have almost always built them outside the official 'legal' city of the élite and contrary to their norms and regulations. They utilize, wherever possible, techniques and settlement lay-outs which, specific to their region and to that period, reveal their own cultural values. Most of Tenochtitlan (the Aztec capital over which Mexico City is built), Delhi or Cairo were built in defiance of official rules and practices.

As Third World cities began to grow as centres of (now independent) government or as centres for production and commerce within an increasingly inter-linked world market, new neighbourhoods began to occupy unused land near the city centre or close to places, such as ports, where jobs were available. The last four decades have seen illegal house construction, either on illegally occupied or illegally subdivided land, become the major source of cheap new housing in most Third World cities. For example, in Nouakchott, capital of Mauritania, a 1981 estimate suggested that 64 per cent of the population lived in largely self-built illegal settlements[19]. Some 60 per cent of the population in Guayaquil, Ecuador's largest city, live in settlements built by their inhabitants on stilts over tidal swamplands.[20] A study of El Salvador in 1975 found that nearly two thirds of the housing stock in the five main urban centres had been produced outside the formal legal, financial and institutional framework.[21] In Alexandria, Egypt's major port and second largest city, 68 per cent of the housing stock is informal housing.[22] (Chapters 3 and 4 give more details and examples of how such housing developed.)

Nearly all forms of housing used by low income groups are "illegal" in some respect although there are degrees of illegality. Housing in squatter settlements is illegal in two senses; land is occupied illegally, and the site and the building are developed and built illegally – contrary to zoning regulations (which specify the use to which land can be put and often the number of units allowed per hectare), sub-division regulations (which specify the standards needed for access roads, water supply, drainage etc, and often the minimum size of plot allowed) and building regulations.

Many illegal settlements are not squatter settlements and do conform to the law in some ways. For instance, in the case of illegal subdivisions, the occupation of the land is legal – at least in the eyes of the person or company who owns it. It is very common for poorer (or even middle income) households to purchase a site on which to construct a house from a landowner (or developer acting for a land owner) who has not satisfied all the laws and regulations governing the subdivision of land for housing. In this instance, it is the landowner who commits the illegal act, although governments usually treat the people who purchase land and develop housing as the guilty parties.[23] In the example given of the city of Alexandria earlier, three quarters of the informal housing is on illegal subdivisions outside the city boundaries with the remaining quarter in squatter settlements.[24]

Then there are settlements which did not really develop illegally, but where the legal status of house-owners remains unclear. This is very common when a rural settlement becomes engulfed by a growing urban centre – as in the case of Olaleye village, in Lagos, whose development is described in Box 1.2.

Box 1.2: The development of Olaleye Village in Lagos, Nigeria

Olaleye village has a central location within metropolitan Lagos, sub-Saharan Africa's largest urban agglomeration with more than 5 million inhabitants. Olaleye first developed as a farming settlement outside Lagos but as the city grew, it became part of the city. In 1983, along with a smaller neighbouring "village", it had around 20,000 inhabitants on a site covering some 35 hectares.

Olaleye village is believed to have been founded about 150 years ago when the chief of the Oloto family (a major land owning family) gave the parcel of land to a certain Olaleye to farm. Olaleye did not live there – at the time the land was forested and uninhabited – but invited Baba Egun to farm the land. Baba Egun invited another person Sadiku to join him and together, they farmed and raised herbs; they invited others to join them and most made a living from palm wine tapping, palm oil processing, fruit growing, market gardening, fishing and trapping.

When Baba Egun died, Sadiku became the village's oldest man and in 1950, the traditional head of the village. Sadiku was asked by Olaleye to bring more people to the village and there was a rapid growth in population; most of those who acquired land did so under a lease tenancy agreement issued by the Olaleye family.

The settlement expanded rapidly when a railway line was constructed through it; the first wave of migrants who came to live there were construction workers, labourers, staff of the railway and petty traders. An estimate for 1967 suggested a population of 2,500 persons. The settlement grew further after the end of the Civil War (in 1970) and the economic boom associated with rapidly growing oil revenues from 1973.

The neighbouring village Iproni is thought to have been founded in 1878 by someone who also acquired the land from the Oloto family. He also farmed the land, planting cashew, mangoes and apples. As his farming prospered, he was joined by other settlers who created adjoining settlements such as Baba Ruth Village, Caterpillar Village, Good-U-Morning and Saro Garden Villages. Most of these villages no longer exist as identifiable settlements. Iproni grew in very much the same way as Olaleye, although it was constrained by a series of government projects which used part of its land for roads and bridges, the construction of offices and housing and shopping estates. Land in Olaleye was not appropriated for public works in this way since parts of it are regularly flooded and the site slopes down, ending in a swamp.

Olaleye village contains within it an enormous range of different economic activities: a large market, beer parlours, night clubs, brothels, a makeshift cinema, tailors, shoe-makers, blacksmiths, tinkers, watch repairers, knife-sharpeners, washermen, mechanics, battery-chargers, shoe-shiners and itinerant beauticians. Many women produce and sell a great variety of cooked foodstuffs. Many inhabitants work outside the settlement – mostly in nearby factories or offices.

The railway track running through the village has become an important centre of economic activity. The slow pace of the trains passing through allows the sale of goods to passengers, and along the "railway line" (the land next to the tracks) around 100 shacks have developed which are rented out by the Nigerian Railway Corporation for a variety of economic activities.

Source: Tade Akin Aina, *Health, Habitat and Underdevelopment – the case of a Low Income Settlement in Metropolitan Lagos* (IIED, Technical Report, 1989).[25]

There is also the problem faced by tenants in illegal settlements who not only live in illegal houses but who have no protection against arbitrary eviction or sudden rises in rent from the landlord. Olaleye village is a good example because many of its inhabitants rent a room. We will return to these problems in Chapter 3.

It is not only the homes that poorer groups build for themselves which are illegal; so too are many other kinds of accommodation used by the poor. For instance, many low income individuals or households rent a room in tenements or cheap boarding houses. Inner city tenement buildings may be structures which were built legally; many were originally middle class houses and apartment blocks and only when their owners moved out to the suburbs were they subdivided. Others were originally built for the purpose of renting rooms to poorer households – often with the approval of government or even government support. But most are illegal because they contravene standards for lighting, ventilation, space per person and facilities for washing, cooking and sanitation.

Many other aspects of the poorer city dwellers' lives are deemed illegal because in one way or another, they contravene official laws – labour, health, safety or environmental legislation for example. Water for drinking, cooking and washing often comes from an unauthorized source such as a river or an illegally dug well or from water drawn illegally from the water mains. Electricity is often only obtained when the inhabitants illegally connect wires to a nearby pylon and construct their own informal electricity network from them.

Illegal food supplies are often important: food from scavenging in the garbage of richer residents or on the city rubbish tip, or food deemed spoilt and unfit for human consumption by food inspectors. Cooked or prepared food purchased from street vendors often forms an important part of low income groups' diet but governments often deem these vendors illegal.[26] In many cities, small privately run buses or vans are often considered illegal yet are widely used by poorer groups either because no legal bus service comes to their settlement or because it does not match their needs. Children do not complete their mandatory schooling – often because they have to leave at a young age to begin earning so they can contribute to the family income. Many of the health services used by poorer groups are not run by licensed, qualified professionals; official services are too expensive or too distant and costly to reach. The places where many people work do not meet government regulations for working hours or for health and safety standards. In addition, many rely on selling goods or services on the street (sweets, trinkets, clothes, food-snacks, shoe shine etc), but this too is illegal. In many illegal settlements, there are also considerable numbers of illegal or unregistered foreign workers.

It is ironic that the city governments and institutions which deem these people and their activities 'illegal' benefit from them. Much of the cheap labour on which city businesses depend has its home in illegal settlements. Much of the so called 'informal sector' in which many poor individuals or households earn an income may be considered illegal but in reality, the goods and services provided are essential to the functioning of the legal city.[27] Governments acknowledge that there are not enough legal jobs in registered businesses. Most implicitly recognize that informal jobs provide the only means of livelihood for a high proportion of all households. But as a gesture to existing regulations and to established businesses, the police still subject many informal businesses to harassment, fines and arrest.

The law is not equal for all

All too often, it is assumed that all citizens are equal before the law. When national constitutions were written and approved, citizens were assumed to enjoy equal rights. In theory, the law should be each citizen's safeguard from exploitation – whether by landlords, employers, other family members or the state itself. The law should help protect consumers from sub-standard goods and services. Of course, it should also protect people from arbitrary arrest and imprisonment.

From the legislative framework are derived the standards which set minimum wages, maximum working hours, health and safety standards for homes and workplaces, infrastructure and density standards for land development for housing, and health related standards for food preparation, storage and sale. They also delineate land suitable for buildings, keeping clear the sites subject to such natural hazards as floods or landslides or other dangers.

But as noted in the previous section, the laws and the rules derived from legislative frameworks deem most aspects of the poor majority's lives illegal. In most cities, only a small proportion of the working population actually work in enterprises which meet labour, health, safety and environmental legislation. Most have to find other ways of earning a living – such as selling goods on a street or hawking with no license, working at home running a small retail store, cafe or workshop which contravenes zoning regulations, or which is in an illegal settlement; or they work in enterprises where health and safety standards are ignored or rules on working hours and minimum wages are contravened. Rules regarding workers' rights to sick pay, redundancy pay or pension rights are almost universally ignored.

In most Western cities, there are also substantial numbers of people who live and work illegally – for instance, the squatters who invade empty property, those working in illegal sweatshops which also contravene minimum wage, social security and health and safety regulations, and many of those working in what has come to be termed the "black" economy.

But there are two major differences when First and Third World cities are compared. The first is the difference in scale; it is the majority, not the minority who live and work illegally in Third World cities. The second difference is that in virtually all Third World cities, government provides no safety net for those who find no way of earning an income or of finding a shelter. While this safety net for the poor and unemployed has been eroded in the past decade in many Western nations, most citizens who are out of work can obtain a subsistence income and free or subsidized goods and services to prevent them starving and living in the street. This provision may be inadequate and bureaucratic but it greatly reduces severe physical deprivation such as starvation or exposure. The poor majority in Third World cities have no safety net; they have no choice but to find some activity which allows an income to be earned and find some form of accommodation. In such circumstances, the extent of their exploitation by employers and the extent to which rules and regulations are contravened is much greater.

Much of what we have learned – or rather what lower income groups have learnt – about the basic preconditions for a more egalitarian construction of cities will be very difficult to incorporate into government programmes and projects. For it will cut across some of the principal precepts on which current legislation is based. Basic concepts about the ownership of land and the inheritance of privileges will have to be changed if we are to fulfil our objective of better cities.

The setting of any standard is relative – whether it is to promote health or safety or to protect people from inadequate pay or overlong working hours. There is no single 'ideal' applicable in all societies. Standards must be relative to what can be achieved nationally and locally. But most official standards bear little relation to local needs and possibilities. Virtually all were originally conceived with some ideal in mind – whether as urban legislation, health and safety or environmental legislation, commercial or building regulations. All are attempts to regulate the actions of individuals or enterprises. Perhaps in theory, the approach is correct. But in most Third World cities, the standards have become so complex, so rigid and so beyond any possibility of implementation, both in relation to local circumstances, and the possibilities open to poorer groups, that they are transgressed daily. They provide no protection for those who are most vulnerable and in greatest need.

There must be something wrong with a law or code if it is broken daily by so many people as they go about their daily lives. To put this in perspective, one can envisage a standard which would be inappropriate for a Western city. All new housing could be required to have large gardens – say a minimum of 300 square metres. Setting such a standard could be considered as "improving living conditions". But in any major city, the effect would be to price most people out of the market since the cost of including a garden of this size in all new units would enormously increase their price. In effect, this is exactly what happens in most Third World cities – existing codes and standards price most Third World citizens out of the legal housing market.

But the issue is not one of 'lowering' standards. In theory, standards should be a consensus as to what should be achieved within one particular context; they should be rooted in the needs and preferences of that particular society. Each society, each culture has its own parameters within which such standards could be developed. For instance, building regulations should be intimately linked to local climatic conditions, the availability of local building materials, the availability of building skills and the likelihood of hazards such as earthquakes or floods. They should be linked to cultural needs and preferences which are also particular to each society. Legislation on land should be based on the way that a society views public interest and private responsibility. To be effective, a standard or code has to be related to local reality. If set too high or too much at odds with local preferences, it cannot promote 'better practice' which should be its objective. If it cannot be implemented, it loses its meaning. If it contradicts deeply held societal beliefs, it will create conflicts.

Not surprisingly, most poor people have little faith in laws. Many may know little or nothing about existing laws. If the laws are too complex or irrelevant to their needs or threaten their survival, they will live by their own values and codes. Box 1.3 describes the development of Brasilia Teimosa – a squatter settlement in Recife, Brazil. After a struggle against eviction which lasted nearly 40 years, the public authorities claimed to have changed their minds and said that they wanted to provide basic services. But the inhabitants remained sceptical; as one of them said "we decided to create our laws . . . our urban plans".

Box 1.3: "Stubborn Brasilia" – the development of a squatter settlement in Recife, Brazil

Recife, a state capital in the northeast of Brazil, has more than 1.3 million inhabitants. Some 193 squatter settlements were counted in 1985 in which nearly half the city's population lived.

Brasilia Teimosa ("stubborn Brasilia") is a squatter settlement on the shores of the Atlantic Ocean; it is a 50 hectare site just 5 kilometres from Recife's city centre (to which it is linked by good quality roads). The site was first developed by the State government which purchased it to build a fuel park in 1934; they landfilled the site and built some walls to protect it from flooding. But nothing was built there and a few families moved onto the site and built rudimentary housing. One of the first squatters talked of these early struggles. "In 1938, there was landfill. There was barbed wire everywhere. The police came to destroy people's shanties but we built them again." Over the next 20 years, the number of people living there gradually grew, as new households arrived and built shelters.

In 1953, the State Federation of Fisherman Colonies received permission to lease the site to build a headquarters for the fishermen. They transferred 0.6 of a hectare to the Recife Yacht Club but this broke the terms of the lease and the State Governor sought to have the lease annulled (although unsuccessfully). At this time, more households were moving onto the site - especially in 1957-8 during a period of severe drought which forced many rural people to move to Recife. This was also the time when Brasilia, the new capital of Brazil was beginning; the squatters christened their new settlement Brasilia Teimosa (literally "stubborn Brasilia") in acknowledgement of the stubborn spirit they had to show in the face of threats from police, City Hall, would-be owners and some fishermen from the State Federation.

In April 1958, a local newspaper announced that 3,000 wooden houses had been built clandestinely and that City Hall considered itself powerless to stop this. Recife's Port Authority which owned 10 hectares of the site demanded that City Hall expel the squatters but City Hall maintained that it was not meant to cope with invasions of public land. Brasilia Teimosa's residents had to defend themselves against the police: "For six months, we had to use clubs and knives. . . Police destroyed houses in the daytime, we rebuilt them at night."

In 1961, residents began demanding urban infrastructure and legal tenure of the land; many street demonstrations were organized. But such actions had to lessen after 1964, with the coup which brought a military dictatorship to power in Brazil, because many residents' associations came to suffer under the military régime's persecution.

However, the residents remained well organized; in 1966, they elected a Residents Association. Its formation and subsequent activities were helped by the work of Dom Helder Camara who had arrived in Recife to become Archbishop and had encouraged church members to organize within their settlements. The church helped support the Residents Association, especially through the Justice and Peace Commission. It was probably the fact that the Residents Association was well organized which helped them survive another attempt in 1977

to evict them – this time by the Urbanization Enterprise of
Recife who wanted to develop the site for tourism. But a year
later, with the political momentum from Brazil's move back to
democracy, the plan to remove the settlement changed to one
which would improve it for its residents and provide them with
land rights. But the residents remained sceptical; as a long-time
resident said:

> We decided to create our laws, our urban plans. . . How
> can you trust in URB (the Urbanization Enterprise of
> Recife) or FIDEM (The Foundation for the Development
> of the Metropolitan Area of Recife) or the President if
> what they want is to drink from the coconuts on Brasilia
> Teimosa's beach? We do not know the techniques but no
> technician can appraise the value of my shanty. It is worth
> 26 years of struggle.

Since 1979, work has been continuing to obtain legal rights
for the residents. In 1982, there were elections for the State
Assembly and for councillors; the lawyers on the Justice and
Peace Commission were the most voted-for councillors in
Recife's history and received most of the votes from Brasilia
Teimosa's electorate.

Source: Alexandrina Sobreira de Moura, "Brasilia Teimosa – the organization
of a low-income settlement in Recife, Brazil", *Development Dialogue*, no.1
(1987).

In 1985, an Indian journalist friend took us to visit some squatter
settlements in Delhi; in one, we asked its inhabitants (with the
journalist acting as our interpreter) what had happened to the house
which had obviously existed in what was now a small empty plot in
the middle of a very densely built up settlement. The answer was:

> A family lived here. During the last monsoon, the rains des-
> troyed the shelter. As the family did not have enough money to
> buy the materials to build a new shelter, they moved out of the
> settlement to seek other sources of income. But they said that
> they plan to return and we are keeping the plot for them.

Despite the desperate shortage of land and the fact that every square
metre of the settlement was crowded with huts, the people living

there had decided to assume the responsibility of keeping a place for one of their families – even if the entire community was occupying the site illegally.

A law's relevance can only be judged by the benefits that the population as a whole receives from its application. If judged by this criterion, most laws concerned with protecting the health and safety of people in Third World cities – at work or within their homes – are irrelevant. Laws are seldom changed to take account of new realities.

Not surprisingly, the laws – and the multiplicity of government agencies which administer them – seldom take account of the very low average incomes of most citizens or differences in income distribution or the diversity of cultural groups. Furthermore, since independence, foreign aid and foreign consultants have helped reinforce inappropriate foreign models for many urban laws governing the built environment. Few governments have modified these so they reflect local needs, local possibilities and local resources. If any modifications are made, they are made in the largest cities. Little thought is given to the fact that the standards set for the largest cities might be totally inappropriate in smaller urban centres. Yet in many nations, much of the urban population lives in relatively small urban centres (see Chapter 9). If and when standards are adopted for smaller urban centres, these are usually only simplified replicas of those adopted for large cities.

In summary then, laws are unjust when the poverty of the majority of people makes it impossible for them to comply with them. If for most urban citizens, the basic tasks of daily life – building or renting a shelter, earning an income, obtaining food and water – are illegal, it would be wise for governments to change the legislation or simply to eliminate unrealistic laws. Urban legislation should be more flexible in adapting to the great variety of circumstance and the rate at which these can change. But it should also incorporate the particular objectives and priorities of low income groups as well as the experience gained by community organizations in the construction and management of their neighbourhoods. If building codes are meant to promote health and safety, then perhaps they would have more impact if they sought to guide and advise the people who are actually managing most new house construction – the poorer households – and thus help them meet health and safety requirements at minimal cost. As Patrick McAuslan has pointed out, it is hardly appropriate for poorer groups building their own houses to be told that the level of foundation (for their new house) should be such that a minimum depth of the foundation to prevent the soil moving laterally under pressure shall be according to Rankine's theory[28]

with Rankine's theory then set out in mathematical symbols with no diagrams, drawings or simple explanations of what is required. Yet this is part of Madras City Corporation's building rules which apply to all buildings within the city. As the old Masaii proverb says "one government cannot hold all wisdom".

2. One Government Cannot Hold All Wisdom

Although circumstances vary greatly from city to city and from nation to nation, nearly all Third World governments are failing to adopt the policies and to make the investments which actually address the basic needs of lower income groups. Among urban centres, the few already privileged cities, and the consolidated urban districts within such cities, receive a much higher share of total expenditure and investment than do the illegal settlements – usually largely self built – of poorer groups. One result of this is that the differences between the health status of the richer groups and the poorer groups within a large city can be greater than the differences between the health status of city dwellers and rural dwellers. Evidence for this can be found in an increased number of health studies.[1]

Most governments – whether through unwillingness or incapacity – are not even beginning to meet the problems which derive from the expansion of cities and their population growth. Part of the reason is the very weak and inadequate institutional structure of local and city government; for much of Africa and Asia, this is another legacy of colonial rule but again one which has not been addressed by independent governments. National and provincial governments usually limit the actions of city and municipal governments to providing infrastructure and services – such as roads, water supply and garbage collection. Never in the history of cities in the Third World have there been so many projects for sanitation or conventional housing or industrial parks. But they have contributed very little to improving the living conditions of the poor majority (see Chapters 3 and 4). Not only are public housing programmes very small in relation to need but in addition, they usually benefit relatively well off households. Public housing projects are politically useful as tangible proof that the government is doing something but the impact on the problem is minimal and most of the limited allocation of funds end up benefiting the middle class.

Governments often reduce the problem of building and managing cities to one of lack of funds for projects. Money is seen as the universal solution - money to build more homes, pipes, roads and pavements, money to buy more buses and build an underground, a hospital or schools. Each ministry or municipal department and each social group wants more money to satisfy its own plans and ambitions. Each has its own, usually self-serving priority. Very few serious efforts are made by governments to rethink what is appropriate and effective for their cities in their own economic, social and cultural context with the resources they have to hand. Little consideration is given to a more equal distribution of existing resources used in ways which relate to local economic possibilities and meet general needs. Building regulations could help rather than hinder every citizen in finding a legal solution to their housing problems; they should be sufficiently flexible to encourage and support upgrading. Reform of local government could allow municipal decision-making to be based on a broader, more participatory approach which would allow for closer cooperation between government and the community organizations formed by low income groups in illegal settlements.

Inappropriate models and concepts

Underlying many of the inappropriate actions by government are a series of questionable judgements as to what the problem is. Many governments are still trying to plan and build cities for societies which only exist in the minds of their technocrats and politicians. Perhaps the most common example is the national or city government which tries to plan and build a city based on alien or outdated ideas or models. One reason for this is the nature of professional training; many Third World professionals trained in schools and universities in Europe and North America and neither they nor their teachers questioned the validity of transferring the approaches that they were taught to the Third World. Another is pressure from the aid agencies of Western nations, whose aid is so often tied to purchasing their own equipment or following the advice of their own consultants. But the blindness of Third World ministers or civil servants must also be considered; they often want to emulate the Metro system in Paris or the public-housing programme in Singapore and give little thought to its appropriateness to their cities and their citizens' needs.

The attitude to illegal housing developments is an example of this lack of realism. Not long ago, it was common to find maps in use by city planners still representing large squatter settlements as unbuilt areas or open space, as if the illegally developed sites occupied by thousands of households somehow did not exist. Such maps illustrate official attitudes to these settlements, even when such settlements house a third or more of the entire city's population and workforce. Another is the common practice of hiding low-income settlements behind large walls or poster hoardings so nothing is done about housing problems except to make them less visible.

Slums or sub-standard housing only exist because specific housing structures or residential areas are so labelled (usually by a government agency). The criteria used to make such judgements are often based on Western models. Box 2.1 illustrates how subjective the judgement can be by highlighting the differences between the perceptions of the inhabitants and those of the government in a central Lagos slum. People who live in slums or sub-standard housing often have different accounts of both the problem and the solution.

Box 2.1: A slum is only a slum in the eyes of some

When the representative of the British Crown visited Nigeria at Independence, part of the city along her route from the airport was fenced off, out of sight. The Nigerians did not want her to see the central Lagos slum. This was defined as a slum not because of the condition of its houses nor because of the circumstances of its residents but because of the image of Nigeria it presented to politicians and administrators. In this slum:

a stock of houses . . . had been adapted by a mixed population of shopkeepers, traders, clerks, artisans and labourers, ranging from poor to prosperous, who lived congenially in the courtyards off its narrow lanes. For most of its inhabitants, central Lagos was not squalid, overcrowded or dirty, despite the undrained alleys, the chickens and goats. It was the centre of small-scale commerce, a nub of trading activities reaching hundreds of miles into the hinterland; and through its courtyards ramified a network of family relationships sustaining an intricate exchange of mutual support.

For most of its inhabitants, it was a home that suited their needs. It was also an important centre for commerce and thus for jobs. There were serious problems – ones which no doubt both government and residents could agree on – for instance the lack of sewers and drainage, inadequate services to collect household garbage. However, these could have been solved without slum clearance.

Source: Peter Marris, "Slums and patterns of change", *International Journal of Urban and Regional Research*, vol. 3, no. 3, 1979.

Government agencies also tend to think of illegal settlements as disorganized or unplanned and this becomes a justification for demolishing some or all of the houses to allow for a planned development. It is very difficult for any outside observer to understand why a particular illegal settlement developed in a particular way. The location of the settlement, the site plan and the connections it has with other neighbourhoods and with the rest of the city are often carefully thought out by its inhabitants. The sheer diversity of the ways that different illegal settlements develop and the complexity of each settlement's connections to the wider city, society and economy defy academic or bureaucratic approaches which seek to classify them. Each settlement must be understood as a particular process of social transformation – usually in a continuous and vital period of transition. Even well-motivated government efforts to improve conditions may result in damage to this process, if such efforts are not based on a real understanding of the inhabitants' needs and priorities.

Third World governments often act as if they were dealing with populations whose incomes are comparable with those in Western cities. It is one thing to think of building a city where most people have steady incomes and can pay for the houses and services they use, or even where people have lower or unstable incomes but can none the less can afford to pay modest amounts for housing and services. It is quite another to consider how to build and develop a city and serve its citizens when a high proportion can afford to pay little or nothing for their housing and who subsist on such an inadequate income that virtually all is spent on food and other goods on which survival depends. Models and precedents from Western cities have little relevance for governments faced with these circumstances.

Attitudes to housing

Few Third World governments gave much attention to housing problems in the 1950s and early 1960s. The United Nations was pointing out that most Third World nations would need to maintain a house construction rate of between 8 to 12 new units per 1,000 inhabitants per year but in most nations, only one or two new conventional houses were being constructed and in many, the average was below one. There was a widespread belief that the diversion of scarce capital to such ends was a waste since economic development would create the conditions for improved housing and a more productive economy. This in turn could provide more resources to invest in social provision. The literature about development from this period is characterized by a considerable optimism that governments could create the conditions for "take-off" and then self-sustaining economic growth so resources should be concentrated on removing key bottlenecks.[2] The rapidly growing illegal settlements were often regarded as a transitory phenomenon which would soon disappear as the economy developed. Such an attitude proved convenient for governments since it justified taking no action at all.

In time, however, many governments became increasingly worried about the rapid growth in the size and population of their major cities and of what they called slums or shanty towns. These were often seen as "a cancer" and thus in need of eradication;[3] the most common reaction was large slum and shanty clearance – usually by bulldozing (see Box 2.2).

Box 2.2: The bulldozing option

LATIN AMERICA: By the 1950s and 1960s, there were large scale squatter bulldozing programmes in many Latin American cities, and attempts by low income groups to invade land were usually quickly suppressed. In many Brazilian cities, there was the major drive to eradicate squatter settlements (or *favelas*) during the 1960s and early 1970s. In Caracas, Venezuela, throughout much of the 1950s, there was large-scale bulldozing of the *ranchos* combined with attempts to rehouse their population in high rise public housing estates –

the *superbloques*; those living in the *ranchos* often had no more than a few hours warning before the bulldozers arrived. More recent examples include the squatter eradication programme of the Military Government of Argentina between 1977 and 1980, the eviction and control of squatter invasions in Chile after 1973 under Pinochet and a city "beautification" programme in Santo Domingo started in 1988 in preparation for the celebrations planned to commemorate the 500th anniversary of Columbus's journey to America. In Santo Domingo, 7,000 households had been evicted by October 1988 while a further 12,000 were under threat of eviction; some 100,000 people in all are affected. Evicted home-owners are in theory authorized to live in a new public housing development but most cannot afford such housing. Tenants receive no compensation at all.

AFRICA: In Nigeria, a major slum clearance scheme was undertaken in Lagos during the 1950s. In 1984-5, the so-called "War Against Indiscipline" included mass demolitions in many cities. In newly independent Tanzania, during the First Five Year Plan (1964-69), slum clearance schemes were launched in several urban centres and almost as many housing units were destroyed as were built by the public housing programme. In Senegal, the government undertook

> a systematic campaign to destroy squatter areas in the city
> centre of Dakar, culminating in the destruction of Nimzatt
> and Angle-Mouse in 1975. . . Echoes of the Senegalese
> initiatives (both before and after) were the Nairobi "clean
> up" campaign of 1970 which left 50,000 homeless . . . and
> the Ivorian government's destruction of the homes of 20
> per cent of the Abidjan population from 1969 to 1973.[4]

ASIA: Large slum clearance programmes were common in many Asian cities between 1950 and 1975 and some have continued up to the present. Seoul, capital of South Korea, has probably had the most forced evictions of any city in the world in the last 30 years; since 1966, millions of people have been forced out of accommodation they own or rent against their wishes. Home-owners have received inadequate compensation and little or no help in finding alternative accommodation; tenants received no help and most received no compensation. Between 1983 and 1988, 720,000 people lost their homes in "redevelopment" programmes; most of the houses destroyed were solid one-storey houses and 90 per cent of those evicted did not obtain an apartment in the redeveloped site. In Manila, over the last 40 years, hundreds of thousands of people have been forcibly evicted from their homes; four relocation sites at considerable distances from the city centre have been developed to accommodate over 400,000 people. The first recorded squatter eviction was in 1951 and after that, they became common occurrences. Perhaps the largest was the eviction of 90,000 people between December 1963 and March 1964. There was also what is known as "the last campaign" in 1982 when Mrs Marcos, Mayor of Metropolitan Manila and wife of the (then) President launched a large squatter eviction campaign. In Bangkok, a study published in 1985 found that 269 slum areas housing 272,000 people were under threat of eviction. A study of slum areas in 1981 found 39 where the population had already been evicted (some 61,600 people) while a further 148,600 people were being evicted or under threat of eviction. In Delhi, during the 1960s, there was a major redevelopment programme with tens of thousands of people relocated to transit camps and urban villages on the fringe of the city. Between 1975 and 1977, this redevelopment programme was revived as part of a city "beautification" programme and some 150,000 people were moved. Large scale evictions have also taken place in Delhi, Bombay, Calcutta and other Indian cities since 1980.

Sources: See note 5.

Slum clearance was often encouraged by Western "experts" or by Third World professionals trained in Western schools and universities[6] who used precedents both from Third World nations under colonial rule and from the West's own cities. No doubt, the approach was made more attractive because the land cleared by such actions was often used for profitable commercial developments; those displaced by slum clearance rarely received accommodation on the redeveloped site, even where this was promised.

Many studies have shown how these clearance schemes greatly exacerbate the problem. They destroy some of the few housing options open to poorer groups; the result of such actions is usually to make conditions even worse in other settlements as those evicted have to double up with other households or build another shack in another illegal settlement. Perhaps more serious than this is the damage done by eviction to the network of family, friends and contacts which individuals and families build up within their neighbourhood. This network often has enormous importance for poorer households since it is through this that they find out about new jobs, borrow money or goods during difficult periods, share child-minding to allow more adults to go to work etc, all of which have considerable importance to their survival.[7] For instance, a study in the *suburbios* in Guayaquil (Ecuador) where families invade and take possession of municipally-owned land on a tidal swamp showed the importance of these links. The lack of water, electricity and provision for the disposal of household wastes forces women living there to rapidly develop mutual aid links with previously unknown neighbours. Such links are often formalized as neighbours are asked to become godmothers at the birth of children. Such links are not only of great importance to day to day survival but they also provide the basis for the community to mobilize to request some public investments in the area from the local authorities.[8]

As Box 2.2 suggests, where government does take some responsibility for rehousing those evicted, the most common response is to dump them onto an undeveloped site at some distance from the city centre. Not surprisingly, the result is usually further impoverishment for those evicted. It is also common for many of those moved to such new locations to move back to another illegal development or inner-city tenement. More central locations are essential to many families' survival; such locations allow more than one adult and often children to find work and contribute to the household income. In the relocation site, not only does the main income earner have high transport costs in terms of the journey to and from work but it makes it impossible for other family members to work. The Sapang Palay relocation site in Manila provides an example. When some 90,000 people were evicted from central Manila in late 1963 and early 1964, 30,000 of them were registered for relocation in Sapang Palay, some 37 kilometres away from Manila. The site proved so poorly suited to the needs of those evicted that many moved backed to central Manila. By the end of 1965, less than 17,000 people remained.[9] Other relocation sites have proved just as inappropriate for poorer households in terms of poor location, poor local job prospects and inadequate infrastructure and services (see Box 2.3).[10]

Box 2.3: The impact of squatter relocation in Manila, the Philippines

Despite the fact that relocation sites were planned to rehouse hundreds of thousands of squatters, the sites themselves were ill-prepared, the promised facilities were not available and people had to make do with hastily constructed shelters. The relocation uprooted squatters from an environment which had become vital to them and their families. They were brought to sites outside Manila far from their places of work, their net-work of friends and relatives and the schools attended by their children. Children had to leave their schools. For people who looked after infants and children, there were far fewer opportu-nities to earn secondary incomes in the relocation sites. Before being relocated, household heads and spouses usually earned livings as drivers of jeepneys (jeeps converted into taxis), as factory or construction workers, security guards, streetsellers, scavengers, laundry women, maids and dressmakers. Those lacking regular jobs needed to live close to the central city to find casual work. All could walk to and from work or at least keep transport costs down. Relocation meant a significant increase in transportation costs and time spent commuting to and from work. Those who relied on casual work had far more difficulties, after relocation, not only because of the time and cost of going to and from central city locations but also because of the disruption to social networks which in their former settlements had provided information about where casual work was available.

Source: Perla Q. Makil, "Slums and squatter settlements in the Philippines", *Concerned Citizens of the Urban Poor* series, no. 3 (Manila, 1982).

Governments usually justify evictions in one of three ways. The first (and perhaps the most common) is to "improve" or "beautify" the city. In Manila and Seoul, many evictions took place just before major international events there: in Manila, prior to the Miss Uni-verse contest and the visit of the Pope[11]; in Seoul, prior to the Olym-pics.[12] The active involvement of the late Sanjay Gandhi (the son of the then Indian Premier) in the large-scale eviction programme in Delhi between 1975 and 1977 was part of a city "beautification" programme. No doubt, the fact that Delhi is India's capital was also used to help justify the redevelopment programmes implemented during the 1960s which dumped tens of thousands of households in transit camps and urban villages on the fringes of Delhi.[13] In Kenya, President Kenyatta defended the large-scale squatter demolition programme undertaken by Nairobi Council in 1970 by saying that he did not want Kenya's capital to turn into a shanty town.[14]

Authoritarian governments are more likely to implement large "city beautification" plans with large-scale evictions; a lack of dialogue with citizens and their organizations, a lack of representation for citizen views within government and a style of government which represses popular protest greatly limits the possibility of successful opposition to such plans.[15] Not surprisingly, the negotiation of a compromise between those undertaking the redevelopment (the state or a private company) and those to be evicted is more common in nations with representative forms of government.

A second way in which government justifies evictions is the idea that slums are centres of crime and havens for criminals. In their eyes, evictions not only make the city more beautiful but rid it of concentrations of crime. When a new eviction programme was launched in Manila in mid-1982, Mrs Marcos (then Mayor of Metro Manila) talked of "professional squatters" who were "plain landgrabbers taking advantage of the compassionate society".[16] In Malaysia, illegal settlements were said to "harbour criminals and racketeers, pose fire and disease hazards . . . tarnish the image of the capital at home and abroad" and furthermore, "promote juvenile delinquency, challenge the status of the government as the source of law and order, and threaten the economic, social and political stability of the city".[17]

Governments have also used the health problems evident in innercity tenements or squatter settlements as a justification for their clearance. This argument was put forward in Nigeria to justify slum clearance in the mid-1950s.[18] But eviction and slum or squatter clearance will usually increase rather than decrease health problems. If no alternative accommodation is provided for those displaced, they have to find space in other cheap areas and increase overcrowding there. And as noted already, even where those displaced are rehoused, this is usually done in such a way as to further impoverish these people and is likely to lead to even poorer health. In this way, the people whose health problems were used to justify the evictions are likely to end up with worse health problems than before.

Of course, the underlying reasons for evictions often differ from official justifications. Alejandro Portes illustrates this in the case of Rio de Janeiro where a large *favela* (squatter) eradication programme between 1968 and 1972 destroyed 16,647 *barracos* (shacks). The government justified this by using inaccurate stereotypes about the "pathological" character of *favelas*, the impossibility of improving them and the need to "free" their inhabitants from cultural and physical disintegration. Although never made explicit, the eradication had more to do with the desire of the Brazilian Federal Government to intervene in housing policy which, traditionally, was a state responsibility. In the late 1950s and early 1960s, the state government had promoted community organization and upgrading in Rio's *favelas*. Such approaches were then rejected, especially by the military government which took power in 1964.[19]

A comparable gap between underlying reasons and official justifications can be seen in the eviction of squatters from central locations in the city of Pune (India) and their relocation to more peripheral sites after 1983. These were justified by the need to protect water quality in a canal which runs through the squatter settlement – a more likely reason is that these settlements were on a valuable central site of historic importance and were easily visible from large parts of the city.[20]

A third justification for evictions is redevelopment, to use the cleared land more intensively, or to build public works or facilities. Here, underlying reasons and official justifications are more likely to coincide. Centrally-located areas in a city and strategically-located areas (for instance, close to airports or main roads) become increasingly valuable as the city's economy develops. Cheap tenement districts often develop in city centres but as the city grows, so too does the pressure to redevelop central locations for offices or other uses which yield higher returns. Similarly, squatter settlements which developed on what was once the city's periphery some decades ago are often on land which has become very valuable as the city expands. Land-owners or developers can make very large profits redeveloping such sites, especially if they can avoid the cost of rehousing those evicted from these sites. If settlements are judged to be "illegal" – even if they have been there for many decades – this is a convenient excuse to bulldoze them with no compensation paid to former inhabitants.

In "redevelopments" of areas where the housing is legal, house-owners usually receive compensation although not necessarily enough to allow them to purchase another house of comparable quality and value to the one they will lose. But it is very rare for tenants to receive any compensation. In many redevelopment schemes in Seoul, home-owners received some compensation although not enough to allow them to purchase another house or flat in the new development. But tenants – who often made up 60 per cent or more of all those displaced – usually received nothing but a notice to quit and, at best, a small token payment. When government officials were asked about this by the Asian Coalition for Housing Rights,[21] it became obvious that they had never considered the idea of tenant rights and indeed had difficulty understanding the concept. The implication is that government views tenants as second-class citizens with fewer rights than those rich enough to afford the purchase of their own house or flat. The same is true of the large scale evictions in Santo Domingo, initiated in 1988 and currently underway. Here too, home-owners received very inadequate compensation but tenants (again, the major-ity) received nothing.

Portes summarizes the benefits brought to middle and upper income groups, and to industry and construction firms as a result of the *favela* eradication programme in Rio de Janeiro. He also looked at comparable benefits that have come to similar interests in eviction programmes in other cities.

> The re-organization of space . . . freed land from occupation by the most deprived classes and placed it at the disposal of the wealthier groups. The program aimed to stimulate upper and middle class residential construction by clearing the most desirable areas of the city from the presence of the poor. "Clear-ing" took the double meaning of physically opening new sites for construction and symbolically freeing the well-to-do from daily confrontation with the misery of the *favelas*. Other sites were cleared to serve the needs of industry and construction firms were given an additional boost by receiving government contracts to build public housing projects. Needless to say, all of this was done in the name of the government's concern for the welfare of the "less favoured" families.[22]

Many evictions are extremely violent. In some, the inhabitants get little or no warning before the bulldozers move in. Box 2.4 tells the story of an eviction in 1987 in Seoul, South Korea.

Box 2.4: Eviction in Sang Kye Dong in Seoul, South Korea

Sang Kye Dong was initially established as a result of people evicted from other areas of Seoul being moved there in the 1960s. With the development of a subway system (one of the projects associated with preparations for the Olympics in 1988) and a new station being located nearby, this became an area slated for redevelopment as a new city with 57,000 apartments.

There were around 1,100 houses on a 4 hectare site. When local residents organized to resist this redevelopment (and their eviction), they were subjected to a series of violent attacks. Between 26 June 1986 and 14 April 1987, they were attacked 18 times. Around 400 people (half of them young people and children) resisted eviction. Most of these attacks involved several hundred riot police and men hired by the construction company to intimidate and assault the residents. Many of the residents, including grandparents and babies, suffered serious injuries as a result of these attacks. The cost of treating those injured totalled some US$15,000.

On 24 December 1986 the most senior South Korean Catholic, Cardinal Kim, had planned to come to the community to celebrate a Catholic Mass for Christmas Eve. On the afternoon of 24 December, an attack was mounted specifically to stop him doing so and two large tents used as community centres were burnt down; so too were all the items stored in the tents. The site was then dug up to prevent the Cardinal being able to celebrate the Mass, the city water pipes used by the residents were destroyed, and the electricity was cut off. As in previous attacks, the local police were also there and did nothing to halt a violent attack organized by a private company on a group of people, with the illegal destruction of private property.

On 14 April 1987, a force of 3,500 people and 77 trucks moved into the area – against 380 citizens. The belongings of the residents were loaded onto the trucks and driven away. The tent headquarters were demolished and the residents carried off the area. Wide trenches were dug at the entrances to the area and large barricades erected to prevent re-entry. Riot police and guards hired by the construction company remained to guard the site.

The former residents lived for several months in tents set up in the grounds of the Roman Catholic Cathedral in central Seoul. With the political changes which saw a move towards democracy, the public authorities appear to have become less intransigent. A plot of land was provided for the Sang Kye Community members – but when they began to erect their dwellings, these were torn down by the local authorities. The people were refused permission to build their houses because the plot they had been allocated happened to be in sight of the road where the Olympic torch was to be carried in September 1988. The residents were forced to dig holes in the ground in which they lived for the worst of the winter months and then with the advent of the rains, to live in plastic shelters.

Sources: Urban Poor Institute, *Information Packet on the Urban Poor of Korea*, Seoul, 1988; and Catholic Institute for International Relations, *Disposable People: Forced Evictions in South Korea* (London: CIIR, 1988).

This is not to imply that no redevelopment can take place within cities. Inevitably, in any rapidly growing and developing city, there will be a need to redevelop certain areas and for public agencies to acquire land for infrastructure and services. The issue is not that such redevelopments should never take place but the way they are currently implemented with little or no dialogue with those who will be displaced and with little or no respect for their needs. In many cities, both the scale of evictions and the motivations of government in allowing or implementing them are open to question. In this context, note should be made of changes in government attitude to evictions in Thailand which coincide with the move to a more open and democratic form of government. Most of the recent evictions in Bangkok have been from public land although there are many instances where a compromise has been reached between the inhabitants of illegal settlements and the land-owner. Such compromises – known as 'land sharing' arrangements – give part of the site to the inhabitants on which houses or flats are constructed to house them with the rest returned to the land-owner for redevelopment.[23]

It is difficult to assess whether the scale of evictions in the Third World is growing or lessening. Existing documentation suggests that evictions are now less common than in the 1960s and early 1970s, and Chapters 4 and 5 will describe the alternative policies which some governments have developed. But it may be that evictions continue in many Third World cities on a large scale without us being aware of them. Researchers prefer to document what are regarded as successful policies rather than evictions. It is worth noting that much of the information about recent evictions in Seoul and Manila came from documentation produced by citizen groups there trying to fight the evictions.[24]

Urban growth as a problem

Most governments have identified urban growth as a problem and many have used repressive measures to control it. For instance, in Senegal in 1977, there was a major effort to remove beggars and small traders from the streets of Dakar while in Nigeria in 1983, there was a massive "clean up" of urban traders.[25] In Tanzania, in 1983, elaborate administrative machinery was established for the "transfer, training and rehabilitation of unemployed (urban) residents"[26] which led to thousands of arrests in Dar es Salaam. In Manila in 1982, Mrs Marcos ordered the creation of a special commission "to prevent and control the entry of squatters in Metro Manila" with the powers and the equipment to immediately remove squatter families and drive them to a relocation site.[27]

Other governments have sought to control migration to cities in other ways. For example, an attempt was made in Indonesia in 1970 to control migration to Jakarta. All migrants had to obtain a residence card to be allowed to remain in the city and to qualify for the card, they had to prove they had a job, accommodation and permission to leave their destination. They also had to make a deposit, equivalent to their return fare. In addition, attempts were made to exclude hawkers and streetsellers from certain districts.[28] In South Africa, one of the various aims of the apartheid system is to control the migration of black citizens by providing the legal basis to deny them the right to live in cities. In certain centrally planned economies, large scale programmes to force people out of cities and into the countryside have been implemented.[29]

Such policies usually derive from the mistaken belief that poor people flood into cities attracted by the lure of the bright lights. As late as 1976, a UNESCO Expert Meeting on Urban Problems talked of "the ever increasing migratory movement – in practice beyond control – of families from rural areas attracted to the glitter and fallacious promises of consumer society", with the migrants described as "potential parasites".[30] But numerous case studies have shown that most people come to cities because that is where economic opportunities are concentrated or survival is more certain. People's movements to or from cities are logical responses to the pattern of economic opportunities across a nation; Chapter 8 will document the heavy concentration of economic activities in the largest cities which underlies rapid migration flows to these cities. Most decisions to move to cities are based on careful, logical and rational judgements; many result from information from people in the cities about job opportunities there. Such judgements are more solidly based on an understanding of economic change than government programmes which try to control population movements. And migrants are not parasites; indeed, the prosperity of cities often largely depends on the jobs that they do for very low pay with long hours and very poor working conditions. Thus, government attempts to control city growth by trucking the poor out to the countryside, or to control movement into the city through some form of licence, are simply addressing the effects, not the causes.

Governments might decry the fact that a city is growing rapidly but they rarely ask why – or consider the extent to which their own policies are one of the main causes. Nor do they look at why people are leaving their original homes. In many cases, the migrants are small farmers forced off their lands or agricultural labourers whose livelihood has disappeared because of soil erosion, low crop prices or the increasing concentration of land ownership, with consequent changes in crops and the means of producing them. Many other migrants come from smaller urban centres whose economies stagnate and whose potential for development is stifled by inappropriate government policies (see Chapter 9). These are causes about which governments could take action, if they wanted to slow migration to cities.

But it is also possible to question whether population growth or the "flood" of migrants is in fact the problem. Most of the Third World's urban centres are not growing very rapidly (see Chapter 8), and the natural increase in population as children are born to parents already residing in urban areas contributes much more to urban population growth than new people coming into the city.

Many of the cities which have grown most rapidly during the last 20 to 30 years have done so because their booming economy attracted a large number of people. Many others grew rapidly because they were the location of most new investments and job opportunities within the nation, even if the national economy was not growing rapidly. In theory, government should have been able to recapture some of the profits from such expanding city economies to pay for infrastructure and services for both the inhabitants and for city businesses. In this way, government could not only tackle the problems but also provide the basis for continuing economic expansion. Of course, there are also many cities which grew rapidly because they became the homes of those fleeing drought, floods or war or those pushed off land that had been their livelihood so that rapid city growth was not associated with an expanding city economy. But this should not disguise the fact that many city problems could have been greatly reduced if governments had more effectively drawn resources from expanding economic activities to provide the capital needed for infrastructure and service investments.

There are many examples of Western cities which grew at rates comparable to most of the Third World's fast-growing large cities, and these have shown that it is possible for governments to deal with rapid city growth. For example, the population of the Los Angeles–Long Beach urban agglomeration has grown more rapidly than Calcutta since 1900 and the population of the Tokyo agglomeration has, in recent decades, grown on a scale comparable to that of Mexico City. While there are serious housing problems in both Los Angeles and Tokyo, they do not compare with those in Calcutta or Mexico City. Nor is their population growth associated with comparable levels of poverty, malnutrition and disease.

The problems for Third World cities are not the result of rapid population growth itself, but of growth within the context of a legal and institutional structure unable to cope with the needs of the population and the tasks of providing and running city services. Central to this is the weakness of municipal and city government. More recently, problems have been further compounded by declining public investment capacity, the giving of low priority to investments in basic services, and inappropriate models of public intervention. As Otto Koenigsberger commented in 1976, "rapid population growth does not create poverty; it merely makes poverty more visible".[31]

There is evidence in recent years that some governments are beginning to appreciate the gap between their plans and the reality around them – perhaps partially as a result of conferences, projects, better knowledge and closer ties between researchers and community leaders. These will be described in Chapter 3 which looks at how citizens find shelter and Chapters 4 and 5 which examine the role of government within this. But more effective pressure on governments has come directly from community groups formed by the poor, even if these usually receive neither official recognition nor representation within government.

Local government – responsibility without the resources

Urban centres of whatever size need competent, representative government to make them work, especially for poorer groups. No other institution can ensure that infrastructure and basic services are provided to all citizens, even if local government does not itself provide all services. No other institution can manage and co-ordinate new urban developments to ensure they contribute to a safe and healthy built environment and to reserve sufficient space for roads, pathways and public areas for recreation and leisure. No other institution can provide on-the-spot checks on the over-exploitation of workforces, and the dumping of polluting wastes. No other institution can provide tenants with protection against landlords, or address such problems as traffic congestion.

Largely in recognition of this fact, local government usually has an enormous range of legal and institutional responsibilities in the planning, maintenance and rehabilitation of urban centres. It is usually responsible for regulating building construction, for paving streets and sidewalks, for regulating traffic and public transport, for enforcing (and perhaps legislating on) environmental matters including sanitary measures and, at least in principle, in deciding on the location, characteristics and sequences of public and private investments within their area of jurisdiction. In exchange for these services, it can exact certain taxes or revenues – typically real estate taxes or taxes on certain industrial and commercial goods or activities. It also sets rates and collects charges for many publicly provided services and is often an important source of employment – especially for unskilled labour.

Urban plans and socio-economic plans for cities are, in most instances, also the responsibility of local government. Individually, or through agreement with other local governments and provincial (or state) and national government, metropolitan or even regional plans can be initiated. So all plans, programmes and policies for an urban area should in theory be subject to decisions by local government. In practice, in the Third World, this is very rarely the case. Most local governments have very little positive influence on urban development and fulfil very few of their responsibilities for management and public service provision. Most lack the staff to prepare and implement projects and the revenues to pay for needed capital investments, and the up-to-date data about their area including something as basic as a cadastral survey.

Local government has a long tradition in many Third World nations but its role in socio-economic development has declined – even in those countries where it was never particularly strong or well defined in the first place. The structure of most local governments is obsolete; their professional and intermediate level staff totally inadequate for their jobs. Their tax collecting systems and the ordinances which generate local incomes are usually obsolete; so too are the measures to control the evasion of tax. As one paper on local government in the Third World commented, many such governments are "fragmented, confused about their functions and all too often either invisible or largely ceremonial".[32]

Virtually all local governments lack the funds to permit the expansion of basic infrastructure and services in line with expanding needs. National government usually reserves for itself the most lucrative and easily collected taxes - like income tax[33] while local governments are faced with "a formidable list of restraints" on their taxing powers and "access by urban area governments to the most productive tax sources is commonly denied or severely restricted".[34]

But perhaps more importantly, only local government can perform a range of tasks which are critical to local development. As a review of experiences with decentralization in the Third World noted – the centralization of decisions and resources imposes a heavy cost:

> Central administrators cannot know the complex variety of factors that affect the success of projects in local communities throughout the country. In their attempt to cope with uncertainty, they create highly centralized and standardized procedures; or through fear of making mistakes, they do nothing about urgent decisions that are essential for implementing local projects and programmes.[35]

Central governments' failure to provide local government with power, resources and trained personnel means that government plans rarely fit in with local needs and that local revenues remain untapped. A training exercise in the Philippines for local government officials found that if the property tax from just a few of the largest property tax delinquents was collected, it would equal one year's total local government revenue.[36] A similar exercise in Ghana found that the potential returns from local revenues from various taxes, fees, tolls and licenses were usually five times or more than the amount collected.[37]

Local governments often serve cities with several million inhabitants with structures, levels of representation and political ideas which might have some validity for urban centres with a few thousand inhabitants, but which are totally ineffective in larger metropolitan centres. Their ability to negotiate with provincial/state or national government, and with the private sector, is also weak.

The increasing economic and political decline of local government over the last few decades reflects the growing centralization of power within national governments and their indifference to sub-national levels of government. National political parties and formal power groups show little interest in local government, possibly because they fear its potential as a breeding ground for politicians with real popular support. In predominantly urban societies, as in most Latin American and many Asian nations, the situation is even more serious as there is also poor co-ordination between national or provincial agencies and the local governments responsible for urban centres.

Poor inter-sectoral co-ordination in local government and among different government levels also inhibits necessary action. Investments in public works, health, education, housing etc, are controlled by sectoral agencies. As a result, in any urban area, there are several sectoral investment programmes, both public and private, operating simultaneously – and yet none of them will be working in coordination with each other.

The rigid systems of tax collection and the sporadic contacts between tax assessment agencies and those responsible for public services help explain the low revenues which come to local government – whether raised from direct or indirect sources. This is made worse in periods of high inflation and recession – but these are now common characteristics for many nations. The possibility of resolving such problems is limited both by central government controls on their capacity to raise funds and by the poor technical knowledge of most local officials.

Thus, despite the plethora of books and articles about what government is doing or should do, cities continue to grow and evolve in a manner over which local government has a relatively little control. In most cities, municipal politicians and planners have not been able to influence the land market for housing so as to increase the proportion of households which can buy, rent or build a legal house. They have not even begun to keep pace with the growth in the need for basic infrastructure and services. And they have shown little or no capacity for providing a framework for the city's physical growth.

National policies

Most governments will not state explicitly what they intend to do with their human settlements. Their national plans may express concern for "rapidly growing cities" or "unbalanced regional development" or "backward regions", but the policies they propose show little or no concern for the spatial distribution of social and economic investments – investments which, after all, underlie the development of settlements. During the 1950s and 1960s, the emphasis in national plans was on economic development, on productive investment (which meant mostly industry but sometimes export crops) and on the infrastructure they needed such as dams, roads, ports and airports. The Five Year Plans (or shorter or longer term plans) formulated by national government had titles which emphasized economic development. By the early 1970s, these plans increasingly came to include the phrase "social development" somewhere in their title. An interest in slowing the growth of their largest cities also became more apparent.

But rather than explicit policies and projects based on careful analyses of what was causing or contributing to urban trends judged to be unsatisfactory, national plans included a number of broad objectives like slowing migration to the major cities, developing backward regions or dynamizing rural growth points. Some were more explicit with the identification of specific growth poles, growth centres, growth-axes, counter-magnets, secondary cities and the like which were to serve as alternatives to large cities. Most of these were based on Western precedents and ironically, they seemed to become more popular among Third World governments just at the time when their high cost and their limited impact in the West was becoming better appreciated.

More recently, many governments have launched special programmes to develop some of their smaller urban centres – often in the hope that these would provide alternatives for migrants who were heading for the major cities. Many governments have also developed national urban strategies. In addition, a new interest emerged in moving national capitals – as in the cases of Argentina and Nigeria, following earlier precedents set by nations such as Brazil, Pakistan, Malawi and Tanzania.

The measures proposed to achieve these objectives have usually been at odds with the objectives and very often have been far beyond the capacity of the government to implement them. But perhaps more worrying is that even if the measures proposed had been implemented, they would have brought little or no benefit to those most in need. On occasion, where such plans have been carried out, they have actually made things worse for poorer groups. Government programmes to push some industries or other developments to poorer regions "to benefit the poor there" rarely had much impact; many assessments of such special regional development projects show high costs to the government but little or no benefit to poorer groups.[38] Given the highly centralized nature of governments, the technocratic style of national and local planning and the political structure of most nations, popular opinion was almost always ignored. Indeed, many of the special programmes for backward regions or for small urban centres initiated by Third World governments in the last 30–40 years can be judged as smokescreens; they are there to conceal the fact that these same governments are tackling neither the fundamental causes of poverty nor the weakness in the economic base and in the local governments of smaller urban centres.[39] We will develop these points further in Chapter 9.

The impact of the economic crisis

Most Third World nations are currently experiencing an economic crisis which has had, and will continue to have, enormous repercussions on all aspects of urban life. Their governments face severe recession, large deficits in their balance of payments and, linked to this, insuperable problems in debt repayment. Application to the International Monetary Fund for help results in pressure to reduce public spending, especially in social programmes. As a result, the number of government jobs falls and living costs for poorer groups rise. Government subsidies provided to lower the price of certain goods or services – for instance certain basic foods or public transport – are often among the first things to be cut. Very often, they had come to represent a considerable proportion of government expenditure, as inflation had greatly increased the cost to the government but the price at which they were provided was fixed.

But many poorer groups have come to depend on these subsidies so a sudden increase in basic food or bus prices hits them very hard. When this is combined with the declining purchasing power of many salaries and informal incomes, it can lead to social and political clashes of unpredictable dimensions. In recent years, the bread riots in Morocco and Tunis, the problems of popular protest faced by the governments of Venezuela, Jordan, Nigeria, Senegal and Cameroun, and the difficult negotiations with labour unions of the recently elected governments of Argentina, Brazil, Peru and Uruguay, provide some examples.

It should be recalled that many national debts were contracted between international banks and non-elected and often highly repressive military governments. In certain instances, these governments only gained power with the tacit approval of governments or private companies in Europe or North America. Today, how can a democratically elected government, committed to social justice, ask additional sacrifices of its population to pay for a debt run up by the ousted military dictatorship for which neither they nor their electorate were responsible? In addition, both lenders and borrowers knew or should have known the difficulties governments would face in meeting repayments later – even if in the late 1970s, real interest rates went up to unexpected levels. Furthermore, many governments did not use the loans they received for the purposes for which they were requested and many social loans contributed little or nothing to social development.

Today, Third World governments and the banks who lend to them still see the way out of the crisis as being expanding and diversifying their exports, especially in manufactured goods. Additional foreign loans often help finance this. But the chances of success for most nations are much reduced when the richest foreign markets – those of the EEC, Japan and the United States – remain highly protected.

Every economic crisis imposes increasing pressure on already scant resources and in such periods, all citizens, businesses and institutions have to rethink their strategies for survival. For governments, this usually means the postponement of new investments in city infrastructure and no expansion in the provision of basic services. It usually implies little or no investment in maintenance – and this is reflected in the deterioration of countless city bus and train services, in road repairs, in maintenance to water mains, sewers, drains, public buildings and the like. Home-owners, landlords and businesses also postpone investments in maintenance and repair. This has important repercussions on the architectural and urban fabric and on the quality of life of urban dwellers. But even in such times, government policies and actions remain concerned with sectoral or isolated decisions; little or no thought is given to ways in which limited public resources might best be used to stem the most damaging impacts of recession.

Whatever the ultimate outcome of the economic crisis – perhaps, in the longer term, a tragic end to the move towards more democratic government in the Third World – it is obviously the urban and the rural poor who are hit hardest. They have little or no safety margin to allow them to absorb or survive its impacts. The crisis only helps to highlight their permanently unsatisfied needs. Increasing numbers of people are forced to organize the construction of their own shelters; many who took part in the invasion of private lands in Buenos Aires (Box 1.1) were forced out of reasonable accommodation because of the decline in their real incomes. The economic crisis is also a heavy blow to the expectations of lower-middle income groups, and many with stable jobs but declining real incomes are forced to seek additional incomes. In many nations, the salary levels for many local and even national government employees is so low in relation to the cost of living that many take on other jobs – often during the hours in which they are meant to be performing their government job. The result in terms of deterioration in the efficiency and competence of government is obvious.

Blocks to change

If governments persist in current attitudes and approaches, they will never successfully meet the basic needs of their urban populations. A fresh view is needed but there are various blocks that stand in the way of change. Two have been stressed already: the fact that most governments are not elected and can hardly claim to have the political support of their people; and the poor understanding government has about their people's needs and priorities.

There is also the inherent conservatism of the legal profession and, therefore, of the legislative framework which underlies governments' powers and actions. Even in democratic societies where public pressure has more chance of promoting change, laws tend to evolve by precedent and they tend to protect the interests of the more powerful.[40] Given the power of private interests in urban land, it is hardly surprising that so little has been achieved in formulating and implementing laws more in keeping with the needs of poorer citizens.

This conservatism is reinforced by the dominance of Western models, technology and training. An architect, engineer or doctor trained in the West, or in institutions with curricula based on a Western model, is rarely capable of avoiding the trap of transferring to their own cultures, the theories, techniques and experiences developed in First or Second World nations. Third World professionals have few guidelines as to how to develop more realistic norms and codes. But even to try to do so is to risk censure or to be blamed for any failure which might occur. For example, there are systems and techniques which can greatly improve sanitation in illegal settlements at a much lower cost than the standard Western-style waterborne sewage system; the range of possible options is sufficient to allow local solutions to be developed which match local conditions, resources and cultural preferences.[41] Even in sewage systems, standards might be set so high that they double the cost with no improvement in the quality of the services.[42] Project designers, technical agencies and elected officials all find it safer to stick to techniques they know and standards that minimize the possibility of failure. In addition, fees for design and profits from construction are often based on a percentage of the total project costs and this hardly acts as an incentive for the designer and the contractor who are building the system to reduce costs.[43]

Conservatism is also promoted by many aid agencies. Third World governments who seek to limit the right of individuals to own or use land so as to guarantee that poorer groups can get access to land know that this is contrary to the ideological base of many aid giving governments; to seek to change the legislative base for such matters is to risk the possibility of losing all aid. More radical attempts by Third World governments to restructure a society towards more egalitarian models often invite overt or covert military attack - as the past few decades in Latin America have shown all too many times.

3. The Search for Shelter

"The value of my house – 26 years' struggle"

Box 3.1 tells the story of the Ramirez family's search for shelter; this story was used on a United Nations poster to illustrate the struggle of a family of recent rural migrants to find a home in a large metropolis. It illustrates the kinds of political, environmental, cultural and economic problems that the family had to overcome. After 20 years struggle and the loss of one of their children (who died after drinking contaminated water), the Ramirez family finally obtained their goal of a conventional house in a legal urban development with basic services. As one householder in the squatter settlement Brasilia Teimosa said, "the value of my house – 26 years struggle".[1]

Box 3.1: The search for shelter

Below is the text of a poster printed by the United Nations during the International Year of Shelter for the Homeless in 1987. It illustrates the difficulties faced by a poor family in finding a decent house in the city. Their struggle for shelter is presented in the form of a series of steps which the family have to move through. It was designed in the form of a game known in English as Snakes and Ladders; each player would start at the beginning and take turns to move through the steps, after throwing a dice. Below is a slightly shortened version of the text taken from the game.

BACKGROUND: Mr Ramirez (31), his wife Ines (25) and their children Carlos (8), Clara (5) and Rosa (3) find that they cannot survive on their rented farmland. The rains have been poor and the one hectare plot they farm has been producing less each year. Ramirez decides to go to the city to see if he can find a job. His cousin Juan moved to the city two years earlier and has offered to help Mr Ramirez.

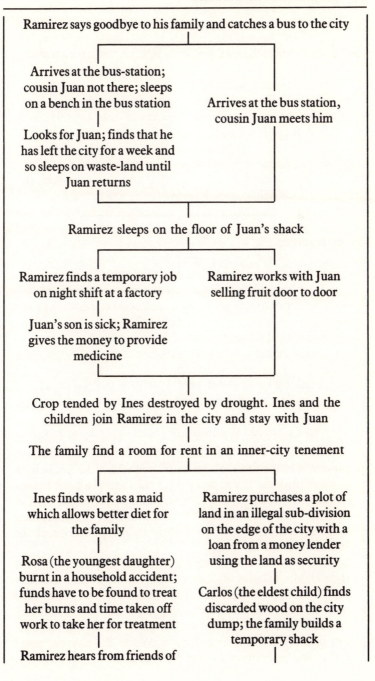

Ramirez says goodbye to his family and catches a bus to the city

Arrives at the bus-station; cousin Juan not there; sleeps on a bench in the bus station

Arrives at the bus station, cousin Juan meets him

Looks for Juan; finds that he has left the city for a week and so sleeps on waste-land until Juan returns

Ramirez sleeps on the floor of Juan's shack

Ramirez finds a temporary job on night shift at a factory

Ramirez works with Juan selling fruit door to door

Juan's son is sick; Ramirez gives the money to provide medicine

Crop tended by Ines destroyed by drought. Ines and the children join Ramirez in the city and stay with Juan

The family find a room for rent in an inner-city tenement

Ines finds work as a maid which allows better diet for the family

Ramirez purchases a plot of land in an illegal sub-division on the edge of the city with a loan from a money lender using the land as security

Rosa (the youngest daughter) burnt in a household accident; funds have to be found to treat her burns and time taken off work to take her for treatment

Carlos (the eldest child) finds discarded wood on the city dump; the family builds a temporary shack

Ramirez hears from friends of

a squatter invasion being planned; he joins the organization of the invasion

|

The family takes part in an invasion of land; on the plot of land they occupy, they build a makeshift shack

|

Police suppress the invasion and destroy the Ramirez shack;

Private firm which sells water to those in the illegal sub-division from a tanker raises prices

|

Rise in the price of bus-fares increases cost of travel to work

|

Ramirez loses his job; cannot pay the loan used to purchase the land and so they have to sell the land

the family return to a room rented in an inner-city tenement

|

The family acquire another plot of land either through a squatter invasion or by buying another illegal subdivision and manage to hold onto it and build a shack

|

A flood inundates the site of their house which delays construction and means they live in a plastic tent

|

A candidate for Mayor of the city promises that if elected, he will give Ramirez and others in their settlement legal tenure

|

Ines buys a second hand sewing machine; the extra income from selling the clothes she makes, and which Rosa helps deliver, helps speed up house construction

|

Clara goes to school; extra cost for family for books and clothes delays house construction

|

Carlos drops out of school to work as a builder; extra income helps speed up house construction

|

Candidate for Mayor who promised legal tenure wins election and after lengthy negotiations between the community organization formed by the residents of Ramirez's neighbourhood, they receive legal tenure

|

A group of people in the newly legalized settlement form a co-operative and apply for a loan to the national housing bank
|
The Ramirez have a fourth child
|
The co-operative receive the loan from the housing bank and the Ramirez, as members of the co-operative, receive a loan to allow them to purchase materials to build a permanent first storey to replace the wooden shack
|
Neighbours help the Ramirez family to pour and form the concrete for the first storey
|
The youngest child dies of dysentery because the water supply is polluted
|
Ramirez contracts TB which slows down the construction of the house
|
Clara qualifies as a teacher and finds a job teaching; she contributes to the family income and this allows the construction of a second storey to the house
|
The City Council provides piped water to the settlement with a public tap installed close to the Ramirez house
|
Clara gets married and moves out; the family rent out a room in the house to obtain extra income
|
THE END: The Ramirez family finally have a safe, well-built home of their own; it has taken them 20 years of struggle to do so, since they moved to the city. Ramirez is now 51 years old while Ines is 45, Carlos 28, Clara 25 and Rosa 23.

Source: This text was written by Jorge E. Hardoy and David Satterthwaite for a poster prepared at the request of the United Nations Centre for Human Settlements (Habitat) for the International Year of Shelter for the Homeless in 1987; Pat Crooke designed the poster and both he and John F.C. Turner helped develop the text.

Tens of millions of individuals and households who move from small towns or rural areas to major cities face comparable or worse problems in finding accommodation. Comparatively few will be as fortunate as the Ramirez family; many will spend their entire lives in an endless struggle to survive with little chance of finding a stable income and acquiring legal, good quality housing. Migration is not the problem. In many cities, there are more city-born people living in very poor accommodation than recent migrants; it is not origin but lack of income which prevents people from acquiring better accommodation. Most of those who took part in the land invasion which formed the settlement of San Martin in Buenos Aires (Box 1.1, p. 12) had been in the city for many years and many had been born there.[2]

The diversity of need

Chapter 1 already described some of the more common ways through which poor people find accommodation – building or buying a house or shack in an illegal settlement. Others will rent a room – in an inner city tenement building or a cheap boarding house or in a house in an illegal development; whole families or groups of friends will usually share just one room to keep down the cost. Others will live and sleep in public spaces – parks, graveyards, railway stations etc. Tables 3.1 and 3.2 list some of the more common ways through which poorer individuals or households find accommodation.

Within most cities, there is a considerable variety of ways through which poorer people find some form of accommodation. Each individual and each household has its own particular needs; accommodation within easy reach of jobs or places where incomes can be earned is usually the most important. Each person will also have preferences in terms of the size and cost of the dwelling – and each will have its own preferred trade off between between cost, size of dwelling, housing quality and access to services. Some will want temporary accommodation; others want a more permanent arrangement.

For many of the poorest individuals or households, accommodation within easy reach of jobs or of places where income can be earned (for instance, a busy square where goods can be sold) is more important than the size and quality of accommodation. This helps explain the tens of thousands of people whose "accommodation" is the pavement or some public open space or building. In Bombay 150,000 people live on the streets. They do so because this is the only accommodation they can afford close to the markets or docks from where their main income is derived. Some of these people could afford cheap accommodation in some of the outer parts of Bombay but they could not afford the journey to and from the centre of town. Many build makeshift huts on pavements in Central Bombay and even if the public authorities demolish their huts two or three times a year, they have little option but to rebuild – and to put up with the lack of basic services, the tiny, cramped huts and the constant fear of eviction. An Indian non-government organization, SPARC, has worked with the women pavement dwellers in Bombay and their experiences and census of pavement dwellers have revealed not only the important economic contribution that these people make to Bombay's economy but also how their pavement dwellings represent the most logical response to their housing and income needs.[3]

The housing needs of a young single person wanting to spend as little as possible on accommodation while he or she saves (and perhaps sends a proportion of their income to help support their family in rural areas or abroad) are very different from those of a family with several children and a stable (if low) income. The poorer the individual or household and the less stable their source of income, the less flexibility they have in terms of where they can live and how much they can pay. The needs of each individual or household also change over time. Government failure to understand the particular needs of poorer groups – or the diversity of need – is a major reason why government housing projects are so ineffective. Government projects provide standard solutions in one particular location with little or no choice in terms of price, repayment conditions and size, and these, at best, match the priorities of only a few poorer individuals or households.

The possibilities open to low income people to find housing vary greatly from city to city. They are influenced by the rate at which the population is growing and new households are forming, as well as the extent to which poorer households can acquire land on which they can organize the construction of a house or shack – whether legally or illegally. This in turn is influenced by the pattern of land ownership or tenure and the rights given to individuals or the community under the legal framework. Inevitably, government attitudes and actions also powerfully influence the possibilities open to the poor. Attitudes to existing or to new illegal settlement, their regulations, norms and procedures for building and subdivision (and the extent to which these are enforced), and their provision of infra-

Table 3.1: Types of rental housing used by lower income groups in many Third World cities

Types of rental accommodation	Common characteristics	Problems
Rented room in sub-divided inner city housing (tenements)	Often the most common form of low-income housing in early stages of a city's growth. Buildings usually legally built as residences for middle or upper income groups but subdivided and turned into tenements when these move to suburbs or elsewhere. Advantage of being centrally located so usually close to jobs or income earning opportunities. Sometimes, rent levels controlled by legislation. Infrastructure (e.g. paved streets, sidewalks, piped water, sewers) available. Access to schools and hospitals. Certain Third World cities never had sufficient quantity of middle/upper housing suited to conversion to tenements to make this type of accommodation common.	Usually very overcrowded and in poor state of repair. Whole families often live in one room, sometimes with no window. Facilities for water supply, cooking, storage, laundry and excreta/garbage disposal very poor and have rarely been increased or improved to cope with much higher density of occupation brought by sub-division. If subject to rent control, land lord often demanding extra payment "unofficially". Certain inner city areas with tenements may be subject to strong commercial pressures to redevelop them (or their site) for more profitable uses.
Rented room in custom built tenements	Government built or government approved buildings specially built as tenements for low income groups; sometimes publicly owned. Common in many Latin American cities and some Asian cities and usually built some decades ago. Some quite recently constructed public housing estates fall into this category although now quite rare for governments to sanction private sector tenement construction.	Similar problems to above in that original building never had adequate provision for water supply, cooking, ventilation, food storage, laundry, excreta and garbage disposal. Inadequate maintenance common.
Rented room or bed in boarding, rooming house, cheap hotel or pension	Often most in evidence near railway station or bus station though may also be common in other areas, including illegal settlements. Perhaps common for newly arrived migrant family or single person working in city to use these. Single persons may hire bed for a set number of hours each day so more than one person shares the cost of each bed. Usually relatively cheap and centrally located.	Similar problems to above in terms of overcrowding, poor maintenance and lack of facilities. A rapidly changing population in most such establishments prevents united action on part of users to get improvements.

Renting room or bed in illegal settlement	In many cities, rented rooms in illegal settlements represent a larger stock of rental accommodation than in tenements which are legally built (see above). May take form of room or bed within room rented in house or shack with *de facto* owner-occupier; may be rented from small or large scale landlord even though it is within an illegal settlement.	Problems in terms of quality of building and lack of infrastructure (paved roads, sidewalks, storm drainage ...) plus site often ill-suited to housing as in squatter settlements and in illegal subdivisions (see Table 3.2). Also insecurity of tenure which is even greater than for *de facto* house/shack owners.
Renting a plot on which shack is built	The renting of plots in illegal subdivision or renting space to build a shack in some other person's lot, courtyard or garden is known to be common in certain cities; in some cities, space is even rented to people to build a shack on the flat roofs of houses or apartments. Its extent in these and other Third World cities is not known.	Similar problems to those listed above in terms of insecure tenure and lack of basic services and infrastructure. Additional burden on household to build, despite no tenure and no incentive to improve shack.
Renting room in lower-middle income or formal sector worker districts	Declines in purchasing power for many lower-middle income or formal sector worker households has encouraged them to rent out rooms to supplement their incomes and to help pay off loans or mortgages on their homes.	Probably relatively good quality compared to above options. Tenant landlord relationship not subject to contract. Such rooms frequently in areas at a considerable distance from concentrations of employment.
Employer-housing for cheap labour	Some large enterprises provide rented accommodation for their workforce. This is common in plantations but also evident in some cities.	The quality of this housing is usually very poor with several people crowded into each room and very inadequate provision of basic services. Rules often prevent families living there so workers' families have to live elsewhere.
Renting space to sleep outside	Where there are large numbers of people who sleep outside or in public places (e.g., temples, railway stations or graveyards) local officials or protection gangs may demand payment informally, especially in the best locations.	The problems are obvious – not only the insecurity and lack of shelter and basic services but also the need to pay for this space and pay people who have no right to demand such payments.

Source: Adapted from Table 1 in Jorge E. Hardoy and David Satterthwaite, "Shelter, infrastructure and services in Third World cities", *Habitat International* Vol. 10, No. 3, 1986.

Table 3.2: Examples of "owner occupation" housing used by low income groups in many Third World cities

Types of owner occupation	Common characteristics	Problems
Building house or shack in squatter settlement	As city grows and number of people unable to afford a legal house or house site grows, illegal occupation of land sites on which occupants organize construction of their house or shack usually becomes common. Advantage of what is usually a cheap (or free) site on which to build – although as the settlement develops, a monetized market for sites often appears and land sites can be expensive in better quality, better located settlements. The extent to which households actually build most or all their house varies considerably; many lack the time to contribute much or all and hire workers or small firms to undertake much or all the construction.	Lack of secure tenure; settlement often subject to constant threat of destruction by government. Lack of legal tenure inhibits or prevents use of site as collateral in getting loan to help in construction. No public provision of water, sanitation, roads, storm drainage, electricity, schools, health care services, public transport – or even where government does so, this is long after settlement has been built and is usually inadequate. Poor quality sites are often chosen (e.g. subject to flooding or landslides) since these have lowest commercial value and thus give the best chance of avoiding forceful eviction.
Building house or shack in illegal sub-division	Together with housing built in squatter settlements, this represents the main source of new housing in most large Third World cities. Site is bought or rented from landowner or "middleman" who acts as developer for landowner. Or where customary law is still common, access to a site through the permission of the appropriate chief who acts for the "community". Governments often prepared to tolerate these while strongly suppressing squatter occupation. Often relatively well-off households also organise their house construction on such illegal developments. As in squatter settlements, the extent to which people build their own houses varies considerably.	Comparable problems to those above except land tenure is more secure and landowner or developer sometimes provides some basic services and infrastructure. The site is also usually planned (although so too are some squatter settlements). The better located and better quality illegal subdivisions are also likely to be expensive. If the city's physical growth is largely defined by where squatter settlements or illegal subdivisions spring up, it produces a haphazard and chaotic pattern and density of development to which it will be very expensive to provide infrastructure and services.

Building house or shack in government sites-and-services or core housing scheme	An increasing number of governments have moved from a concentration on public housing schemes (which were rarely on a scale to make any impact) to serviced sites or core housing schemes. Very rarely are these on a scale to have much impact on reducing the housing problems faced by lower income groups.	Public agency responsible for scheme often finds it impossible to acquire cheap, well located sites. Sites far from low income groups' sources of employment chosen, since they are cheaper and easier to acquire. Extra cost in time and bus fares for primary and secondary income earners can make household worse off than in squatter settlement. Eligibility criteria often bar women headed households. Regulations on repayment, building schedule and use of house for work or renting rooms often make many ineligible and bring considerable hardship to those who do take part.
Invading empty houses or apartments	Known to be common in a few cities; its overall importance in Third World is not known.	Obviously insecure tenure since occupation is illegal. May be impossible to get electricity and water even if dwelling was originally connected.
Building or developing a house or shack in a "temporary camp"	Many examples known of governments who develop "temporary" camps for victims of disasters or for those evicted by redevelopment – usually on the periphery of the city. Many become permanent settlements.	Land and house tenure is often ambiguous; the provision of basic infrastructure and services at best inadequate, at worst almost non-existent; the location is often far from the inhabitants' main centres of employment.

Source: Adapted from Table 2 in Jorge E. Hardoy and David Satterthwaite, "Shelter, infrastructure and services in Third World cities", *Habitat International* vol. 10, no. 3, 1986.

structure and services (especially the location of roads and the availability of public transport) are all influential. But because the relative importance of such factors differs from city to city and from government to government, it is difficult to generalize. Below we try to outline the most common ways through which poorer people have found accommodation in existing cities.

The development of tenements

In the cities of Latin America's south-eastern coast such as Sao Paulo, Rio de Janeiro, Montevideo, Buenos Aires and Rosario, the highest rates of population growth took place in the late nineteenth and early twentieth centuries (though during different decades for each of these cities). At this time, renting rooms in tenement houses in the central districts of the city was the way most most poorer households found shelter. The period 1880–1910 is considered the heyday of the tenement house in these cities. Many tenements were made by converting existing buildings originally built for middle or upper income groups who had moved out to the suburbs. By putting up a few new partition walls, three or more families could be squeezed into a house or flat originally designed for one. In other instances, custom built tenements were developed where, from the outset, the design and construction of the buildings sought to pack in as many households as possible. Their construction was encouraged by local governments as an inexpensive way of providing housing. Tenements were also one of the most profitable investments for the local firms and bourgeoisie. Tenement housing also became a common form of accommodation in Havana, Lima, Santiago de Chile and various international ports.[4] In Mexico City, from about 1850, when the population began to grow, low cost housing was created by converting existing family dwellings into multi-family tenements. Up to 1900, with a growing population and a limited stock of buildings which could profitably be converted, the private sector constructed tenements (today's *vecindades*), and these increasingly became the main source of new cheap accommodation. By 1950, three quarters of Mexico City's housing stock was rental accommodation.[5]

Although illegal settlements developed in the late nineteenth and early twentieth centuries, they usually housed only a small proportion of a city's population. Their construction and expansion was inhibited by a lack of cheap public transport, the central location of most possible sources of income, and long working hours for workers, often 12–14 hours a day, six or seven days a week. Poorer groups cannot live in squatter settlements located on the periphery of the city if their sources of income are in the central city and there is no possibility of travelling to and from work each day.

Although the early development of low income housing in Asia and Africa has not been so well documented, there are comparable examples both of custom built slums and of the conversion of existing buildings into tenements. For instance, in Colombo, the capital of Sri Lanka, the slum gardens which today house around 20 per cent of the city's population were built to house workers by businesses, colonial corporations and real estate developers. They used nineteenth century English factory tenements as a model. The slum tenements of Colombo which today house around 8 per cent of its population arose from the sub-division of middle income housing.[6] The construction of tenements was a profitable investment for many local businesses who were unable to break into the more lucrative area of plantation investment.[7] In Bombay, *chawls* which today house more than 1.5 million people were originally built by factory owners and landowners to house their growing workforce,[8] while the *vahavelis* and *mohallas* in old Delhi provide examples of tenements created by internal sub-division. In many areas in the older parts of other cities, comparable tenements developed and many remain today as important, cheap, centrally located rental accommodation. Examples are found in the walled city of Lahore (Pakistan), in old Dhaka (Bangladesh) and in the old walled cities (*medinas*) which now form the old city centre in many Arab cities.[9] In Nigeria, between 1910 and 1930, tenement districts became established in the older sections of the traditional cities, usually in areas enclosed by the town walls as in Ibadan, Kano and Zaria; they also developed in central Lagos but most disappeared after major slum clearance schemes in the 1950s.[10]

In slum areas of cities in South and South-East Asia, the process of sub-division has reached the point where tiny windowless cubicles are being let to low income urban dwellers.[11] In Seoul, capital of South Korea, the extreme shortage of cheap housing has led to the development of what are known as "beehive" buildings where landlords sub-divide buildings into rooms of five square metres or less and rent them to young industrial workers; the rent often takes more than half the tenant's wages.[12] In Calcutta, the "hotbed" system represents perhaps the most extreme case of maximizing landlord's return from very poor people; here, beds are rented by the hour with two or three persons using the same bed over a 24-hour period; as many beds as possible are crowded into each room with beds also stacked as bunks, one above another. In other cities, even marshy land, flat rooftops, tiny city gardens or small boats are rented and small shacks erected by the tenants.

The growth of illegal settlements

At some point in any growing city, the supply of existing buildings which could profitably be converted into tenements was fully utilized. The pressure of rising numbers and often the fact that there were more profitable sources of investment than tenements led to illegal settlements becoming the main new source of low income accommodation. Improved systems of public transport – generally a mixture of suburban train lines and buses – often made undeveloped land around the city more accessible to inner city employment. Job opportunities began to develop outside the central districts as richer consumers and certain businesses became concentrated there. In some countries, notably nations least urbanized in the early 1950s, including many in Sub-Saharan Africa, the main cities never had a large middle income housing stock which would be easily converted into tenements. At relatively early stages in the physical and demographic growth of these cities, illegal settlements became the main source of new cheap housing. These often developed in and around what had previously been temporary native compounds, the settlements which the colonial rulers had permitted to house the indigenous population whose labour they needed to ensure the functioning of the city.

In some of the largest cities of the late-nineteenth and early-twentieth centuries, a considerable number of illegal or informal settlements had developed before World War II. Cities such as Caracas, Rio de Janeiro and Montevideo already had extensive illegal settlements by the 1940s. In India, the fact that Calcutta was much the largest city in the late nineteenth century helps to explain the early development of what are known as *bustees*. These were originally informal land sub-divisions on what was then the fringe of Calcutta's built up area; in the late nineteenth century they were not considered illegal in that they were seen as temporary rural phenomena. They were parcels of land let out by their owners, through agents, for hut buildings. The builders might live in the huts or rent them out. As in many informal or illegal sub-divisions since, there was no systematic planning or provision for infrastructure. Sometimes, government and company housing were also provided in *bustees*.[13] By 1980, there were some 3,000 *bustees* scattered all over the Calcutta Metropolitan District, their population varying from 100 to 20,000 people. In Calcutta, today, most poor people live in these *bustees*, or in squatter settlements or in refugee colonies where the inhabitants have not been granted legal tenure of the land they occupy.[14]

But in most cities, it is within the last four to five decades that illegal house construction either on illegally occupied or illegally sub-divided land has become the major source of new, cheap housing; Box 3.2 illustrates the extent to which city populations have come to live in illegal settlements. New tenement construction was inhibited in many nations as governments introduced regulations demanding certain minimum standards and maximum rent-levels.

Box 3.2: Housing conditions in selected cities

BANGKOK (Thailand): Estimated population of 4.7 million in metropolitan area in 1977. An estimate in 1978 suggested that 1.2 million people lived in slums and unauthorized settlements, while many more lived in factory houses and dormitories and in servants quarters. Many of the unauthorized settlements are on swampy land prone to flooding and along rail lines or canals. It is common for households in these settlements to receive the land-owner's permission to build a makeshift house but only temporary tenure is given, so occupants can be removed when the owner wants to sell or develop the land. A major eviction programme in Bangkok is now threatening people living in low income settlements. By 1981, 61,600 had been evicted and 148,600 were in the process of being evicted.

DELHI (India): A paper in 1982 reported that half or more of Delhi's population of more than 5 million lived in very poor conditions. 1.3 million lived in what are officially defined as slum areas in or close to the historic old city, while 600,000 or more lived in over 1,380 squatter settlements (the so-called *Jhuggi-Jhompri* clusters). In addition, 700,000 live on unauthorized sub-divisions and 150,000-200,000 lived in what are essentially camping sites (*Jhuggi-Jhompri* colonies) which is where squatters were moved to after being forcibly evicted from public lands. Most of the households in these settlements exist with grossly inadequate water supplies and little or no provision for the sanitary removal of household and human wastes and for basic community services such as primary health care centres.

GUAYAQUIL (Ecuador): Estimated population in excess of 1 million in 1980. On the edge of the city's commercial centre, there are the inner city slums, the *tugurios*. These rooms, either sub-divisions of decaying middle class housing or purpose built tenements, accommodate up to 15 people in very overcrowded and insanitary conditions. But much of the city's rapid growth in population since 1930 has been housed in squatter communities built over an area of tidal swampland to the west and the south of the city centre which has little commercial value in its natural state. Population in this area (known as the *suburbios*) has grown far more rapidly than the rest of the city. In 1975, it was estimated to contain 60 per cent of the city's population. The major part of the *suburbios* are kilometre upon kilometre of small, incrementally built bamboo and timber houses standing on poles above mud and polluted water. The houses are connected by a complex system of timber catwalks which also link them to the nearest solid land. In some areas, solid land is a forty minute walk away.

LIMA (Peru): Population of 4.4 million in 1981. Much of Lima's rapid population growth over the last 40 years has been accommodated in inner city slums (*tugurios*) which house around 15 per cent of the city's population, and squatter communities, originally known as *barriadas*, but later called *pueblos jovenes*, which house around one quarter of the population. Precise statistics on the *pueblos jovenes* are difficult to get since new ones are continuously appearing both in tiny areas within the city and on the outer fringes of the continuously expanding metropolitan area. There are over 300 *pueblos jovenes* in and around Lima and most do not have piped water, sewer lines or provision for garbage removal. Virtually none have paved streets.

MANILA (Philippines): Estimated population of over 5 million in 1980. A 1978 report suggested that there were 328,000 squatter families with a total population of close to two million inhabitants living on 415 sites dotted through the whole urban region. These do not include families living in legal but otherwise sub-standard housing. Manila's squatter settlements vary in size from the very large Tondo Foreshore area, with 27,600 families, or Bagong Barrio in Caloocan (part of Metropolitan Manila) with 16,800 families, to mini-squatter settlements. Estimates suggest that only around 12 per cent of Manila's population can afford to buy or rent a legal house or flat on the open market.

MEXICO CITY (Mexico): Estimated population of 16 million in the metropolitan area in 1982. At least seven million people live in some form of uncontrolled or unauthorized settlement. Up to the 1940s, most lower income groups lived in rented rooms in custom built slums (*vecindades*) or in sub-divided middle and upper income housing. Since the late 1940s, most new low cost housing has been in unauthorized developments which usually developed in one of two ways. Either landowners or real estate companies sold illegal sub-divisions, or land allocated to rural communities under the long-standing agrarian reform was illegally sub-divided and sold. In both cases, occupants' tenure is insecure since the sub-divisions contravene official regulations and the infrastructure and service standards demanded by such regulations are not met. The land on which they are developed is frequently ill-suited to residential development because of rocky, steeply inclined land, instability of subsoil, or dry, dusty environments.

NAIROBI (Kenya): Estimated population of 827,800 in 1979. Unauthorised units house around 40 per cent of the city's population since 60–70 per cent of Nairobi's population cannot afford the housing erected by the state or City Council. These unauthorized units include houses or shacks built on land which is illegally occupied (which could be designated squatter occupation) and unauthorized shelters on land either owned by the developer or used with the permission of the land-owner. Mathare Valley, one of Nairobi's squatter areas, grew from 4,000 inhabitants in 1964 to 90,000 in 1979 and is perhaps 200,000 today, while other areas with illegal developments grew at comparable rates. The unplanned and unauthorized settlements are typified by structures of simple and usually low quality construction, often in a poor state of repair with very inadequate provision for sanitation and water supply. In addition, the settlements have no paved access roads and no public lighting and densities are very high.

NOUAKCHOTT (Mauritania): In 1965 it was a small town with 5,800 inhabitants; by 1977 it had 135,000 and estimates suggest that by 1982 it had 250,000 or more. Most of this incredibly rapid growth in population has been housed in illegal shanty/tent settlements. The government has distributed 7000 plots of land since 1972 but these received little or no services. An estimated 64 per cent of the population now live in largely self-built communities on these 7000 plots and in illegal settlements. More than two-thirds of the city's inhabitants have no direct access to water. Water frequently has to be bought from a water merchant with no guarantee as to quality and with the price up to 100 times that paid by those with piped water connections.

Sources: See note 15.

In many inner city areas, the availability of cheap accommodation has been reduced as new commercial or residential developments for higher income groups have taken the place of tenements. For instance, in old Delhi, between 1961 and 1981, the population dropped from 420,000 to 362,000 while the number of jobs and commercial establishments multiplied several fold. In Bombay, new commercial and residential developments have squeezed out slum populations; the same processes is evident in Karachi and Bangkok. In Santiago, the inner city's population declined from 97,122 to 55,061 between 1952 and 1982. In Lima, as much as 10 per cent of the central area has been affected by the demolition of buildings and their subsequent conversion into car parks.[16] This decline in cheap centrally-located accommodation has been exacerbated in many cities by the conversion or replacement of tenements or cheap boarding houses by houses or apartments for middle and upper income groups. Inefficient public transport, congested roads and the fact that suburbs are ever more distant from central city jobs have encouraged this process; so too has the rapid growth in the number of households. Ironically, as in the West, middle or upper income houses or apartments formed by converting relatively old tenement buildings or cheap boarding houses now have considerable prestige in many cities. Single people or childless couples can fit very comfortably into what were previously very overcrowded apartments which housed one or even two large families. Also, in many illegal settlements which developed in good locations and which survived the threat of demolition, it is common for poorer households to be pushed out by middle and even upper income 'improvers'.

A large number of cities have seen a proportional decline in the availability of cheap rental accommodation in or close to central city areas; in many it has declined in absolute terms. But in some of the largest cities, this trend might be changing. Poorer groups seeking accommodation in illegal settlements have been pushed so far away from city centres that the cost (in time and money) of getting to and from centrally located jobs is becoming prohibitively expensive. New tenement areas are likely to be developing in relatively central city areas. In some instances, these are developing in the more centrally located illegal settlements; in others, it is in consolidated neighbourhoods which had previously been predominantly owner-occupied, middle or lower-middle income neighbourhoods.

Acquiring land for housing

Land for the illegal settlements which came to form such a large part of most Third World cities was acquired in many different ways. Sometimes it was through a group of households carefully organizing an invasion. Sometimes it was through quiet encroachment – one or two households moving onto a piece of wasteland or a river bank or some other vacant site. Sometimes it was through people receiving permission to build a house from the landowner or the person or family who traditionally had the right to give such permission – as in the early development of Olaleye Village in Lagos (Box 1.2 p. 26). Often it was through each household purchasing a house plot in a commercial transaction with the landowner or company acting for the landowner – the illegal sub-division – although the procedures for doing so vary greatly from city to city.[17]

Paul Baross looked at this question in many different nations and suggested that there are at least seven different kinds of land which were commonly used for illegal settlements in different cities: customary land (as in Port Moresby and Blantyre); government land reserves (as in Lima, Karachi, Valencia and Istanbul); abandoned land – for instance that left after foreign settlers emigrate when a nation achieves independence (as in Manila and Lusaka); marginal land (as in Jakarta, Rabat, Madras, Beirut and Manila);

"mini-plots" which include the sub-division of existing, already developed, sites in illegal settlements (Lusaka); land rental (as in Bangkok and Butterworth and in Maputo before independence) and finally illegal sub-divisions (with examples from San Salvador, Bogota and Evora).[18] Box 3.3 outlines the history of Jabra in Khartoum which simply evolved from a small rural settlement to a densely populated urban settlement, as the city itself grew. Like Olaleye village in Lagos, it is neither the result of an invasion nor the result of an illegal sub-division. But it was many decades after Jabra had become a part of the city of Khartoum when the authorities were finally prepared to consider it a legal settlement.

Box 3.3: The development of Jabra, Greater Khartoum

Jabra is a predominantly residential settlement to the south of the centre of Khartoum, capital of the Sudan. Greater Khartoum – made up of the three contiguous cities of Khartoum, Khartoum North and Omdurman – had over 1.5 million inhabitants by 1983 and in recent decades has been one of the world's fastest growing large cities.

Jabra had about 7,600 inhabitants in 1983, settled on a site of some 1.2 square kilometres. Before it became part of Khartoum, it had supported the raising of sheep and cattle. In the 1920s, it became an important water station for milk-men and cattle merchants. By the early 1940s, local residents re-excavated a well on the site which had previously been filled in and abandoned. Opening up a well attracted more people to the settlement – even though at this time, it was at a considerable distance from the city of Khartoum. It is said that the name Jabra is derived from *jubara* which means co-operation and solidarity. The re-excavation of the well demanded a co-ordinated co-operative effort since the well was "nine men deep".

Most people settled in one room dwellings without boundary walls – dispersed over the site so their sheep and cattle could graze. The only enclosures were animal pens. By the late 1950s, there were seven established houses and the well; the vegetation was still dense enough "to conceal the feeding cat-tle". But from then on, with the rapid growth and physical expansion of Khartoum, it attracted a growing number of new settlers and developed into what is essentially an outer suburb of Khartoum. Growth was particularly rapid in the late 1960s which coincided with the legal recognition by the government of the settlement next to Jabra. Some people in Jabra were given plots or permission to settle by the government during the 1960s and 1970s, but only in 1983 was official recognition given to the settlement and to the right of its inhabitants to live there. Within the settlement have developed two mosques, two primary schools, a police station, the co-operative society (which runs two shops), two markets for building materials, a private clinic and a newspaper kiosk. 80 per cent of the population work in Khartoum.

Various public works have been undertaken by the residents. For instance, for the construction and paving of a main street in 1972, residents had to pay for the gravel and the professional workers' overtime while the government agreed to provide the asphalt, the skilled personnel and the machinery. The bus fare from Jabra to Khartoum was raised by 33 per cent which went to a special fund to pay for paving the road. The same technique was also used to pave other roads and the organizing group also introduced electric lighting, planted trees and provided grilles to protect the trees. It is generally community leaders rather than organizations which start new initiatives or form pressure groups and the groups they organize are often defined by tribe. However, apart from the temporary, *ad hoc* committees set up to undertake particular tasks, there are several organizations such as a national committee, which includes all the community leaders, two women's units, three parent-teacher councils, two co-operatives and two benevolent societies.

Source: Omer M.A. El Agraa, Adil M. Ahmad, Ian Haywood and Osman M. El Kheir, *Popular Settlements in Greater Khartoum* (Khartoum SGAHS, 1985).

The distinction between illegal occupation of land (squatting), and other illegal settlements which develop without conflict between the inhabitants and the landowners, such as illegal sub-divisions or as in the case of Jabra above has already been noted. All kinds of illegal settlements have little or no government provision for water supply, sanitation, garbage disposal, roads, storm drainage, electricity and public transport. All kinds of illegal settlements also develop on land ill-suited to housing such as on hillsides prone to landslides or flooding. But governments generally show less readiness to bulldoze illegal developments where there is no conflict between landowners and inhabitants.

In Bogota, Colombia's capital, most new housing for lower income groups is on illegal sub-divisions, the so-called "pirate developments"[19]; in 1973 a calculation suggested that 59 per cent of the population lived in houses or shacks built on these and that less than one per cent live in squatter settlements.[20] One reason for this has been the government's refusal to allow squatting; the squatter invasions which have taken place were usually rapidly destroyed. Another reason is the lack of municipal land or land to which ownership rights are uncertain – as these tend to be the preferred sites for squatter invasions. Pressure can be brought to bear on municipal government to sanction squatter settlements on municipal land. This is especially so just before municipal elections – in those countries where there are local elections. If squatters occupy land where ownership is unclear or in dispute, there is less chance of an owner pressing the authorities to evict them. Over time, many illegal sub-divisions in Bogota have been "regularized" (i.e., their inhabitants have been given legal tenure although the public provision of infrastructure and services has been slow in coming). A survey of 135 pirate sub-divisions in 1977 found that more than half lacked sewers and more than a third lacked water and electricity; 13 per cent had no water, sewers, electricity, streets or sidewalks. When these are installed, it is usually the developer and the community who pay most of the cost.[21]

In the metropolitan areas of Mexico, of the eight million or so people living in largely self-built illegal settlements, most live in illegal sub-divisions, not in squatter settlements. When illegal settlements first came to house a significant proportion of the city's population after World War II, squatter settlements were much more common but more recently, the illegal land market has become commercialized.[22] People acquired house-plots by payment, either to landowners and real estate companies, or to the leaders of agrarian communities who illegally allowed them to build on *ejido* land.[23] From the beginning of the 1970s, the government increased its programme to regularize tenure in illegal sub-divisions.[24]

In Delhi, a 1982 estimate showed some 700,000 people living in illegal sub-divisions[25]; these, too, have a good chance of being legalized, especially just before elections. However, squatter settlements are more likely to face forceful eviction; there was a large scale squatter eviction programme between 1975 and 1977 and large squatter demolitions were also reported in 1980 and 1981.

In Sao Paulo up to 1972, squatter settlements were usually destroyed (especially those in central areas) while house or shack construction on illegal sub-divisions was by far the most important source of new low income housing. One such was the ironically named "Garden Flowers of Spring" (Jardin Flor do Primavera), located on the periphery of the metropolitan area. In 1969 the landowner sold the first land-plots to people who could afford nothing better or closer to the city. The inhabitants not only had to build their own houses but also develop roads and paths, and construct a bridge over a gully to connect their neighbourhood to a road with public transport. Such developments increased the value of the remaining unoccupied lots and the landowner sold these at a substantially high price. The owner made no investment either in infrastructure or in services.[26] In Sao Paulo, many illegal sub-divisions have been legalized, especially just prior to the November 1982 elections.[27]

By contrast, squatter invasions have been the principal means by which lower income groups acquired land for housing in cities such as Lima, Caracas, Ankara, Santiago de Chile between 1969 and 1973 and Rio de Janeiro during the 1950s and 1960s. Box 3.4 tells the story of one in Lima where, although the squatters failed to secure the land-site they invaded, their invasion prompted the authorities to provide them with an alternative and, since 1971, this site has developed into Villa El Salvador, a settlement with over 160,000 inhabitants.

Box 3.4: The planning of a squatter invasion in Lima, Peru

The population of Lima's metropolitan area grew from half a million to over 4 million between 1940 and 1981. Much of this increase was housed in squatter settlements around the city and today, over 1.5 million people live in such settlements.

In 1971, a group of between 80 and 100 families decided to organize a land invasion. They had been promised land-sites by the government after organizing another invasion two years previously but these had not materialized. They invited Mr Perez, a self taught man of Indian origin, to organize the new invasion. He had two important advantages. First was his knowledge of a 1961 law which provided the basis for allowing illegal settlements to be given semi-official status and basic services like water.[28] Secondly, he had contacts within the Peruvian Ministry of Housing. Mr Perez advised each family on how to prepare for the invasion – each should bring a mat (to set up a largely symbolic shelter as soon as they moved onto the invaded site), a whistle (to warn each other of the arrival of the police) and Peruvian flag (to demonstrate that they were patriotic, and to provide a visual symbol of the national flag all over the invasion site which would discourage the army or the police from forcibly ejecting them). The site selected for the invasion was outside the city and there were plans to build housing on it for low-level government employees.

The invasion was planned for 1 May 1971 to coincide with meetings in Lima between the Government of Peru and the Inter-American Development Bank (one of the largest and most influential aid agencies and development banks operating in Latin America). The presence in the city of officials from the Bank might discourage the Government from violently repressing the invasion. A few families invaded two days early and were forced by other families involved to leave and wait until May 1st.

The invasion took place at dawn. A priest from a nearby settlement quickly told the police, since he thought that land designated for a new church had been occupied. Five truckloads of troops arrived. Mr Perez quoted the 1961 law to them which he interpreted as giving Peruvian adults the right to a place in a "young community"; the military government at that time under General Juan Velasco Alvarado had given considerable support to legalizing squatter settlements (which were renamed *pueblos jovenes* – "young communities") and to providing some basic services for their inhabitants. The troops withdrew, although representatives from public authorities continued to demand that the squatters disperse. Mr Perez and a committee of five began to negotiate with the Ministry of Housing and incorporated themselves as a Housing Association with the Ministry of Justice. Meanwhile, as reports of the invasion were relayed on the radio and in the newspapers, hundreds of other families came to join in and by the morning of the fifth day, 9,000 families were reported to be occupying the hillside and the adjacent land.

A large contingent of troops came to disperse the squatters, and a major shot and killed the brother of one of them. At the funeral which followed, the Archbishop of Lima preached a strong sermon in support of the invasion. The Minister of the Interior then ordered the arrest of the Archbishop and two other priests who had supported the invaders. This caused a considerable stir in the meeting of the government with the Inter-American Development Bank and finally led to the Minister's resignation.

On 7 May, the government offered Mr Perez a large tract of land less commercially valuable than the site that the squatters had occupied. Here, the invaders could have housing sites with the government's permission and after occupying them for two years, could apply for legal title for a token charge. Some of the squatters refused to move but most accepted and some 7,000 families from the invasion and many other families in search of a housing plot went to the new site. Mr Perez was arrested the next day and remained in jail for three months.

The new site developed into a thriving self-governing community and by 1986, 168,000 people had settled there. By 1984, there were over 31,000 housing plots (half with permanent brick and concrete houses). Most of them had electricity and over half had domestic water and sewerage. Despite originally being a desert site, the area now has many trees and gardens, the main roads are paved and bus services link it to central Lima, some 20 kilometres away. Most of these improvements were made by the inhabitants and their organizations, not by government.

Sources: The story of the invasion comes from a case study of Villa El Salvador by Lisa Peattie. Details of current developments in Villa El Salvador: Andrew Maskrie, "Low income Peruvians build a new township", *Building Community – a Third World Case Book*, Bertha Turner (ed.), (Habitat International Coalition, 1988).

Owners and renters

In many illegal settlements, there is a large rental market for housing. This differs greatly in size and kinds of rental arrangement, but rental markets are likely to develop in the illegal settlements which survive in the city areas close to markets, ports or other locations where poorer people can find work.

Many households in illegal settlements rent out a room to individuals or to another family to supplement their income. In many cities, there are more cheap rooms available for rent within illegal settlements than within the more traditional tenement and cheap boarding-house districts. In some settlements, quite extensive landlordism has developed – to the point where it is large scale and often highly profitable. One example of this is to be seen in Kibera in Nairobi, Kenya (Box 3.5).

Box 3.5: The growth of large-scale landlordism in Kibera, Nairobi

Kibera, a large unauthorized settlement in Nairobi (Kenya) had some 60,000 inhabitants in 1980 – and will probably have considerably more by 1989. At first sight, it looks like a settlement where the inhabitants have built, and now live in, their own shacks. Most houses are made of mud, or mud brick, with corrugated iron roofs – and there are many small shops and industries.

There is a great lack of basic infrastructure and services – few roads or paths are paved, drains are, at best, rudimentary and very few houses have piped water. An estimate by the Catholic Relief Service for one section of the settlement suggested that 50 per cent of the children suffer from malnutrition. But a high proportion of Kibera's inhabitants are in fact only renting their rooms – and very often paying to a landlord who does not live in Kibera.

Kibera's origins go back to colonial times when the government allowed some Nubians to build their shelters there – although no official documents were ever drawn up to confirm this. The settlement grew and by 1972 had some 17,000 inhabitants. From the mid 1950s, many households constructed additional rooms to rent out. Up to the early 1970s the government had not intervened. Then in 1974, it threatened to demolish any new building put up in Kibera without official permission. In addition, it began to give permission to certain individuals to construct buildings there.

But it was largely people from the Kikuyu – the largest tribe in Kenya and the one which has dominated government since independence – who obtained permission. This helped underpin the rapid growth of large-scale landlordism in Kibera with Kikuyu landlords displacing Nubian landlords; a survey in 1980 found that two thirds of the large landlords were Kikuyu. Most of the landlords with 20 or more units do not live in Kibera; many own 30 or more rooms and it seems that once a potential landlord manages to obtain informal permission from local authorities to build there, the returns are very high. The four largest landlords between them owned 571 rooms and landlords were able to recoup their investments within one year.

Source: Philip Amis, "Squatters or tenants: the commercialization of unauthorized housing in Nairobi", *World Development*, vol. 12, no. 1, 1984.

Recent studies in informal settlements in Lusaka (Zambia), Khartoum (the Sudan), Lagos (Nigeria) and Karachi (Pakistan) also show that renting is widespread, although not necessarily accompanied by the largescale landlordism found in Kibera. In George, Lusaka, a squatter settlement which was legalized and upgraded in the late 1970s, had, between 1977 and 1985, an increasing number of absentee owners who rented out their houses and an increasing proportion of houses with one or more rooms let to tenants.[29] In Greater Khartoum, close to half of all households living in the poorest "legal" areas rent their accommodation.[30] In Olaleye, an informal settlement in Lagos, most inhabitants are tenants.[31] In Umbadda, another settlement on the outskirts with some 180,000 inhabitants in 1983, around a third of all households are renters and there are many different kinds of financial arrangements and of arrangements for sharing space between owners, tenants and sub-tenants.[32] In Baldia, the first squatter settlement in Karachi for which there was a largescale legalization and upgrading programme, an average of around 10 per cent of the houses are rented out although there are considerable differences in the proportion of rented accommodation in different areas within the township.[33] Census data for 1970 for Mexico City shows that as many as 60 per cent of the buildings in the older, more consolidated illegal settlements were rented or 'loaned'.[34]

Even if there has been a decline in the proportion of poorer people living in rental housing in traditional inner-city tenement districts, it may be that rental housing in other areas and in other kinds of housing is becoming increasingly important in many cities. For instance, in Seoul, 60 per cent of the population live in rental accommodation and that proportion has increased since 1960.[35] This may represent an extreme case since the government has not allowed illegal settlements to develop on a large scale as an alternative for poorer groups, and its redevelopment programmes over the last 20 years have evicted millions of people with little or no compensation and provision of alternative accommodation. The result is a very high level of overcrowding in existing housing stock; in 1985, for the poorest 30 per cent of the population, there was an average of just two square metres per person and three families per house.[36] In addition, a complex series of rental sub-markets has developed, the most common of which requires tenants to make a large lump sum deposit with the landlord at the beginning of the contract period with this deposit refunded at the end of the contract.[37] The lump sum demanded often represents a third or more of the value of the room or house being rented. By 1987, the lack of cheap accommodation in Seoul had become so serious that a thriving market had developed in renting out small areas in greenhouses for families to live in; the greenhouses (covered in plastic) had formerly been used for raising flowers and pot plants. By late 1988, around 8,000 families were estimated to be living there.[38]

Studies of rental housing in other cities have shown its scale and diversity. A study in Bucaramanga which, with some 500,000 inhabitants in 1980, is not among Colombia's largest cities, found nine different kinds of rental accommodation used by lower income groups.[39] A study of low income housing in Rio de Janeiro found six different kinds of rental accommodation.[40]

These studies, and the others from which we have drawn examples, have great relevance for they show that the poor do not live in slums or squatter settlements but in a more complex and diverse series of housing sub-markets. Thus, the ways through which poorer groups find accommodation in any city are likely to be particular to that city. Comparisons can be made between cities but in the end, the opportunities open to poorer groups to find accommodation will be influenced by many factors particular to each city. One of the most important is the attitude of government to illegal settlements.

Government attitudes to illegal settlements

The attitude of governments to illegal settlements varies greatly from nation to nation – or indeed from government to government within the same nation – ranging from extreme hostility and suppression through various degrees of tolerance to occasional out-right support.[41] Attitudes also vary according to the ways in which the inhabitants acquired the land; from examples given already, it is evident that some governments have been more tolerant of illegal sub-divisions than of squatter settlements. But even the distinction between illegal occupation and illegal sub-division is often blurred. For instance, in Karachi (Pakistan), what are referred to as squatter settlements may have some of the hallmarks of illegal sub-divisions, since an entrepreneur with political connections obtains tacit approval to occupy and sub-divide government land and the lay-out often follows municipal regulations.[42] In Bangkok, many private land-owners allow low income groups to build shacks on their land but only on a temporary basis so there is no long term tenure.[43]

Perhaps the two most important factors in determining the balance between illegal sub-divisions and squatter settlements in any city are the attitudes of city or national authorities to squatter settlements, and the availability of land suited to their development. If, within or around a city, there is unused government land, land whose ownership is uncertain or land of very low commercial value, squatter settlements usually have a better chance of developing.

Thus, in Ankara, the existence of land owned by the government or of which ownership was uncertain, and a tolerant (even, at times, supportive) attitude on the part of government led to the rapid growth of squatter settlements called *gekekondus* (literally "to land by night"); most new low income housing was developed in these illegally occupied areas.[44]

In Pakistan's largest city, Karachi, the fact that so much land is under public ownership has made it easier for the government to support programmes giving tenure to squatters.[45] Box 3.6 tells the story of Islam Nagar, a squatter settlement formed in 1979, which illustrates the long and usually complex negotiations which squatter communities must endure if they are to safeguard their homes and settlements.

Box 3.6: The development of Islam Nagar in Karachi, Pakistan

During the night and early hours of 31 March 1979, some 30 families erected huts of simple reed-matting in one of the many open spaces within the built-up area of Karachi. Over the next few days, some 50 families joined them.

The formation of this new settlement was organized by Mr Sharif, a local politician who probably wanted to enhance his position as a leader, as well as wanting to help the people he represented. He lived in an adjacent middle class settlement where there were many poor tenants. Some of these tenants took part in the initial invasion. The date of 31 March was chosen because it was the end of former Prime Minister Bhutto's rule and those undertaking the invasion expected protection from the party to which Mr Sharif belonged.

Mr Sharif made a provisional map, demarcating 60-square-yard plots to guide the settlers, when they moved onto the land. On 14 April, the Karachi Development Authority's demolition squad destroyed 40 huts with no prior warning. Mr Sharif filed a complaint against the Authority but it was he that the authorities blamed for the invasion; he was put in jail and sentenced to one month's imprisonment.

The residents of Islam Nagar applied to the Commissioner and the High Court to set him free; it also seems that the local Party élite used their influence, and he was freed on 3 June. Meanwhile, together with the police, the demolition squad had again returned to Islam Nagar, had demolished all the houses, taken away building materials and, according to one of the residents, even "our pots and pans, sugar and flour". The residents stayed in the open for a couple of days; some then left while the majority began to rebuild their houses. Mr Sharif died in August and the court case against him was cancelled.

In January 1980, the Authority sent notice to the inhabitants to vacate the area; the inhabitants' committee made contact with the police and an agreement was reached; that unfinished or temporary buildings would be left undisturbed. When the demolition squad came at the end of January, they only inflicted some damage to some parts of a few houses that had one or more walls built of concrete blocks – ie. on those which were developing into permanent houses. In mid-1981, a stay order was obtained which forbade the Karachi Development Authority to touch any structure, pending investigation into an allegation that the land the settlement was on was in fact a graveyard.

In 1982, Islam Nagar had some 140 families; the most common reason given for moving there was to escape paying rent. More than three quarters of the families had previously lived in the adjacent settlement or within walking distance of it. It is probably because of their generally poorly paid or insecure jobs that they were unable to move to more distant places. For those in irregular employment, proximity to the informal network of information about jobs is essential. Nearly three-fifths of the heads of household were semi- or unskilled labourers and a further 11 per cent were skilled labourers. The other most common jobs were salesworkers, drivers, postmen or servants.

Source: Jan van der Linden, "Squatting by organized invasion in Karachi – a new reply to a failing housing policy", *Third World Planning Review*, vol. 4, no. 4, November 1982.

The case of Chile shows how official attitudes to squatting can change with a new government. The government of President Frei (1964 to 1970) was tolerant of most squatter invasions; under the government of President Allende (1970 to 1973), many people and agencies in government actively supported squatter invasions. Under Pinochet, when a long history of democratically elected governments came to an end, a highly repressive form of government prevented, by force, any chance of successful squatter invasions in Santiago between 1973 and 1981, and has recently sought to destroy all those which have taken place since then.

In many African nations, the change in attitude went the other way. While under colonial rule, the formation of illegal or informal settlements for the indigenous population was strongly controlled, independent governments have generally been more tolerant

– although, in some instances, only after an initial period when unsuccessful attempts were made to control their development.

In nations where much or all the land is under public ownership, as in Zambia, Tanzania and the Sudan, governments were among the first to accept the right of low income city-dwellers to land on which to build a shelter. Perhaps one reason is the influence of traditional attitudes to land which were more concerned with the community's needs than an individual's rights.[46] Another reason might be the fact that the land markets in their cities are less commercialized than in (say) the multi-million inhabitant cities in Asia with rapidly expanding economies.

In one of the Third World's largest and most prosperous cities, Sao Paulo, the government became less antagonistic to squatter settlements. After 1972, squatter invasions were not repressed, as they had been in the previous period; the population living in squatter settlements between 1972 and 1982 increased fourteen-fold to reach a million people. One reason is certainly the increasing impoverishment of many; the more accessible illegal sub-divisions on land close to city jobs had already been developed and anyway, were expensive. Cheaper illegal sub-divisions were increasingly distant from the city; the cost in time and money commuting from these to central city jobs was too high. And with the rise of unemployment, there are more people competing for cheap housing; it is not uncommon to find households which previously enjoyed relatively good housing and living standards coming to compete with lower income groups for access to cheap accommodation when the main income earner loses their job or real incomes fall.

A second reason for the change of attitude in Sao Paulo is the decline in the power of the state to control such invasions since 1974, and the growing power of civil society and social movements.[47] This is a point to which we will return, for the power of civil society and social movements to influence government policy on housing can be crucial in influencing its orientation. But the example of Sao Paulo and previous examples show the complexity of forces and factors which determine the housing options open to lower income groups, and how these change over time.

But even where governments have been tolerant towards the illegal settlements, there are very few instances where a government will actually try to provide a legal alternative to them. Some have resorted to the expropriation of any private land on which illegal settlements have developed, and compensation for the owner. By turning the land into public property, the government resolves the conflict between the interests of the squatters and the landowners. But as an author from Venezuela commented on Caracas:

> this paradox seems to reflect a broad ambiguity in state policy. On the one hand, the state recognizes that a significant proportion of the population lacks adequate housing and resorts to squatting. Plans are drawn up to resolve the problem, different measures are introduced and substantial resources are invested in low income areas. At the same time, however, the state pays generous compensation both to the land-owners and to the occupants of the *ranchos* (illegal settlements). One interpretation of this reaction is that rather than trying to solve the problem effectively, officialdom is concerned to disperse resources as favours to its chosen beneficiaries.[48]

It is evident that types of accommodation available to poorer groups vary enormously from city to city. However, some common threads can be identified. Perhaps the most important is that even the illegal housing markets are becoming increasingly commercialized in many cities – or at least in the best located illegal housing areas. This can be seen in the commercialization of illegal land markets (for instance illegal sub-divisions replacing illegal land occupation) and in the growth of commercial markets for rooms in illegal settlements (which also reflects the commercialization of illegal land markets).

If low income groups can obtain cheap, well-located house sites on which they can organize the construction of their own house, this will help limit the size of the rental sector, help moderate rents and keep down prices for illegal sub-divisions. In any city, there is always likely to be a group of people who want rented accommodation – for instance those who regard their stay in the city as temporary or young people who do not want a more permanent arrangement. In some cities such as Cusco in Peru and Quito in Ecuador, demand for rental housing is particularly high since so many people from surrounding areas commute from their villages to these cities to stay a few days to sell their produce and then return home.[49] In other cities, perhaps most especially those in some sub-Saharan African nations, many people only want temporary accommodation because they plan to return to their home town, and indeed may be funding the construction of their house in their hometown, despite living most of the time in the main city.[50] But the more poorer groups

who want more permanent solutions can find and afford them –
either through buying or building a shelter – the less chance large
scale and highly exploitative landlordism has to develop.

4. Shelter: The Response of Government

Housing policies of Third World governments from (say) 1950 to the mid-1970s usually show evidence of an important change at some point. This stems from a recognition that the rapid growth of the major cities is not likely to stop and that considerable social and political dangers may arise if the housing problem is not addressed. It is also recognised (perhaps grudgingly) that squatter settlements or other forms of illegal housing development are a permanent part of a city's growth. One sign of this change is less emphasis on slum or squatter clearance; the fact that these simply destroy some of the few cheap housing options open to the poor has become evident to both city and national city governments; eradication policies began to be seen not as part of the solution but as contributing to the problem.

Despite this change in attitude, new squatter settlements – especially on high quality high value sites – were still rarely tolerated. But governments became more reluctant to bulldoze existing illegal settlements unless the land was needed for public projects. As noted in Chapter 3, many became more tolerant towards the development of illegal settlements on poor quality land (e.g. land subject to flooding or landslides) or on land around the periphery of the city. This was partly due to the sheer scale of illegal developments. By the late 1970s, most of the Third World's multi-million cities had more than a million living in settlements which had developed illegally – Sao Paulo, Rio de Janeiro, Bogota, Lima, Mexico City, Manila, Karachi, Delhi, Bombay, Lagos, Cairo and Bangkok among them. Many smaller cities had between a third and a half of their population living in illegal settlements; some had more than half. In almost all of them, most new house construction was taking place in illegal settlements. In democratic societies, an increasing proportion of the urban electorate lived in these illegal settlements. Those seeking election as city officials could count on a very large vote if they could convince the people in such settlements that they had the people's real interests at heart. Furthermore, squatters in many nations had shown themselves to be politically adept at negotiating for basic services in return for votes.[1]

The change in attitude was also helped by powerful interests who benefit from the growth of illegal settlements. City businesses benefit from the cheap pool of labour that their inhabitants provide or the cheap goods and services produced by the workshops and businesses which develop in many of them. Illegal settlements help to keep housing costs down – so wages can be kept low. There are also many large businesses who farm out work to the inhabitants of illegal settlements – for instance producing shoes or clothes in their homes. These businesses cut costs since no factory or machinery is provided (the out-workers have to supply their own machines), no provision made for workers' social security (sick pay, pension etc.) and it is difficult for workers to join together to demand better wages. Box 4.1 gives an example of these invisible workers. Meanwhile, the fact that the government spends little or nothing on housing programmes for lower income groups, or on providing the illegal settlements with infrastructure and services, also keeps government expenditures down and taxes low.

Box 4.1: The "invisible workforce": the hammock industry in Fortaleza, Brazil

Fortaleza is one of the largest cities in the Northeast of Brazil; it is the third largest industrial centre and by 1980, had over 1.5 million inhabitants. It is a major centre for the production of hammocks – both standard hammocks for use by Brazilians (a high proportion of the people in the North and Northeast sleep in hammocks) and luxury hammocks for tourists, foreign markets and richer Brazilians.

According to official figures, in 1976, there were 866 people working in the hammock industry but these were only the "registered" workforce in registered factories. This figure excluded thousands of people involved in hammock production who work in clandestine workshops or at home or in registered factories but not registered. In registered factories, it was usually women, not men, who are not registered.

Registered factories use unregistered workers because this produces a considerable saving for them. They avoid making contributions to social security in one of three ways: directly employing labour but not registering it; sub-contracting work to clandestine workshops; and farming out work to people working in their homes (typically women, children and older people). One factory visited in 1978 had seven registered employees but fifteen employees were counted and the owner said that he employed several hundred people working in their homes. This may be an extreme case but the finishing of a "luxury" hammock is a delicate and laborious process and virtually all hammock-makers put out such work to people working in their homes. The large hammock-makers usually use intermediaries to organize this. For instance, one large hammock producer used women working in the interior of the state at some distance from Fortaleza but organized through intermediaries. These women would come to Fortaleza every fortnight to deliver to the intermediary what they had finished and receive payment and new unfinished hammocks. One of these intermediaries provided work for more than 100 women. Working on hammock finishing at home does not provide an adequate income for survival; even where this is done full time, it produces substantially less than the minimum wage.

Many registered factories also sub-contract a lot of work to clandestine workshops. One such factory had 100 employees and 160 working in clandestine workshops. The owner said that if he had to pay all 260 people minimum wages and health insurance and social security, he would not be able to compete with other businesses. Registered factories find that sub-contracting is very useful not only for the costs saved but also to allow them to meet sudden rises in demand; sub-contracting can then be cut if demand falls. Those people running clandestine workshops and accepting subcontracts from the registered factories would like to be independent but they usually lack the capital to buy sufficient yarn for hammock production. In addition, they cannot buy the yarn direct from the cotton spinning industry because they are unregistered so they have to purchase this at a higher price from some intermediary.

Source: Herbert Schmitz, *Manufacturing in the Backyard – case studies on accumulation and employment in small-scale Brazilian industry* (London: Frances Pinter, New Jersey: Allanheld, Osmun and Co., 1982).

There are also many individuals and businesses who make money out of the development of illegal settlements or the needs of their inhabitants. First, there are the businesses which sell goods and services. For instance, in the absence of publicly-provided piped water, private water vendors are common and there are instances where they charge 20 or more times the price per litre of public supplies. There are also many businesses selling basic goods or services at the edge of illegal settlements; these often include those run by relatively large and prosperous business concerns. There are also the many producers and vendors of building materials, components, fixtures and fittings used in construction. Second, there are the land-owners, land developers and businesses who make money out of buying and selling land illegally – as in illegal sub-divisions. Third, there may be profitable possibilities for landlords; in Chapter 3 we noted the rental markets which develop in many illegal settlements and how profitable these can prove to be. Perhaps this is not so surprising; historically there are many examples of rental housing for poorer groups, based both on custom built tenements and on sub-divided older properties which proved very profitable for their landlords. If you pack enough people into a limited space and build cheaply with little investment in infrastructure and services, you can make money even from the relatively small rents that the poorest groups can afford. Certain land-owners also profit from land invasions; there are many cases of land-owners organizing or encouraging squatters to invade their land because they could receive more money in compensation from the government than the land itself was actually worth before it was invaded.[2]

Thus, governments could afford to be tolerant, as long as low income groups did not try to invade prime real estate and where the settlements they developed were not too easily visible. This change in attitudes and policies is certainly not universal – as shown by the many recent examples of large scale slum and squatter bulldozing (see Chapter 2), the example of policies in South Korea, and in Chile under Pinochet. It is perhaps significant that many of the governments which in recent years have continued with slum or squatter clearance schemes are non-elected governments – the military government in Argentina between 1977 and 1980; the eradication programme in Delhi between 1975 and 1977 during the Emergency when democratic law was suspended; the redevelopment schemes in Seoul, South Korea evident throughout the 1970s and 1980s; the squatter clearance programmes in Manila under Marcos; and the programmes of the Chilean Government 1973–1988.

The more tolerant attitude towards illegal developments may change back to repression. This is most likely in cities with rapidly growing economies and populations where there is a rapidly growing demand for land for new businesses, government offices and middle- and upper-income-group residential developments – and for the improvements in roads and other infrastructures to serve the expanding population and economy. Here, the pressures to redevelop the better-located areas which have developed as low-income low-rise settlements (whether legally or illegally) will be very great. The scale of evictions in Seoul and the way in which they have been implemented may be an indication of what will happen in many other major cities.

The cost of government inaction on land

There is a strong case for recommending a tolerant attitude on the part of government to the development of illegal settlements; at least it is more realistic than seeking to control or destroy these settlements. But if this is all that government does – what might be termed "benign tolerance" – it has several negative consequences.

Perhaps the most serious is the social and economic segregation it will allow. Such an attitude condones uncontrolled speculation in urban land and the establishment of haphazard and often dangerous settlements, since poorer groups are allowed to live on dangerous sites of low commercial value. It results in the segregation of lower income groups in the worst quality, worst-serviced and often worst-located sites and the concentration of richer groups in the best located, best quality, best-serviced sites. By relegating low income groups to overcrowded tenement districts (often in inner-city areas) and squatter settlements and illegal sub-divisions at ever greater distances from the city centre, the spatial segregation of the old colonial cities is being recreated. This means an acceptance of segregated urban societies ruled from above in ways which can only limit the potential of their citizens and undermine their dynamic and fruitful interactions. Once established, these segregated patterns of urban development cannot easily be changed; their deficiencies in regard to (say) overcrowding and lack of public space for recreation and leisure are very difficult to resolve once built up.

Benign tolerance also leaves all those living in illegal settlements open to exploitation; no laws or codes can be used in their defence since they are living in illegal settlements. Large-scale landlordism can develop with no protection for the tenants. Or if an illegal settlement is in a relatively good location, powerful commercial interests can push out the inhabitants to allow them to develop the land for their purposes (often through intimidation or arson). This has become quite common within many of the better-located illegal settlements.

Living in an illegal shelter has serious disadvantages. First, there is the obvious problem of lack of public services – not only those associated with housing (water, sanitation etc), but also services such as police and emergency services to cope with fires, accidents or serious health problems. Second, their inhabitants are not usually eligible for loans to buy, build or improve a house or to start or expand a business since their illegal shelter or land-site is not accepted as collateral. In other instances, the inhabitants cannot obtain subsidized goods or services; for instance, the inhabitants of squatter settlements in Allahabad (India) could not obtain subsidized food from the government's "fair-price" shops since the authorities would not provide the necessary card because they lived in an illegal settlement.[3] In Seoul, South Korea, households have to live in a legal, authorized address in order to register their children in the local school.[4] In these and other ways, the inhabitants of illegal settlements suffer discrimination.

A tolerant but passive role also increases the costs of infrastructure and services. The expansion of cities is haphazard when most new housing is illegal. Illegal settlements develop in small and large clusters, dotted around the city area, wherever there happens to be a plot of land where such a development is possible. This creates an ever-expanding patchwork of hundreds of high-density settlements where poorer households are concentrated – scattered all over the city region. This means a pattern and density of housing development to which it is very expensive to extend water, sewers, roads and public transport. Illegal settlements built on swampy land on hillsides subject to landslides or other sites ill-suited to human habitation (because only here did the inhabitants stand a good chance of avoiding forceful eviction), present difficult and costly problems if conditions are to be improved.

In most cities there is no lack of undeveloped or partially developed land on which low-income housing-sites could be developed, with costs much reduced because they are already close to existing roads or highways and water-mains. Large areas of land well-suited to housing developments and well-located with regard to employment centres are left vacant. Such land is owned by individuals or institutions who keep it vacant because the growth of the city and the development of its economy is rapidly pushing up its value, despite the fact that no investment is made in developing it. In this way, the owners receive the increment in the value of the land which they do nothing to create. Such land is rarely invaded; low income groups know that any attempt to do so would be crushed. There are hundreds or even thousands of hectares of vacant land in and around cities such as Manila, Bombay, Delhi and Bangkok.[5] In Sao Paulo, the present urbanized area could accommodate a two-thirds increase in population without any further expansion if undeveloped land was put to use.[6] In Karachi, the development plan for the period 1974-85 states that "over 12,000 acres of land (around 4,850 hectares) sufficient to accommodate 1.2 million people at the current residential density of 100 persons per acre (around 250 persons per hectare) lie unutilized at the heart of the city and in other parts of the built up area, with public utilities and roads still being extended expensively into outlying areas in response to pressures that are primarily speculative".[7] In Greater Bombay, "a conservative estimate would put the amount of surplus land ... at 20,000 hectares" (i.e., 200 square kilometres!) and one family alone owns 2,000 hectares of vacant land, enough to house most of the city's population currently living on pavements, inner city tenements and illegal settlements.[8]

In most cities, large areas in or close to city centres could be redeveloped for housing, public space and new traffic solutions (for instance, express bus-ways). Most major, and many less important, cities have large areas of unused or under-utilized land owned by public entities such as different branches of the armed forces, railway companies, port authorities, public utilities or other public companies. Railway companies often own large amounts of valuable but under-utilized land. When they first built the railways, they obtained land or land-use rights each side of the track and around the major stations. In the many nations where British or French companies built the railways, including not only their colonies but also independent nations such as Chile, Uruguay, Mexico and Argentina, most of the land concessions they received are still owned by the railways. This includes well-located sites no longer used or with activities which could be transferred elsewhere so the site could be redeveloped. The armed forces are often among the largest city land-owners or users with barracks and even large expanses of land for parades, sports and training in central city locations; when first acquired many years or decades ago, the location may have been appropriate and of strategic value. But with the rapid development of the city and with such locations no longer valid for strategic reasons, these could be redeveloped – again for housing, public space and improving transport systems – with facilities for the armed forces developed in less expensive areas. Old airports often exist close to city centres; these too often have surplus land or could be moved to more appropriate locations to free land needed to tackle housing problems.

Evaluating government housing policies

Table 4.1 summarizes constrasting government attitudes to housing – the "ignore or repress them" attitudes discussed in chapter 2, and then three more positive attitudes. It also outlines the implications that each attitude has for government policy on housing, basic services, finance, building- and planning-codes, land, building materials and relations with community organizations.

Subsequent sections in this and the next chapter will describe and assess the results of these different kinds of policies. But care should be taken in reading Table 4.1. It is included to illustrate the kinds of housing policies which arise from different conceptions of the housing problem. No government's housing policy can be fitted into one of these stages; government policies are never rational responses to carefully-researched problems but the result of complex interplays between different groups and interests in each particular society. Each policy, both in its formulation and implementation, is shaped by complex economic, social and political forces particular to each nation. Each nation has its own particular legal and institutional framework which will influence this. When two governments appear to have similar policies, these probably arise from different motives and may have very different implications for their citizens. In addition, we do not suggest that governments change their housing policies going from stage 1 to stage 5 on the Table; there are too many

Table 4.1: Different attitudes by governments to housing problems in cities and the different policy responses

	Stage 1	Stage 2	Stage 3	Stage 4	Stage 5
Government attitude to housing	Investment in housing provision a waste of scarce resources. Problems will be solved as the economy grows.	Government worried at rapid growth of city populations and of more rapid growth of tenements and illegal settlements. Seen as a "social problem"; squatter settlements often referred to as a "cancer".	Recognition that the approach in stage 2 is having very limited impact. Still seen as "social problem" but with political or social dangers if not addressed. Recognition that squatter settlements or other forms of illegal development are "here to stay".	Recognition that approach tried in stage 3 is having very limited impact. Recognition that people in slums and illegal settlements contribute much to cities' economies – providing cheap labour and cheap goods and services with the so called "informal sector" being key part of city economy and employment base.	Recognition that major institutional changes are needed to make approach first tried in stage 4 effective. Recognition that improving housing conditions demands multisectoral approach including health care and perhaps food programmes. Recognition that low income groups are real builders and designers of cities and government action should be oriented to supporting their efforts. Government action to ensure that all the resources needed for house construction or improvement (cheap, well-located sites, building materials, technical assistance, credit...) are available as cheaply as possible.
Government action on housing	No action.	Special institutions set up to build (or fund) special public housing programmes supposedly for lower-income groups. Slum and squatter eradication programmes initiated; often destroying more units than public agencies build.	Public housing programmes with increasingly ambitious targets. First sign of sites-and-services (or core housing) projects. Reduced emphasis on slum and squatter eradication programmes.	Reduced emphasis on public housing programmes. Far more emphasis on slum and squatter upgrading and serviced site schemes. Ending of squatter eradication programmes.	

	Stage 1	Stage 2	Stage 3	Stage 4	Stage 5
Government action on basic services	Very little action; not seen as a priority. Richer neighbourhoods in cities only ones supplied with basic services.	Initial projects to extend water supply to more city areas.	Water supply (and sometimes sewers or other sanitation types) included in site and service schemes and upgrading projects.	Major commitment to provision of water supply and sanitation.	Strengthening of local/city governments to ensure widespread provision of water supply, sanitation, storm drainage, garbage removal, roads and public transport to existing and new housing developments. Health care also provided; link between poor housing conditions and poor health understood. Perhaps supplemented by cheap food shops or school meal project to improve nutrition.
Government action on finance	Discourage housing investment; considered waste of resources.	Set up first publicly-supported or guaranteed mortgage/housing finance agency.	Attempt to set up system to stimulate saving and provide long-term loans for low income groups.	Improve efficiency of formal housing finance institutions to allow cheaper loans; flexible attitude to collateral and to small loans for land purchase and house upgrading. Encourage and support informal and community finance institutions to serve those not reached by formal institutions.	
Building and planning codes	No action.	No action. Unrealistic standards in public housing one reason why unit costs are so high.	Recognition that these are unrealistic in that low-income households cannot meet them. Not used in site-and-service and upgrading schemes.	Most public programmes to provide services, land etc. not following existing laws/codes on standards and norms because they are unrealistic.	Building/planning standards reformulated – advice and technical assistance as to how health and safety standards can be met.

	Stage 1	Stage 2	Stage 3	Stage 4	Stage 5
Government action on land	No action.	No action.	Cheap land sites made available in a few sites and services projects.	Provision of tenure to illegal settlements. Recognition that un-regulated land market a major block to improving housing and conditions.	Release of unutilized/under-utilized public land and action to ensure sufficient supply of cheap well-located sites plus provision for public facilities and open space.
Government action on building materials	No action.	No action.	Acceptance of use of cheap materials in low income housing which are illegal according to existing building codes.		Government support for widespread production of cheap building materials and common components, fixtures and fittings – perhaps supporting co-operatives within each neighbourhood for production of some of these.
Government attitude to community groups	Ignore them.	Ignore or repress them.	Some "public participation" programmed into certain projects.	More acceptance of low income people's rights to define what public programmes should provide and to take major role in their implementation.	Recognition that government support to community groups formed by lower income residents is a most effective and cost effective way of supporting new construction and upgrading.
Impact on problems	None.	None or negative.	Usually minimal although certain projects may be successful.	Substantially larger impact than in previous stages but still not on scale to match growing needs.	Impact becoming commensurate with need.

examples of national policies and attitudes which have gone in the other direction.

There is always a danger of discussing different governments' policies outside the particular context in which they are implemented. For instance, the extent to which urban land is publicly or privately owned has an influence on the extent to which governments tolerate illegal settlements. So too has the nature of government; we noted already that non-elected governments seem more ready to repress squatter invasions and repress the community organizations formed by low income groups. The extent to which the national population is living in urban areas may have an influence since urban groups have greater possibilities of organizing than rural groups – especially in large cities. Economic changes in cities also have an influence; as noted earlier, in a booming city with a rapidly-growing population, there will be more pressure to redevelop the more central or more strategically-located areas and evict any squatters from those areas. The nature of the government will also influence the extent to which those displaced by such redevelopments receive compensation or rehousing.

The cost of inappropriate action: public housing for the few

In most nations, the first major government initiative to do something positive about housing problems was a large public housing programme (what could be characterized as Stage 3 in Table 4.1). Most were launched after 1960, although there are examples of government-financed projects or programmes much earlier than this. Some of the earliest were tenements constructed with public funds in certain Latin American nations. For instance, the municipality of Buenos Aires built one *barrio* (neighbourhood) for low income groups in 1885, although four had been planned.[9] In Venezuela and Chile, government-financed housing schemes intended for low income groups are in evidence before 1930. In other Latin American nations, especially those which first began to urbanize rapidly, direct government intervention in housing becomes more common after 1930. This intervention usually began with housing finance institutions and then became direct involvement in construction. In Mexico City, Colonia Balbuera, built in the early 1930s, was intended for a low income population. So too was Vistahermosa *barrio* built in Panama City in the late 1940s. These, like so many other government-financed housing projects in subsequent years, proved too expensive for their supposed target group.[10]

By the 1950s, public housing programmes were underway not only in many Latin American nations but also in Africa and Asia – including Egypt, India and the Philippines (under independent governments), and Singapore and various sub-Saharan African nations (under colonial governments). In Singapore, a public housing programme constructed approximately 21,000 units between 1947 and 1960.[11] But in Africa, government-financed housing programmes were almost all for colonial staff or cheap, overcrowded tenements to house the labour force for certain key institutions or industries.

However, it was during the 1960s and early 1970s that most Third World governments either launched large public housing programmes or enlarged existing programmes.[12] Initially, many were explicitly linked to slum or squatter clearance but as public housing programmes developed, many governments stopped or at least cut the scale of their clearance programmes. Governments also claimed that the public housing programmes were targeted to poorer households. In Latin America, for the first time, aid was available on a large scale for financing housing projects in the early 1960s – this was from the Inter-American Development Bank but funded largely by the U.S. Government under the "Alliance for Progress".[13]

Large public-housing programmes were initiated during the 1960s in Brazil, Colombia, Egypt, South Korea and Tunisia – with efforts during the early 1970s to expand them. In Indonesia, the Philippines and Thailand new public housing agencies were set up during the 1970s (although in the case of the Philippines and Thailand, these consolidated existing agencies). The Nigerian government began its first major public housing programme for low income groups in 1973 and greatly increased its targets in the 1976–80 Plan. In Kenya, targets for public low cost housing expanded greatly first in the 1970–74 Plan and then in the 1974–78 Plan. During the late 1960s or early 1970s, Malaysia, Bangladesh, Iraq, Jordan and India, among others, had a high proportion of government funds allocated to low income housing being spent on public housing progammes. Many governments also set up new housing finance institutions or overhauled existing ones.

But three problems dogged public housing programmes: unit costs were high, so that few units were built relative to needs; middle or upper income groups ended up as the main beneficiaries; and designs and locations were ill-matched to poorer groups' needs. It was rare for the ambitious targets set for numbers of units built to be met. The cost of each public housing unit was generally very high. If little or no unit subsidy was given (so that more units could be built), the new units could only be afforded by relatively well-off households. Alternatively, if sufficient unit subsidy was given to allow lower income groups to afford them, relatively few could be built.

Box 4.2 gives examples of the quantitative inadequacies of public housing programmes – and their failure to meet ambitious targets – in Nigeria, Kenya, Egypt, the Philippines, Pakistan and Bangladesh.

Box 4.2: The shortfalls in public housing programmes

NIGERIA: The Nigerian government's target of 202,000 units between 1976 and 1980 was not met; by the end of the plan period, just 25 per cent of the units planned had been realized and many of these were allocated to relatively well-off households. The initial investment planned for this programme was an astonishing $3.5 billion; the impact that such funds could have had on improving housing and living conditions could have been enormous if spent in more appropriate, effective ways. In an analysis of public housing in one state, the federal government had planned the construction of 21,000 units between 1970 and 1985 but just 1,268 were completed. The state government had planned 12,750 for this period but completed 324 units.

EGYPT: Cairo Governorate's construction of nearly 39,000 public housing units between 1955 and 1975 can be compared to the growth in Greater Cairo's population by some 2 million inhabitants in that same period. In Egypt's second largest city, Alexandria, in 1984, public housing production made up less than half of one percent of the housing stock while informal or illegal housing represented 68 percent.

KENYA: The Kenyan Government's 1979–83 Plan noted that "over the last plan period (1974–8) only 8 per cent of the low costs units planned were in fact completed and these cost an average five times the expected cost".

THE PHILIPPINES: The target for the Economic Housing Programme in 1975 was for more than 15,000 units; actual production was slightly over 2,000.

PAKISTAN: In Karachi, Pakistan's largest city, the Karachi Development Authority aimed to build between 30,000 and 40,000 flats to rehouse those living in very poor conditions as part of the Jacob Lines Redevelopment Scheme; 10,000 units were to be built within the first year. By 1976, after four years, 475 flats had been built; after eight years, when the project was discontinued for lack of funds, 800 has been built.

BANGLADESH: During the first five year programme (1973–78), some 45,000 government funded shelters and flats were planned plus an additional 16,000 flats and shelters for public servants; estimates suggest that just 8,500 housing units were built between 1973 and 1980.

Sources: See note 14.

The problem with public housing programmes is not only that relatively few units are built. It is also that their construction takes a major proportion of (and often virtually all) public funds allocated to housing. And often, the units so produced are rented or sold at prices which lower income groups cannot afford. None of the 800 flats produced in the scheme in Pakistan described in Box 4.2 went to the originally targeted beneficiaries.[15] A World Bank paper noted how a substantial proportion of the population of Manila, Cairo, some Indonesian cities and Rabat (Morocco) could not afford to take part in publicly funded projects despite what were often high unit subsidies.[16]

One way around this problem was to reduce the level of subsidy, so that public funds went further. This is what the National Housing Bank in Brazil, set up in 1964, sought to achieve. The Bank was set up to provide loans for the construction of housing for low income groups; at first, direct to households – later to institutions building the houses. Its intention was to develop alternatives to the *favelas* (squatter settlements) for low income families and to stimulate employment in the construction industry. The Bank's loans were largely funded by compulsory savings; each employer had to deposit 8 per cent of employees' wages in a savings account in the Bank. These savings accounts were severely limited as to uses they could be put to – except for purchasing a house. The Bank did help to stimulate construction and expand employment in the construction sector and during 20 years of operation (it was abolished in November 1986), it provided the core of a housing finance system which produced around 4 million units.[17] But the Bank brought little or no benefit to lower income groups. One assessment in 1975 stated: "eleven years after the creation of the housing finance system, workers still have no house and those who believed the Bank's promises cannot pay their instalments because salaries have not risen in the same proportion as these have".[18] Indeed, the programme drew more resources from low income registered workers through the compulsory savings than it returned to them in terms of affordable housing.

Another criticism which applied to many public housing projects was that poorer households simply did not receive the units built, at great public expense, supposedly for poorer households. In some instances, only relatively well-off people were allowed to apply for them; in Indonesia, military personnel and mid-level civil servants received priority allocation. In Port Harcourt in Nigeria, a survey of residents living in highly subsidized public housing units found that over three-fifths had had a university education; "high-ranking public servants inhabit highly subsidized good quality housing even though many own property both in the city and elsewhere and they would all qualify for mortgages from commercial sources".[19] In Bangladesh, between 1980 and 1985, virtually all the housing units and plots constructed by the Housing and Settlement Directorate (central government's main housing agency with responsibility for public housing) went to military personnel or civil servants.[20]

In other instances, the application procedures automatically rule out many poor households. For instance, women-headed households are often not eligible, even though up to a third of all households, and up to half of the households in many low income areas, are headed by women. In some instances, only men may apply on behalf of a household. In others, proof of formal, stable employment is required; women-headed households are rarely able to find a formal job – given both the discrimination against women in the job market and the fact that a formal job is very difficult to combine with rearing and caring for infants and children.[21]

One final criticism of public housing programmes is that many of the units produced were very unpopular with their residents. Even if they did reach poorer households and were built in sufficient quantities to have an impact, they still had major drawbacks. During the 1970s, an increasing number of case studies showed that most public housing estates were not only an expensive solution but also a very bad one with regard to meeting poorer households' needs in terms of size, location and cost. In some instances, they were far too small; their design was based on Western concepts of small nuclear families but they had to house larger families, and many families needed space to work at home – for instance making clothes or food for sale. They were often based on Western designs and so proved poorly suited to tropical or sub-tropical climatic conditions. In many nations, poorer families keep some livestock and this is hardly possible in five storey apartment blocks. They failed to consider cultural needs; for instance, in Tunisia, public housing did not include inner courtyards, a critical need within any Islamic household where women have little or no possibility of using public open space.[22] Repair and maintenance were a continual problem; tropical climates with high humidity and rainfall often ensure more deterioration while ineffective local government proved incapable of implementing a maintenance programme. Box 4.3 provides an example of how a family's move from a shanty town to a subsidized public housing unit in Mexico City helped impoverish them. It is drawn from *Housing by People* by John F.C. Turner, published in 1976, one of the most widely-read critiques of public housing – or indeed of any centralized programme of state provision where citizens have little or no control over what is provided and how it is provided.

Box 4.3: Impoverishment after a move from a shanty town to a public housing unit

A mason and his family living in Mexico City received a house in a public housing project, after their previous home in a shanty town had been threatened by the government authorities. In this shanty town, the family had lived on the mason's irregular employment as a semi-skilled mason and from running a small shop serving tourists. Because of low housing and transport expenditures, the low income these activities produced allowed them to eat reasonably well and remain relatively healthy. Just 5 per cent of their income went on housing and travelling to and from work.

The move to the new house meant a much increased standard of housing with basic modern services. But the family found that it needed 55 per cent of its income to meet the cost of the rent-purchase arrangement and payment for utilities like water and electricity – even though they were not charged the full cost of these. The cost of getting to and from work also increased – to take another 5 per cent of income. And one of their previous sources of income finished since they were not allowed to run a shop in their new house.

Source: John F.C. Turner, *Housing by People* (London: Marion Boyars, 1976).

Many governments have accepted the validity of the various critiques of public housing; others still retain faith in large-scale public provision. The example of Singapore's large-scale public housing programme still attracts attention and even now, "the relevance of the Singapore model" is still discussed. In Singapore, a public agency, the Housing and Development Board, constructed some 230,000 housing units between 1960 and 1975 and around as many again between 1975 and 1985. By 1985, close to three quarters of the population lived in housing units built by this government board.

A review of 17 Third World nations' housing policies published in 1981 noted that Singapore's public housing programme was the only one on a scale sufficient to have a significant impact on improving housing conditions.[23] But even leaving aside the issue of the appropriateness of the housing so provided, hundreds of thousands of people were forcefully evicted from their homes as the area they inhabited was redeveloped. This study also pointed to three characteristics which made the example of Singapore of little relevance to other Third World nations. The first is that the city had enjoyed a very rapid growth in its economy (one of the most rapid and sustained increases in the Third World) and yet had had very little in-migration; Singapore Island had virtually no rural population and immigration was strictly controlled. In virtually all other Third World nations, a city which experienced comparable rates of economic growth would have been the centre for very rapid in-migration which would have swamped any public housing programme. The second reason, related to this, is the fact that with rapid economic growth but relatively slow growth in the economically active population, most households had steadily rising real incomes and thus increases in what they could afford to spend on housing. This too considerably eases the problem noted earlier, namely the gap between the cost of reasonable quality accommodation and what lower income groups can afford. The third reason is that in 1960, when the public housing programme greatly increased its scale, the government already owned large tracts of land amounting to around half the island's total area, including land close to the city centre. Thus, public housing could be built on well-located sites with no high land-cost and with no lengthy land-expropriation procedures. The public housing programme was also supported by stronger land use control and public expropriation powers than in other Third World nations which have tried similar approaches. As will be discussed later, the unwillingness or inability of Third World governments to ensure sufficient supply of cheap well-located land for low income housing (a problem that Singapore's government did not face) underpins their failure to successfully address city housing problems.

The myth of the housing gap

One of the main justifications used by governments for public housing programmes is the idea that a "housing gap" of enormous proportions is developing in their cities. This housing gap is calculated in three stages. First, government sets some criteria to judge the quality of housing and thus define what they regard as an "adequate" house. Secondly, it judges existing housing against these criteria and thus determines the number of housing units which are "sub-standard". Thirdly, it calculates the degree of over-crowding. The figure for the housing deficit is then calculated by adding together the number of sub-standard housing units and the number needed to eliminate overcrowding. Governments often then add to this figure the number of housing units which will be needed in particular cities or regions over the next 5–10 years. This is then announced as the housing deficit, usually to justify government plans to build or finance enough units to reduce this deficit.

But rarely do these figures have any validity. The criteria used to judge which houses are sub-standard and what constitutes over-crowding are often based on western models and their validity within the national context is open to question. There is little or no consultation with the people who live in sub-standard housing as to their judgements. The criteria used often condemn half a city's housing stock and nine out of ten of all new housing units currently being produced as sub-standard and by implication, having zero value. This includes vast numbers of houses built, repaired and extended by their inhabitants which represent not only these people's homes but also their most valuable asset. These houses also function as these people's long-term savings bank.

In Egypt, the urban housing deficit in 1975 was said to have reached 1.5 million units with the housing deficit in Cairo alone being 750,000 inhabitants.[24] In the Philippines, the housing deficit was put at 1.8 million units in 1980[25] while it was put at 750,000 in Colombia's urban areas in 1974.[26] In effect, because the government regards the housing in which these millions of people live as worthless, these people are considered homeless. The fact that Cairo had a housing deficit of 750,000 units in 1975 implies that around half the city's population was homeless, if one assumes that on average, there are between five and six people for each household. It is ironic that most of these millions of homeless people who make up the housing deficit and live in worthless housing are not homeless because they found or organized the construction of their own housing, often with nothing but hostility from the governments.

Public provision in centrally planned economies

In centrally planned economies, there has also been a tendency to see the housing problem in cities as a quantitative problem rather than a qualitative one. Housing problems are also often defined as a deficit of so many hundreds-of-thousands of units.

In Cuba in 1959, the government talked of a housing deficit of 700,000 units (the housing problem was conceived in the same way by the Egyptian government in 1975 and the Philippine government in 1980). Annual production of publicly supported housing units never met the original hopes – although the size of the construction effort was higher relative to population than in most market or mixed economies. During the 1970s, some 143,000 units were built (including those constructed by micro-brigades[27]). But the number constructed by private initiative during this period was substantially higher. There have been changes in the Cuban government's approach in recent years. There is now more support for private or co-operative house construction and families' right to own their own dwelling has been sanctioned by law. This frees up scarce public resources for other investments.[28]

But the example of Cuba cannot be discussed only in terms of housing production. In terms of improving housing and living conditions, Cuba's comprehensive health care service and food rationing system which considerably improved nutrition levels, and education programmes which gave Cuban citizens a level of literacy comparable to many European nations should be noted. A Rent Law reduced rents and an Urban Reform Law transferred ownership of rented accommodation to tenants. An Agrarian Reform Law and a major programme to improve housing and living conditions in rural areas, and in urban centres other than Havana, reduced the pressure to migrate to Havana for survival. While the Cuban government's efforts to improve the quality of the physical structure in which people live may be open to criticism, it is undeniable that the majority now have much better housing and living conditions than they had in 1959.

The same seems to be true in China where levels of health, nutrition and education have improved considerably since 1949, even if urban housing conditions have not. Richard Kirkby, writing on urbanization in China, divides the period 1949–84 into three distinct phases. During the first, 1949–1960, there was a very rapid growth in urban population but relatively little public action to improve housing or living conditions; the average floorspace per capita in urban areas is reported to have halved between 1949 and 1962. Then between 1961 and 1976, aggregate urban population fell as a result of mass deportations and controls on rural to urban migration. While this produced a rise in the amount of floorspace per city-inhabitant, housing conditions probably continued to deteriorate. Private sector initiatives in housing were severely restricted and public investment both in housing and in infrastructure was regarded as a wasteful use of resources. The period 1977–1982 saw a return to very rapid urban population growth and a rising public commitment to the construction of new housing in urban areas. "In terms of re-allocation of the state's resources the urban housing sector has emerged as the single greatest beneficiary."[29]

During the 1981–85 Plan, public housing programmes are likely to have constructed nearly as much new housing as in the entire period 1950–1977. But as in Cuba, with public resources being scarce, there seems to be an increasing recognition that mobilization of private savings, for house repair and maintenance, or for house purchase, can play an important role in improving conditions. In 1982, pilot schemes to sell housing were set up in four cities. And private sector construction is no longer discouraged.[30]

The final example from a centrally planned economy is drawn from a paper by Allan Cain on Luanda, capital of Angola.[31]

Luanda had around 1.25 million inhabitants by the mid-1980s and around three quarters of these lived in *musseques* (largely unplanned, dense settlements) or peri-urban settlements. When Angola finally achieved independence from Portugal in 1975, perhaps not surprisingly, the new government wanted to move fast and decisively on housing. At Independence, it was confronted with very rapid urban growth fuelled by the return of thousands of Angolans who had taken refuge in villages or neighbouring nations during the liberation struggle. In addition, the urban economy virtually collapsed with the flight of the Portuguese who had controlled it. The Portuguese had taken every movable object with them and sabotaged much of what they could not take. The government was attracted by the idea of mass housing using industrialized building systems rather than rehabilitating the existing housing stock including the traditional *musseques*. The scarcity of people with a technical training also made such systems seem attractive since, in theory, they minimize the amount of skilled labour needed on the site where the housing is to be constructed. Several schemes were put forward to eradicate specific *musseques* and replace them with modern blocks and flats with little investment considered in existing *musseques*, even though these housed much of Luanda's population. As Cain comments,

> many nations at a similar stage of development have found ...
> that prefabrication, rather than being a short cut to housing
> the masses, tends to produce housing well out of the reach of
> the most needy, costing more, sometimes several times more
> than housing built by conventional means. Rather than being
> efficient in resources, industrialized building only begins to be
> comparable in cost to conventional construction in situations
> where there already exist high levels of infrastructural support,
> such as transport, energy and skilled labour. Such situations are
> still rare in Africa today.[32]

By the early 1980s, the inappropriateness of such schemes was better appreciated and official housing policy broadened with the publication of the first "auto-construction" law designed to support those organizing the building of their own houses.

Thus, the evidence of the last 20 years from both centrally planned and capitalist nations suggests that if governments try to solve the problem by public agencies seeking to construct sufficient units, in quantitative terms, they will almost always have limited impact. This is especially so in market or mixed economies where much (or most) investment comes from the private sector and where lower income groups have too little income to spend on housing to represent effective demand, and thus encourage the private sector to invest in housing. Private sector investment may still be an important source of low income rental accommodation or an important source of cheap sites (as in illegal sub-divisions). But to make these profitable, given the low level of effective demand, this will mean little or no provision of infrastructure and services. It also usually means that the whole operation is undertaken illegally, so the clients have no protection from the law.

In countries with centrally planned economies, governments can make more impact on the housing problem because they own the land, control most investments and control the location of most productive investment. In theory, this allows a match between the location of new jobs and new housing in a way which is rarely apparent in market or mixed economies. It also makes housing provision less expensive because land costs are avoided (and land acquisition is much easier) and it allows the control of cities' physical expansion. But as the examples of recent changes in the attitude of the Chinese, Angolan and Cuban governments show, ignoring the potential for even relatively low income households to fund part of their own house construction, improvements or extension (if sites and materials are cheap and easily available) ignores an important source of investment in improving housing. It also prevents those households who wish to contribute some of their time to housing construction or improvement from doing so.

Allowing or encouraging private investment by owner-occupiers in housing is now acknowledged as a way to lessen the burden on public agencies to maintain the housing stock; the problem of maintaining (or, rather, not maintaining) the public housing stock is one which virtually all nations share. In addition, as noted earlier, governments in both market and centrally planned economies have increasingly recognized that public programmes to build housing units rarely produce units which match the great diversity in needs and preferences among lower income groups in terms of chosen trade-offs between size, quality, location and cost.

5. The Emergence of New Attitudes and Policies for Housing

Over the last 20 years, increasing numbers of governments have recognized that a concentration on public housing was having little impact. Many began to recognize that illegal settlements were simply logical responses by city dwellers solving their own accommodation needs. They also recognized that the exclusion of the low income majority from any possibility of entering either the legal housing or the legal land market was the fundamental cause of the housing problems. In some instances, they also recognized that inappropriate official building and planning norms and codes and inefficient government procedures for allowing legal land-sub-divisions contributed to the problem. The dynamism shown by those who organize the construction of their own housing in illegal settlements, began to be better appreciated – with illegal housing developments viewed less as a problem and more as a solution. In some instances, there appears to be a growing awareness that public housing projects are often ill-matched to the needs of many low income individuals and households.

It is impossible to point precisely to the origins of these new attitudes. Part of it came from the experiences of people who worked with low income groups in housing and community development projects in the 1950s and early 1960s; many of these were priests and religious groups affiliated to the World Council of Churches. Part of it originated from the work of researchers and professionals working in illegal settlements. For instance, a Peruvian anthropologist, Matos Mar, was among the first to write about squatter settlements, mapping their sites and seeking to relate their expansion with the policies of different governments.[1] In the late 1950s, evaluations of the huge public housing *superbloques* in Caracas were documenting not only how inappropriate they were for poorer households needs, but also the disastrous impact of the forced relocation of their inhabitants on community links, which had been such an important part of the illegal settlements from which they had been evicted.[2] During the 1960s, the writings of John F.C. Turner and William Mangin elaborated and developed new attitudes to illegal settlements and reached a much larger audience.[3]

Although no concensus was ever reached as to the "right attitude" and the "correct policy", certain new elements became apparent in various government programmes which implied a break with the past.

First, the legal right of those living in illegal settlements to be there was recognized; this can be seen at project level in many cities with the legalization of tenure for people living in certain identified illegal settlements. In certain instances this recognition went beyond project level – for instance in many municipalities in Peru or urban centres in Tanzania or in Lusaka, Zambia. This recognition also underlies the various land-sharing schemes negotiated between squatters and landowners, with the help of non-governmental organizations and government agencies in Bangkok (see Box 5.1).

Box 5.1: Land sharing as an alternative to eviction

In Bangkok, the inhabitants of illegal settlements threatened with eviction have organized and bargained successfully for a share of the land they occupy and landlords have agreed to sell or lease them the land – although usually after long negotiations. The inhabitants then develop new housing on part of the site while the rest reverts to the land-owner. Several land-sharing schemes have been implemented or are underway. Although these are not the ideal solution for the inhabitants, they do represent a successful compromise which is much preferred to eviction.

In 1985, 272,000 people lived in settlements in Bangkok which were under threat of eviction. Rapid growth in Bangkok's economy has meant rapidly rising land prices in central areas and thus increasing pressure to redevelop central sites. A study in 1981 suggested that the main reasons for evictions were the need for road construction, to make way for commercial development and for public buildings.

By 1985, five land-sharing agreements had been signed: Rama IV where the company developing the site had to finance and build 850 flats for the residents; Manangkasila

where houses were constructed for 181 families; Wat Lad
Bua Kaw where residents took responsibility for constructing
houses; Samyod where 175 houses were constructed by the
government's National Housing Authority; and Klong Toey
where 1,440 families received flats built by the National Housing Authority and 1,300 families rebuilt their own homes on
serviced sites.

To give one example of a land-sharing scheme. In
Manangkasila the community was established some 60 years
ago on public land. The site runs along a railway track and is
close to the city centre and next to a busy commercial artery –
and thus well placed for its inhabitants in terms of access to jobs.
In 1978, the Treasury Department decided to redevelop the site
and to do so by leasing it to the highest bidder for commercial
development; a bid was won by a company with the stipulation
that the dwellers would be moved within one year. The company
offered the inhabitants compensation for evicting them but only
32 dwellers accepted.

The inhabitants organized a demonstration in front of
the Prime Minister's house; the Prime Minister instructed
the Ministry of Finance to resolve the matter. Negotiations
between representatives from the Ministry of Finance and
the Treasury Department, the company and the community eventually led to agreement on a land-sharing scheme.
Virtually all the organization, site-planning and negotiation for
land-sharing was done by a few leaders – with technical support from staff members of the government's National Housing
Authority and voluntary agencies. Once the division of the site
between the company and the inhabitants' new housing was
agreed, the housing was constructed by a private contractor,
supervised by members of the community committee and the
house owners; there was little self-help construction, but the
units were left unfinished for the dwellers to complete themselves.

While on average, those taking part in land-sharing schemes
end up paying only six per cent of the market value of the land
they occupy, the developers also obtained their portion of the
land relatively cheaply, despite their share in paying for the
accommodation of the residents.

The move towards more democratic government with the
increasing involvement of elected politicians in decision

making processes, which were previously the domain of the established bureaucracy or the armed forces, was an important factor in land-sharing schemes gaining government acceptance. This and increasing public exposure to the problems of the poor increased support for negotiated compromises which benefited poorer groups; they also encouraged a change in the orientation of the government's National Housing Authority, towards upgrading projects and towards support for land-sharing schemes.

Source: Shlomo Angel and Somsook Boonyabancha, "Land-sharing as an alternative to eviction – the Bangkok experience" *Third World Planning Review*, vol. 10, no. 2, 1988.

Another innovation was the recognition of the right of people living in what were previously considered slums and illegal settlements to basic infrastructure and services – as in the many slum and squatter upgrading projects and programmes. National programmes for upgrading poorer areas in urban centres are also evident in some instances – notably in Indonesia[4] and Tanzania.[5]

A few governments began to reformulate building and planning codes so that they do not demand unrealistically high standards which lower-income groups cannot attain. Again, the evidence for this is mainly at project level; most innovative and successful projects for upgrading or for new low income housing have ignored existing building and planning norms and codes – including the housing units built in the land-sharing schemes described in Box 5.1.[6] Examples which go beyond specific projects include the revision of sub-division norms in Colombia[7] and the flexible standard approach in the Sudan described later in this chapter.[8] Governments have also begun to support the production of cheap building materials and common components, fixtures and fittings used in housing production; again, this is most evident at project level rather than city wide programmes.

Some governments have released unutilized and under-utilized land, and taken other measures to ensure land-sites for housing are available which provide legal alternatives to squatter settlements. This too usually occurs at project level through government sponsored "serviced site" projects. In such projects, households receive a plot of land supplied with basic infrastructure and services and then organize the construction of their own house on it. This lowers the initial cost for the purchaser (since they are only paying for a site, not a house) but of course means that they have no shelter, until they have organized and paid for the construction of a house. Dozens of governments have implemented serviced-site projects, but very few have gone beyond a few projects to a continuous programme. In Managua, Nicaragua, there was a large programme to release unutilized land for housing, while in Tunisia, the government has initiated a continuous programme to develop sites for housing with services and this has been implemented in many urban centres over a number of years (see p. 130). In 1987, the Presidential Commission for the Urban Poor set up by the Philippines government under Corazon Aquino facilitated the release of 600 hectares of government land for allocation to 37,400 families (some 223,900 people). This Commission has also helped to implement land-sharing schemes with private developers and landowners and has officially recognized the community organizations formed by poorer groups.[9]

The strengthening of local/city governments to permit them to fund and manage a steady improvement in the provision of water, sanitation, storm drainage, garbage removal, health care services, roads and public transport to new and existing residential areas is an important aspect of the new approach. This is much discussed although there are few examples where national government has decentralized sufficient power and resources to city/municipal governments to undertake this. One relatively recent example is the municipal reform in Colombia where centrally appointed mayors were replaced by elected mayors and where the fiscal base of local governments was considerably strengthened.[10] In other nations, there are also many examples of new national agencies set up to give technical and financial support to local governments.[11]

Some governments have given support to community groups formed by lower income residents so that they can provide a more coherent and effective way of improving existing illegal settlements and developing new low income settlements. Examples include the support provided to community groups by the Municipality of Hyderabad's Urban Community Development Department in India,[12] the support given to *favela* organizations by the Municipality of Rio de Janeiro[13] and the Mexican government's creation of FONHAPO – a National Fund for Popular Housing.[14]

Non-governmental organizations (NGOs) based in Third World cities can be valuable intermediaries between government and the community or neighbourhood organizations formed by the inhabitants of low income settlements. NGOs with architects, planners, health specialists, engineers and community motivators on their staff can be used by community organizations for technical advice or for help in co-ordinating and implementing projects or in helping negotiate with government agencies. Again, most of the cases which are documented are for particular projects rather than for long term programmes. There are hundreds of examples of small NGO projects but among the NGOs which have implemented large scale projects or programmes on low income housing with official approval and support are FUNDASAL in El Salvador[15], Human Settlements of Zambia[16] and CENVI and COPEVI in Mexico.[17] The scale and diversity of such NGO involvement is also better recognized.[18]

A few governments have supported informal finance organizations such as co-operatives, savings and loans associations and credit unions, or made the formal financial system more responsive to people's needs for housing finance. One example is FUNDASAL, a foundation supporting mutual self-help housing in El Salvador which found a very low rate of arrears or defaults on loans despite the low income of those participating. The sense of community and household responsibility within the project – since the participants helped establish priorities as well as in the construction – was one key reason.[19] Community-based finance institutions have also been able to provide housing finance to poorer households who could not obtain such finance from conventional banks.[20] But it is also possible for governments to support large, formal institutions which become more flexible both in the size of loans given, and in their demands on households before loans are given (for instance in the amount of collateral required). The Housing Finance Development Corporation in India is reaching many households normally excluded by conventional housing finance systems with commercial loans to buy or improve their own housing or land-site for housing. One reason is a more flexible attitude in regard to collateral; a second is cheaper interest rates because loan defaults are kept to a minimum.[21]

Pilot schemes and institutions to resolve the complex housing and housing tenure problems for long term tenants have been implemented. Here, the aim is usually to increase tenants' control over their accommodation and to give them the possibility of purchasing it – either individually or collectively. New approaches to this problem are being tried by a state foundation in Salvador, Brazil in rehabilitating the units (with self help from the tenants), in the transfer of ownership to the tenants, and in job creation. The transfer of ownership of the *vecindades* (old, cheap-rental housing) from the previous owners to the tenants and their reconstruction with much improved standards after the earthquake in Mexico City[22], and the building repair and reconstruction programme in Bombay, where financial support is given to tenants to organize the repair and maintenance of the tenements in which they rented rooms, provide two more examples of this.[23] There is also the example of Ganeshnagar in Pune where tenants formed a group to resist landlords who were charging protection money and harassing them for higher rents. Eventually, the tenants gained control of the settlement, forced the landlords to sell them the houses and organized an upgrading programme.[24]

One government housing programme which has sought to combine many of the innovative elements listed already is the Million Houses Programme of the Government of Sri Lanka. This changed the focus of government intervention from public housing programmes which were costly and reached relatively few people to the provision of secure tenure, basic infrastructure and services and housing finance to much greater numbers of households. The programme covered both rural and urban areas and included upgrading of squatter settlements and inner city tenements and serviced site schemes. Many initiatives had a strong community focus.[25] But independent evaluations as to the success of this Programme have not yet appeared, although evaluations of several projects implemented within the broader programme have been favourable. Furthermore, the context within which such a programme has been implemented includes considerable civil disturbance and violence which further complicate any evaluation.

It is difficult to assess whether these many examples represent a trend towards new approaches by governments or are mostly small, isolated incidents which arise because of some particularly favourable political conjuncture in particular cities at particular points in time and thus can never serve as the basis for action on a much larger scale. Most of the examples of innovations given were for particular projects, not large scale programmes.

It can also be argued that most of these innovative projects cannot be transferred to other societies. For instance, if the land-sharing schemes could only be implemented in Bangkok because of a process of democratization, a high degree of public land ownership and a culture which values compromise, this would limit the possibility of their application elsewhere. Bangkok's land-sharing schemes provide a valuable example of a compromise negotiated between illegal settlers and landowners and the documentation of these schemes describes in detail how and under what conditions such schemes were possible in Bangkok[26]. The example can stimulate and encourage those individuals and institutions seeking such compromises in other cities – but these compromises can only be conceived within the cultural, social and political context of each nation and each government.

Of course, political changes can open up the possibility of implementing new approaches – just as they can bring to an end a new approach tried by the previous government. Box 5.2 gives an example – outlining the contrast in policies between Argentina's military government and that of the government after the return to democratic rule. In Manila, immediately after the overthrow of the Marcos government, thousands of people invaded vacant private and public land; as the squatter leaders commented, they expected a more generous and humane attitude from the new, democratic government.[27]

Box 5.2: Political change and changes in government attitudes – the example of Argentina

The democratically elected government which replaced a military government in 1983/4 has shown a far more open attitude to squatter settlements than its predecessor, accepting land invasions, eliminating the repression of illegal settlements and stopping evictions. After the military government took power in 1976, lower income groups found it increasingly difficult to find accommodation. For most people, real incomes declined. A law in 1976 abolished rent control; this led to innumerable tenant evictions. And many of those who had formerly rented rooms were forced to compete with the lowest income groups for space in tenements or cheap boarding houses. The military government's public works programme concentrated on such aspects as highway construction which brought little benefit to the poor. And the programme to demolish squatter settlements (*villas miserias*) simply meant a decline in the housing options open to lower income groups, and an increasing number needing cheap accommodation. These were the conditions which prompted over 20,000 people to invade land in the suburbs of Buenos Aires; the story of this invasion is told in

Box 1.1, p. 12. Since 1984, with the new democratically elected government, the municipal and national authorities have been more sympathetic to the squatters' problems – although only a few municipalities have formulated explicit plans to support the upgrading of such settlements. Municipalities are now taking the initiative, promoting self-help co-operatives, devising new ways of regularizing illegal settlements, providing technical assistance and lending equipment.

Sources: Beatriz Cuenya, Hector Almada, Diego Armus, Julia Castells, Maria di Loreto and Susana Penalva, "Habitat and health conditions of the popular sectors: a pilot project of participative investigation in the San Martin settlement, Greater Buenos Aires", CEUR, Buenos Aires; and Ernesto Lopez Montana, "PRODIBA – integrated basic service provision for low income groups in Greater Buenos Aires" in UNICEF Urban Examples 15, *Improving Environment for Child Health and Survival*, March 1988.

Obstacles to scaling-up and institutionalizing the new approaches

This section will review some of the difficulties inherent in developing the new approaches into larger and more continuous programmes. First, it will look at upgrading programmes and site and service programmes; then it will consider the difficulties in tackling the question of poorer groups' access to land and in changing official norms and codes on building and planning.

In the case of upgrading programmes, the difficulties centre on how to sustain the initial impetus. The Indonesian Kampung Improvement Programme can be taken as an example, since this was one of the first large upgrading programmes and remains one of the largest ever implemented. This was started in Jakarta in 1969 and later expanded to cover a very large range of urban centres; it is generally judged to have been a success because, at a relatively low cost, it improved infrastructure and services for a high proportion of lower income households. However, there are signs that in some cities or some districts within cities, upgrading also led to rising land prices, and a marked decrease in cheap rental accommodation.[28] In addition, where no provision was made to work with the inhabitants of the *kampungs* in designing and implementing the upgrading – and thus no provision made to ensure there was maintenance for the new infrastructure and services – considerable problems with maintenance soon arose.[29]

An upgrading programme tries to make up for a lack of past investment in basic infrastructure and services. In effect, it suddenly makes a series of basic investments which should have been made on a continuous basis by the local government. It may improve conditions considerably at first but very rarely does it increase the capacity of local government to maintain the new infrastructure and services and to continue with the process of upgrading. Upgrading momentarily makes up for a deficiency in local government but over time, this deficiency returns. As Johan Silas suggests, fully involving the residents in the upgrading can provide a substitute – so that local residents and community organizations take on the responsibility for maintenance but this is rare in upgrading schemes. In addition, it is somewhat inequitable for poorer communities to have to take on responsibility for maintenance when richer areas not only receive higher quality public services but also have the influence to ensure that these are maintained by local government.

The limitations of site-and-service projects are also becoming more evident. Serviced-site projects are only cheaper than public housing projects because the public authorities make the recipients of the plots responsible for house construction (and perhaps additional cost savings are achieved by having lower standards for plot sizes, and infrastructure and services). Many serviced-site schemes have suffered from exactly the same kinds of problems that public housing projects experienced, being too expensive for poorer groups, in the wrong location and with plot sizes and site lay-outs which were ill-matched to the needs and priorities of the intended beneficiaries.[30]

To return to the case of Indonesia, the National Housing and Urban Development Agency (PERUMNAS) was set up in the mid-1970s to work alongside the upgrading programme and it had a target of 30,000 units a year during the 1979–84 Plan for the whole nation (including serviced sites, core housing and complete units). But even if this target was met, it would make little impression; in Jakarta alone, the population was growing by some 250,000 inhabitants a year. In addition, the new agency has experienced considerable difficulties in acquiring sites for low income developments and many of the "low cost solutions" it provides are not allocated to lower income groups. Meanwhile, it seems housing built on informal or illegal sub-divisions, often over prime agricultural land, account for three quarters of the new housing in Jakarta.[31] PERUMNAS's plans for the 1984-89 Plan received similar criticisms; $933 million was allocated for the construction of 300,000 serviced sites and low cost houses to serve 1.5 million people but just $13.3 million was allocated to upgrading schemes which are also aimed at reaching 1.5 million people.[32]

There are many other examples of governments who have, with positive results, accepted the right of those living in illegal settlements to live there and provide some basic services but have had far more difficulty in stimulating the supply of cheap, legal, serviced alternatives; the governments of Tanzania and the Sudan fall into this category. In both, the commitment to upgrading and regularizing illegal settlements and a concentration on serviced (or on occasion unserviced) sites to guarantee lower income households access to cheap land-sites became a central part of national policy in the early 1970s. But governments in both nations have experienced difficulties in actually implementing the serviced-site programmes (or even unserviced-site programmes) on the desired scale[33]. Clearly, shortage of trained personnel is one major hindrance; so too are the severe economic problems each national economy has faced in recent years.[34]

At the core of the limited impact of serviced-site schemes (and indeed of other government initiatives to guarantee poorer groups access to legal housing solutions) was the failure of government to ensure a larger and cheaper supply of legal land sites for housing. In market or mixed economies, official government reports or United Nations reports are almost unanimous in pointing to high land costs and the lengthy procedure involved in public land acquisition as the major constraint on any programme to provide legal, affordable alternatives to squatter settlements or illegal subdivisions. In a recent United Nations Report on Human Settlements in Asia and the Pacific,[35] it is interesting to note the similarities in comments about urban land. Thus, in Indonesia, one of the major problems facing the national agency responsible for sites-and-services schemes was land availability.

> While the government has powers to condemn land, it is reluctant to do so and relies on negotiating purchases with landowners. This means that lowest-cost land available is not always the most appropriate for a given facility. Problems are compounded, moreover, by the poor state of cadastral records in the country.[36]

For the Philippines,

> government resources will never be sufficient to maintain a
> continuous subsidy for housing for low income families and
> there is a need for policy reinforcements especially in the matter
> of land acquisition and strategies to lower the cost of housing in
> order to make it accessible to the poor.[37]

In Thailand,

> the government (i.e., the National Housing Authority) is ham-
> pered in its shelter programme by inability to expropriate land.[38]

In Bangladesh,

> although the government has powers of expropriation, land
> acquisition for shelter has proven extremely difficult due to
> litigation and costs. It is estimated that as many as ten years are
> needed to acquire a housing site.[39]

Comparable comments could be drawn from official government or
United Nations reports for nearly every Third World nation with
urban land markets dominated by private-sector ownership.

Government sponsored site-and-service projects can be seen as an
attempt to come to terms with the lack of cheap, legal housing
plots but however successful they are at project level, their limit
is precisely that they are one-off projects. Site-and-service projects
appear to tackle the problem of too little cheap land for housing but
they do so on such a small scale that they have little impact. They fail
to tackle the real problem – an urban land-market which excludes
poorer groups. When governments try to scale up site-and-service
projects into a continuous programme, they run into problems
in implementing and financing this because they cannot acquire the
land they need. They are not prepared (or able) to challenge the
power of private land owners. Landowners can challenge the government's right to expropriate their land in the courts, and even where
the courts decide in favour of the government, the legal system can
be used to delay the whole process to such an extent as to prevent its
effectiveness. To avoid the long delays which usually accompany the
government's expropriation of sites well-located for poorer groups'
employment needs, governments may acquire only cheaper, lower

value sites which are easier to obtain. These will probably be the ones whose locations *least* suit lower income groups.

Furthermore, governments usually pay inflated prices for the land they acquire. In cities, private land-owners find the value of their land rises as the city's economy expands and as the quality of infrastructure and services improves. They do nothing to earn this increment in value – and part of it is paid for by government. But when governments purchase land, they usually pay landowners for this unearned increment. Governments purchasing land for serviced-site programmes usually pay market rates, so the main beneficiaries of expanded programmes will be the landowners, not the poor. And the costs of the land will probably be so high that the scale of the programme will be much reduced. A study of a site-and-service project in Guatemala City showed that because no initiative was taken to recapture the value added to adjoining areas as a result of the project, the cost of acquiring land in later stages had been increased sufficiently to force a redesign of the entire project and lower the originally planned standards and size of plots.[40] In addition, the profits made by the subcontractors (36 per cent of total costs) almost exceeded the cost of all salaries, wages, materials and infrastructure.[41]

Perhaps not surprisingly, a recent review of serviced-site projects commented that most governments have adopted this kind of project on a trial basis and not as a central part of housing policy.[42] The review also found that pressure on public agencies to reduce unit costs was the main reason for their implementation – rather than a genuine attempt to develop more appropriate solutions for low income groups. In pursuit of such cost reductions, the government used cheap land-sites which were in locations too distant from employment sources to suit poorer households. They were cheap only because they transferred to the recipient of the plot additional costs not only of housing construction but also of travel to and from work. Not surprisingly, many low income recipients either default on payments or sell out to middle income groups.[43]

One reason why the Tunisian government's intervention in improving lower income groups' housing and living conditions has proved more successful than most other governments is that the government set up special land development agencies; one such agency, operating from regional offices, acquires, sub-divides and develops land and sells it at cost for residential developments. This greatly increased the supply of land for housing – but since the land was sold without subsidy, it was at no cost to the government. Meanwhile, the public agency responsible for social housing was able to expropriate land it needed or to use public land. This has been complemented by a large political and financial commitment to improving housing conditions and, from the mid-1970s, a move away from public housing projects to a more varied mix of projects better suited to lower income groups' needs. Public projects offered a range of serviced-site or core houses or apartments. They were implemented with projects to upgrade and legalize inhabitants' land tenure in illegal settlements; this contrasts with the policy in previous years which sought to eradicate such settlements and build conventional public housing.[44] Although criticisms can still be made of government housing programmes in Tunisia – perhaps most especially in the failure to involve poorer groups in decisions about the most appropriate solutions – they have certainly had a greater impact on improving housing and living conditions than most other Third World governments' programmes.

Building and planning codes and standards can be changed to reduce the cost of the cheapest legal house or land development and to increase the proportion of buildings and land developments which are legal. As such, they too need changing although this presents most governments with difficulties since they are usually embedded in a legal system and implemented by professionals who are resistant to change. One way around this is to designate certain settlements or areas as "special development zones" where the building and planning codes are not enforced; this has been tried in the Philippines, Kenya and Jamaica.[45] But this can create segregated societies – the poor restricted to special zones.

The approach to building and planning codes in the Sudan – inherited from colonial times – is a more comprehensive version of this. No doubt its original intention was to segregate the rich from the poor, but in fact it also provides considerable flexibility. Most urban land is owned by the government so householders lease plots of land on which their houses stand. Residential areas within a city may be designated first, second, third or fourth class areas. In fourth-class areas, the inhabitants have a lease from the government for their plots but no building standards are demanded. In third-class areas, longer leases are given, plot sizes are larger and some infrastructure and services provided. Then second- and first-class areas get longer leases, better infrastructure and services and larger plots. While government agencies have managed neither to release sufficient land in third- or fourth-class areas nor to keep up with infrastructure and service provision to residential areas, the principle by which no building standards are demanded in the poorest areas allows households there to have secure tenure without having to build to standards they cannot afford to meet. Fourth-class areas can be upgraded to third-class areas, as households there find themselves able to improve their houses; this also entitles them to better infrastructure and services.[46] This system has merit in that it recognizes the need to provide households with secure tenure of their land without necessarily demanding standards which are beyond the financial means of many people – but provides them with incentives to improve standards. Of course, the system is open to abuse and could reinforce the segregation of income groups and deny the poorest areas basic infrastructure and services.

It is not only the attempt to enforce unrealistic standards which ensures that illegal sub-divisions or squatter invasions predominate; so too do slow, inefficient bureaucratic procedures. For instance, in Manila, the incentive for landowners to develop legal sub-divisions is enormously constrained by laws which demand that a whole host of different agencies have to approve the plans for each development, and the legal requirements that each agency has are often contradictory. To satisfy the conflicting demands of different utility agencies (for instance for water and sewers) and national regulations and local municipal requirements is almost impossible and so time consuming as to act as an enormous disincentive to legal sub-division development. It is notable that in Bogota, where the government changed the regulations to require lower standards for sub-divisions (what were termed "minimum norms") and speeded up the time taken for their approval, the proportion of legal to illegal sub-divisions increased.[47]

While many governments have simply accepted that existing buildings codes and norms should not be applied in officially sponsored squatter upgrading, slum improvement and serviced-site schemes, there has been far less readiness to rethink how new standards could be used to actively promote the improvement of housing conditions.

Governments and the market

It has become fashionable for governments to talk of "unblocking" the market as a solution to housing problems and the lack of services. Certainly, a lot of government funds have been wasted in heavily subsidized public housing projects or serviced-site projects which went to relatively rich households who could afford to pay market prices for housing. Some governments have also blamed existing housing problems on constraints placed by previous governments on the supply of housing – what economists would call supply constraints. In most nations, there is evidence of such supply constraints arising from past government actions or inefficiencies which push up the cost of legal housing but these alone are certainly not the cause of the problem. Above all, it is demand constraints which underlie housing problems – poorer groups' lack of power and resources to allow them to obtain better housing.

However, the debate about the role of the market has become so polarized that proponents of market solutions reject the importance of demand constraints while their opponents refuse to accept any validity in the idea of unblocking markets. In market or mixed economies, unblocking the market is an important component of much-needed action. Many of the new initiatives noted above sought to do this and in doing so, to lower the cost of legal housing or land, finance and materials for housing. More appropriate building and planning standards can lower the cost of legal housing. Innovative housing finance systems can reach relatively poor households with commercial loans and still maintain very high standards of loan repayment (which then allows lower interest rates).

There are also initiatives that can help "unblock" a city's land market. For instance, improving a city's land registration system can make it easier to buy and sell land legally since buyers and sellers know who owns what – or, where land is not owned privately, who has land-use rights over what; in most Third World cities, land registration systems cover only small parts of the urbanized area and are often out of date. A complete, up-to-date land registration system should make the process of buying and selling legally both quicker and cheaper. Speeding up and simplifying government procedures to approve private landowners' sub-division of their land for sale for housing can also reduce the costs of legal plots and perhaps expand the proportion of city-dwellers who can purchase land or housing in the legal market. They can help expand housing finance markets, since an individual with a legal document to prove their ownership or right to use a plot of land can use it as collateral for a loan. This in turn can lead to cheaper housing finance. These initiatives have much to recommend them.

But if a government's sole concentration is on unblocking markets for land, housing and housing finance, in most nations this will not help a large proportion of the urban population. Indeed, in some instances, it could make things worse. To unblock the market governments can so reduce standards for the size of housing plots, the quality of materials and services and the protection of tenants that they end up legalizing the most exploitative kinds of landlordism and the most unhealthy and dangerous forms of illegal land development. The very poor conditions that exist today in most illegal settlements are an indicator as to what happens in an uncontrolled market. If unblocking the market is meant to solve housing problems, why is it that housing conditions are so poor and service provision so inadequate in the many illegal settlements which have developed outside any government regulation of the market?

If governments choose to rely only on market solutions, virtually all the benefits from unblocking the markets will go to landowners, landlords, construction firms and housing finance institutions. As Alfredo Stein comments in a study of different approaches to self-help housing programmes, the possibility of making (urban) land markets efficient and accessible to the poor depends among other things on overcoming the political obstacles posed by the private sector itself. If governments are serious about reaching poorer groups with improved conditions, not only must they unblock markets but also tackle such sensitive issues as the distribution of land ownership, financial resources, infrastructure and the participation of the poor in housing related projects.[48]

Reaching poorer groups with improved housing in cities is not a technical issue amenable to market solutions. Legal market solutions can only work for households which have the purchasing power to enter the legal housing market. Initiatives to unblock markets can increase the proportion of middle income or lower middle income households who can find legal housing solutions. They can increase the proportion of people able to afford market solutions but in all nations, there will still remain a percentage of individuals and households too poor to enter this market. In virtually all Third World nations, this will include a substantial proportion of the population of cities.

Many of the initiatives described earlier helped to solve poorer households' housing problems by allowing them to acquire land or housing at far less than market prices. In effect, they involved some redistribution of resources in favour of certain poorer households. The land-sharing schemes, the legalizing of squatters' tenure and the projects where tenants acquired the right to purchase their accommodation were not market solutions but negotiated solutions where concessions were made to the households concerned. Many of the concessions were made as a reaction to popular pressures, within democratic systems of government. Most projects or programmes, which have provided poorer households with land-sites and services in locations which suited their needs, were not market solutions since poorer households could not afford the market price for well-located land sites. Obviously, the more prosperous a city and the more equitable the distribution of income and capital assets within its population, the higher the proportion of people likely to find satisfactory market solutions. But in all cities, there is a need for carefully directed government action to ensure the fulfilment of the housing needs of those whom the market cannot serve. The city of Seoul provides a good example; few cities in world history have experienced such a rapid growth in prosperity over so short a period. As documented already, housing conditions there remain very poor for much of the population and hundreds of thousands of households have been forcibly evicted, against their wishes, from legal housing.

Concentrating solely on unblocking markets also implies a reduced role for government at all levels, including local government. Yet there is an urgent need to strengthen the capacity of local government to ensure that basic infrastructure and services are available to all citizens and to guide urban development to avoid the problems caused by uncontrolled physical expansion. In addition, effectively implementing new initiatives to unblock the market also depends on competent local government. So too does the task of being a watchdog to prevent poorer groups being exploited by landowners, landlords and businesses; one can hardly expect the private sector to police itself.

Yet we noted earlier that most local governments are weak and fragmented. Not only is there a strong centralization of power within most national governments but also a high degree of administrative decentralization within sectoral ministries or agencies. Thus, a national ministry will have within it agencies working at different levels – but with little or no co-ordination between themselves. Basic tasks and investments which should be controlled and coordinated by local government continue to be the responsibility of national agencies and each fights within government to enlarge its own budget and preserve its own interests. Public investments in infrastructure and services should be co-ordinated within any district or neighbourhood – water supply and storm drainage, roads, electricity, housing, health care, education, schools. But these are so often the responsibility of different agencies or ministries, some controlled by local government, some by city (or metropolitan area) government and some by national government. Each has its own interests which practically guarantees inadequate co-ordination and duplication of efforts.

Building on the last thirty years' experience – the popular approach

If a government is able to draw on the experiences of the last 30 years in designing and implementing a more effective urban housing policy, it might contain the elements outlined in Stage 5 of Table 4.1 (p. 103). This draws on lessons learnt from the innovative projects or programmes already outlined. But it recognizes that these have little impact on the problem, if they remain isolated examples. In Stage 5, the aim is to stimulate, encourage and support continuous programmes. The key issue is how to provide the legislative and institutional framework for this.

In effect, the popular approach combines the new elements already referred to described as the emergence of new attitudes and policies (pp. 119–24).On the one hand, government action concentrates on increasing the supply and reducing the cost of all the components of an adequate house: cheap, well-located sites, cheap building materials and credit, knowledge and advice on how to build cheaply, piped water supplies, services or facilities to remove household and human wastes and waste water; all this is sometimes referred to as the "enabling approach".[49] This is backed up with a redistribution of power and resources in favour of poorer groups.

Such an approach depends on new attitudes to the problem. Perhaps the most important is for governments to accept that the building of cities must be rooted in their own particular culture and society and that the current processes by which cities are being built, as long as they receive appropriate help, support and regulation can help *solve* the problem rather than be it. This implies discarding many foreign models and most foreign concepts. It includes discarding the common stereotype of the poor living in slums and shanty towns. It includes a much greater effort to understand how poorer groups find accommodation – or build it – and the problems they face. It includes a recognition that within the poor's need for housing is a large range of individuals and households, each with different needs and priorities with regard to their preferred trade-off between quality, size, location and cost. As a recent review of African cities stated

> Ultimately solutions to problems of urban finance, housing, public transport, the siting and standards of urban infrastructure, public health and public cleansing services, water, electricity and numerous other urban amenities *must be formulated locally, by local people, on the basis of local experience and information.*[50] [our emphasis]

A second change in attitude is for government to accept that they themselves have been instrumental in creating the problem. Squatter settlements, illegal sub-divisions, cheap and overcrowded boarding houses, exploitative landlords, settlements built on land subject to floods or landslides etc are simply the response of the market to the combination of very low incomes for large proportions of the city population and government inaction. Governments, either through inaction or repression, are a powerful influence on how and where poorer groups take action to build new settlements, whether legally or illegally.

A third change in attitude is an appreciation of the limitations of target-group approaches; this implies that government action moves from short-term project intervention aimed at identified target groups to long-term collaboration with citizens and their community or neighbourhood associations. The idea of a target group implies that some outside agency identifies a target and concentrates action on that target over a short-project period. By implication, the target has little or no voice in design and implementation. Perhaps this approach can be justified for certain short term emergencies. But it is inherently limited because poverty and ill health are the result of so many factors and target group projects neither consider all the factors nor set in motion continuous processes to allow these factors to be tackled. Such processes must involve the residents, the organizations they form, and the local government in whose jurisdiction they fall. Each has to be equipped with the resources and knowledge to collaborate in tackling problems. Poorly-housed citizens do not want one-off projects or campaigns so much as a continuous process through which services are improved, infrastructure installed and encouragement given for house construction or improvement. They also want a voice in deciding what is done and how scarce resources should be used.[51]

The fourth change in attitude is an understanding of the constraints faced by low income residents and community organizations in contributing time and energy to community-based projects. Many poor households have little or no time available to contribute to community projects. Assumptions made by governments (and aid agencies) on the free time that low income groups can contribute to a community project or construction on their own house often prove false. This is illustrated by the fact that governments and agencies still talk of unemployment or under-employment as a major problem for low income groups, when the problem for many is over-employment but underpayment. Many of the so called unemployed or under-employed are working long hours, six or seven days a week.[52] They are classified as unemployed because their work is not official or registered. It is often assumed that women have more free time. Women are also expected to manage and help run community food programmes or crêches or other externally funded initiatives. But a high proportion may be working full time (especially where they are *de facto* heads of household) and even if not working full time, they are expected to undertake virtually all domestic and child-rearing responsibilities. These take up all available time, especially as those living in peripheral illegal settlements have to spend so much time collecting water and travelling to and from jobs, shops, health centres and most other services and facilities.[53]

There is also the issue of who benefits from community participation. Many government agencies or aid agencies regard community participation as a way of cutting their costs – saving labour costs by demanding that residents contribute their time free, saving maintenance costs because maintenance becomes a community responsibility, saving professionals' time through community organizations having to design new internal road networks and move the houses which stand in the way of these new roads. It is ironic that the poor with the least incomes and often the least free time are asked to contribute labour to the installation and maintenance of infrastructure and services while richer households receiving far better quality infrastructure and services (often at below market costs) have no demands on their time to help install and maintain it.

A recent paper on community participation points to "the intense individualism generated by the survival strategies of low income populations" which can prevent or inhibit the "the collective solidarity necessary as the basis for community level organization".[54] It also describes how many projects are designed with little understanding of the contradictory demands within households and the community. Some have already been mentioned, such as the different needs and priorities of men and women from the same household. Another is the assumption that all residents in a settlement chosen for upgrading have similar priorities. Settlements often have too diverse a population to be regarded as a community and yet many parts of the project rely on community organization for their implementation. Existing community organizations may represent the needs of only some of the inhabitants. Such organizations formed by residents of illegal settlements lobbying for legalization are hardly likely to include tenants' interests. This should not discourage either governments or aid agencies from closer engagement with low income groups and community organizations. Most of the "success stories" involved such a close engagement, but only when project officers understood the potentials and the limits on community participation.

These changes in attitude have yet to come about in most national government ministries and agencies. But if attitudes do change in this direction, they provide one of the most powerful justifications for a decentralization of power and resources to city/municipal level and a democratization of the political system. No national agency or ministry can fully understand the particular circumstances within each city and the problems faced by poorer groups there, let alone acquire the ability to act on them. No local government is likely to respond effectively to the diverse needs of poorer groups unless there are effective channels for citizens to influence government policies and priorities. As Julius Nyerere, the former President of Tanzania commented:

> Our nation is too large for the people at the centre in Dar es Salaam always to understand local problems and to sense their urgency. When all the power remains at the centre, therefore, local problems can remain and fester, while local people who are aware of them are prevented from using their initiative in finding solutions ... at present (local) officials have, in reality, very little local power. They have to consult the ministries in Dar es Salaam for almost everything they wish to do, and certainly about every cent they wish to spend.[55]

Implementing the popular approach

A group of practioners and researchers from ten different nations met in 1986 to discuss "Rethinking the Third World City". A section of their report called "Building the City from the Bottom Up", suggests the following:

> The mismatch between what government agencies provide to support lower income groups who build or improve their community, and what such lower income groups need, disappears when government action and support is determined by and defined by the lower income groups themselves. The poor's understanding of "participation" is so often very different from that understood by governments. For it means participation in determining the forms of tenure and property rights they are granted as part of a process by which squatter settlements are legalized. It means their full involvement in determining how land use will be defined as their settlement is regularized. It means their control over which houses (or shacks) have to be moved to allow access roads to be built and water and sewer systems installed. It also means giving them access to information and know-how which can make such levels of participation more effective: information on how to undertake studies to determine community needs and capabilities in terms of implementation, on available credit systems, on planning and building laws, on what procedures must be followed to obtain some particular public service. Ultimately, community participation is not only having the power to determine how their urban environment is planned, developed, financed, produced and maintained but also about re-shaping what is produced – the kind of house, the nature of health services, the form of public transport services provided.[56]

In turning these new ideas into practice, it is at the crucial point of contact between "neighbourhoods" and government action at which new approaches must be tried. Once governments accept that they should support individual and co-operative efforts to build or upgrade their homes and neighbourhoods, the question arises as to how this should be done.

There are examples of where organized low income groups have been able to improve their habitats by applying sufficient pressure to governments to provide legal tenure or to provide some basic infrastructure and services – an all-weather road or landfill to consolidate sites subjects to flooding; piped water; the construction of a school or health care centre; improved provision for garbage collection. It is possible to envisage a local government structure which from the outset is designed to respond efficiently to such pressures – to the needs defined by lower income groups through community or neighbourhood organizations.

Government agencies responsible for paving roads, installing water pipes, digging drains and so on can then have their inputs guided and co-ordinated by representatives of the inhabitants of each settlement. Government's task would be made easier if it provided support for architects, planners, engineers and health specialists to work closely with the representatives of each settlement or neighbourhood.

This is where local non-government organizations (NGOs) can contribute so much to local developments. They can serve as independent advisors to low income households and their community organizations – for technical advice, training and negotiation. They can also serve as "animators", encouraging and supporting the formation of community organizations.[57] They could act as guarantors for loans made to community organizations.[58] They can also serve as research groups which provide non-governmental evaluations of new plans or proposals and lead the move against the imposition of inappropriate foreign models and ideas. Each Third World city needs such an independent group to help develop local solutions based on local knowledge and resources.

Community organizations could turn to such local NGOs for advice and for help in designing and implementing new projects. This already happens in many nations, although most local NGOs face great difficulties both in receiving sufficient support to survive and, perhaps most especially, in gaining recognition from local governments as to the value of the role they can play.

To give one example, in Khartoum, the government's public works agency achieved a considerable cost saving by negotiating with residents' associations over road surfacing: the public works agency provided the lorries, materials and bulldozers to help with road surfacing on the understanding that the inhabitants provided much of the labour force on that particular day and had, in advance, cleared the spaces needed for access roads.[59] The removal of houses from the path of needed access roads, as an illegal settlement is upgraded, *can* be achieved without strong opposition from residents if the residents themselves appreciate the value of such roads, and are involved from the outset in the formulation, design and implementation of the upgrading.[60]

Box 5.3 illustrates how governments and community organizations working together can enormously increase the effectiveness with which limited resources are used.

Box 5.3: Three different options for a government spending US$20 million on housing problems

OPTION 1: $20 million is spent on the construction of two bedroom low cost housing units for low income groups. The cost of each unit is $10,000, once the land has been purchased, the site prepared, the building contractor paid and the infrastructure and the units allocated. Thus, 2,000 households or 12,000 people receive a good quality house – if we assume that on average, there are six persons per household. Cost recovery would be difficult if these were from among the poorer households.

OPTION 2: $20 million is spent on a serviced-site project, so that more households can be reached than in public housing projects. Knowing that poorer households need to live close to the main centres of employment, a relatively central site is purchased for $12 million, with the other $8 million spent on site preparation and installing infrastructure and services. At a cost of $2,000 per plot, 10,000 households (or 60,000 people) could benefit. It would be easier to recover some costs than in the public housing project but for the poorer households, $2,000 for a site on top of the cost of having to construct their own house would be too much.

OPTION 3: Local government makes available to any residents' organization formed by the majority of the inhabitants of any area the sum of $100,000 for site improvements. These residents' organizations have considerable flexibility as to how they choose to spend these funds and who they turn to for technical advice. For instance, they can use local NGOs for technical advice, as long as certain basic standards are met. Although what can be achieved with such a sum will vary greatly depending on site characteristics, local costs and the extent to which residents contribute their skills and labour free, within an area with 500 households, it should be possible to "reblock" the site to allow better access roads and to pave them and also to greatly improve site drainage, water supply and sanitation. Support could be given to local artisans to fabricate the materials, fixtures and fittings which are most cheaply and effectively made on site – for instance, a carpenter's co-operative to make doors and windows or cheap building block fabrication. Of the $100,000, an average of $150 is spent per household on improved infrastructure and services with $10,000 spent on technical advice and $15,000 on support for local businesses. The "reblocking" of the site also frees up sufficient land to allow 50 more housing plots to be developed within the existing site, or on adjacent land as yet undeveloped, and the cost of providing these with infrastructure and services and of building a community health centre is paid for by selling them.

With $100,000 provided to 150 community organizations with an average of 500 households (3,000 people) the total cost was $15 million and the whole programme reached 450,000 people. Since an average of 50 new housing plots were produced in each reblocking, not only did 450,000 people benefit from improved housing, infrastructure and services but 7,500 new plots with services were developed and new health centres constructed in each site. The possibility of cost recovery was much better than for options 1 and 2 since most households could afford to pay $150 – or take out a loan which allowed repayment over a few years. Spending $15 million in this way still left $5 million from the original $20 million which could be used to improve some city-wide service – for instance, providing medical personnel to run health clinics and health campaigns in each settlement.

Source: Developed from an example given in a briefing paper prepared for the World Commission on Environment and Development by Jorge E. Hardoy and David Satterthwaite, April 1986.

In a city of 1 million inhabitants with a population growing at 5 per cent a year, each of the options in Box 5.3 would take several years to implement. Option 1 would do nothing to improve conditions in existing settlements and would not even provide sufficient new housing for the growth in population in one year. Option 2 would also do nothing to improve conditions in existing settlements and would only just provide sufficient new housing for one year's growth in population. Option 3 would reach nearly half the population with improved infrastructure and services and contribute considerably more than the other options to employment creation. It would also support the development of local NGOs as centres of advice and support for low income organizations and contribute almost as many new serviced-sites as Option 2. Furthermore, $5 million would be left for investment by the local government in improving some city-wide service and prospects of cost-recovery were much better than in the other options.

Partnership between local government and local associations of residents is likely to make governments take action on the health problems that lower income groups face; few governments appear to realize the sheer scale of premature death, poor health and disablement which result from (or are exacerbated by) poor housing conditions and lack of infrastructure and services[61]. There is a wide range of basic interventions which municipal government can make, with the help of local residents associations, which at relatively low cost can transform the health status of low income groups. But it is worth noting that very few slum or squatter upgrading schemes – whether funded by governments or aid agencies – have even considered a health care, disease control and accident prevention component.

The popular approach requires institutional changes above all; these are more important than funds (although of course funds will also be needed). The projects which are regarded as success stories usually succeed because within the project area they ignore the usual legal and institutional blocks such as inappropriate building and planning codes and tackle other problems such as a lack of integration between national and local agencies with *ad hoc* arrangements. Such *ad hoc* arrangments also ensure a high input of staff time liaising with community organizations. But the ways in which small, discrete projects avoid or get round these obstacles cannot be repeated for larger, continuous programmes of the kind outlined in Option 3, Box 5.3. Such programmes will demand changes in building and planning codes and more professional staff whose job it is to talk to, work with and help mobilize low income groups. They demand respect for community organizations and support for their efforts. They demand more power and influence to the staff who form the intermediaries between low income groups and government agencies. They involve technical and management training too; problem identification and assessments as to alternatives are needed. The more active, developmental role local governments must take means that they too need more competent, trained staff in many areas. Perhaps a new kind of local government is necessary – less centralized, more open to giving support to group efforts in planning, setting norms and priorities, and evaluating projects. Perhaps many tasks have to be decentralized to district or neighbourhood level offices where community organizations have a better chance of participating in decisions and in influencing resource allocations. Community groups are aware of their potential; supported and enabled by appropriate public and private action, their self confidence and the scope of their initiatives can be greatly enhanced. This would also reinforce their strength as an association of such groups develops.

But ultimately, government action to address problems of housing and living conditions for lower income groups cannot be separated from their actions in other sectors. The state is usually interested in reducing the problems of a particular settlement or neighbourhood to specifics – lack of infrastructure or poor-quality site. It does not want the links made with the functioning of the economy (and governments' role within this) because of the obvious political implications – so it reduces the problems of squatter settlements to shelter, infrastructure and services. Specific investments can be controlled and employed to manage popular resentment. Dialogue with community groups on (say) public service provision favours the fragmentation of the potential challenge presented by community organizations.

These points raise more fundamental questions about governments' orientation on broader social and economic issues, and the extent to which they represent their citizens' needs and priorities, than can be tackled here. It also raises questions about nations' role within the international market and the dozens of nations which under present circumstances never seem likely to develop a sufficiently stable, productive base to generate the means either to eliminate or to greatly reduce poverty. If their governments simply accept such a role, conditions in their cities will reflect that acceptance; inevitably, providing basic services to city (or for that matter rural) inhabitants demands a certain level of development within the national economy.

6. Environmental Problems in Third World Cities – in the Home, Workplace and Neighbourhood

The term "environmental problems" covers many areas; this and a subsequent chapter consider environmental problems in terms of an inadequate supply of a resource essential to good health (for instance, water) or the presence of toxic substances or pathogens (disease causing agents) in the environment which can damage human health or physical resources such as forests, agricultural land and fisheries. Such problems will be discussed under four different headings. The first two, the focus of this chapter, are those within the home or workplace and the district or neighbourhood. The second two, the focus of Chapter 7, are the wider city environment (i.e., the environment that cities provide for their inhabitants in terms of air and water quality) and regional impacts, the links that cities have with their wider locality and the extent to which city-based activities draw on limited resources such as fertile land, fossil fuels and fresh water, and create environmental problems which impact on the wider region.

Information about environmental problems in the Third World is relatively scarce so these two chapters will only give a somewhat impressionistic sketch. Very few Third World nations have a range of citizen groups working on environmental issues comparable to those in Europe, North America and Japan. In the First World, it is largely through the efforts of individual activists, citizen groups and non-governmental organizations that attention was drawn to environmental problems. Although First World governments have been slow to react, the fact that most have taken some action despite the opposition of powerful vested interests is a demonstration of democratic processes at work.

Such democratic processes are strongly controlled or even repressed in many Third World nations. This is one reason why there are so few Third World environmental NGOs, although their number and influence is growing. Third World NGOs also suffer severe lack of funds to develop sustained programmes of research, monitoring and lobbying. The examples of environmental problems in this chapter cannot claim to point to the worst cases for many of them have probably not been documented. This chapter draws on the publications of Third World based citizen groups working in this area, and these publications are listed on pp. 362–5.

The indoor environment – at home and at work

Chapter 3 described the very poor quality of different kinds of accommodation used by poorer groups. This section will concentrate on the impacts on inhabitants' health. Of course, different kinds of housing present different health problems; the health problems of a family renting one room in an inner city tenement with one kitchen, bathroom and WC shared among 30–40 people are not the same as, for example, those of a family who have built their own shelter on illegally occupied land where there is no piped water, sewers and the collection of garbage.

But almost all the different kinds of housing used by poorer groups share two environmental problems: the presence in the human environment of pathogens because of no infrastructure or services to remove and safely dispose of them; and crowded, cramped conditions. A lack of readily available drinking water, of sewage connections (or other systems to hygienically dispose of human wastes), of garbage collection and basic measures to prevent disease and provide primary health care ensure that many diseases are endemic among poorer households – diarrhoea, dysenteries, typhoid, intestinal parasites, food poisoning among them. Most cities in Africa and many in Asia have no sewage system at all – including many cities with a million or more inhabitants. Rivers, streams, canals, gullies and ditches are where most human excrement and household waste water ends up, untreated. For those cities with a sewage system, rarely does it serve more than a small proportion of the population – typically the richer residential, government and commercial areas. Box 6.1 gives some examples of the inadequacies in the supply of water and sanitation in different cities.

Box 6.1: Inadequacies in water supply and sanitation

BANGKOK: About one-third of the population has no access to public water supplies and must obtain water from vendors. Only 2 per cent of the population is connected to a sewer system;

human wastes are generally disposed of through septic tanks and cess pools with their effluents, as well as waste water from sinks, laundries, baths and kitchens discharged into stormwater drains or canals.

CALCUTTA: Some 3 million people live in *bustees* and refugee settlements which lack potable water, endure serious annual flooding and have no systematic means of disposing of refuse or human wastes. Some 2.5 million others live in similarly blighted and unserviced areas. Piped water is only available in the central city and parts of some other municipalities. The sewage system is limited to only a third of the area in the urban core. Poor maintenance of drains and periodic clogging of the system have made flooding an annual feature.

COLOMBO: About 31 per cent of houses have water piped indoors and another 20 per cent have piped water outside. A waterborne sewage system serves half the city's population.

DAKAR AND OTHER SENEGALESE TOWNS: Senegalese towns have no provision for the removal of household and public waste. Of the five urban centres with sewage systems, generally only the inner urban population has access to these facilities. In Dakar, the capital, a survey in 1980–81 found that 28 per cent of households have private water connections while 68 per cent rely on public standpipes and 4.2 per cent on buying water from carriers. A survey in Pikine, the outer part of Dakar, found an average of 696 persons per standpipe with 1,513 in one neighbourhood. In Dakar, nearly one-sixth of human solid wastes is dumped outside proper toilet facilities.

DAR ES SALAAM: From a survey of 660 households drawn from all income levels in 1986/87, 47 per cent had no piped water supply either inside or immediately outside their houses while 32 per cent had a shared piped water supply. Of the households without piped water, 67 per cent buy water from neighbours while 26 per cent draw water from public water kiosks or standpipes. Only 7.1 per cent buy water from water sellers. Average water consumption is only 23.6 litres a day. For sanitation, only 13 per cent of the dirty water and sewage produced is regularly disposed of. Of the 660 households, 89 per cent had simple pit-latrines. Only 4.5 per cent had toilets connected to septic tanks or sewers. Most households have to share sanitary facilities. Overflowing latrines are a serious problem, especially in the rainy season and provision to empty septic tanks or latrines is very inadequate.

JAKARTA: Less than a quarter of the city's population have direct connections to a piped water system. Some 30 per cent depend solely on water vendors with water costing five times that of piped water. The city has no waterborne sewage system. Septic tanks serve about 25 per cent of the city's population; others use pit latrines, cesspools and ditches along the roadside. Much of the population have to use drainage canals for bathing, laundering and defecation.

KARACHI: Potable water has to be brought more than 160 km from the Indus and is available for only a few hours a day in most areas. One third of households have piped water connections and most slum dwellers and squatters must either use public standposts or buy water from vendors at inflated prices.

KHARTOUM: The systems of water supply, sewage disposal, refuse disposal and electricity supply are all inadequate both in the coverage of the urban area and the maintenance of the service ... the water supply system is working beyond its design capacity while the demand continues to rise. The coverage is poor, with the low income groups in squatter settlements suffering the cost through paying the most for water, often bought from vendors. Breakdown and cuts in the supply system are common ... The municipal sewage system serves only about 5 per cent of the Khartoum urban area. Even that system is susceptible to breakdowns when waste is discharged either directly into the river or onto open land.... for most people in the low income areas, there is no system of sewage disposal.

KINSHASA: There is no sewage system in Kinshasa. Around half the urban population (some 1.5 million people) are not served by a piped water network. High income areas are often 100 per cent connected while many other areas have 20-30 per cent of houses connected – essentially those along the main roads. The sale of water flourishes in areas far from the network – in these areas water is usually obtained from wells, the river or deep wells.

MADRAS: Only 2 million of the 3.7 million residential consumers within the service area of the local water supply and sewerage board are connected to the system. On average, they receive some 36 litres per day per capita. The rest within the service area must use public taps which serve about 240 persons per tap. Another million consumers outside the service area must rely on wells – but supplies are inadequate too because of falling groundwater levels. The sewage system serves 31 per cent of the metropolitan population and raw sewage flows freely into the Metropolitan Area's natural watercourses in many points.

MANILA: Only 15 per cent of the population of Metro Manila is served with sewers or individual septic tanks. Some 1.8 million people lack adequate water supplies – and educational, community, health and sanitary services. Inadequate services to collect domestic wastes also means that garbage blocks canals and drains and makes flooding problems much more serious.

SAO PAULO: Of the more than 13 million people living in the metropolitan area, 64 per cent lived in households not served by the sewage system in 1980 and very little sewage was treated.

Sources: Most of the above data was drawn from K.C. Sivaramakrishnan and Leslie Green, *Metropolitan Management: the Asian Experience*, (Oxford: Oxford University Press, 1986); and Kankonde Mbuyi (Kinshasa), Thiecouta Ngom (Senegal), Satiel Kulaba (Tanzania) and Mohamed El Sammani *et al.* (Khartoum) in Richard E. Stren and Rodney R. White (eds), *African Cities in Crisis* (Westview Press, USA, 1989). For complete references, see note 1.

Many of the health problems are linked to water – its quality, the quantity available, the ease with which it can be obtained and the provisions made for its removal, once used. Hundreds of millions of urban dwellers have no alternative but to use contaminated water – or at least water whose quality is not guaranteed. A small minority have water piped into their homes while rather more have piped water nearby which has to be collected. As one specialist in this area commented, "those not served are obliged to use water from streams or other surface sources which in urban areas are often little more than open sewers or to purchase water from insanitary vendors. It is little wonder that their children suffer frequently, often fatally, from diarrhoeal diseases".[2]

The quantity of water available to a household and the price which has to be paid for it can be as important to a family's health as its quality.[3] The cost of water and the time needed to collect it influence the quantity used. Where public agencies do not provide any water supply – as is common in illegal settlements – the poor often obtain water from private vendors and can pay 20–30 times the cost per litre paid by richer groups with piped supplies.[4] Water vendors probably serve between 20 and 30 per cent of the Third World's urban population.[5]

Where there is a public supply – a well or public standpipe – consumption will depend on the time and energy involved in collecting and carrying it back to the home. In many instances, there are 500 or more persons for each tap; in one part of Dakar, there were 1,513 persons per tap.[6] One can imagine the time needed to queue for the water – and very often, water will only be available in the piped system for a few hours a day. There is also the fact that water is very heavy, so water consumption will be much influenced by the distance that it has to be carried.

Because low income people often work very long hours, time spent queueing for the use of a tap or transporting buckets takes up time which could be used in earning an income. Limited quantities of water mean inadequate supplies for washing and personal hygiene – and for washing food, cooking utensils and clothes. Eye and ear infections, skin diseases, scabies, lice and fleas are very difficult to control without sufficient supplies of water. No drains or sewers to drain away waste water – and rainwater – will lead to waterlogged soil and stagnant pools which can transmit diseases like hookworm. Pools of standing water can convey enteric diseases and provide breeding grounds for mosquitoes which spread filariasis, malaria and other diseases. Inadequate or no drainage often means damp walls and damp living environments.

Some statistics on domestic water consumption in the metropolitan zone of Mexico City reveal the differences between the consumption of the rich and the poor. Consumption among residents in the high income Chapultepec zone averages 450 litres per person daily while in low income Nezahualcoyotol, it averages only 50 litres. Just 9 per cent of the domestic consumers account for 75 per cent of all consumption and more than 2 million people have very limited access to any supplies.[7]

Removing and safely disposing of excreta and waste-waters coming from washing, bathing and other domestic uses is also a critical health need. Around two-thirds of the Third World's population have no hygienic means of disposing of excreta and an even greater number lack adequate means to dispose of waste waters.[8] For instance, in India, defecating in the open is common practice since one-third of the urban population (over 50 million people) have no latrine of any kind while another third rely on bucket latrines. A third may use latrines connected to sewers but only 10 per cent have sewage connections in their homes.[9] As many as 50 different infections are caused by the ingestion of excreta and the diseases these cause rank among the chief causes of sickness and death in the Third World.[10]

Although official figures suggest that people in urban areas are better served than in rural areas, public provision to remove and safely dispose of human excreta is usually no better in the housing and neighbourhoods used by poorer groups than it is in rural areas – and the health problems are usually greater, as higher densities make more difficult the protection of people from contact with excreta. Box 6.1 helps illustrate the scale of the problem; for instance, in Dar es Salaam virtually all the population rely on pit latrines but these regularly over-flow and the public authorities only have the equipment to empty a tiny proportion of them[11]; in Jakarta there is no waterborne sewage system so much of the population uses the canals for bathing, laundering and defecation.[12] Even in the larger and richer cities, where a higher proportion of homes are connected, millions still suffer; for instance, although 70 per cent of metropolitan Mexico City's population has sewers serving their housing, there are still 3 million people not served.[13] It is also common for official statistics to over-state the proportion of people adequately served; for instance, people in neighbourhoods with public latrines are often considered adequately served when there are 100 or more persons per latrine and the maintenance and cleaning of the latrines so poor that they are a major health hazard and many people avoid using them.

Official statistics or those produced by aid agencies as to how many people they have reached with "adequate" services are often open to doubt. For instance, claims by governments in Bolivia, Jordan and Kenya that 100 per cent of their urban populations were adequately served with piped water in 1980 cannot be taken seriously. Nor can the claim that 100 per cent of the urban population in Bolivia and Jordan had adequate excreta disposal facilities.[14] The figures presented by many aid agencies as to the number of households their projects have reached with "adequate water" or "sanitation" are also open to question. The criteria used to make such claims are often not revealed. All too often, visits to project sites where everyone has apparently been provided with "adequate water supplies", reveal a few water standpipes serving hundreds of households, some of which no longer work while at those that do, there are long queues and many households have to carry water hundreds of metres. A family of six needs at least 300–400 litres a day to ensure enough for drinking, washing, cooking, laundry and bathing. That is equivalent to some 30–40 buckets a day. Anyone who has carried two full buckets of water will appreciate the difference between the level of service people need and what many governments or certain aid agencies might choose to call "adequate standards".

Removing and disposing of excreta in ways which prevent human contact is central to reducing the burden of disease; Box 6.2 helps illustrate the health impacts of doing so.

Box 6.2: The health effects of improved water and sanitation

There is overwhelming evidence that the economic burden of disease and ill-health which is in large part the result of deficiencies in both water supply and sanitation is very great in the Third World – particularly for the poor. Some studies have suggested that around one tenth of each person's productive time is sacrificed to disease in most Third World nations.

It has proved difficult to quantify the benefits of improved sanitation as distinct from other influences such as improved availability and quality of water, better nutrition arising from increased incomes and changes in personal hygiene. But the impact of improved sanitation on just one health problem – diarrhoeal disease in young children – gives some clue as to its importance. A recent review of the literature by the World Health Organization suggests the following:

	% median reduction in diarrhoeal morbidity (disability)
Improved water quality	16%
Improved water availability	25%
Improved water quality and availability	37%
Improved excreta disposal	22%

It also noted that reductions in the number of deaths can be even greater. But it should be stressed that water supply, sanitation and personal hygiene should all be improved together, for substantial improvements in communities' health.

In addition, the changes necessary for an effect on health are most likely to occur where there is a real demand for sanitation – such as in high density urban areas.

Source: Gehan Sinnatamby, "Low cost sanitation"; Cairncross *et al.* (eds); *The Poor Die Young: Housing and Health in the Third World* (London: Earthscan Publications, forthcoming); the statistics on the typical effects of improved water supply and sanitation conditions on diarrhoeal morbidity: S.A. Esrey *et al.*; "Interventions for the control of diarrhoeal diseases among young children: improving water supply and excreta disposal facilities", *Bulletin of the World Health Organization*, vol. 63, no. 4, Geneva, 1985, p.72.

A second characteristic shared by most kinds of housing used by poorer groups is crowded, cramped conditions which mean that diseases such as tuberculosis, influenza and meningitis are easily transmitted from one person to another – their spread often being aided by low resistance among the inhabitants due to malnutrition. In Kanpur, one of India's major industrial centres, the development authority estimates that 60 per cent of the children in slums have tuberculosis.[15] Diseases like mumps and measles also spread more rapidly; while measles holds few worries for children in richer households, among poorer households it is often one of the most common causes of infant or child death. Household accidents are also common, perhaps not surprisingly when five, six, seven or more persons live in one room and there is little chance of giving the occupants (especially children) protection from fires, stoves and kerosene heaters. Where open fires or relatively inefficient stoves are used for cooking and/or heating, smoke usually causes serious respiratory problems for most or all inhabitants. The impact on those who spend most time in the home – usually women and children – is particularly serious.

Increasing numbers of health studies in Third World cities show the degree to which lower income groups' lives are dominated by ill health, disablement or premature death. Box 6.3 gives examples of the health problems evident in illegal settlements in Allahabad (India) and Buenos Aires (Argentina). Virtually all of the deaths and most of the diseases and injuries to infants and children would not have occurred if the children had been born into households in the same city with sufficient income to ensure adequate diets and in reasonable quality houses with piped water and sanitation.

Box 6.3: Health problems in low income settlements in Third World cities

In Chheetpur, a squatter settlement in the city of Allahabad with some 500 people in 1984, 55 per cent of the children and 45 per cent of the adults had intestinal worm infections while at the time of the survey 60 per cent had scabies. Most inhabitants had food intakes of less than 1,500 calories a day; among infants and children up to the age of four, 90 per cent had intakes significantly below the minimum needed. Over a period of 14 years, 143 children's deaths had been recorded; malaria was the most commonly identified cause of death followed by tetanus, injuries from accidents or burns, and diarrhoea, dysentery or cholera. Malnutrition was an important contributing factor in many of these deaths. The settlement's site is subject to flooding in the rainy season and a lack of drainage means stagnant pools for much of the year. Two standpipes serve the entire population's water needs and there is no public provision for sanitation or the removal of household wastes.

In San Martin, a squatter community in one of the municipalities which ring the central city of Buenos Aires, clinical tests on a small sample of inhabitants showed that more than half had intestinal worms. Many children were underweight and malnutrition was widespread, especially in terms of protein, vitamin and mineral intake. Physical examinations for a larger sample found 15 per cent of children with inflammations in the upper breathing passage; among adults who underwent physical examination, one in four men and one in ten women had chronic bronchial afflictions. Diarrhoea was a major problem, especially in the summer. Although 60 per cent of the households obtained water from piped public supplies – since the inhabitants simply tapped into a nearby mains supply – the quantity of water available was frequently inadequate and many households could not afford the cost of piping water into their houses. Most of the 40 per cent who did not have access to piped water used water pumped from wells; tests on water quality found that first level ground water had high levels of bacteriological contamination. There was no site drainage apart from some open drains dug by inhabitants.

Sources: H.N. Misra, "Housing and health in squatter communities in Allaha-bad"; and Beatriz Cuenya, Hector Almada, Diego Armus, Julia Castells, Maria di Loreto and Susana Penalva, "Housing and health in Buenos Aires – the case of Barrio San Martin" in S. Cairncross *et al.* (eds) *The Poor Die Young: Housing and Health in the Third World* (London: Earthscan Publications, forthcoming).

According to the World Health Organization, in many illegal settlements, an infant is 40–50 times more likely to die before the age of five than an infant born in a Western nation.[16] A review of nutrition and health by S. S. Basta published in 1977 stressed the extent to which poor urban groups suffer from very poor health.[17] A study in the slums of Haiti's capital, Port au Prince, found 200 infants dying per 1,000 live births with another 100 dying before their second birthday. Comparable infant mortality rates were found in the *bustees* of Delhi, where the rate was 221 per 1,000 live births. Among the lowest castes, the infant mortality rate rose to more than double this figure – more than two in five infants had died before their first birthday.[18] In Manila, the infant mortality rate in squatter communities was found to be three times the average for the rest of the city; the proportion of people with tuberculosis was also nine times higher and diarrhoea was twice as common.[19]

Studies of the health problems of poorer groups point not only to the high proportion of infant and child deaths but also high rates of death, disablement and serious injury from household accidents, and high proportions of people in each age group suffering from ill health for substantial proportions of their lives. Malnutrition is very common. The studies also suggest that it is in the house and its surrounds that most injuries and diseases are contracted and that there are many problems involving poisoning or chemical hazards. It is hardly possible to prevent children from coming into contact with harmful chemicals used in the household (for instance bleach or kerosene), or keep medicines in a secure place, when whole families live in one or two rooms.

Poor people have very little chance of obtaining a healthy house – that is one with sufficient space, security, services and facilities. Poorer groups also have the constant concern about eviction from their homes; this is a permanent worry for most tenants, temporary boarders in cheap rooming houses, those in illegal settlements and land renters on which a house has been built.

The environmental health problems evident within the homes of so many inhabitants of Third World cities are a direct result of their low incomes and of the refusal by government to provide basic services. If an individual or household finds minimum standard accommodation too costly, they have to make certain sacrifices in the accommodation they choose to bring down the price to what they can afford. And they usually make sacrifices in environmental quality. Although this means health risks and considerable inconvenience, these are less important for their survival than other items. For instance, expenditure on food or on children's education or on (say) purchasing a second-hand sewing machine to allow a member of the family to earn additional income all are more important for survival than minimum standard accommodation. Each low income individual or household will choose their own sacrifices in terms of size of accommodation, terms under which it is occupied, suitability of site, housing quality, location and access to infrastructure and basic services. For example, to bring down housing costs, a household of five persons might sacrifice space and live in one room, or sacrifice secure tenure and access to piped water and live in a self-constructed house on illegally occupied land. To understand the possibilities for improving the housing environment of such people, one must understand their very diverse needs and priorities. Complex questions have to be explored, including legality of site or house occupation, legality of the housing structure, and the terms under which the occupants live there (ie. are they guests, legal tenants, illegal tenants, sub-tenants or owners).

Environmental problems arising in the workplace are also a major problem in most Third World cities – and are evident in workplaces from large factories and commercial institutions down to small backstreet workshops and work done in the home. Among the hazards are dangerous concentrations of toxic chemicals and dust, inadequate lighting, ventilation and space, and inadequate protection of workers from machinery and noise. These environmental factors are made all the more serious by the lack of social security; there is little or no provision by most employers of sick pay or of compensation if workers are injured or laid off.

A paper on Bangkok's environmental problems noted that a remarkable number of Thai workers are exposed to poor working environments but that the number of workers suffering from occupational diseases is small. "This may be a reflection of the difficulties of linking disease to working conditions rather than revealing a satisfactory condition."[20] This point has relevance to virtually all Third World nations since people's long term exposure to dust, excessive noise, inadequate lighting and pollutants in the workplace often contributes much to ill health, disablement and premature death but it is difficult to link them – or to prove the link, if compensation is being sought. There are many examples of industrial workers killed or permanently injured from chemicals they handle or inhale at work[21], but the health impacts which take longer to become apparent are more worrying in that these affect such a high proportion of all industrial workers.

A report in 1983 stated that one third of those working in asbestos factories in Bombay suffer from asbestosis while many of those working in cotton mills suffer from byssinosis (brown lung).[22] A study of workers in the Bombay Gas Company found that 24 per cent were suffering from chronic bronchitis, tuberculosis and emphysema.[23]

It is perhaps appropriate to consider environmental problems associated with work in the home in that many poor city-dwellers use their homes as a workshop to produce goods for sale or as a store for goods sold on the street or as a shop, bar or cafe. The environmental problems which arise here are too diverse to be covered in a short summary. But clearly, there are often problems with levels of light and ventilation. There are also major problems for many home-workers arising from the use of toxic chemicals or flammable chemicals in the home as part of the work done there. One common way in which this happens is through out-working; here, well organized (and often large) enterprises commission people (usually women) working in their homes to fabricate some product, for instance, sandals or articles of clothing. These enterprises will often supply the out-workers with the raw materials and chemicals they need and collect the finished articles. Many of these chemicals are a serious fire-hazard and should only be used in carefully controlled conditions in factories with special provisions to limit inhalation or skin contact and to guard against fire hazards. The advantages of such home-workers to the enterprise are obvious – low wages, no costs involved in building and running factories, no costs for social security and usually few problems with labour unrest since the workforce is too scattered to allow them to organize.

Most nations have legislation of some sort which is meant to curb such abuses but it is rarely implemented. Quite a lot of attention has been paid to improving the legislation but, in our experience, too little attention is given to its implementation.

The neighbourhood environment

Added to health risks associated with the presence of toxic substances or pathogens inside the home must be added dangers from the sites on which many poorer households live. The two are not easily separated since deficiencies in the one impact on the other – as in the case of no sewers to remove excreta and waste water so these are dumped in open drains which then present health dangers for the whole neighbourhood. But three problems are worth emphasizing within the neighbourhood environment – dangerous sites, no collection of household garbage, and inadequate site infrastructure.

With regard to the site, large clusters of illegal housing often develop on steep hillsides, floodplains or desertland. Or they develop on the most unhealthy or polluted land sites – for instance around solid-waste dumps, beside open drains and sewers or in and around industrial areas with high levels of air pollution. They also develop in sites subject to high noise levels – for instance close to major highways or airports. Poor groups do not live here in ignorance of the dangers; they choose such sites because they meet more immediate and pressing needs. Such sites are often the only places where they can build their own house or rent accommodation. The sites are cheap because they are dangerous. Polluted sites next to industries are close to jobs. Finally, if they occupy such land illegally, they are less likely to be evicted because the land is unsuitable for commercial developments. To the dangers inherent in the site are added a lack of infrastructure – for instance, storm and surface water drains are rarely installed in most new residential developments. Frequent flooding, water-logged sites, lack of paved roads or paths, damp housing all take a serious toll on health. Examples can be seen on hillsides prone to landslides in Rio de Janeiro (Brazil), Guatemala City, La Paz (Bolivia) and Caracas (Venezuela) or on sandy desert as in Lima (Peru), or on land prone to flooding or tidal inundation or under water as in Guayaquil (Ecuador), Recife (Brazil), Monrovia (Liberia), Lagos and Port Harcourt (Nigeria), Port Moresby (Papua New Guinea), Delhi (India), Bangkok (Thailand), Jakarta (Indonesia) and in many other cities.

In Mexico City, approximately 1.5 million people live on the drained lake-bed of Texcoco. This area "is the most unhospitable part of the Valley of Mexico, plagued by constant flooding, dust storms in the dry season and an almost complete lack of urban services".[24] The use of this land for housing developments is illegal. Yet these *colonias populares*, in common with many others in and around the city, were built because no more suitable sites were within the economic reach of lower income groups.[25] The hundreds of people killed or seriously injured and the thousands made homeless by mudslides in Rio de Janeiro in 1988, in Medellin in Colombia in 1987 or in Caracas in 1989 are illustrations of a much larger and more widespread problem. Low income groups have no option but to occupy such dangerous sites since no other site is available to them within reach of possible sources of employment. The dangers inherent in such sites can often be greatly reduced by paving access roads and installing drains and other safeguards.

House sites, structures and surrounds increase the risk of burns, scalds, cuts, bites and injuries in and around the house. Children are particularly at risk from pathogens or toxic substances within the neighbourhood – from the problems of (say) contracting diarrhoea through ingesting pathogens from fecal matter which contaminates the land on which they play, or from coming into contact with some toxic chemical in a nearby stream or dumped on a land site nearby. Risks posed by road traffic are often particularly serious since many illegal settlements have developed next to major roads or highways.

There is the additional problem of inadequate or non-existent collection of garbage. It is estimated that 30–50 per cent of solid wastes generated within urban centres remains uncollected[26] and such refuse accumulates on wasteland and streets (sometimes to the point where it actually blocks roads).[27] Of course, it is the poorer areas of the city which have inadequate or no garbage collection service. The resulting problems are obvious and almost always given far too low a priority by government – the smells, the disease vectors and pests attracted by garbage (rats, mosquitoes, flies, etc.), the drainage channels which become clogged with garbage and overflow. Uncollected garbage can also be a serious fire hazard and a serious health hazard for children playing on the site.[28]

Box 6.4: Household garbage collection in nations' largest cities

BOGOTA: Around half the 1.5 million tons of garbage generated every year is collected and disposed of by local authorities. Every day, some 2,500 tons is left uncollected – some is partially recycled informally while the rest is simply left to rot in small tips or in canals, sewers or the streets.

BANGKOK: Although 80 per cent of the population is served by a refuse collection service, in 1987 24 per cent of solid wastes were dumped, mostly onto vacant land or in canals and rivers.

DAR ES SALAAM: Just 24 per cent of daily refuse is collected.

JAKARTA: Around 30 per cent of the garbage is not collected and ends up in canals and rivers and along the roadside where it clogs drainage channels and causes extensive flooding during the rainy season.

KARACHI: Only one-third of the solid waste produced in the city is being removed.

KINSHASA: The collection of household waste is only undertaken in a few residential areas. In the rest of the city, household waste is put out on the road, on illegal dumps, in stormwater drains or buried on open sites.

SAO PAULO: One-third of the population are living in areas without any service to collect solid wastes.

Sources: See note 29. These are simply cities for which data is available; several of them seem relatively well-served compared to many cities which could not be included here for lack of accurate data.

The impact of the burns, cuts, scalds and other injuries contracted in and around the home is further magnified by a lack of provision of first aid within the neighbourhood, and the difficulties in rapidly transporting a sick or injured person to hospital (and, of course, ensuring that the person will receive rapid treatment once at the hospital). A lack of paved roads and house sites which are on steep slopes, waterlogged or in other ways difficult to cross with motorized vehicles also mean that in the event of fires, neither fire engines nor ambulances can reach the settlement, at least not without long delays.

In concluding this section, it is worth asking why the environmental health problems associated with housing have been ignored. One reason is that the architects, planners and engineers who work for government departments of housing or public works know very little about the health problems faced by those they are meant to serve. Their training may not even consider this as being an issue – especially if the curriculum for their training is based on Western models. Where a government department or ministry of the environment is set up, these problems may also fall outside their brief.

In looking at health problems associated with the home, it is important to look beyond the house's structure. It is the environment provided for people by the house, the services and facilities it should contain, and the neighbourhood within which each house is located which should act as a defence against injury and disease.[30] In most Third World cities, the largest and most pressing environmental issue is to improve the housing and living environment of the poor majority of citizens by reducing or eliminating the most serious health hazards present within their homes, workplaces and neighbourhoods – and by guaranteeing prompt action in the event of an accident. Since there is a growing interest among governments in the problems of managing and disposing of toxic wastes, it would seem appropriate to put human excrement as the most serious "toxic waste" – and, indeed, one whose safe disposal is relatively cheap.

Tackling environmental health problems

As Chapter 7 will outline, the idea that environmental quality and pollution control are expensive luxuries to be pursued when a country is rich enough is slowly being eroded, at least with regard to city-based industries. But attitudes regarding the cost of safe and hygienic disposal of household and human wastes and the provision of safe water supplies seem more rigid. It has taken 30 years or more for many governments to accept that land invasions are not a threat to established institutions but a growing movement that emerges out of poor people having no alternative way of securing a house site. Let us hope that it does not take so many years for governments to accept the need for action to tackle environmental problems. One reason for little action is certainly that this has the heaviest impact on poorer groups. It is common for richer residential areas and the main commercial and industrial concerns to receive good quality water supplies, sewers and drains while 30 per cent or more of the population in the poorer residential areas receive little or nothing.

There is also the question of costs and cost-recovery. National and city governments frequently claim that extending piped water, sewers and drains to poorer areas is too expensive, but the claim is based on the cost of systems in Europe and North America.

Take first the question of excreta disposal. There are various alternatives that are far cheaper than conventional waterborne sewerage systems and sewage treatment plants, but far more effective and hygienic than the standard pit latrine or bucket latrine systems. World Bank research involving field studies in 39 communities in 14 nations found a wide range of household and community systems which could greatly improve the hygienic disposal of human waste. Within this range were options which could be implemented to match local physical conditions, social preferences and economic resources. Several of these options had a total annual cost per household of between one-tenth and one-twentieth that of conventional sewerage systems. Most demanded far lower volumes of water to allow for their efficient operation. Some demanded no water at all, although of course household water needs for drinking, cooking and washing were essential. And it is also possible to install one of the lowest cost technologies initially and then upgrade it in a series of steps over time; an example of this is given in Box 6.5.

Box 6.5: Incremental development of improved sanitation

Initially, ventilated improved pit latrines, could be installed in a settlement where there are serious water shortages since these demand no water for their operation. Of course, it is important to minimise water use in sanitation if water is scarce and members of the household have to collect it by hand. This latrine is likely to cost a tenth (or less) that of a system based on sewerage or a septic tank. Then, if households' access to water is improved (say a supply piped to the house or yard), dry latrines can be converted into a pour-flush latrines. This too can be upgraded when piped water into the house is installed so the system is connected to a small bore sewer system. Many other combinations and upgrading options are possible.

Source: John M. Kalbermatten, DeAnne S. Julius and Charles Gunnerson, *Appropriate Technology for Water Supply and Sanitation – a Summary of Technical and Economic Options* (Washington, DC: World Bank, 1980).

Improvements in the quality of water and its availability are also often possible at relatively low cost and with good possibilities of cost recovery. In many cities, largely self-financing water supply systems can reach poorer groups with much improved levels of service. Given the high cost to poorer households from paying private water vendors for the water they need, a proper piped water system can often replace water vendors, and provide these same households with a more economical and convenient supply for the same price that they previously paid to vendors.[31] A case study in Lima, Peru found that lower income groups were spending three times the amount per month on water from water vendors than that paid by those with piped house connections, despite the fact that lower income groups' daily consumption was less than a sixth that of those with house connections.[32] In effect, poorer groups were paying more than 18 times the amount per litre of richer groups. In a review of water supply options for the urban poor, Sandy Cairncross notes that a thriving informal market for water is evidence of a demand unsatisfied by the formal sector. It is also evidence of the money value which even the poorest are ready to give to the time they would have to spend carrying water if they did not buy from vendors. It is an indication of how much they would be willing to pay for an adequate conventional water supply, were it made available to them.[33]

Cairncross also points out that better management and maintenance of existing water systems can improve services more cheaply than increasing capacity. Many water supply systems lose 60 per cent of their water to leaks in the pipes. Reducing the leakage rate from 60 per cent to 12 per cent (the typical figure for systems in Britain or the United States) would more than double the amount of water available for use.[34] Often, just 20 per cent of the leaks account for 80 per cent of the water losses.[35] In Sao Paulo, the proportion of water leaking out of the system has been reduced by some 50 per cent over a ten year period.[36]

Again, the approach needed is one which analyzes local problems and assesses which combination of actions best utilizes local resources. Cairncross suggests various approaches which may be considered unconventional by Western-trained engineers but which may prove to be the cheapest and most effective option in certain localities.[37] For instance, in some localities, government support to make water vendors more efficient and to improve water quality might be the most cost-effective option. In others, making use of local water sources for small independent networks for particular city areas may be more cost effective than extending the water mains system. In areas with sufficient rainfall, grants to households to install guttering and rainwater tanks may be a cheap way of improving supplies. Where piped systems are installed, modifications to the official standards can often produce major cost savings with little or no reduction in performance; for instance, the size of pipes and depth to which they must be sunk according to official regulations are often inappropriate, because they copied foreign practices without modification to local circumstances; the minimum depth set for laying sewage pipes hardly needs to be to a depth to protect it from 40 ton trucks if the pipe is being installed in a high density, low income settlement.[38] Standards appropriate to local circumstances does not always mean lower standards; indeed, higher standards may be appropriate in some cases to compensate for lower levels of maintenance.[39]

Involving residents in decisions about the level of service they want and what level of payment they can afford can also produce surprises; assumptions made by professionals and technicians as to what people can afford for piped water are often too low because they under-estimate the value placed by poorer households on the saving in time and energy in collecting water from a public standpipe.

But virtually all the above measures are forms of better local practice which depend on competent local government. One returns to the fact that most municipal governments lack the trained personnel and the financial base and autonomy to provide the needed investments. This weakness of city governments also makes other changes difficult to implement – from the enforcement of environmental legislation to the efficient collection of garbage, management of solid waste sites and improvement of traffic management.

The role of privatization

Low income groups need safe and sufficient supplies of water close to their homes (preferably piped into their homes). They need drains to take away waste water and, where possible, sewers to take away excreta. Where this is too expensive, they need regular services to empty pit latrines or septic tanks. They need regular services to collect garbage, health-care services and all-weather roads. Many governments and aid agencies are promoting privatization as a way to improve provision for such basic needs. The idea that privatization can improve provision and solve the problems already outlined is greatly overstated.

In the Third World, the justification for privatization given by its proponents is usually that the government is short of capital. Their hope is that the private sector will provide the capital needed to expand and improve services, if offered the opportunity. In this instance, the private sector would be taking over some of the responsibilities of local government.

In most Third World cities, many of the poorest inhabitants already rely on "private" services. Private (often informal or illegal) enterprises are already the substitute for local government since they are the main suppliers of certain services in illegal settlements. In illegal settlements, private enterprises are often the main supplier of water through water vendors. In many, they are the providers of rental housing. Illegal sub-divisions are the private sector taking on the task of supplying building plots outside government regulation. The lack of infrastructure and services supplied in most illegal sub-divisions, the level of tenant exploitation and the very poor conditions in most rental housing does not support the idea that privatization will necessarily improve standards for poorer groups. The high price and the often poor quality of the water sold by water vendors also suggests problems with privatization.

Most of the services which are the main concern of this chapter are natural monopolies since they require large capital investments to set up the supply but once set up, the cost of extending it to more people is relatively low. Piped water supply or sewers are good examples. They are very costly to set up but once in place, extending them to another household or neighbourhood nearby is relatively cheap. Once a water supply or sewer system is built, it is virtually impossible for another business to compete by starting to build another piped water or sewer system. It is also ridiculous to think of two or more companies, each with their own piped water or sewer system, competing against each other to serve the same households.

There is also the complementary nature of the services, and the large cost savings if they are installed together. Water supplies piped to each house require drains connected to each house and, preferably, sewers. Sewers need sufficient supplies of water to stop them getting blocked. House sites need drains for rainwater. Roads and other paved areas need drains. Drains need efficient garbage collection otherwise they get blocked with garbage; so on occasion do sewers. The public good is served when all four are undertaken since this brings the greatest improvement in health; if only water supply is improved, this may increase health problems as waste water forms stagnant pools which then serve as breeding grounds for insects which spread diseases.

But private companies are unlikely to want to take on water, sanitation, drainage and garbage disposal. Water supply is probably the most attractive to them because people pay as they consume and often pay for the initial cost of connection. Enforcing payment is easier because supplies can be cut off, if payment is not made. Garbage collection may also be attractive since the capital costs needed to set up the service need not be high and again, services can be stopped to households who do not pay. But site drains cannot be cut off when a household cannot pay. In addition, there are large cost savings if the installation of piped water, drains and sewers are done together, along with the paving of roads and footpaths.

If a natural monopoly is privatized, it has to be very carefully regulated both in terms of prices charged and quality of the service provided. If a private firm runs the water supply in a city, residents have no other piped supply they can turn to, if prices get too high or quality too low. But if water supplies are privatized because local governments are so weak, how can local governments regulate the private firms? How can they ensure that water quality is guaranteed?[40]

In particular cities or parts of cities, the weakness or inefficiency of local government or of national agencies providing, say, electricity and telephones, may provide a strong case for the private supply of certain services or certain kinds of infrastructure. Public companies which fail to provide adequate services to businesses who can pay for such services constrain the growth in production and employment. As Lee has pointed out in his study of deficiencies in infrastructure provision in Nigeria, the failure of government to supply businesses with adequate standards of water supply, electricity, telephones and drains means that these businesses make very large investments to guarantee their own supplies, that is their own electricity generators, wells for water, and microwave telephone systems. The costs to each business are enormous and any larger scale supplier (public or private) could meet their demands far cheaper.[41]

In other services, especially those which are not a natural monopoly, private enterprises can help improve quality. In public transport, private enterprises often provide a cheaper, more flexible service than public sector bus companies; private buses, mini-buses, shared taxis, powered rickshaws and a whole host of other kinds of paratransit either replace or supplement public-sector buses in virtually all Third World cities. Garbage collection may also be improved at an affordable cost, with appropriate encouragement and regulation by local government.

Where household water comes mainly from vendors, supplies should be cheaper and of better quality if different vendors compete with each other. Here, one option for local government is to help water vendors and private paratransit firms to improve services as well as regulating quality.[42] But it is more difficult to conceive of private companies helping to improve and extend piped water supplies, sewers, drains, roads and pavements, especially to poorer households and poorly-located residential areas.

One reason why private companies can operate more profitably than public enterprises is that they are often more efficient at collecting payments for the services provided. Public companies which are lax about collecting payments for, say, a water supply are subsidizing those who do not pay (often not among the poorer households) and penalizing those who do. They are also penalizing all households that have no piped water service since this lowers the returns to the company and thus inhibits new investment to expand the service. Improving cost recovery – in terms of reducing the proportion of households who do not pay for some service – is one important way to pay for better maintenance of the system and its expansion to reach new households. But improved cost recovery cannot be at the expense of the poorest households not receiving services.

Improved cost recovery in a privatized service may penalize the poorest households. It may also not result in improved services but in higher profits for the owners. Private companies will always be reluctant to extend their services to poorer areas especially if this requires a large investment. For instance, it would not cost much for a private company to see if a new bus service to a squatter community would be profitable. If this does not prove profitable, the company loses no capital investment. But laying water pipes or sewers to a squatter community is a much greater risk, since it is far more expensive and the company can hardly dig up the whole system and try again elsewhere.

In effect, allowing private enterprises to provide certain services now inadequately provided (or not provided at all) by local government can be useful and worth considering, especially in the services which are not natural monopolies. But in the services which are the main concern of this chapter, there will be problems with quality and with reaching poorer households without a strong and competent local government to supervise levels of private service and charges. If local government is strong and competent, it should be able to provide such services more cheaply and effectively itself. It is worth considering one of the underlying causes of the failure of govern-ment provision in the larger and faster growing cities: the physi-cal expansion of the city and its demographic growth outstripping the needed expansion of the powers, capacities and revenue base of city and municipal government. The institutions have changed far slower than the growth in the scale of their responsibilities. It is counter-productive for government to inhibit private enterprises that can provide people with a better level of services for which they can pay, if government itself cannot deliver such a service.

In the final analysis, the aim is to seek a compromise between guaranteeing a basic level of service to everyone and to maximiz-ing cost recovery. New technologies and innovative institutional arrangements can greatly cheapen the cost of supplying a basic level of services – and thus greatly narrow the gap between basic service cost and what poorer households can afford. They can also make it easy for households to obtain better services, once they can afford to pay more – ie. bring piped water into the house rather than in the yard outide. Privatization is only valid if considered within the more important long-term goal of strong, competent and representative local government.

Another role for NGOs

A more interesting and more relevant debate about privatization has to do not with private commercial enterprises, but with non-profit organizations and with organizations set up by residents of particular areas. Such organizations can not only match private enterprise's rec-ord in cost recovery but also provide cheaper services (since no profit is made) and be more immediately accountable to their customers. There is tremendous potential in new partnerships between local governments and local community organizations – which could be regarded as privatization in another form, but where control of some service rests largely with representatives of the consumers of that service.

The possibility of tackling the most serious health problems with limited resources needs co-operation between local government and community-based or neighbourhood-based citizen groups. Joint programmes can be set up, for example to drain stagnant pools, to reblock existing settlements so pipes, drains and access roads can be installed and space made for schools and clinics, to locate and destroy disease vectors within homes and their surrounds, to design educational programmes on health prevention and personal hygiene, to set up emergency life saving systems through which first aid can be provided immediately in each neighbourhood and through which seriously ill or injured persons can be rapidly transported to a hospital. In most instances, none of these can be provided at an affordable cost without the support of those living in low income settlements. It is not simply that money is saved because local residents contribute labour free (many poor households lack free time because of long working hours). There are major savings in the time of architects, planners, surveyors and other expensive professionals, as community consultations work out and resolve such issues as moving certain houses which stand in the way of access roads, and collect funds from households to pay for improvements. There are also major savings as specialized equipment and materials are used to install not only piped water but also provision for sanitation, drainage and all weather roads and paths.

As in new policies to improve housing conditions, intermediary non-profit organizations can become particularly important in health. Consider the example of the Orangi Pilot Project where an NGO formed by local professionals worked with community organizations in an unauthorized settlement to build sewers (Box 6.6).

Box 6.6: The Orangi Pilot Project in Karachi, Pakistan

Orangi is a unauthorized settlement with some 700,000 inhabitants; most inhabitants built their own houses. There was no public provision for sanitation; most people used bucket latrines which were emptied every few days, usually onto the unpaved lanes running between houses. More affluent households constructed soakpits but these filled up after a few years. Some households living near creeks constructed sewage pipes which emptied into the creeks. The cost of getting local government agencies to lay sewage pipes in Orangi was too much for local residents – who also felt that these should be provided free.

A local organization called the Orangi Pilot Project (OPP) was sure that a cheaper, more appropriate sanitation system could be installed and paid for, if local residents were fully involved. OPP staff organized meetings for those living in

10–15 adjacent houses each side of a lane, showed them the benefits of improved sanitation and offered technical assistance. Where agreement was reached among households, they elected their own leader who formally applied for technical help. Their site was surveyed, with plans drawn up and cost estimates prepared. Local leaders kept their group informed and collected money to pay for the work. Sewers were then installed with maintainance organized by local groups. As the scope of the sewer construction programme grew – as more local groups approached OPP for help – the local authorities began to provide some financial support. By December 1985, over half of the lanes within Orangi had sewage systems.

Women were very active in local groups; many were elected group leaders and it was often women who found the funds to pay for the sewers, out of household budgets. But women had difficulty visiting health centres since custom dictates that they should stay at home. OPP has set up mobile training teams to visit local groups with information about sanitation and preventive measures against common diseases. In addition, women's work centres have been set up.

Sources: Arif Hasan, "A low cost sewer system by low-income Pakistanis" in Bertha Turner (ed.), *Building Community: a Third World Case Book*, Habitat International Coalition, 1989; and "Orangi Pilot Project, Karachi" in Czech Conroy and Miles Litvinoff (eds), *The Greening of Aid* (London: Earthscan Publications, 1988).

Table 6.1 sketches the actions needed to tackle environmental problems in the home and the neighbourhood. It suggests that these must be linked to actions at the level of the district and city. Support is needed from national government. The actions in Table 6.1 are in effect the health aspects of what was termed the "popular approach" to housing in Chapter 5.

The actions described in Table 6.1 are not beyond the means of most Third World governments. They do demand a decentralized, multi-sectoral approach with government agencies' inputs guided by low income groups and the organizations that they form. Ironically, the fact that resources are so scarce actually requires local governments in the Third World to be more sophisticated, innovative and flexible than First World local governments. Ideally, each house should be provided with piped water and sewers and each residential

Table 6.1: Links between health and government action at different levels to improve housing conditions in urban residential areas

Health risks	Action at individual and household level	Public action at neighbourhood or community level	Action at city or district level	Action at national level
Contaminated water – typhoid, hepatitis, dysenteries, diarrhoea, cholera etc.	Protected water supply to house; promote knowledge of hygienic water storage	Provision of water supply infrastructure. Knowledge and motivation in community	Plans to undertake this and resources to do so	Ensure that local and city governments have the power, funding base and trained personnel to implement actions at household, neighbourhood, city and district level. Review, and where appropriate, change legislative framework and norms and codes to allow and encourage actions at lower levels and ensure infrastructure standards are appropriate to needs and the resources available. Support for training courses and seminars for architects, planners, engineers etc
Inadequate disposal of human wastes – pathogens from excreta contaminating food, water or fingers leading to faecal-oral diseases or intestinal worms (eg hookworm, tapeworm, roundworm, schistosomiasis)	Support for construction of easily maintained latrine/WC matching physical conditions, social preferences and economic resources; washing facilities; promote handwashing	Mix of technical advice, equipment installation and its servicing and maintenance (mix dependent on technology used)	Plans to undertake this plus resources. Trained personnel and finances to service and maintain	
Waste water and garbage – water logged soil ideal to transmit diseases like hookworm; pools of standing water becoming contaminated, conveying	Provision of storm/surface water drains and spaces for storing garbage that are rat, cat, dog and child proof.	Design and provision of storm and surface water drains. Advice to households on materials and construction techniques to make	Regular removal or provision for safe disposal of household wastes and plan framework and resources for drains	

Health risks	Action at individual and household level	Public action at neighbourhood or community level	Action at city or district level	Action at national level
enteric diseases and providing breeding ground for mosquitoes spreading filariasis, malaria and other diseases. Garbage attracting disease vectors.		houses less damp		on the health aspects of their work
Insufficient water, washing facilities and personal hygiene – ear and eye infections (including trachoma), skin diseases, scabies, lice, fleas	Adequate water supply for washing and bathing. Provision for laundry at household or community level	Health and personal hygiene education for children and adults. Facilities for laundry at this level, if not within individual houses	Support for health education and public facilities for laundry	Technical and financial support for educational campaigns. Co-ordination of housing, health and education ministries
Disease vectors or parasites in house structure with access to occupants/ food/water e.g. rats, cockroaches and other insects (including vector for Chagas disease)	Support for improved house structure – eg tiled floors, protected food storage areas, roofs/ walls/floors protected disease vectors	Technical advice and information; part of adult/child education programme	Loans for upgrading house. Guarantee supply of cheap and easily available materials, fixtures and fittings	Ensure building codes and official procedures to approve house construction/improvement are not inhibiting individual, household and local government actions. Support for

Health risks	Action at individual and household level	Public action at neighbourhood or community level	Action at city or district level	Action at national level
Inadequate size house/ventilation – helps spread diseases like TB, influenza and meningitis (aerosol drop transmission) and increases frequency of diseases transmitted through inter-human contact (eg mumps and measles). Risks of household accidents increased with overcrowding; it becomes impossible to safe guard children from poisons and open fires or stoves	Technical advice and financial support for house improvement or extension and provision of cheap sites with basic services in different parts of the city to offer low income groups alternatives to their current shelter	Technical advice on improving ventilation; education on over-crowding related diseases and accidents	Loans (including small ones with flexible repayments); support for building advice centres in each neighbourhood	nationwide availability of building loans, cheap materials (where possible based on local resources) and building advice centres. Produce technical and educational material to support this
Children playing in and around house site constantly exposed to dangers from traffic, unsafe sites or sites contaminated with faeces or pollutants	Organization of child-care services to allow care for children in households where all adults work	Provision within each neighbourhood of well drained site separated from traffic, kept clean and free from garbage and easily supervised. Ensure first aid services are to hand	Support given to neighbourhood level play, sport and recreation facilities.	

Health risks	Action at individual and household level	Public action at neighbourhood or community level	Action at city or district level	Action at national level
Indoor air pollution through open fires or poorly designed stoves – exacerbate respiratory illness, especially in women and children	Posters/booklets on improved stove design and improving ventilation etc	Ensure availability of designs and materials to build improved designs and investigate possibilities of promoting use of alternative fuels		
House-sites subject to landslides or floods as result of no other land being affordable to lower income groups	Regularize each household's tenure if dangers can be lessened; relocation through offer of alternative sites as last resort	Action to reduce dangers and encourage upgrading or offer alternative sites	Ensure availability of safe housing sites that lower income groups can afford	National legislation and financial and technical support for interventions by local and city governments in land markets to support lower level action. Training institutions to provide needed personnel at each level
Illegal occupation of house-site or illegal sub-division with disincentive to upgrade, lack of services and mental stress from fear of eviction	Regularize each household's tenure and provision for piped water, sanitation and storm and surface water drainage	Local government working with community to provide basic infrastructure and services and incorporation into 'official city'	Support for incorporating illegal sub-divisions and for providing tenure to squatter households	
Nutritional deficiencies and low income	Action to reduce worm burden and worm transmission. Support for income generating work within the house	Food supplements/school meals. Support for enterprises in low income settlements or set up by their inhabitants. If land is available, promote its use for growing vegetables. If malnutrition is serious, consider most appropriate programme to		Structural reforms, funds for food supplement or other emergency nutrition programmes and other

Health risks	Action at individual and household level	Public action at neighbourhood or community level	Action at city or district level	Action at national level
		reach most seriously affected groups		measures to improve poorer groups' real income
No or inadequate access to curative/preventive health care and advice	Widespread availability of simple primer on first aid and health in the home with home visits by health workers to promote its use	Primary health care centre; emphasis on child and maternal health, preventive health and support for community action and for community volunteers	Small hospital (first referral level) and resources and training to support lower level services and volunteers	Technical and financial support for nationwide system of hospitals and health care centres. Preventive health campaigns (e.g. immunization) and nationwide availability of drugs and equipment.
No provision for emergency life saving services in event of injury or serious illness	Widespread availability of simple primer on first aid and health in the home with educational programme on minimizing risks	Basic equipment (eg stretchers, first aid) available and accessible 24 hours a day. Community volunteers with basic training on call and arrangements for rapid transfer of sick person to hospital. Equipment to rescue and treat people saved from burning houses	Support for neighbourhood level equipment plus organization of training programmes for community volunteers. Fire fighting equipment, contingency plans for emergencies	Set up training system for paramedics/community health workers. Provide guidelines for setting up emergency services and planning and risk minimization in risk prone areas to minimize injuries and damage if disaster occurs

Health risks	Action at individual and household level	Public action at neigh-bourhood or community level	Action at city or district level	Action at national level
	Discussions with individuals and community organizations about some minimum changes in site layout to improve emergency vehicle access and create fire breaks			

Note: Many of the above actions to improve or extend houses or to improve the quality of the services and facilities that the house contains will often be constrained for houses, flats, rooms or house sites which are rented. One should recall that a high proportion of the lowest income individuals and households rent their accommodation in most Third World cities and improving their quality and reducing health risks will need government programmes and actions which are not summarized in this Table

Source: Jorge E. Hardoy and David Satterthwaite, "Housing and Health: Do architects and planners have a role?", *Cities*, vol. 4, no. 3, 1987.

area with paved roads, electricity and storm/rain-water drainage. There should be regular collection of household wastes, nutrition programmes for vulnerable groups and health care and emergency life saving services. But this may be too expensive so local governments in consultation with citizen organizations must make pragmatic choices as to where limited funds should be spent. They need considerable sophistication and sensibility to detect the major health problems and to design and implement appropriate interventions.

The issue is certainly about making the suppliers of services more responsive to consumer demands. It is about local government giving the private sector more power in decision making, more role in service provision and more rights in determining priorities. But the private sector is made up of low income citizens and their community organizations – and the non-profit professional groups who pioneer new ways of working with them.

7. Environmental Problems at the City and Regional Level

The city environment

Environmental problems such as air and water pollution might be assumed to be less pressing in the Third World than in the West for two reasons. First, a smaller proportion of the population lives in cities. Second, the Third World is less industrialized; in 1980, the Third World (excluding China) with half of the world's population had 11 per cent of the world's industrial production.[1] Rural and agriculturally-based environmental problems such as deforestation, soil erosion, loss of topsoil, water pollution and deaths and disablements from biocide use (and over-use) may seem more urgent even if, as described later, some of these have important linkages with cities. Thus, industries' and cities' appetite for water (and its subsequent pollution and disposal), and problems of air pollution and solid waste disposal might be assumed to be less of a problem than in the more urbanized and industrialized West.

However, the aggregate picture hides the fact that there are hundreds of Third World cities or wider city-regions which do have high concentrations of industries. Nations such as China, India, Mexico, Brazil and South Korea figure prominently amongst the world's largest producers of many industrial goods. Not surprisingly, Third World cities or city-regions with high concentrations of industries (especially heavy industries) suffer comparable industrial pollution problems to those experienced in Europe, Japan and North America.

Indeed, the problems may be more serious. Industrial production has increased very rapidly in many Third World nations in the last 30 years in the absence of a strong and effective planning and regulation system. More than 35 nations recorded annual average growth rates for industrial production of 5 per cent or more during the 1960s and/or the period 1970–85.[2] The more rapid the growth in industrial production, the more serious the problem is likely to be. Very few governments have had much interest in controlling industrial pollution (at least until recently). And governments' concern to create more jobs usually meant that when a new factory was proposed – by national or international businesses – little attention was given to the likely environmental impacts.

A second reason why pollution can be particularly serious is the concentration of industry in relatively few locations; in most Third World nations, industrial production is heavily concentrated in one or two city regions or core regions within each nation (see Chapter 8). In Thailand, a high proportion of all industry is located in the metropolitan area of Bangkok or in neighbouring provinces. This region has three-quarters of all factories dealing with hazardous chemicals. Within Bangkok and five satellite towns are five of Thailand's seven lead-smelting plants and over 90 per cent of its chemical, dry cell battery, paint, pharmaceutical and textile manufacturing plants.[3] While some governments have managed to support a decentralization of industry away from the largest cities, many new industrial plants have set up outside the main city but still within or close to its metropolitan area.

Environmental problems arise from activities other than industrial pollution. The large proportions of the population not served by sewers and garbage disposal add greatly to land and water pollution problems, while very congested traffic and inefficient and poorly maintained engines in most road vehicles add greatly to air pollution. Other factors also increase pollution problems – for instance many households using inefficient heaters and cookers (especially those using solid fuel). Local conditions can also exacerbate the pollution. For instance, thermal inversions (where a mass of warm air well above the city helps trap the pollutants in the cool air underneath it) is common in the winter for northern Chinese cities.[4]

Certain South-East Asian cities have long periods in the year with very little wind to help disperse air pollution and with high concentrations of automobiles and an abundance of sunshine, photochemical smog has become an increasing problem.[5] The world's most populous metropolitan area, that of Mexico City, has an environment ill-suited to the very large concentration of industries which have developed there. The valley in which it has developed is some 2,200 metres above sea level and is surrounded by mountains. These provide the conditions for thermal inversions which trap pollutants within the valley.

It is difficult to judge the magnitude of industrial pollution problems in comparison to the other environmental problems already discussed such as the lack of piped water supplies, sewers, drains or services to remove garbage. There are hundreds of incidents where a group of workers or many members of the public died or were seriously disabled as a result of direct exposure to industrial pollutants; some will be given later in this chapter. There are also hundreds of examples of much larger numbers of people suffering ill health or permanent disablement arising from pollutants in the air or water; some of these will also be given later in the chapter. We also know that an enormous number of cases of ill health, disablement and death to which industrial pollution has contributed goes unreported. It is likely that the known and documented cases represent only a tiny proportion of all cases. This is especially so for ill-health, disablement or death which arises from continued exposure to pollutants over a long period of time. We suspect that the next 20–30 years will show that the health impact of pollutants in the Third World, in the air and water, and through direct exposure in the home or workplace, has been greatly underestimated. Large-scale tragedies such as Bhopal (over 3,000 dead and perhaps 100,000 seriously injured) or the natural-gas explosions in Mexico City in 1984 (over 1,000 dead) alerted us to the scale of death and human suffering which can arise from an industrial accident. The attempts by European and North American industries to dump their toxic wastes in Third World nations has also received a lot of publicity. But we suspect that there is a far larger and more widespread problem of premature death and human suffering arising from pollution which goes undetected and remains undocumented.

In Europe, North America and Japan, only through long and well organized citizen action and protest did governments begin to act on the environmental problems created by industries. Citizen groups did much to document the scale and nature of the problems and alert people to the dangers. As noted earlier, there are far fewer environmental NGOs in the Third World and those that do exist often have to work in much more difficult circumstances; funding is less easy to find and government legislation to control pollution is less clear. In many instances, such NGOs suffer from harrassment or repression from government. The examples which follow are drawn from the (limited) documentation which does exist. (The fact that so many examples come from India reflects the fact that Indian NGOs have been among the most active and well-organized – and among the first to identify the critical links between environmental issues and poverty.)

Toxic/hazardous wastes

In the Third World, as in the West, one sees the familiar list of pollution problems: the heavy metals (which include lead, mercury, cadmium and chromium), oxides of nitrogen and sulphur, petroleum hydrocarbons, particulate matter, polychlorinated biphenyls (PCBs), cyanide and arsenic as well as various organic solvents and asbestos.

Some of these and certain other industrial and institutional wastes are placed in a special category of "hazardous" or "toxic" waste because special care is needed for disposal, so they are isolated from contact with humans and stored in ways which prevent them polluting the environment. If such wastes are buried, great care must be taken that they could not contaminate underground water sources. If stored in drums, great care must be taken that the drums do not corrode. Most toxic wastes remain toxic so simply storing them does not solve the long-term problem.

Most toxic wastes come from chemical industries although several others such as primary and fabricated metal and petroleum industries, pulp and paper industries, transport and electrical equipment industries and leather and tanning industries also produce significant quantities of hazardous wastes.

There are many different kinds of hazardous wastes. Some are highly inflammable, such as many solvents used in the chemical industry. Some are highly reactive and can explode or generate toxic gases when coming into contact with water or some other chemical. Some have disease-causing agents: for instance, sewage sludge or hospital wastes often contain bacteria, viruses and cysts from parasites. Some wastes are lethal poisons, such as cyanide, arsenic and many heavy-metal compounds; and many are carcinogenic (cancer inducing).

Box 7.1: Examples of toxic chemicals, their use and their potential health impacts

ARSENIC	pesticides/some medicines/glass	dermatitis/muscular paralysis/damage to liver and kidney/ possibly carcinogenic and teratogenic

ASBESTOS	roofing insulation/air conditioning conduits/ plastics/fibre/paper	carcinogenic to workers and even family members
BENZENE	manufacture of many chemicals/gasoline	leukaemia/chromosomal damage in exposed workers
BERYLLIUM	aerospace industry/ ceramic parts/household appliances	fatal lung disease/lung and heart toxicity
CADMIUM	electroplating/plastics/ pigments/some fertilizers	kidney damage/ emphysema/possibly carcinogenic, teratogenic and mutagenic
CHROMATES	tanning/pigments/ corrosion inhibitor/ fungicides	skin ulcers/kidney inflammation/possibly carcinogenic/toxic to fish
LEAD	pipes/some batteries/ paints/printing/plastics/ gasoline additive	intoxicant/neurotoxin/ affects blood system
MERCURY	chloralkali cells/ fungicides/pharmaceuticals	damage to nervous system/kidney damage
PCBs	electric transformers/ electrical insulator	possibly carcinogenic/ nerve, skin and liver damage
SULPHUR DIOXIDE	sugar/bleeding agent/ emissions from coal	irritation to eyes and respiratory system/ damage to plants and buildings
VINYL CHLORIDE	plastics/organic compound synthesis	systemically toxic/ carcinogenic

Source: C.R. Krishnamurthi, "Toxic chemicals", *State of the Environment: Some Aspects*, National Committee on Environmental Planning, New Delhi quoted in G. Anandalingam and Mark Westfall, "Hazardous waste generation and disposal: options for developing countries", *Natural Resources Forum*, vol. 11, no. 1, February 1987.

Only in the last 15 years has the scale of the problem of hazardous wastes and the potential danger to people's health been recognized. The United States, for example, industrialized rapidly, giving little consideration to the safe disposal of hazardous wastes. Now it is faced with the problem of some 50,000 land-sites where hazardous wastes may have been dumped without control, and without provision to ensure that the wastes do not pollute groundwater. The cost of dealing with the backlog created by inadequate or non-existent control runs into tens of billions of dollars.[6]

Today, most toxic wastes are either dumped in liquid wastes which run untreated into rivers, streams or other nearby water bodies, or are dumped on land-sites with few safeguards to protect those living nearby or nearby water sources from contamination.

Very few Third World nations have effective government systems to control the disposal of hazardous wastes; indeed, in most, there are no regulations dealing specifically with such wastes, let alone the system to implement them. Such systems need a competent well-staffed regulatory authority with the ability to make regular checks in each industry using or generating toxic chemicals, and with power to penalize offenders. This authority needs the backing of central government and the courts. For the control of toxic wastes to be effective, industries must keep rigorous records of the kinds and quantities of waste they produce and the dates and methods by which these are disposed of. Businesses which specialize in collecting and disposing of these wastes must be very carefully monitored; so too must the specialized facilities which need to be created to handle toxic wastes. Since the safe disposal of toxic wastes is extremely expensive, there are enormous incentives to cheat in any regulatory system.

Reports of problems arising from the careless disposal of chemical compounds with heavy metals (including mercury, cadmium, lead, nickel) are increasingly frequent. The problem of mercury contaminated wastes being discharged into water bodies, which received such publicity through the hundreds of deaths and disablements it caused in Minamata, Japan and which has caused serious problems in many North American water bodies, has also been noted in Bangkok, Perai (Malaysia), Bombay, Managua, Alexandria, Cartagena and in various Chinese cities.[7-13] Significant build-ups of mercury, lead, cadmium, copper and chromium have been reported in recent years in almost every industrializing nation in Southeast Asia.[14] The Kalu river which runs through two of Bombay's industrial suburbs receives the liquid effluents of over 150 industrial units and these include heavy metals. This causes dangerously high levels of mercury and lead in the water near the village of Ambivali and the villagers are slowly being poisoned as heavy metals enter the food chain through cattle browsing on the river bank vegetation.[15] On the South-East Pacific coast of Latin America, heavy metals have been detected in practically all areas that receive industrial and municipal wastes and worryingly high concentrations of mercury, copper and cadmium have been found in some fish species.[16] Lead and cadmium concentrations in drinking water were found to exceed the guideline values in about a quarter of the 344 stations which monitor water pollution within the Global Environmental Monitoring Network.[17] Thirteen children were reported to have died of mercury poisoning in Jakarta in 1981 after eating fish caught in the waters of Jakarta Bay tributary, while mercury levels in the water polluted by nearby factories were found to have dangerously high concentrations.[18] Jakarta Bay remains the source of much of the fish consumed in the city.

Reports from China in 1980 and 1981 note "some astonishingly high cadmium and mercury concentrations in rivers and underground wasters".[19] For instance, downstream from Jilin, a major industrial city with a high concentration of chemical industries, the Songhua Jiang river had organic mercury pollution for a stretch of more than 20 kilometres. The concentration reached between 2 and 20 mg per litre which is between 2,000 and 20,000 times the concentration recommended for inland surface waters by the European Commission. Fish in the Zhaoyuan Jiang river have a mercury content of 5.35 mg per kg body weight, 18 times the maximum concentration level set by the European Commission.[20]

One final kind of toxic waste which deserves special attention is radioactive wastes. The problems are best illustrated by an accident in Goiania, Brazil where a scrap-metal dealer broke up an abandoned cancer-therapy machine and released the radioactive chemical caesium–137 from inside it. Because the powder and some of the metal glowed in the dark, the scrap dealer and his family and friends handled it. Around 240 people were contaminated and several people have died; many of those that survive will probably develop cancer.[21] Even for nations which have no nuclear power stations, radioactive chemicals are widely used in other activities. Wherever governments seek to develop waste disposal sites for these or other toxic wastes, local citizens are likely to mount strong protests. For instance, there was a long battle in Malaysia between a firm called Asian Rare Earth and local residents (aided by environmental groups) over the siting of a dump for radioactive wastes near their town.[22]

Transferring the First World's pollution to the Third World

Since governments in the North enforced more stringent regulations on pollution control and on the disposal of hazardous wastes, many companies from the North have tried to transfer the problem to the Third World. In some instances, dirty industries have been transferred; in others, the hazardous wastes have been transferred.

To take first the transfer of production; there has been a trend towards the relocation of industries manufacturing asbestos from the United States to Latin America, with Brazil and Mexico as the most frequent recipients. Asbestos textile imports into the United States from Mexico, Taiwan and Brazil grew rapidly between 1969 and 1976 and Taiwan and South Korea have been displacing Japan as a source of asbestos textiles for the United States, as new regulations on this industry have been introduced in Japan.[23] There has been a comparable transfer of production by Japanese and North American subsidiaries in other dirty industries with Taiwan, South Korea, the Philippines and Thailand being among the recipients.[24] For instance, the Nihon Chemical Company closed its polluting factory in Tokyo and constructed a replacement in Ulsan, South Korea and many Japanese companies have invested in petrochemical industries in South-East Asia.[25]

To meet demand for the products of certain dirty industries in Japan, Western Europe or North America, multinational corporations may increasingly transfer production to Third World nations to avoid the costs associated with meeting workplace safety and pollution standards. Arsenic production, lead refining and battery manufacture, metal smelters and biocide production are among the industries where this transfer may increasingly take place. This transfer, allied to increasing dirty industry production in Third World cities to meet local and regional demand, has serious implications for the health of city populations both now and in the future. The lessons learnt in the West over the last 15 to 20 years on the enormous health costs associated with the uncontrolled disposal of toxic wastes by certain industries do not seem to be heeded by government, and are often being ignored by the industrial sector.

The case of mercury pollution in Managua illustrates this problem. In 1980, an investigation by Nicaragua's new government found that Electroquimica Pennwalt (Elpesa), an affiliate of a Philadelphia-based multinational, was responsible for mercury contamination of Lake Managua from where some of the drinking water for the capital city is drawn. The lake, more than 1,000 square kilometres in size, had been a major source of fish for city inhabitants. But the problem was not only the contamination of fish and drinking water source. Workers at the factory were also affected. An inspection in 1980 found the level of mercury in the air was 12 times the recommended safety level by the US National Institute of Occupational Safety and Health and that the workforce had not been warned about possible health hazards. An examination of workers found that 37 per cent had evidence of mercury contamination.[26]

There is also the issue of the export of hazardous wastes to the Third World, which recently gained a lot of attention in the press, as it was discovered that certain European or North American businesses were dumping toxic wastes in certain Third World nations with little or no provision to protect the people living there. It also became evident that the scale of this exporting operation was likely to grow very rapidly, since the cost of transporting and dumping toxic wastes to Third World nations was only a fraction of the cost of safely incinerating or storing them in the West and meeting government regulations in doing so.

Box 7.2: The West's export of toxic wastes

BANGKOK: Large quantities of chemical wastes have been stored in Bangkok's main port, Klong Tuey. Most came from unknown shippers in Singapore although some also came from the United States, Japan, West Germany and Taiwan. Officials from the government's National Environment Board have expressed fears that the barrels may contain PCBs or dioxin which can only be destroyed in high temperature incinerators which Thailand does not possess.

BENIN: European firms were seeking a contract to send 5 million tons of wastes each year from Sesco, a company registered in Gibraltar. It was reported that Benin was to receive $2.50 for each ton received while Sesco would charge firms up to $1,000 a ton or more to dispose of the wastes. Benin is one of the poorest nations in the world and lacks virtually all the infrastructure and the government system needed to handle and manage even a small fraction of the 5 million tons a year proposed.

GUINEA-BISSAU: It was reported that Lindaco, a firm based

in Detroit, applied to the US government to ship up to 6 million tons of chemical waste to Guinea Bissau, one of the world's poorest nations. Other contracts have been signed for importing chemical and industrial wastes from Western nations.

GUINEA: A Norwegian firm dumped some 15,000 tons of burnt or partially burnt industrial waste and incinerator ash from the United States and Norway on the island of Kassu, near the capital Conakry. Toxic wastes could filter down to pollute ground-water supplies used by the islanders and into the sea to damage fisheries.

NIGERIA: 3,800 tons of European chemical wastes were dumped by Italian ships in the southern port of Koko on the Niger river with a payment to the landowner of the equivalent of around $100 a month; the cost of disposing of these in Europe would be of the order of $350–1,750 a ton. The wastes are stored in 45-gallon (around 200-litre) drums, many of them leaking and most in poor condition. Many drums have volatile chemicals which in a hot climate, present a serious risk of a spontaneous fire or explosion.

PERU: Negotiations were reported between a Peruvian company and a US company to dispose of barrels of toxic wastes from US industries – solvents, burnt oils and chemical wastes.

VENEZUELA: In October 1987, 11,000 barrels of chemical wastes were returned to Italy after a private Italian company had tried to store them in a warehouse in Puerto Cabello; local inhabitants claimed that some barrels leaked and caused various diseases.

Sources: See note 27. There are also many other examples of wastes from the First World being dumped in the Third World or negotiations underway to do so.

Box 7.2 gives some examples of this export trade; the publicity coming from press coverage has helped mobilize environmental groups and some governments both in the West and in the Third World to guard against this. There are reports of this problem having existed for some years – especially in Northern Mexico with the illegal dumping of toxic wastes produced by US firms which have been shipped across the border.[28] But a lot more attention needs to be given to the dumping of toxic wastes in exactly this same manner by branches of multinational firms or by domestic industries within Third World nations. Most Third World nations do not have the special facilities needed to safely store such wastes. It is likely that most toxic wastes are currently dumped on land-sites with no provision to ensure these remain isolated from contact with plants, animals and humans or simply dumped in sewers, drains, wells or nearby water courses – rivers, lakes, estuaries.

Water pollution

In terms of their impact on human health in Third World cities in general, the dangers from heavy metals and from most toxic industrial wastes are probably more localized and more open to swift and effective government control than those from other industrial pollutants. In many Third World cities environmental problems such as smog or smoke irritating the eyes, and noxious and polluted rivers, lakes, or sea-coasts are usually all too evident. These have serious health implications and often cause, or contribute to, ill health in much of the population.

To take first the question of water pollution, there are usually four different sources: sewage, industrial effluents, storm and urban run-off and agricultural run-off.[29] Agricultural run-off is often an urban problem too since water sources from which an urban centre draws may be polluted with agricultural run-off, and contain dangerous levels of toxic chemicals from fertilizers and biocides. Box 7.3 outlines the most common kinds of pollution arising from these sources.

Box 7.3: Water pollution

Most water pollution falls into one of three categories: liquid organic wastes, liquid inorganic wastes and pathogens.

LIQUID ORGANIC WASTES: These can be termed "oxygen demanding" wastes since when disposed of into water, bacteria and other micro-organisms combine with oxygen dissolved in the water break them down. The biochemical oxygen demand (BOD) of such wastes is a measure of how much oxygen dissolved in the water they will need to be broken down and as such, is one of the most widely used indicators of pollution. Liquid organic wastes include sewage, many liquid wastes from industries (especially from industries processing agricultural products) and run-off from rains and storms which pick up organic wastes from land, before flowing into streams, rivers, lakes or seas. Too great a volume of organic wastes can overload the capacity of the water's bacteria and other micro-organisms to the point where all dissolved oxygen becomes exhausted. As the concentration of dissolved oxygen decreases, so fish and plant life suffer or die. Some portions of rivers or lakes which receive large volumes of organic wastes can have all their dissolved oxygen used up and thus lose their ability to break down these kinds of wastes, and become black and foul smelling.

LIQUID INORGANIC WASTES: Most inorganic liquid wastes come from industry. These are not broken down in water in the same way as organic wastes but for most, their dilution in large bodies of water renders them harmless. Many such wastes kill animal and plant life, unless sufficiently diluted. Some can become concentrated in fish or other fresh- or sea-water products (shellfish, seaweed) to a point where they kill or do severe damage to the health of humans who eat them. Wastes which include certain chemical elements known as the heavy metals or some of their compounds can be particularly dangerous. Many of the pollution incidents which resulted in the largest number of deaths and serious injuries have arisen from human contact with a heavy metal or one of their compounds.

PATHOGENS: Disease-causing agents (for instance bacteria, viruses and worms), many of which are spread in water. Much the most common and widespread problem are pathogens from human excreta which contaminate water subsequently used by people. Typhoid, hepatitis, dysenteries, diarrhoea and cholera are among the diseases spread by contaminated water. Contaminated water also plays a central role in the transmission of many intestinal worms.

Earlier sections have already documented the lack of sewers (or other means to safely dispose of human excreta) and the inadequacy in garbage collection services. This adds greatly to water pollution problems since many of the uncollected wastes are washed into streams, rivers or lakes and add greatly to the chemical oxygen demand. Many rivers in Third World cities are literally large open sewers.

Take the case of India, as documented in two volumes on *The State of India's Environment: a Citizen's Report* produced by a network of Indian NGOs, co-ordinated by the Centre for Science and Environment in Delhi. This points out that of India's 3,119 towns and cities, only 209 have partial sewage and sewage treatment facilities and 8 have full facilities. On the river Ganga alone, 114 cities each with 50,000 or more inhabitants dump untreated sewage into the river every day. "DDT factories, tanneries, paper and pulp mills, petrochemical and fertilizer complexes, rubber factories and a host of others use the river to get rid of their wastes."[30] The Hooghly river which branches off the Ganga passes through Calcutta and Howrah, with very high concentrations of people and industries. "The Hooghly estuary is choked with the untreated industrial wastes from more than 150 major factories around Calcutta... raw sewage pours into the river continuously from 361 outfalls."[31] While Delhi does not have comparable concentrations of industry, every day the Yamuna river which passes through it "picks up nearly 200 million litres of untreated sewage. Twenty million litres of industrial effluents including about half a million litres of DDT wastes enter the Yamuna in this stretch."[32]

Box 7.4: Examples of water pollution

KARACHI: The Lyari river which runs through Karachi (Pakistan's largest industrial city) is an open drain from both chemical and micro-biological points of view; a mixture of raw sewage and untreated industrial effluents. Most industrial effluents come from an industrial estate with some 300 major industries and almost three times as many small units. Three-fifths of the units are textile mills. Most other industries in Karachi also discharge untreated effluents into the nearest water body.

BOGOTA: High degree of pollution in the Tunjuelito, a tributary of the Bogota river. Many tanneries and plastic processing plants pour wastes untreated into it and the dissolved oxygen in the water is almost depleted. The wastes include heavy metals such as lead and cadmium. Other rivers are not so heavily polluted with chemical wastes but receive large volumes of untreated sewage waters.

ALEXANDRIA: Industries in Alexandria account for around 40 per cent of all Egypt's industrial output and most discharge liquid wastes, untreated, into the sea or into Lake Maryut. In the past decade, fish production in Lake Maryut has declined by some 80 per cent because of the direct discharge into it of industrial and domestic effluents. The lake has also ceased to be a prime recreational site because of its poor condition. Similar environmental degradation is taking place along the seafront as a result of the discharge of untreated waste waters from poorly located outfalls. The paper, textile and food industries contribute most to the organic load.

KUALA LUMPUR: The city's name means "muddy confluence" since it is located at the meeting of Gombak and Kelang rivers – running through densely populated areas. The Sungai Kelang is dubbed an open sewer. The Kelang river has very depleted levels of dissolved oxygen.

SHANGHAI: Every day some 3.4 million cubic metres of industrial and domestic waste pour mostly into the Suzhou Creek and the Huangpu river which flows through the heart of the city. These have become the main (open) sewers for the city. Most of the waste is industrial since most houses do not possess flush toilets. The Huangpu may be the most heavily polluted stream in the world; essentially dead since 1980. It is a chemical cocktail of raw sewage, toxic urban wastes and huge volumes of industrial discharges. The entire river area and lower reaches of Woosung river smell terrible. Less than five per cent of city's wastes treated. A high water table means that a variety of toxins from industrial plants and local rivers find their way back into ground water and contaminate wells which also contribute to city water supplies.

SAO PAULO: Two main rivers are completely dead – most residential sewage and industrial effluent flows directly into rivers and other water reservoirs. Only ten per cent of solid wastes collected and treated; most remains in open air deposits some dangerously near water sources and most in areas completely uncontrolled by public authorities.

Sources: See note 33.

Box 7.4 gives other examples of cities with serious problems of water pollution. Another Third World NGO which has helped highlight serious pollution problems in their own nation is the Consumers Association of Penang. This has documented how in peninsular Malaysia, many rivers are grossly polluted: the three principal sources being organic wastes from sewage, and discharges from oil palm and rubber factories. The range and complexity of water pollution problems caused by the discharge of other (non agro-based) industrial effluents has increased, especially in industrial centres such as Kuala Lumpur, Petaling Jaya and Penang. The main industrial sources of pollution come from electroplating industries, tanneries, textile mills, food processing industries, distilleries, chloro-alkali plants, sulphuric acid plants and electronic factories. Many of these industries discharge wastes containing different compounds, including heavy metals, into public water courses without prior treatment. Significant levels of toxic heavy metals such as mercury, lead, chromium and cadmium have been encountered in the Juru River Basin. Measurements in coastal waters and estuarine waters in various locations showed very high concentrations of coliform bacteria. In addition it is not uncommon to see large quantities of solid waste in the form of plastic bags, wood and other debris floating in the water and deposited on the beaches. A survey of accessible beaches on the eastern coast of peninsular Malaysia found that more than half were contaminated by oil residues.[34]

A shortage of water also adds greatly to the problem of disposing of wastes, especially liquid wastes from industries and sewage. Large volumes of water dilute wastes and can render them much less dangerous; in addition, bacteria in the water break down organic wastes, as long as the volume of wastes relative to the volume of water is not too great. Mexico City, like most of the largest cities and many smaller cities, is also facing mounting costs in increasing water supplies. Over-exploitation of underground water sources has made the city sink – in some areas by up to 9 metres.[35] New sources of water are at a considerable distance and these have to be pumped up to the city, up to 1,000 metres, which adds considerably both to costs and to fuel consumption.[36] Mexico City is just one of many cities which developed in an area with limited water resources and has now out-grown the capacity of the region to provide adequate, sustainable supplies. Hundreds of urban centres which developed in relatively arid areas have grown far beyond the point where adequate supplies can be tapped from local or even regional sources. Many others are simply facing problems with finding the funds to allow them to keep up with demand: Bangkok and Jakarta are two among many major cities and ports close to the coast with serious problems of subsidence from drawing too much from underground aquifers, and also saline intrusion into such ground waters; in Jakarta, many shops, houses and offices can no longer drink the water from the wells they use because of saline intrusion.[37]

Air pollution

There are four major sources of air pollution – industry, fuels for heating and electricity generation, solid waste disposal and motor vehicles (including cars, buses, trucks, motorbikes etc).[38] The scale of the problem and the relative contribution of the different sources varies greatly from city to city. Local conditions can decrease the problem; for instance in Bangkok, the location close to the coast on a flat plain means that a prevailing wind helps disperse pollutants. Local conditions can also increase the problem as noted earlier for Mexico City. The limited evidence which does exist suggests that city-wide air pollution problems are most serious in the larger industrial cities of the Third World, in large cities where solid fuels are widely used for cooking and heating in homes, and in large cities where local conditions inhibit the dispersal of air pollutants. More localized problems with air pollution occur more widely, in and around particular businesses with high levels of polluting emissions.

Box 7.5: Air pollution

Most air pollution falls into one of the six categories below:
CARBON MONOXIDE: Mostly coming from the incomplete combustion of oil, coal and natural gas and other organic matter, carbon monoxide reduces the capacity of the blood to carry oxygen and in prolonged, high concentrations, can cause death. More generally, it contributes to headaches and fatigue and aggravates heart and respiratory diseases. Within the city environment, motor vehicle exhausts are usually the major source. It is also a problem in homes and factories with open fires or inefficient heating or cooking appliances allied to poor ventilation.
HYDROCARBONS: A group of chemicals made up of hydrogen and carbon. As air pollution, most comes from incomplete

---

combustion of fuel by motor vehicles but also from oil spills and the evaporation of industrial solvents. These can injure the respiratory system and some cause cancer. They also contribute to photochemical smog (see below).

OXIDES OF NITROGEN: Mostly derived from high temperature fuel combustion in motor vehicles, power plants and industries, these can aggravate respiratory and heart diseases, irritate lungs and, when dissolved by rain, become acid rain.

OXIDES OF SULPHUR: Mostly coming from the burning of coal or oil containing sulphur in homes, factories or powerplants, these can (like the oxides of nitrogen) aggravate respiratory diseases and cause acid rain, when dissolved from the air by raindrops. They can also irritate eyes and the respiratory tract.

SUSPENDED PARTICULATES: Smoke, dust, soot and liquid and other solid particles which become suspended in the air. Depending on their size and composition, these can cause cancer and aggravate respiratory and heart diseases. They can cause coughing and irritation of the throat and chest. They also reduce atmospheric visibility and block out sunlight.

PHOTOCHEMICAL SMOG: Sunlight acting on hydrocarbons and oxides of nitrogen forms various chemicals including ozone which aggravate respiratory and heart diseases, irritates eyes and throats, damages plants and decreases atmospheric visibility.

The most tangible evidence of high levels of air pollution within a city is a high level of respiratory diseases – although in the case of airborne lead, it shows up in blood tests. If the incidence of, say, cancers and respiratory diseases are drawn on a city map, this often pinpoints certain areas where residents suffer most from air pollution – directly linked to one industry or one industrial complex. Bombay, with its concentration of population and heavy industry probably suffers more than India's other cities. There is a large concentration of industries in the Trombay-Chembur area along the eastern coast of the island which is the core of the city and in the Lalbaug area which includes a thermal power station, a chemicals and fertilizer plant, a gas company and numerous petrochemical plants, oil refineries and textile mills. In one study in 1977–78, the health of residents in Chembur and Lalbaug (with heavy concentrations of industry) was compared to that of residents in a cleaner suburb, Khar. People living in the congested industrial areas suffered from a much higher incidence of diseases such as chronic bronchitis, tuberculosis, skin allergies, anaemia and irritation of the eyes. The rate of absenteeism by workers was much higher, particularly in Lalbaug's textile mills, and there was a notable rise in the number of deaths from cancer in Lalbaug.[39] A survey by the Bombay Municipal Corporation states that tuberculosis and respiratory diseases are the major killers in the city; between 1971 and 1979, deaths from tuberculosis went up from 83 to 101 per 100,000 people although deaths from breathing impairments came down from 170 to 143, largely due to the use of low sulphur gas in the most polluting industries.[40] A report in Calcutta estimated that 60 per cent of its residents suffer from respiratory diseases related to air pollution.[41] In Mexico City's metropolitan zone, emissions of sulphur dioxide, nitrogen oxides and carbon monoxide all increased substantially between 1972 and 1983, and air pollution is a likely cause or contributor to 90 per cent of the respiratory illnesses and infections suffered by the population.[42] Sulphur dioxide emissions from oil refineries and thermal-electric industries and carbon monoxide from car exhausts are a particular problem. In addition, the thermal inversion helps trap pollutants in the valley within which the city is located; it was recently reported that schools were shut down because air pollution levels had reached such high concentrations.[43]

In China, the industrial sector is the dominant consumer of fossil fuels and its heavy concentration in some 20 cities, with most of them using coal in outdated furnaces and boilers, ensures high levels of air pollution. Lung cancer mortality in China is four to seven times higher in cities than in the nation as a whole and the difference is largely attributable to heavy air pollution.[44] In Shanghai, clear days are rare and chronic smog is referred to as "Yellow Dragon"[45] while rain can be so acid that it burns holes in nylon shirts.[46]

One of the most drastic examples of unchecked industrial pollution and its impact on human health comes from the city of Cubatao in Brazil as outlined in Box 7.6. What is difficult to gauge is whether this is an extreme but unusual example, or representative of what has happened and what continues to happen in many industrial complexes in the Third World. It is perhaps revealing that only with the return to democracy in Brazil has the scale and nature of the pollution there become widely known. Again, it was local citizen organizations who helped document and publicize the problem – and set up a system to monitor emissions from certain factories. Under the military government, there were restrictions on all press reports on Cubatao.

In 1985, environmentalists in Brazil gained the right to sue companies for damages to pay for cleaning up the damage to the environment that they have caused, and a local environmental group in Cubatao and the state government attorney have filed an $800 million suite against 24 industries there.[47]

Box 7.6: Cubatao, the valley of death

The City of Cubatao in Brazil, close to Sao Paulo and to the major port of Santos, has long been known as the "Valley of Death". The city contains a high concentration of heavy industry which developed rapidly under Brazil's military government from 1964 with little or no attempt on the part of government to control pollution. The industries there include branches of multinational firms – for instance a Union Carbide fertilizer factory and the French Rhodia company – and Brazilian oil, chemical and steel companies. Very high levels of stillborn and deformed babies, of tuberculosis, pneumonia, bronchitis, emphysema and asthma, and a high infant mortality rate are all linked to the very high levels of air pollution. There are even cases of children being born without brains; almost daily, young children come to a hospital to breathe medicated air. The Cubatao river was once an important source of fish; now there is little or no fish. There are crabs but these contain far too high a level of toxic chemicals to be safe to eat. Toxic industrial wastes have been dumped in the surrounding forests and are contaminating surface and ground water which is used for drinking and cooking. Vegetation in and around Cubatao has suffered substantially from air pollution and from the rain that returns pollutants to the land to the point where there have been landslides on certain slopes as vegetation died and no longer helped retain the soil.

Many of those who work in the city live in shanty towns built on stilts above swamps. Hundreds of the inhabitants of one shanty town there are reported to have been killed in late February 1984 after a pipeline carrying gasoline leaked into the swamp under the shanty town and then caught fire. There has been little or no protection for the workers in many of the industries and many suffer from serious diseases or disabilities arising from their exposure to chemicals or waste products while at work.

Sources: H. Jeffrey Leonard, "Confronting Industrial Pollution in Rapidly Expanding Industrializing Countries – Myths, Pitfalls and Opportunities", Conservation Foundation, USA, 1984; film on air pollution by Bo Landin produced in 1987 by the Television Trust for the Environment as part of the series "Battle for the Planet"; and Debbie Macklin, *South*, March 1989.

Substantial progress has been made in Cubatao in the last few years in forcing companies to reduce the emission of air pollution – especially the more dangerous ones. The volume of industrial effluents dumped into local rivers and solid wastes dumped in local landfills has been cut substantially. Some companies there have publicly committed themselves to a far more responsible attitude to the local environment, as they substantially reduce polluting emissions. But for many people, this is too late, since they are already permanently disabled. The longer term impact of pollutants already in the local rivers or leaking into groundwater is also uncertain.

The highly urbanized Kelan (or Klang) Valley in Malaysia (which includes the capital Kuala Lumpur) has two to three times the pollution level of major cities in the United States, according to the Director General of the Government's Environment Division.[48] Kuala Lumpur has a concentration of suspended particulates in the air 29 times the desirable goal recommended by the Malaysian Environmental Quality Standards Committee. In Cairo, the prevailing winds blow north or south; one brings toxic fumes into the city from the lead and zinc smelters in Shubra al Khaymay; when the winds shift, they bring poisonous pollutants from the steel and cement factories in the south of Helwan, an area noted for its many dead trees.[49]

But many activities other than industries contribute to air pollution. Stone quarries, so often located on a city's periphery, are usually major sources of particulate matter. Motor vehicles are a major source in most cities through emissions of carbon monoxide, oxides of nitrogen, lead and hydrocarbons, and they contribute to suspended particulate matter. Air pollution from motor vehicles might be assumed to be less of a problem than in Western nations because poorer nations have fewer automobiles. This may be so in most urban centres but is not the case in most major cities. Virtually all the largest cities and many smaller ones have high concentrations of motor vehicles and traffic flows too large for existing road networks. The major cities of richer Third World nations have as many automobiles per capita as many Western cities. But even where the ratio is lower, a combination of narrow congested streets and old and poorly maintained vehicles with much higher levels of polluting emissions can ensure there are serious problems.

Alarming levels of airborne lead and/or carbon monoxide have been noted in Kuala Lumpur alongside busy roads and in the heart of the capital, in Calcutta, in Lagos and Ibadan in Nigeria, and alongside busy roads in Zimbabwe, in Rio de Janeiro and in Manila.[50-54] In a study of lead exposure conducted between 1979 and 1981 in 10 nations (with follow up in 1984 in 4 nations) 10 per cent of the population sampled in Mexico City and Bangalore (one of India's largest cities) had exposure levels well above the maximum recommended level.[55] The problem of lead is exacerbated by the fact that many Third World governments permit a much higher lead content in gasoline than those permitted by Western governments, to boost octane ratings.[56]

In many cities, open fires or inefficient stoves burning solid fuels in homes are also major contributors to air pollution. This is the case in many Indian cities; for instance, one estimate suggests that domestic fuel burning generates about half of Delhi's air pollution. In China, although total fuel combustion by households is small by comparison to industry and power stations, "the burning of raw coal in millions of small inefficient stoves is a very burdensome air pollution source through the colder half of the nation".[57] In Seoul, heavy oil burned in home heating units and power stations, and anthracite briquettes used for domestic heating and cooking, contribute to high levels of air pollution.[58]

Noise pollution

The health impacts of noise on city inhabitants is now being given more serious attention, even if the precise health and environmental effects of noise pollution are not fully known.[59] In the urban environment, there are usually four principal sources of noise – aircraft, industrial operations, construction activities and highway traffic.[60]

Large areas of many Third World cities have high levels of noise arising from aircraft landing and taking off in nearby airports; for instance, in Latin America, many major airports are in the middle of densely populated areas (the international airport of Mexico City and airports in Lima, Bogota, Quito, Guayaquil, Buenos Aires, Port-au-Prince and Santiago de Chile). Noise from major roads or highways is a major problem – especially since few Third World governments have instituted effective noise-control programmes on road vehicles, as in Europe in North America. For instance, in Bangkok, noise pollution is considered a serious problem. Noise from trucks, buses and motor-cycles meant noise levels greater than 70 decibels in many locations; findings from Western nations suggest that outdoor noise levels should be kept under 65 decibels to comply with desirable limits indoors.[61] Motorboats which are widely used in Bangkok frequently exceed the noise standard of 85 decibels at a distance of 7.5 metres set by the Harbour Department, and an examination of motorboat operators found that 80 per cent had hearing loss.[62] While noise pollution remains a major problem in Western nations, at least there are regulations, institutions to enforce them and democratic procedures through which protests can be organized; one or more of these is sadly lacking in virtually all Third World nations.

Environmental problems in smaller cities

It is not only the largest cities or those with a concentration of heavy industry which have serious environmental problems. So too can smaller cities with few industries. Such problems usually arise from a lack of drainage, lack of sewage pipes (or other methods to safely dispose of human wastes), lack of planning controls (to ensure polluting industries are downwind and downstream of city inhabitants) and either a lack of pollution control regulation or its enforcement. Just one or two agricultural processing factories or chemical, pulp and paper or beverage factories can seriously pollute a river. Just one cement plant or one thermal power station burning high-sulphur coal or oil can create serious air pollution problems. There is very little documentation on land, air and water pollution in smaller cities. (Very few sub-Saharan African cities featured in the examples in sections on air and water pollution.) But this does not imply that these problems do not exist.

Douala and Yaounde in the Cameroon, both cities on a much smaller scale than Beijing or Bombay, Sao Paulo, Manila or Lagos provide useful illustrations. They show the range of environmental problems which exist even in relatively small cities.[63] Recent estimates put Douala's population at close to half a million inhabitants and Yaounde's at over 300,000.[64] Yaounde is the national capital and Douala the chief port and main industrial centre. Both cities' populations have grown rapidly over the last three decades; in 1950 neither had reached 100,000 inhabitants.[65] In 1981, 64 per cent of Cameroon's population lived in rural areas.[66]

The environmental problems of these two cities revolve around effluents and emissions from industries; inadequate provision for the hygienic removal of household and human wastes; the concentration of motor vehicles; a high concentration of low income people who have no alternative but to squat on house sites ill-suited to safe, healthy housing; and lack of planning to provide some separation between polluting industries and people (and the water they drink), and to control low density sprawl.

Industries cause serious problems of air and water pollution in both cities[67] and were built in locations which best served the needs of that industry with no logic or plan guiding this location in the wider public interest. There has been little regard for regulations to control industrial emissions.[68] Household and human wastes are also disposed of with little regard to potential health hazards. The company responsible for emptying and cleaning septic tanks and latrines disposes of some of this untreated sewage into Yaounde's waterways or on waste ground. In both cities, these problems are made more acute by the fact that garbage collection is only provided for certain neighbourhoods. In those with no such collections, rubbish heaps build up on streets and sidewalks, providing breeding grounds for rodents and disease vectors. While rain might eventually wash them away, such garbage frequently gets stuck in bottleneck spots and causes flooding. Richer households, however, tend to live upstream on higher ground with the poorer quarters downstream on lower ground. The waterways polluted by sewage and industrial effluents and the run-off from higher ground comes through some of the poorest residential areas.[69] There are also problems of air pollution – from factory dust and ash and the burning of household wastes to the various oxides of nitrogen, carbon and sulphur emitted by internal combustion engines or industries.

In Yaounde and Douala, as in other Third World cities, it is usually lower income groups who suffer most from air and water pollution and from floods and other "natural" hazards.[70] If many (or indeed most) city households cannot afford to buy or rent even the cheapest legal house, apartment or room where the most basic environmental standards are met, they have to resort to some form of housing with one or more major defect to bring down the price. One common solution, is to live in shelters illegally built on dangerous sites – sites subject to flooding or landslides or continual contamination from industrial emissions; or on (or close to) city garbage tips or right next to railways or major highways. One example is a large shanty town which has grown up around a quarry on the outskirts of Yaounde with the residents having to live with the problems of dust, explosions damaging houses, noise, air pollution from tar production and lack of piped water.[71] Other spontaneous settlements in both Yaounde and Douala have grown up on valley bottoms and marshy sites which are usually infested with mosquitoes.

Environmental problems often become particularly acute in smaller cities which grow rapidly because local governments show little or no capability of resolving the problems that accompany rapid growth. Railway tracks, stations and yards often impede physical expansion. So too, in many instances, do large tracts of land owned by the armed forces – a problem which tends to be more acute in provincial or state capitals. No action is taken to move activities which are no longer appropriate in the central city, for instance, moving army barracks and redeveloping land taken from under-used railway yards. Because local government does little to guide physical growth, the expansion of city activities often takes place on unsuitable sites (for instance, land prone to flooding) and industrial and residential areas develop together. For example, in Salta (Argentina), the army owns 10,000 hectares of land, some of it within 1,200 metres of the main square. The army also owns 2,800 hectares in La Rioja and 2,600 hectares in Resistencia and again, some of this is within 1,200 metres of the main square.

The environment of poverty

Obviously, perhaps, it is almost always the poorer groups who live in the places where the smells and the pollution levels are worst: such zones may be the only places where poorer groups can find land close to sources of employment on which they can build houses without fear of eviction. It was the high concentration of low income people around the Union Carbide Factory in Bhopal which caused so many people to be killed or permanently injured. In Mexico City, the highest concentrations of dust particles in the air are found in the south-east and north-east areas which are areas where lower income groups live.[72] In Manila, some 20,000 people live around a garbage dump known as Smokey Mountain where the rotting mass of organic wastes produces a permanent haze and a powerful, rank smell affecting the whole area. Some of these people have lived there 40 years or more. Moving to a cleaner safer location is beyond their means and many of them make a living scavenging on the dump, often sorting it with their bare hands.[73]

The examples of Douala, Jakarta and Bangkok already given are just three among many cities with large concentrations of illegal settlements on the banks of rivers, lakes or streams, because the land is subject to flooding (so they have better possibilities of being allowed to stay there) and because they need a supply of water. But such water supplies are usually very heavily polluted with both untreated sewage and industrial wastes.

It is virtually always the poorest groups who suffer most from the floods, landslides or other "natural" disasters which have become increasingly common occurrences in cities of the Third World. Historically, many cities developed on sites prone to floods, earthquakes, landslides, droughts or hurricanes; but two factors limited the impacts on human populations. First, the most dangerous sites within the locality were avoided, second, cities were relatively small and less densely populated.

Today, there are many large cities in areas prone to natural disasters and many of the most dangerous sites have been occupied. Each time a disaster is reported, most of those who die or are injured and most of those evacuated and lodged in transitory shelters are from lower income groups. Such disasters bring to the surface the poverty which characterizes the lives of so many inhabitants. They lose their housing because no provision was made by their society to allow them a safer site; they lose their source of income as they are moved by some public agency to a different ("safer") site which is too far from their previous source of work. For many who build their own dwellings, they lose much of their capital investment since their house was their bank account, i.e. their main source of capital. Moving to a new site often damages their contacts with family, friends and others who have helped them find work or survive periods of no income.[74] Poorer groups usually suffer most from noise and dangers from airports. Many governments have legislated against the development of land in or close to airports under the main flight paths. But these often develop as densely populated illegal settlements and government does nothing to offer such people safer, less noisy alternatives.

Regional impacts

As the major centres of production and consumption, cities demand a very high input of resources – water, fossil fuels, land and all the goods and materials that their populations and enterprises require. The more populous and spread-out the city and the richer its inhabitants, the larger its demand on resources is likely to be, and the larger the area from which these are drawn. Cities are also major centres for resource degradation. Water needed for industrial processes, for supplying residential and commercial buildings, for transporting sewage (and other uses) is returned to rivers, lakes or the sea at a far lower quality than that originally supplied. The solid wastes from city households and businesses which are collected are usually dumped in land-sites around the city while much of the uncollected solid waste finds its way into water bodies, adding to the pollution. These are termed regional impacts. We look first at the impact of cities drawing resources from the wider region and then at the impact of city-based activities (especially the production of wastes) on the wider region.

The demand for rural produce or resources from city-based enterprises and households can pre-empt their use by rural households. For instance, in cities where wood and charcoal are still widely used for cooking and heating (mostly by lower income households), city-based demand often pre-empts supplies formerly used by rural inhabitants. Where once, poor rural inhabitants gathered wood from what was regarded as common land, now they are barred from doing so, as the wood is harvested for sale. Common land once used

---

Box 7.7: Firewood in the cities

To meet demand for firewood in Delhi 12,423 railway wagons of firewood arrived at Tughlakabad railway siding during 1981–82, some 612 tons a day. Most of this wood comes from Madhya Pradesh, nearly 700 kilometres away. The Shahdara railway siding also receives firewoods daily from the forests in the Himalayan foothills in Assam and Bihar – although in smaller quantities. In addition, the forested area and trees within Delhi yield thousands of tons annually. Yet Delhi has a relatively low per-capita consumption of firewood, because of the ready availability of kerosene, coal and liquid petroleum gas (which are much preferred as fuel if they can be afforded). In Bangalore, an estimated 440,000 tons of commercial firewood are consumed each year, far more than Delhi, even though Bangalore has around half the population of Delhi. Most of it arrives by road – an average of 114 trucks a day. Most firewood comes from private farms and forests within 150 kilometres of Bangalore but 15 per cent comes from government forests, 300 to 700 kilometres away.

Source: The State of India's Environment 1984–5: The Second Citizens' Report, (New Delhi: Centre for Science and Environment, 1986).

for gathering wild produce and grazing is taken over by monoculture tree plantations where this is not permitted.[75] In addition, high demand for fuelwood from cities may be a prime cause of deforestation (and the soil erosion which usually accompanies it) and this may be taking place at considerable distances from the city (see Box 7.7).

This shows how difficult it is to separate "rural" from "urban". The impoverishment of rural people in a region and their movement to cities may be considered a rural problem – but it may be largely the result of the commercialization of agricultural land and crop markets because of city-based demand. Deforestation may be considered a rural problem but it may be intimately linked to the demand for fuelwood or charcoal from city inhabitants and enterprises, even if their effects impinge most seriously on rural inhabitants. Furthermore, the soil erosion linked to deforestation may be destroying rural inhabitants' livelihoods with the result that they migrate to the city. Deforestation of river catchments and associated soil erosion can contribute to floods which devastate large areas downstream, including cities or city-districts built alongside rivers. Electricity demand in cities can also cause problems for rural areas. The environmental impacts of large hydro-electric dams, such as the loss of agricultural land and the resettlement of thousands of rural people, or the introduction or exacerbation of waterborne or water-related diseases are usually rural, even if most of the electricity will be consumed in urban areas. Other examples could be given, including the environmental effects of agricultural or mining operations which produce raw materials for city-based activities, as well as poorly designed and located bridges, highways and roads linking smaller settlements with cities, which might contribute to problems of flooding.

Mike Douglass has considered the long term impact that Jakarta may have on its wider region and this provides an example of the complex rural-urban interations taking place between a city and its surrounding areas, and the serious environmental consequences.[76] The expansion of the urban area and urban activities pushes out farmers from agricultural land; productive agriculture is replaced by urban developments or by commercial ventures for tourism and recreation. Agriculture is pushed onto land less suited to such use in hill and upland areas. Soil erosion there lowers agricultural productivity and causes siltation of water reservoirs, flooding after heavy rains plus reduced flows in rivers during dry periods. Meanwhile, the government must seek new sources of water to supply Jakarta since over-pumping of groundwater has already resulted in serious salt water intrusion into what were previously sweet water aquifers; the supply of water may need to multiply fourfold between 1983 and 2000, especially if the supply of piped water to city households is to improve; in 1980, only 26 per cent of the population were served with piped water. But many of the lowland river and water courses nearby have high concentrations of non-degradable organic chemicals and heavy metals from biocides used in agriculture, which limit their use for human consumption.

Within each nation or region, there are also complex population movements linking rural areas, towns and cities. Such movements can have a major impact on cities' population growth and demographic structure and thus on city environment. Migration to cities can be promoted by high population densities in rural areas, shortage of cultivable land, declining soil fertility, increasing commercialization of agriculture and agricultural land markets, inequitable land-ownership patterns and exploitative landlord–tenant relations as well as government support for cash crops. Such processes are likely to be cumulative and mutually reinforcing. Cities not only feel the effects of these, but their growth as centres of demand for rural produce can in turn cause increasing commercialization of agricultural land markets which pushes peasants off the land. Furthermore, the livelihood of rural-based artisans has frequently been destroyed or damaged by the increasing availability of mass-produced goods made or distributed by city-based enterprises. Factors such as these, allied to the concentration of public and private productive investment in relatively few cities has meant rapid net in-migration to most cities in the Third World, at least for certain periods in their physical and demographic growth. Although a detailed discussion of these regional factors and their contribution to cities' environmental problems is beyond the scope of this chapter, their importance must not be underestimated.

Three particular kinds of city impact on their wider region deserve special attention: uncontrolled physical expansions; solid and liquid waste disposal; and air pollution.

Uncontrolled physical growth impacts most on what might be termed an immediate hinterland around a city; this cannot be described as urban or suburban and yet much of it is no longer rural. If the city has been designated a metropolitan centre, much or all of this hinterland may fall within the metropolitan boundaries. Within this area, agriculture has often disappeared or is evidently in decline, as land has been bought up by people or companies in anticipation of its change from agricultural to urban use, as the city's built-up area expands. The lack of effective public control of such changes in land use or of the profits which can be made from them encourages this process. In many Third World nations it is also encouraged by the lack of other high return investment opportunities.

There are usually many legal sub-divisions in this hinterland for houses or commercial and industrial buildings which have been approved without reference to any city-wide plan. There are also usually many unauthorized sub-divisions. As the built-up city area expands towards this land, development occurs through legal and illegal action by various land-owners, builders, and real estate firms in an *ad hoc* way, producing an incoherent urban sprawl. Illegal squatter communities have often been forced out to this hinterland as well. In cities such as Delhi and Manila, this hinterland also contains settlements formed when their inhabitants were dumped there, after being evicted from their homes by slum or squatter clearance.

Unplanned and uncontrolled city expansion has many serious social and environmental impacts. Chapter 4 already described the vast amounts of land left vacant in and around cities and the social impacts: the segregation of the poor in the worst-located and most dangerous areas and the increased costs of providing basic infrastructure, public transport and social services (p.99). In 1980, the Governor of Lagos State, Nigeria, commented that many of the popular towns and districts in his state, especially those in and around Lagos Metropolis, had sprung up in contravention of official regulations and that in most, there were no services and infrastructure and those which did exist were grossly inadequate.[77] In these, as in so many other Third World cities and their hinterlands, one sees the paradox of extreme overcrowding and chronic housing shortages and acute shortages of infrastructure and services – and yet vast amounts of land left vacant or only partially developed, with all that this implies in terms of increasing the cost of providing infrastructure and services.

The loss of agricultural land is another serious environmental problem arising from uncontrolled city growth. Cities often expand over the nation's most fertile land since so many cities grew up within highly fertile areas. Before the development of motorized transport, no major city could develop too far from the land which produced its inhabitants' daily food and fuel requirements. In addition, many cities first developed as market centres to serve the prosperous farms and farming households around them. For example, almost all the large cities in the nations around the Pacific were established on lowland delta regions and continue to expand into their nation's most fertile agricultural land.[78]

In most cities, this could be avoided by the government guiding the physical expansion and ensuring that vacant or under-utilized land within the city was fully used. In most cities, the problem is not a lack of vacant land but a lack of government action to guide new developments on land other than the best farmland. As a report from Colombia stated: "the belief in private initiative, so necessary in other areas of the economy, has led in urban issues to the supply of a hardly satisfactory, and in many cases chaotic, product. Vast extensions of utility networks and buildings are under-used or deteriorating while the urbanization process, guided by the incentive of private profit, proceeds with no control to the confines of the country's most productive land".[79] In Egypt, more than ten per cent of the nation's most productive farmland has been lost to urban encroachment in the last three decades, much of it through illegal squatting or sub-division, while at the same time prime sites within cities remain undeveloped.[80] Around Lima, between 1965 and 1975, more than 14,000 hectares of irrigated land in the Rimac Valley were lost to the growing urbanized region.[81] Since 1900, the urban area of Delhi (including New Delhi) has grown nearly 13 times, eating into surrounding agricultural areas and absorbing more than

100 villages. This unplanned and uncontrolled expansion has been accompanied by the expansion of brick-making kilns, with fertile topsoil being used to make the bricks.[82]

Uncontrolled physical expansion also destroys or degrades areas and buildings important to the urban environment, because their protection does not represent an economic gain for any individual or enterprise. Natural landscapes in or close to cities should be preserved as parks, natural reserves, historic sites or simply areas of open space for recreation. The need to preserve or develop such areas might seem less urgent than, say, land for housing, but to ignore these now condemns both present and future city inhabitants to never enjoying their benefits. Once an area is built up, it is much more difficult and expensive to develop such areas. But the richer groups usually suffer much less. Their residential areas often have plenty of open space. In addition, it is common for large country clubs to develop in the regions surrounding major cities. Such clubs provide their members with open space for walks, playgrounds and facilities for sport while governments make little or no provision for the recreation needs of poorer groups.

The contamination of rivers, lakes and seashores is an example both of the impact of city-generated wastes on the wider region and of government's negligent attitude to protecting open areas. In cities on or close to coasts, untreated sewage and industrial effluents are often dumped into the sea with little or no provision to pipe them far enough out to sea to protect the beaches and in-shore waters (see Box 7.8). Most major Third World cities located on the sea have serious problems with dirty, contaminated beaches and with the water there being a major health risk to bathers. Oil pollution often adds to existing problems of sewage and industrial effluents. Pollution may be so severe that many beaches have to

---

Box 7.8: Beach pollution

Untreated sewage is the main cause of polluted beaches within the metropolitan limits of Montevideo and Rio de Janeiro and along the northern coast of Venezuela, close to Cara-cas. Untreated industrial effluents and sewage have all but destroyed the recreational value of Lake Maryut in Alexandria and have polluted its Mediterranean beaches. Comparable problems exist in many other cities including Karachi, several cities in Malaysia, Dakar, Panama City, the inner waters of the Gulf of Guayaquil and beaches in Lima and in Concepcion and Valparaíso (Chile), and many beaches in the Caribbean.

Sources: See note 83.

be closed to the public. It is also worth noting that in major cities, it is usually the most accessible beaches which suffer most and these are often among the most widely used recreational areas by lower income groups. Richer households suffer much less; those with automobiles can reach more distant, less accessible beaches.

Liquid wastes from city activities have environmental impacts stretching beyond the immediate hinterland. Fisheries damaged or destroyed by liquid effluents from city-based industries are becoming increasingly common. Worsening water pollution is threatening the livelihoods of millions of river fishermen in India; in the 158 kilometre stretch of the Hooghly River, the average fish yield in the polluted zones is only about one-sixth that in the unpolluted zones.[84] In Malaysia, the livelihood of many fishermen who depended on rivers and lakes has been destroyed by water pollution, while fishermen in the inshore waters reported heavy falls in catches in coastal waters affected by industrial effluents and oil.[85] In Lake Maryut, close to the city of Alexandria in Egypt, fish production has declined by about 80 per cent due to discharges of industrial and domestic effluents.[86] In the Gulf of Paria between Venezuela and Trinidad, pollution produced a band of dead fish 1.5 kilometres long and 300 metres wide in March 1988.[87] Sewage and industrial effluents in the Bay of Dakar have cut fish stocks[88] while they have meant an enormous drop in the shrimp catch around the Indus delta, near to Karachi.[89] "Red Tides" caused by an abnormal growth of phytoplankton arising from high pollution levels have recently engulfed Manila Bay and affected eight other bays with very serious damages done to fish and shellfish.[90] Eight deaths from the consumption of contaminated shellfish have been reported and the ban on eating produce from the affected areas has brought serious hardship to the many people whose livelihood depended on fishing.[91] Red Tides are also a frequent occurence off certain parts of the Straits of Malacca – off the coast of Malaysia.[92] Comparable examples of industrial effluents severely damaging fisheries have also been recently reported in the Han River, South Korea; in China in the Li Jiang river in Guilin, in Hangzhou Bay (close to Shanghai) and in the Wujin County's portion of the Grand Canal; and in Rio de Janeiro's Guanabara Bay.[93-95]

River pollution from city-based industries and untreated sewage can lead to serious health problems in settlements downstream which make use of that water. One example is the river Bogota flowing through Bogota, the national capital where it is contaminated by effluents from Colombia's largest concentration of industries, and by sewage and run-off from a city with close to five million inhabitants. At the town of Tocaima, 120 kilometres downstream, the river was found to have an average fecal bacteria coliform count of 7.3 million, making it totally unfit for drinking or cooking.[96] In a village close to Tocaima, the river was reported in 1980 to be black and despite its distance from Bogota, to smell of sewage and chemicals. Nearly all the children have sores or growths on their skin from swimming in it.[97] The La Paz river, passing through Bolivia's largest city La Paz, has become so polluted that horticultural production downstream of the city has had to be curtailed.[98] This regional impact of water pollution can even extend to international water bodies. For instance, in the Persian/Arabian Gulf, a small, shallow, salty and almost landlocked sea, rapid urban and industrial growth on its shores is helping to endanger one of the world's more fragile eco-systems. While the major danger of marine pollution comes from oil, especially that from tanker deballasting and tank washing, raw sewage from the rapidly expanding coastal cities and industrial liquid wastes dumped untreated into the Gulf are also having a considerable impact, as are the concentration of desalination plants along the coast.[99] The Caribbean also faces comparable problems with the large quantities of untreated sewage discharged directly into bays, estuaries, coastal lagoons and rivers and "highly toxic effluents from rapidly developing light and heavy industries... also often discharged directly into adjacent bays".[100]

Air pollution from city-based activities impacting on the region also needs consideration. Damage to vegetation or falling crop yields often provide the first evidence of damage. For instance, in China, reports in 1978 noted heavy industrial air pollution in a district in Lanzhou (a major city and industrial centre) which had destroyed the fruit trees on nearby villages. Furthermore, dates flowered but did not bear fruit, pumpkins failed to mature, and livestock contracted oral cavities which ulcerated, perforated and kept them from eating, causing high death rates.[101] Smil's book *The Bad Earth: Environmental Degradation in China* suggests that such reported cases are "most certainly just the proverbial tip of the iceberg" and that regional damage to plants and livestock must also be quite considerable near coal-fired power stations, refineries and chemical works with no (or only rudimentary) controls.[102] Smil's comment is valid for most other Third World nations where the industrial sector has grown rapidly. Considerable damage to the Samsoon plains in South Korea has been reported; this was once an important rice-producing area but is now seriously damaged from air pollution arising from power, petrochemical and fertilizer plants, copper and zinc smelters and oil refineries.[103]

Much of the problem stems from acid rain. Sulphur and nitrogen oxides, discharged into the atmosphere from power stations burning high sulphur-coal or oil, and from automobile exhausts, can turn rain into acid rain which falls to earth many hundreds of kilometres away; this can result in declining or even disappearing fish populations, damage to soils and vegetation and toxic metals being leached from the soil and getting into water used for animal or human consumption.[104] Acid rain which has become such a major issue in Europe and North America is also causing concern in the areas surrounding certain Third World cities including the areas around Shanghai, Petaling Jaya, Malaysia, several Indian cities and Cubatao, Brazil.[105-108]

There is growing concern that large cities, especially those growing most rapidly, will reach a size where the beneficence of nature will be surpassed, in terms of providing and purifying air and water, and yielding cheap and easily exploitable energy sources. The costs of the damage are evident in the examples given already. So too are the mounting costs in tackling the problems – perhaps most especially in increasing water supply and in effective disposal of liquid and solid wastes. As is usually the case, it is the poor who bear most of the costs of no regulation. In surrounding regions, it is generally the rural poor who suffer as their cheap or free sources of wood and land for grazing are pre-empted to serve city-consumers, while their air and water suffer from wastes originating in the cities. In cities, it is quite possible to envisage governments in the more prosperous nations or cities taking actions to meet to the demands of richer households and businesses for more water, better drains and a cleaner environment and yet still ignoring the more pressing needs of poorer groups.

Tackling city-wide pollution

The last 15 years' experience has shown that polluting emissions can be controlled, given the resources and political will allied to appropriate legislation and its enforcement. Numerous new industrial plant designs eliminate or reduce polluting wastes or recover and re-use process chemicals which were formerly dumped.[109] It is now common knowledge that for most industrial operations, a substantial reduction in polluting emissions is possible for a small fraction of production costs. Indeed, there are many examples of industries actually reducing costs or increasing profits at the same time as reducing polluting emissions. Box 7.9 illustrates the benefits which flow from active government involvement in promoting the re-use or recycling of material or its reclamation from wastes. Quite apart from the environmental benefits, the Shanghai Resource Recovery and Utilization Company also generates some 29,000 full-time, and many more part-time, jobs. Since a large part of reducing resource use and waste is a substitution of labour and skill for capital, conservation can be strongly linked to job creation.

Box 7.9: Resource recovery and utilization in Shanghai

The Shanghai Municipal Environmental Sanitation Administration serves a 150 square kilometre city and 6,035 square kilometres of suburbs and rural areas around the city core, with a total population of some 12 million. Since 1957, it has developed into a state complex retrieving materials and marketing the reclaimed products and now has some 29,000 full time and many more part time employees.

A network of 502 purchasing stations and 1,500 purchasing agents in rural areas acquire material for reclamation or recycling and get paid on commission. Twenty-six integrated recycling centres reclaim or recycle material from industrial and consumer wastes and a network of sales departments and retail shops sell reclaimed products. Among the materials recovered from wastes are ferrous and non-ferrous metals, rubber, plastics, paper, rags, cotton, chemical fibre, animal bones, human hair, broken glass, glass bottles, old machine parts, chemical residues and waste oil. The company has subsidiaries for copper refining, precious metal recovery and refining, iron and steel scrap recycling, plastics production, ferrous metal production and oil wastes recycling. In addition, there are over 3,600 people employed to work with factories – for instance advising them on setting up containers for wastes and establishing systems by which the company can collect them.

Source: C.G. Gunnerson, *Resource Recovery and Utilization in Shanghai*, UNDP/World Bank Global Programme of Resource Recovery, 1987.

Organic residues from industries, which are usually among the most bulky of solid wastes and among the most serious sources of water pollution (largely through their depletion of water's dissolved oxygen), can be used as feedstocks for the manufacture of animal feed, packing material, chemicals and pharmaceuticals, fertilizers, fuel, food and construction materials.[110] Wastes from many agro-processing industries can be valuable feedstocks for other industrial operations. For instance, *bagasse* (sugar cane waste) is commonly used as fuel for the sugar cane mill or an ingredient in animal feed or building materials. It can also be used as a feedstock in paper production. The Cuban Research Institute for Sugar Cane By-Products has developed a process which allows *bagasse* to be turned into high quality newsprint at a reasonable production cost. This can replace the newsprint which many Third World nations import at high cost.[111] A recently developed process allows rice straw to be used as feedstock for a pulp and paper mill without the continuous dumping of polluting "black liquor" into rivers and streams. The process allows the recovery and re-use of process chemicals, thus reducing operating costs as well as polluting emissions.[112]

Air pollution can also be reduced. In most cities, much of the air pollution from industries comes from relatively few (and often old) factories or power stations; substantial reductions are possible by replacing them or adding on pollution control equipment.[113] New designs for power stations burning coal or heavy oil can greatly reduce the problem of sulphur oxide emissions and increase the efficiency with which the fuel is converted into useful energy. Some Third World nations might benefit from the availability of cleaner technologies as they build or expand their industrial base.

Reducing air pollution from road vehicles is also possible; more efficient engines, mandatory annual checks for all vehicles (so engines are kept properly tuned) and a move to lead free petrol can reduce the volume of polluting emissions; combined with regulations on the use of private vehicles and efficient public transport, problems of pollution and traffic congestion can be tackled at the same time. This can be achieved without resorting to such expensive measures as new subway systems. A judicious mix of taxes and physical restrictions on private automobiles, improved facilities for the most commonly used forms of transportation (from trains and buses to communal taxis and rickshaws, to bicycles and feet) and better traffic management can reduce congestion and greatly increase the efficiency of the whole transport system at relatively little cost. The Brazilian city of Curitiba improved its transport system by relying on an improved bus system with exclusive bus-ways on the main transport arteries.[114]

Furthermore, many of the more modern and rapidly expanding industries, such as electronics, do not require the large consumption of natural resources and lack the potential contribution to air, water and land pollution of, say, the steel or pulp and paper industry. In addition, in most Third World cities, a large and increasing proportion of the labour force work in service jobs; this also implies less problems with pollution and heavy resource consumption.

However, various factors inhibit government action on pollution control. The most serious is their over-riding concern to expand industrial production and increase the exploitation of natural resources. Pressing problems with repayment of debts makes increased exports a high priority. In many nations, this means increasing the export of natural resources, since either their industry cannot compete on world markets, or the largest potential markets (Europe, North America, Japan) have protectionist barriers around them. The pressure on governments to increase exports and create more jobs inhibits more long term considerations about the environmental consequences of their actions.

If a government's main concerns are the survival of the national economy (and/or its own survival) and its priority is avoiding additional unemployment, the formulation of new environmental legislation or the implementation of existing legislation will not be a high priority. The fear that enforcing pollution controls creates unemployment is still strong even if it has been overstated. In the long term, government policies to promote resource recycling and recovery, and to lessen waste are likely to lead to a net gain in employment. But many nations do have problems with a few dirty industries whose survival may be threatened by stringent new pollution standards.

There is also the problem of generating the foreign exchange to pay for the import of new clean technologies – whether for industrial production, water purification, power generation or engines for motor vehicles. Only a few Third World nations have sufficiently sophisticated and diverse capital goods industries to produce most of these new technologies so most new "add-on" pollution control equipment or the new clean technologies will have to be imported. Foreign exchange is usually very limited and in most nations, machinery and equipment already accounts for between a quarter and a third of all merchandise imported.[115] In virtually all nations, numerous commodities will be judged of higher priority than such equipment.

Finally, there is again the problem of so many unrepresentative governments. At root, pollution control involves allocating costs and ensuring their collection among different producers and consumers – i.e. taxing producers and consumers for providing basic services and facilities (water, drains, disposal sites...) and controlling one individual or company dumping their waste problem in ways which affect others. The best, most permanent check on the allocation of most benefits to richer households and businesses with the costs dumped on the poor is a representative form of government, including a legal system which allows rapid redress for those who do lose out.

The last fifteen years has seen most Third World governments set up national environmental agencies. An increasing number of examples can be given where major industries were fined for contravening government pollution standards. But very few governments have set up the institutional structure to implement a sustained and effective environmental policy. While over 100 nations have national environmental agencies of one kind or another, many are small, weak institutions – one person offices or inter-agency co-ordinating committees with no independent authority.[116] Others are better staffed but find that the courts are not prepared to back their actions, or that the penalties for industries contravening regulations are so small as to provide little or no deterrent. As two specialists comment, the enforcement of environmental regulations in the Third World "is a relatively haphazard process, depending heavily on the political power of those who violate the regulations and on the extent to which the government is under pressure to take action to stop pollution and environmental degradation. Enforcement is arbitrary at times, in ways which appear to have more to do with political considerations than concern with the environment".[117] One area of research which appears in great need of reinforcement is the evaluation of whether environmental legislation (including that to protect workers from environmental hazards in industries) is being implemented. There is a tendency to assume that if a government has passed a law and designated an agency as responsible for its implementation, the problem is solved. But governments often pass laws with little or no intention of implementing them.

Most examples of governments acting on environmental problems owe much to well-organized citizen pressure and are usually from societies with representative forms of government. Here, government action consists of largely *ad hoc* responses to specific local pressures, such as a group of fishermen complaining about industrial effluents damaging their livelihood, or a group of farmers or citizens complaining about one factory or industrial complex's damage to their homes or farms. This is more common than coherent, sustained programmes of regulation and enforcement. One recent example comes from Taiwan where villagers living near an industrial zone in the south forced local companies to pay around $35 million compensation for the damage caused by petrochemical plants' waste waters to coastal areas and fishing grounds. But the residents had to invade the industrial zone and force the plants to close down. They had also threatened to cut the supplies of coal to local power plants which would have meant power cuts in the industrialized south.[118]

In the West, most government actions on the environment have only taken place after long and well organized citizen campaigns. Citizen organizations had not only to organize such pressures but in most instances to document the problem in the first place. Virtually all government actions on the environment have been "citizen-led". The critical question is, are Third World governments likely to take action on environmental problems (especially those which impact most on poorer citizens) without democratic pressures pushing them in this direction? If the answer is no, it has important implications for aid – not only in what kinds of aid should be given but also in what Third World institutions deserve support.

It is worth considering why so many examples in this chapter come from India and Malaysia. One reason is that there are national and local non-government organizations active on environmental issues – including some such as the Centre for Science and Environment in India, and the Consumers Association in Penang and

Sahabat Alam (Friends of the Earth) in Malaysia which have built international reputations. It is organizations such as these which can take environmental issues beyond local citizen groups fighting local problems to broader and more co-ordinated national campaigns.

Global concerns and the global commons

This chapter has not considered some important global environmental issues. Two are particularly pressing: the contributions of city-based activities to depleting the atmosphere's ozone layer, and to increasing carbon dioxide concentration in the atmosphere (mainly through fossil fuel combustion and through contribution to deforestation as centres of fuelwood consumption). These are subjects which are increasingly well covered – even in newspapers and popular journals. Indeed, these receive far more attention from most Western environmental groups and researchers than the environmental problems described in this and the previous chapter. The same is true in regard to protection of endangered species, and this distortion is sometimes reproduced within Third World nations, where environmental groups become active to save endangered species but give no consideration to the environmental problems which so seriously affect the health and well-being of many of their nation's citizens.

Issues relating to the modification of global climate – especially through ozone depletion and increasing carbon dioxide concentration – have come to the top of the agenda both of Western governments and of Western environmental groups. This is hardly surprising, given the estimates for the cost to Western economies which could result from ozone depletion and a sustained trend to a warmer climate.[119] These global issues have also come to dominate Western concerns as they consider Third World environmental problems. We do not dispute their importance. But Western environmental groups would find more in common with the growing number of Third World environmental groups and citizen groups if they give a greater priority to the environmental problems outlined in this chapter and in Chapter 6, which daily take such an enormous toll on human health. These pose a much more immediate threat for most citizens and action to provide a healthy living environment today is second to encouraging such an environment for the future. Questions of survival twenty or more years into the future are of little interest to those concerned with surviving today. Western groups could give invaluable support to Third World groups in helping to document and monitor the environmental problems associated with poverty and to publicize their impacts and the means for their resolution.

There is a danger that both governments and environmental groups in the Third World will dismiss the global concerns promoted by the West for two reasons. The first is the obvious question of who will pay; the measures needed to reduce the release of carbon dioxide and to greatly reduce the release of chemicals which deplete the atmosphere's ozone layer will be expensive to implement. The second is that the West has shown little interest in helping Third World nations resolve the environmental problems which impact most directly on their citizens; indeed, certain multinational corporations with their headquarters in Europe, North America or Japan are seen as major contributors to the Third World's environmental problems. In addition, most Western governments' aid programmes still give a very low priority to supporting piped water systems, sanitation, drainage and other critical components of an improved environment for poorer groups.[120]

Many Western groups have shown considerable insensitivity, and on occasion ignorance, in their approach to global problems and their causes. Perhaps the most common example is the inaccurate linking of what is termed "over-population" in the Third World with resource depletion worldwide. In fact, Europe, North America and, more recently, Japan and the Soviet Union account for most of the world's consumption of non-renewable resources. It can also be argued that much of the problem with the changing global climate is the result of over-consumption by Europe, North America and Japan; it is their consumers and businesses which have been responsible for most of the increase in carbon dioxide concentration and ozone depleting chemicals. If strict and costly controls are now instituted worldwide, the Third World would be denied the use of many of the cheapest fuels and cheapest forms of industrial production which enabled the now rich nations to develop their prosperous and diversified economies. There were no controls on the rich nations' pollution of the global commons.

However, perhaps global concerns such as climate modification provide Third World nations with a power in global negotiations which they have never before enjoyed, except for OPEC's relatively short lived power in regard to oil prices. No doubt the West will seek to avoid negotiations with the Third World and will concentrate on individual negotiations with the largest potential contributors to climate modification. But it still remains an interesting prospect – whether Third World nations could once again raise demands for a less unequal world market and for more aid to address their most pressing environmental problems in return for joint agreement on reducing the threats to global climatic modification.

One special concern of this book has been the impact of environmental problems on the health and well being of poorer groups. This too is an aspect given perhaps inadequate attention in the West. Researchers there tend to focus too much on the presence of some pollutant or pathogen and too little on how and why these impact most severely on the health of certain groups of people. In considering environmental problems, one must consider why certain groups of people are worst affected. Poorer households' unstable and inadequate incomes and inadequate diets underlie their poor health and their low resistance to many diseases. Low incomes underlie their inability to move away from dangerous and polluted residential areas. While a lack of drains, piped water and a service to removed garbage may be the main cause of poor environmental conditions and of the high incidence of typhoid, diarrhoea, dysentery and intestinal parasites, inadequate incomes and poor quality diets can greatly increase the toll such diseases take.

Thus, Third World cities' environmental problems are wider in scope than those conventionally considered by environmental groups in the West. The housing environments of lower income groups in Third World cities must rank as among the most life threatening and unhealthy living environments that exist. When confronted with statistics such as one child in three dying before the age of five – as is the case in some of the worst-served illegal settlements – the seriousness of the problem becomes apparent. The need for more documentation, monitoring, and pressure for action, is acute, and should be encouraged by the fact that an enormous reduction in these problems is relatively easy to achieve, even with limited government investments.

The effectiveness of Third World environmental groups and citizen groups can be enhanced with support from the West. Western environmental groups have considerable experience in organizing well-targeted lobbying and publicity campaigns. Working together on the most immediate and serious environmental problems including those in cities would lay an appropriate foundation for joint action on global concerns. Only through joint actions to tackle "the environment of poverty" are the poorer citizens of the Third

World able to share First World citizens' longer term environmental concerns. Only through a redistribution of resources in their favour will they be able to do something about both.

8. The Dimensions of Urban Change

There are signs that most of the Third World will be less urbanized, and far less dominated by very large cities by the year 2000 or beyond than is predicted by most of the literature on urban development. For more than 15 years, it has been widely assumed that by the year 2000, half the world's population will be living in urban centres. For example, a book on Third World urbanization published in 1985 said that "Third World cities are growing at extremely rapid rates" and accepted without comment that half the world's population would be urban by the year 2000 and 90 per cent urban by the year 2050.[1] Another book published in 1986 talked of Third World cities "mushrooming" and stated that by 2000, not just half the world's population but almost half the Third World's population would be urban.[2] Many other authors have translated this into half the world's population living in cities by the year 2000, although the terms "urban centre" and "city" are not synonymous (see Box 8.1). This chapter will draw on the results of recent censuses from many Third World nations, and on studies of particular cities, to suggest that the pace of urban change and the form it takes differs so much from nation to nation that it cannot be described in such general terms. In addition, many nations are not urbanizing rapidly, and by the year 2000 the Third World is likely to be far less urbanized than that suggested by the two quotes given above. In addition, only a small proportion of the Third World's population is likely to live in very large cities (or "mega-cities") – even looking ahead 30 years or more.

Box 8.1: Some definitions used in this chapter

URBAN CENTRE: A concentration of people, buildings or economic activities which a government chooses to call "an urban centre". Each government has its own way of defining what it considers to be an urban centre and there are large differences between nations as to how urban centres are defined (for more information see note 6, p. 340). In this chapter, an urban centre is any settlement considered by the government as being urban, regardless of the definition that they use.

LEVEL OF URBANIZATION: The percentage of the population living in urban centres. In virtually all publications, figures for the level of urbanization in a nation are based on that nation's own definition as to what is an urban centre so strictly speaking, they are not comparable to figures for other nations.

URBANIZATION: The process by which an increasing proportion of population comes to live in urban centres. A nation which is urbanizing has an increasing proportion of its population living in urban centres – but the term 'urbanization' usually implies not only this change in the distribution of population but also the processes which cause this change which are usually a combination of economic, social and political change.

URBAN GROWTH: The growth in the population living in urban centres. This is not the same as urbanization because if the rural population and the urban population are both growing at the same rate, there is urban growth but not necessarily growth in the proportion of people living in urban centres.[3]

CITY: There is no agreed international definition as to what is a city but the term city is not understood in the same way as urban centre. As described in this chapter, many nations include as urban centres many settlements with a few hundred or a few thousand inhabitants which have many of their inhabitants working in agriculture. This does not fit with most people's idea of a "city" since the term implies a larger settlement with most of the inhabitants working in commerce, industry, services or some other non-agricultural occupation.

TOWN: We avoid using the term town in this chapter because it introduces yet another ambiguous word into the discussion; there is no agreed definition as to what is a town. A town is often understood to be an urban centre which is too small or too agriculturally based to be considered a city.

Given the number of books, newspaper articles and television programmes on exploding cities and rapid urbanization, many people
assume first that all urban centres are growing rapidly and secondly,
that rapid urbanization, evident in most Third World nations in the
last few decades, will continue. This is the conventional view and is
supported by a series of publications by the United Nations Population Division. For many years, this Division has been publishing
projections to the year 2000 on each nation's level of urbanization
and on the population of the world's largest cities; in recent years,
projections have also been given up to the year 2025. These have
suggested an ever-increasing proportion of the world's population
living in urban centres and large cities; United Nations projections
made in 1982 (and published in 1985) forecast close to 500 "million
cities" (i.e., cities with a million or more inhabitants) in the Third
World in less than 37 years compared to 119 in 1980.

The number of Third World cities with 4 million or more inhabitants is also projected to multiply several times from 22 in 1980 to
114 in 2025; by this date, more than 1.1 billion Third Worlders are
projected to live in cities with 4 million or more inhabitants, more
than six times the number in 1980.[4] According to such projections,
by the year 2010, a higher proportion of Third World inhabitants will
live in cities of this size than in the First and Second World.

A careful look at recent census data and at the causes of urban
change in different nations raises serious doubts as to the accuracy of
such projections. Before discussing these projections (and the validity of the assumption on which such projections are based), first this
chapter discusses the reliability of urban statistics and reviews urban
change in recent decades in Latin America, Asia and Africa.

The difficulties in describing urban change

The best basis for making projections about city population sizes, or
about the proportion of people who will live in urban centres in the
year 2000 or 2025, is a detailed understanding of urban change in the
past few decades and its causes. But the statistical base to accurately
describe urban change in the Third World does not exist. One problem is a lack of recent, reliable census data for many nations; for
instance, Nigeria's last reliable census was in 1963.[5] Without accurate figures for Nigeria, no accurate figures can be given for urban
trends in sub-Saharan Africa because Nigeria has around a quarter
of the region's population.

Another problem arises from the inaccuracies in international comparisons of the number (or proportion) of people in urban and rural areas. Despite the fact that so many publications have tables which list different nations' level of urbanization (i.e. the percentage of the population in urban areas), there are large differences in the ways that governments define their urban centres and these differences limit the validity of such comparisons.[6] To give one example, if the Indian government decided to adopt the urban definition used by the Peruvian government in recent censuses, India would change from being a predominantly rural nation to one of Asia's most urbanized nations.[7] This in turn would make South Asia much more urban because India's population makes up such a significant proportion of South Asia's population. Even the world's level of urbanization in the world would change significantly. If the Indian government made this change in definition, the world would move from being 41 per cent urban to around 47 per cent urban in 1985.

In fact, the usefulness of dividing any nation's population into rural and urban is diminishing. The assumption is that most of the agricultural population live and work in rural areas while most of the non-agricultural population live and work in urban areas. But most national definitions of urban areas mean that small market centres are included along with the largest cities, when the two have very little in common. In many urban centres, more than half the economically-active population work in agriculture with virtually all the rest making a living either working in agro-processing or selling goods and services to those deriving a living from agriculture.[8] Meanwhile, many examples could be cited of farmers and agricultural labourers living in urban centres and of rural-based high-technology industries and service enterprises. In addition, many rural areas have large concentrations of people working outside agriculture (see p. 241).

The fact that so many statistics are available to compare urban areas with rural areas has encouraged a lot of studies to compare rural incomes with urban incomes and the basic services available to rural and urban inhabitants. These usually show that rural inhabitants are poorer and less favoured with basic services so these help sustain a belief that governments and aid agencies must give a high priority to reducing rural-urban disparities in income and access to basic services.

But simply dividing national populations into urban and rural is a crude and often inaccurate way to identify the people most in need.

For instance, figures on infant mortality in urban areas may be lower than those for rural areas, so the assumption is made that the urban population is better-off than the rural population. But there are likely to be far more significant differences in infant mortality rates between richer and poorer urban districts within the same city or between richer and poorer rural districts. There are likely to be even more significant differences between richer and poorer income groups. Not surprisingly, a report by an Expert Group meeting to review United Nations Human Settlements statistics pointed out that within most nations, there is such diversity between different rural areas and between different urban centres that aggregate statistics for all urban centres or for all rural areas are very misleading. To identify the people most in need of government services and support, one must look in far more detail – for instance by district within rural areas and by neighbourhood within urban centres, since some rural districts will have few poor people while some urban neighbourhoods have a high proportion of poor people, even if the urban centre of which it is part is rich and well served. Then within these districts and neighbourhoods, the identification of those most in need must consider income and gender – since within districts and neighbour-hoods, it is the poorer households, and within households it is usually the women and children, whose needs government programmes most often fail to meet.[9]

Comparing the population growth rates of two urban centres can also be very misleading. Even within the same nation, if two urban centres of comparable size have comparable population growth rates, this can hardly be stated as evidence that they are experiencing comparable economic changes. For instance, the relative contribution to population growth of children born to residents minus deaths (natural increase) compared to newcomers arriving from elsewhere minus those moving away (net in-migration) may be very different. Or one of the centres may have a rapidly expanding population as a result of an inflow of refugees, or rural inhabitants because of a drought, while the other centre's growth is largely due to in-migration by people attracted by a growth in retail and service trade, which in turn was stimulated by rapid growth in production in surrounding farming areas. The contributions of wars and natural disasters to population movements (and urban growth) may be considered a special case; the movements might be assumed to be temporary. But it seems that the influence of such natural disasters on population movements is growing as governments fail to take preventitive measures in areas known to be prone to natural disasters. The impact of such disasters is so often greatly exacerbated by human actions for short term gain (for instance clear-felling of trees in a watershed) with government doing little or nothing to control this, as well as little or nothing to protect people from the consequences of such actions. In many instances, much of the population movements produced by natural disasters are permanent moves.

Accurate comparisons between two cities as to their populations requires similarities in the way in which these cities' boundaries are defined. But there are large differences in the ways that such boundaries are defined. Population figures for some cities include everyone living in a city region of several thousand square kilometres including large numbers of people living in rural areas. For other cities, population figures are just for people within an area of only 30–60 square kilometres who live in the central core of a city region defined by old city-boundaries over which the city-population has long over-spilled. In the first instance, official figures over-state the city's population since the boundary encompasses large areas of agricultural land and substantial numbers of rural inhabitants. One example of this is the figure of over 10 million inhabitants commonly cited for Shanghai urban agglomeration. This figure is actually the population in an area of over 6,000 square kilometres which includes large areas of highly productive agriculture and many villages and agricultural workers.[10]

In the second instance, the population is understated because no change has been made in a city's boundary to include new developments which have grown beyond this boundary. Take the example of Colombo in Sri Lanka whose population is often quoted in books as being around 600,000, with a comment that this is relatively small for the largest city in a nation with more than 16 million inhabitants. But these 600,000 inhabitants live in an area of 37 square kilometres. If Colombo's population was measured according to a city-region of some 1,800 square kilometres, it would be some 4 million inhabitants. If it was measured according to an urban core of 235 square kilometres, it would have a population in excess of 1.3 million inhabitants.[11] Colombo's rate of growth in recent decades also varies greatly, depending on which of these definitions is used.

Different statistics exist for the populations of virtually all large cities – based on different boundaries – but most statistics are reported with no comment as to which boundary has been used. For example, for Metropolitan Manila, in the Philippines, in 1978, there were at least eight different definitions in use by different government agencies, all of which gave different figures for the Metro Manila's population.[12] For Dhaka, Bangladesh, population statistics may refer to the historic city (5.6 square kilometres), the metropolitan area (414 square kilometres), the Statistical Metropolitan Area (1,121 square kilometres), Dhaka Sadar sub-division (1,601 square kilometres) or the District (7,459 square kilometres). A study of Metropolitan Dhaka in 1981 chose yet another boundary which differed considerably from all those mentioned above.[13] The population of Cairo is often given with no reference as to whether this is for the City (with just over 5 million inhabitants in 1976), for Metropolitan Cairo (which includes nearby Giza and a northern industrial city), or for the Greater Cairo Region which covers 29,000 square kilometres, an area larger than some independent nations – about the size of nations such as Belgium or Haiti.

What generalizations are valid for urban change?

Perhaps because it has proved possible to arrive at some generalizations about urban trends in the First World in recent decades, as nations there underwent comparable economic and demographic transformations (although during different decades), it has been assumed that comparable generalizations can be made about the Third World. It is more difficult to point to 'Third World wide' trends than it is to 'First World' trends. There is more diversity between nations in their economic structures, population growth rates, levels of per capita income and population sizes. The Third World includes many large, resource-rich and small resource-poor nations. Differences between the richer, more industrialized nations such as Brazil and South Korea and the poorer nations such as Chad or Mali or Nepal make it difficult to generalize about urban trends. It is even more difficult to generalize about future prospects for urban development 'for the Third World' when it contains dozens of nations which have little possibility of developing stable, viable economic bases and several nations which have become major industrial powers within the world market.

An understanding of urban change in the Third World needs to be built up from detailed national, regional and local studies. These studies point to the complicated mix of local, regional, national and international factors which influence population movements within each nation or region and in and out of urban centres. While many different urban centres may share a common factor which encourages or discourages migration there, its importance relative to other factors and its inter-action with other factors are unique to each urban centre. Of course, for each urban centre, both the range of factors and their relative importance changes over time. A review of population changes and their causes drawn from around 100 studies of small and intermediate urban centres in the Third World found enormous diversity both in the scale of such changes and in their causes. It also found a large number of urban centres with very slow population growth rates or declining populations which calls into question the notion of universal, rapid urban growth.[14]

Even with such diversity, it is useful to seek some generalizations which have validity beyond one particular urban centre, region or nation. It seems that four generalizations about urban processes in the Third World have some validity in recent decades. The first is that most nations experienced a far more rapid growth in urban population than in rural population which means that an increasing proportion of their national populations live in urban centres (however these urban centres are defined). The second is that in most nations, there has been an increasing concentration of population and economic activities in one or two cities, metropolitan areas or core regions; Box 8.2 gives some examples of cities which contain a high concentration of national production or trade. The third is that rapid growth in urban population and rapid growth in rural population have taken place simultaneously; only relatively recently have rural populations declined in a few Third World nations and in most, they seem likely to continue growing rapidly in the foreseeable future. The fourth is that, in aggregate, natural increase has contributed more to the growth in urban population than net rural-to-urban migration. But on this last point, as examples given later will show, for many cities and for some nations, net rural-to-urban migration has contributed more than natural increase in recent decades. And in many instances, a high proportion of migrants into cities are young people, soon to have children, while many migrants from urban to rural areas are relatively old. So a high rate of natural increase in a city's population may owe much to rapid in-migration of young, fertile people in previous years.[16]

Box 8.2: Examples of cities with high concentrations of their national industrial production, commerce or government investment

BISSAU: (Guinea Bissau): With only 14 per cent of the national population, the capital city received 39.1 per cent of total state investments between 1978 and 1980. Ever since the last decades of Portuguese domination – which ended in 1974 after a 10-year war – most of the city's population has depended on external assistance for its survival largely because it is cheaper to import foodstuffs from as far away as Pakistan than it is to transport the agricultural surplus from the south of this small West African nation.

DHAKA (Bangladesh, previously Dacca): Apart from its role as national capital, 60 per cent of all establishments surveyed by the census of manufacturing industries are located in Dhaka while 47 per cent of all manufacturing employment is also concentrated here. Jute processing and textiles, the two principal industrial groups of Bangladesh, are centred here. Dhaka has also been the major beneficiary of public sector employment. The manufacturing sector and the public sector are the two major employment generating activities; they also comprise the formal sector of Dhaka's urban economy. In the 1981 census, the city contained less than 4 per cent of the national population.

LAGOS (Nigeria): In 1978, Lagos Metropolitan area handled over 40 per cent of the nation's external trade, accounted for over 57 per cent of total value added in manufacturing and contained over 40 per cent of Nigeria's highly skilled manpower. It contains only some 5 per cent of the national population.

LIMA (Peru): The metropolitan area of Lima accounts for 43 per cent of GDP, four-fifths of bank credit and consumer goods production and for more than nine-tenths of capital goods production in Peru. In 1981, it contained around 27 per cent of the national population.

MANAGUA (Nicaragua): In 1983, Managua concentrated 25 per cent of the national population and 38 per cent of the GDP.

MANILA (Philippines): Metropolitan Manila produces one-third of the nation's GNP, handles 70 per cent of all imports, and contains 60 per cent of all manufacturing establishments.

Local governments within the metropolitan area of Manila receive one-third of all local government revenues. In 1981, it contained around 13 per cent of the national population.

MEXICO CITY (Mexico): In 1970, with 24 per cent of the national population, it contained 30 per cent of total employment in manufacturing, 28 per cent of employment in commerce, 38 per cent of employment in services, 69 per cent of employment in national government, 62 per cent of national investment in higher education and 80 per cent of research activities. In 1972, it absorbed 50.8 per cent of the national demand for industrial products and 42.5 per cent of the demand for durable consumer goods. Approximately 68 per cent of the banking capital stock and reserves are concentrated in Mexico City as well as 42 per cent of the short-term deposits and 93 per cent of the long-term deposits.

NAIROBI (Kenya): In 1975, Nairobi had 57 per cent of all Kenya's manufacturing employment and two-thirds of its industrial plants. In 1979, Nairobi contained around 5 per cent of the national population.

PORT-AU-PRINCE (Haiti): Approximately 40 per cent of the national income is produced within the capital although only 14 per cent of the national population live there. It virtually monopolizes all urban economic activities. Its primacy is buttressed by both a highly centralized political and administrative system as well as development policies geared towards the manufacturing sector which have favoured a high level of expenditures within Port-au-Prince.

RANGOON (Burma): Located at the centre of the national transport and communications network, Rangoon (now also known as Yangon) is the economic, political and administrative heart of Burma. It is the dominant tertiary service centre and virtually all the import and export trade passes through its port. More than half of Burma's manufacturing industry is said to be located there. In 1981, it contained around 6 per cent of the national population.

SAO PAULO (Brazil): Greater Sao Paulo, with around one-tenth of Brazil's national population in 1980 contributed a quarter of the net national product and over 40 per cent of Brazil's industrial value-added.

Sources: See note 15.

Although serious doubts can be raised about the validity of international comparisons for levels of urbanization, one is faced with the problem that there are no alternative statistics which give Third-World-wide coverage. Many recent censuses do contain sufficient information as to the proportion of national populations in settlements within defined ranges of population size, but as yet, they have not been used to produce a reasonably comprehensive alternative to figures based on each nation's own criteria.

Separate sections for Latin America, Asia and Africa review urban change between 1960 and the early 1980s. Comparisons of different nations' level of urbanization are avoided. However, comments are made about the change in different nations' level of urbanization between 1960 and the early 1980s since this provides some idea of the extent to which national populations are concentrating in settlements which have some urban characteristics. These should be interpreted with caution for the reasons noted already. The sections also discuss the main causes of these changes in urbanization level and highlight the differences in causes between nations and regions.

Latin America

Table 8.1 shows that in 1980, the various regions in Latin America had among the highest proportion of their populations living in cities with more than 100,000 inhabitants, and with more than 1 million inhabitants of all the Third World regions. Indeed, the southern cone of Latin America had a higher proportion of its inhabitants in such cities than the Second World and most First World regions both in 1960 and in 1980. By 1985, four metropolitan centres (Mexico City, Sao Paulo, Rio de Janeiro and Buenos Aires) had populations exceeding 10 million inhabitants and were among the world's 15 largest urban agglomerations.

Nations with the most rapid growth in their economies and in manufacturing output during the 1960s and 1970s such as Mexico, Colombia and Brazil, tended to have the largest increase in the level of urbanization. Between 1960 and 1982, the level of urbanization grew from 51 to 68 per cent in Mexico, from 45 to 69 per cent in Brazil and from 48 to 65 per cent in Colombia. However, urban growth rates in all sub-regions are declining and apart from the Caribbean, they have been doing so since the late 1940s.[17]

The three nations in the southern cone – Chile, Uruguay and Argentina – had much slower rates of urban population growth and less dramatic increases in the level of urbanization; the proportion of Argentina's population living in urban areas only grew from 74 to 83 per cent in these 22 years while that of Uruguay only grew from 80 to 84 per cent. But these three nations are unusual, not only in long being the most urbanized nations in Latin America, and among the most urbanized nations in the world; in addition, they had among the slowest growing economies and slowest growth in manufacturing output in Latin America during the 1960s and 1970s. Argentina and Chile also had a decrease in the proportion of their labour forces working in industry. In 1980, some 36 per cent of their national populations were in million cities, which was a higher proportion than in Japan, North America or West Europe. The causes are rooted in their economic and demographic histories. In Argentina and Uruguay, rapid immigration from Europe in the late nineteenth and early twentieth centuries took place at a time when the *latifundia* and poor transportation networks generally prevented immigrants moving into farming. The only exceptions were a few areas being settled for the first time, and where official colonization programmes were implemented, but these only covered a small percentage of good agricultural land. At that time, it was easier, cheaper and quicker for immigrants from Europe to travel to the east coast of South America than to the Andean nations. It was in the southern part of this coast that investments concentrated, most of them coming from overseas. Urban developments there were much stimulated by investments in industries and in infrastructure such as railways, urban services and ports; most were to serve national or international economic interests located in the largest cities. Cities such as Buenos Aires and Rosario in Argentina, Montevideo in Uruguay and Sao Paulo and Rio de Janeiro in Brazil experienced more rapid population growth in the late nineteenth and early twentieth centuries than they have in recent decades.

In most Latin American nations, over the last four decades, available statistics suggest an increasing concentration of productive activities and of urban populations in only one or two cities, metropolitan areas or core regions – although, as earlier examples suggest, for many nations this process began many decades ago.

Table 8.1: Distribution of the world's population by urban areas and by cities with over 100,000 and over 1 million inhabitants in 1960 and 1980

	Population (millions)		Population in Urban Areas[1] (per cent)		Population in Cities with 100,000+ Residents (per cent)		Population in Cities with 1 million+ Residents (per cent)	
	1960	1980	1960	1980	1960	1980	1960	1980
Third World								
Africa[2]								
Eastern Africa	76.0	136.7	18.4	28.7	2.7	8.4	0.0	3.1
Middle Africa	34.9	54.6	7.4	15.7	7.1	18.7	0.0	9.7
Northern Africa	65.1	108.2	18.2	34.4	19.9	25.0	9.7	14.6
Southern Africa	20.8	32.8	30.0	44.1	22.8	23.0	6.3	13.0
Western Africa	80.7	143.8	13.4	22.8	5.6	15.8	0.0	5.5
Latin America[2]								
Caribbean	20.4	29.5	49.3	65.3	19.1	28.8	7.1	15.6
Central America and Mexico	49.5	92.3	38.7	52.3	23.1	37.2	10.5	22.6
Tropical South America	116.1	198.0	46.1	60.7	24.7	41.5	14.3	26.2
Southern Cone of South America	30.7	42.3	72.7	82.4	46.7	54.2	32.7	35.9
Asia[2]								
China	667.3	1,002.8	20.6	26.6	11.4	11.0	6.6	7.0
Other East Asia (not including Japan)	39.7	63.0	16.8	20.3	26.1	49.1	15.9	32.1
South Asia	864.5	1,408.2	36.3	60.4	9.7	15.9	4.0	8.2
Second World								
USSR	214.3	265.5	48.8	63.2	25.6	36.2	6.0	14.0
Eastern Europe	116.7	134.9	44.5	56.3	19.5	26.4	8.0	10.4

Table 8.1: Distribution of the world's population by urban areas and by cities with over 100,000 and over 1 million inhabitants in 1960 and 1980

	Population (millions)		Population in Urban Areas[1] (per cent)		Population in Cities with 100,000+ Residents (per cent)		Population in Cities with 1 million+ Residents (per cent)	
	1960	1980	1960	1980	1960	1980	1960	1980
First World								
Western Europe	308.4	349.1	66.6	76.8	42.9	48.2	22.6	25.7
North America	198.7	251.9	69.9	73.8	49.5	56.3	28.7	34.7
Japan	94.1	116.7	62.5	76.2	30.5	45.6	21.7	27.0
Australia and New Zealand	12.7	17.9	79.8	85.8	54.8	69.1	31.7	47.0
World[3]	3,013.8	4,453.2	33.6	39.9	19.9	24.7	9.9	13.6

Notes:
1. Percentages in this column are not comparable due to use of different definitions of an urban population in each country.
2. Countries included in list of nations within each of the African, American, and Asian categories are the same as those used by the United Nations. Europe is divided into two categories: Eastern Europe (Albania, Bulgaria, Czechoslovakia, German Democratic Republic, Hungary, Poland, Romania, and Yugoslavia) and Western Europe (all other countries).
3. Columns do not add to world totals since figures have been rounded and Melanesia and Micronesia were not included.
Source: United Nations, Estimates and Projections of Urban, Rural and City Populations, 1950–2025: The 1982 Assessment (UN, New York, 1985)

Note: Figures for this table could have been presented for 1960 and 1990 rather than 1960 and 1980, which would have made them more up to date. But figures for 1990 would have been projections based on data from censuses taken in the late 1970s and early 1980s. Figures for 1980 were felt to be more appropriate and more accurate, given the authors' reservations about the assumptions which underlie the techniques for making projections of urban populations.

A high proportion of Latin America's industry is concentrated in relatively few core regions; three of the most prominent examples are the La Plata-Buenos Aires-Campana-Zarate-San Nicholas-Rosario-San Lorenzo region in Argentina, the triangle of Rio de Janeiro-Sao Paulo-Belo Horizonte in Brazil and Mexico City-Toluca-Cuernavaca-Puebla-Queretaro in Mexico. While the trend in cities has been for much of the new (or expanding) industry to be within or close to city centres, in recent years, industrial and commercial employment has grown more rapidly outside the inner cities. There are examples both of central cities growing more slowly than suburban rings (or even losing population) and of cities beyond the commuting range of the largest centres sustaining population growth rates higher than the metropolitan areas, a process termed polarization reversal.[18] For instance, in Buenos Aires, the central city (the Federal District) lost population between 1970 and 1980 while the population in the counties within the Greater Buenos Aires Metropolitan Area, but outside the Federal District, had a total population increase of 30 per cent.[19] Perhaps more significantly in the long term, Greater Buenos Aires only increased its share of the national population by 0.1 per cent during the 1970s compared to an increase of 2.0 per cent during the 1960s.[20]

Within Greater Sao Paulo, since 1940, the population outside Sao Paulo City has consistently grown more rapidly than that in the City; between 1940 and 1980, Sao Paulo City's population grew more than sixfold while the population within Greater Sao Paulo but outside the city grew more than sixteenfold.[21] During the 1970s, population growth rates in cities close to but outside Greater Sao Paulo had come to exceed that of Greater Sao Paulo itself.[22]

Comparable trends have also been apparent for many years in Mexico City's Metropolitan Zone. The Zone can be divided into three areas – a central core of 4 "delegations"; an inner periphery of 10 "delegations" and an outer periphery of 16 municipalities. The population of the central core (2.8 million in 1980) hardly grew between 1960 and 1970 and fell by over 90,000 between 1970 and 1980. The ten delegations around this core have had far more rapid population growth than the core since 1940 with a population multiplying nearly 30 fold between 1940 to 1980 to reach 6.56 million. However, from 1950, population growth was even more rapid in the municipalities in the outer periphery whose total population grew from 29,000 in 1950 to 5.1 million in 1980.[23] Furthermore, during the 1970s, various cities close by but not within

the Metropolitan Zone had more rapid population growth rates than
that of the Metropolitan Zone. It is also worth noting that between
1972 and 1981, the population growth rate of Lima-Callao in Peru
(with 4.4 million inhabitants in 1981) was among the slowest of any
urban centre in Peru with 50,000 or more inhabitants[24] although this
may be partially explained by a undercount in the 1981 census.

In terms of changes in population distribution, an examination of
migration flows within nations will reveal and clarify trends which
city population growth rates alone obscure. Latin America's large
metropolitan centres may have slower population growth rates than
many other smaller cities but some may still be the dominant centres
for receiving net rural-to-urban migration flows. This was certainly
the case for Mexico City during the 1940s and 1950s. Mexico City
attracted 49 per cent of all migrants between 1940 and 1950, which
was nine times the number received by the next largest migrant
receiving city (Guadalajara). But between 1950 and 1960, Mexico
City's share in attracting migrants for the nation was down to 42 per
cent – only three times that of Guadalajara.[25]

Cuba's pattern of urban development does not bear much relation
to that of other nations which experienced comparable rates of rapid
economic growth during the 1960s and 1970s. Since the mid 1960s, a
declining proportion of its urban population has lived in Havana, the
capital and much the largest city. The agrarian reform implemented
shortly after the revolution in 1959 removed one of the main causes
of rural to urban migration. Since then, a combination of economic
and social development outside Havana (in rural and selected urban
areas), the rationing system and a postponement of new housing and
infrastructure investments in Havana, reduced its dominance of the
national urban system.[26]

Asia

South and East Asia[27] have a lower concentration of population in
cities of 100,000 or more, or one million or more inhabitants, than
aggregate figures for Africa and Latin America. But such aggregated
statistics are heavily influenced by circumstances in China and India
which together represent more than two thirds of Third World Asia's
population. In Table 8.1, the very large differences between China
and the rest of Third World East Asia (which includes Hong Kong
and both North and South Korea) are notable in terms of the level of
population concentration in cities with 100,000 or more, or 1 million

or more, inhabitants. By 1985, Third World Asia had five of the world's largest urban agglomerations: two in China (Shanghai and Beijing), two in India (Calcutta and Bombay) and one in South Korea (Seoul). Each had more than 10 million inhabitants.[28]

Within Asia, during the 1960s and 1970s, it was richer nations with the highest economic growth rates which tended to have the largest increases in the level of urbanization. Between 1960 and 1982, the level of urbanization grew from 30 to 69 per cent in Saudi Arabia, from 43 to 70 per cent in Iraq and from 28 to 61 per cent in South Korea. In Saudi Arabia, immigration certainly contributed significantly to its population growth and perhaps part of this rapid urbanization was due to a rapid growth in the number of urban-based temporary workers.

Meanwhile, in this same period, it was the far poorer Asian nations with relatively low economic growth that generally experienced the smallest increase in their level of urbanization: Bangladesh, Nepal, Burma, India, and, (to a lesser extent) Pakistan and the Philippines. While growth in the output of manufacturing was often rapid during this period – as in the case of Bangladesh and Pakistan where the annual growth in output averaged more than 7 per cent – there was little change in the proportion of the labour force engaged in agriculture.

Urban trends in India between 1971 and 1981 illustrate how aggregate national statistics provide a poor idea of what is happening in large, populous nations. Among the 12 cities with 1 million or more inhabitants in 1981, Lucknow, Kanpur and Calcutta were probably experiencing net out-migration but Bangalore was growing rapidly.[29] A study of population growth rates (and their causes) in urban centres with 20,000 or more inhabitants in a relatively rich, urbanized region and a poor, un-urbanized region, failed to show any clear correlation between the size of urban centres and their population growth rates over eight decades.[30] In India as a whole, most of the more rapidly growing cities during the 1970s had less than 500,000 inhabitants in 1971 and were either single industry cities, centres for raw material extraction, or state capitals. Many were a long way from the most densely populated areas. However, for large metropolitan centres such as Bombay, Calcutta and Hyderabad, cities close to but outside the metropolitan area often grew more rapidly than the metropolitan centre; examples include the two major industrial centres of Asansol and Durgapur close to Calcutta, and for Bombay, Nasik, Khopoli or, further away, Aurangabad. These are not so much residential or industrial suburbs, although many enterprises there have very strong economic links with the metropolitan centres.

It may be that polarization reversal is taking place in many of India's largest urban centres. Certainly within several of India's metropolitan areas, population growth outside the central city exceeded that within the city during the 1960s and 1970s.[31] The population of Calcutta City hardly grew slowly in the period 1961–1981 and its share of the metropolitan area's population has fallen rapidly since 1951.[32] In Bombay, population in the original city grew very slowly between 1971 and 1981; population in its inner suburbs have grown far more rapidly than in the city since at least 1941, while since 1951, population growth rates in the outer suburbs have exceeded those of both the city and the inner suburbs.[33] Both Bombay and Calcutta provide examples of where the traditional concept of a city as a concentration of non-agricultural economic activities is no longer very useful. The original cities have grown into much larger urban agglomerations but more significantly, they have become part of even larger core regions which in some ways are comparable to those noted in Latin America. If population movements within core regions are analyzed, they point to a decentralization of population and economic activities. But nationally, the trend still seems to be towards centralization within core regions.

Within Asia, China stands out in terms of urban trends for it had very rapid economic growth and very rapid growth in industrial production during the 1960s and 1970s but relatively little increase in the level of urbanization. Richard Kirkby, in his study of urbanization in China, suggests that an understanding of such trends is best achieved by considering three periods in China's development since the revolution in 1949. The first is between 1949 and 1960 when there was very rapid growth in urban population, most of it from net rural to urban migration. These 11 years included both the First Five Year Plan and "The Great Leap Forward"; while having very different approaches as to the form that development should take, both shared a common purpose of accelerated industrial growth. The period 1961–76 can be characterized, in terms of urban trends, as a period of de-urbanization. A combination of forced mass resettlement and strict state control of individuals' access to jobs, housing and food provided the means. Urban population growth was also kept down by the practice of recruiting peasants to work in industry but not allowing their dependents to live with them in the city, a technique widely used by colonial governments in sub-Saharan Africa to limit urban growth in earlier decades. The third phase, between 1977 and 1982, saw a return to rapid growth in urban population, once again with net rural-to-urban migration playing a larger role than natural increase. And much of the increase in urban population has been the officially sanctioned return to urban areas of many of the millions of people removed during the previous period.[34]

The so called "Newly Industrialized Countries" in Asia – Singapore, Hong Kong, Taiwan, South Korea – would be expected to have urbanized rapidly in the period 1960–82 as their economies grew rapidly. This is certainly the case in South Korea where, as noted already, the level of urbanization grew from 28 to 61 per cent. Singapore and Hong Kong were so urbanized in 1960 that they could not urbanize rapidly after that; both have such small rural areas that they can be considered as 100 per cent urban. Taiwan did not urbanize as rapidly during this period but it was already much more urbanized than South Korea in 1960.[35]

Nations such as Indonesia, Thailand and Malaysia are notable because they had much smaller increases in the level of urbanization, despite relatively rapid economic growth. Three possible explanations can be suggested. The first is that this is due to statistical inaccuracies which hide the fact that these nations urbanized rapidly in this period. Urban populations in 1982 could be under-stated, if the government made no adjustments to the boundaries around growing urban centres, so that much of the growth in population took place outside their boundaries and did not register as growth in their population. Alternatively, new urban centres may have been left out of the figures for 1982. In recent decades, in many Third World nations, many new urban centres grew up – for instance new mining towns, tourist centres, frontier towns or centres serving areas where new land was brought into cultivation. In addition, many villages have grown to sufficient size or have been selected as a centre for local government to qualify as urban centres; if no allowance was made to add the populations of these new urban centres to those of more longstanding urban centres, this too would mean that urbanization levels were understated. One specialist suggests that close to 30 per cent of Indonesia's population would be defined as living in urban areas in 1980, rather than the official figure of 22.4 per cent, if a more realistic definition is used for Jakarta and Surabaja, the nation's largest and third largest cities.[36]

Two other possible explanations can be suggested for the relatively small change in urbanization levels of these three nations. One is that booming agriculture helped to keep the workforce in rural areas and this may have special relevance to Thailand where, between 1960 and 1982, the growth in agricultural output was very rapid and the fall in the proportion of the labour force working in agriculture was low. Another explanation could be a rapid growth in jobs and incomes in rural areas, but not in agriculture. Many studies in Asia have shown this in particular regions.[37] For instance in Kelantan, the poorest state in Malaysia, a survey of rice/paddy farming families found that 50 per cent of their income came from "off-farm" activities.[38] A study in Java, Indonesia's main island, points to highly diversified rural industries and services – "from small textile and cigarette factories to batik-making and brick-making, repair of bicycles and agricultural implements, production of coconut oil or tempe (fermented soya bean cakes) to weaving of mats and hats. Trading ... provides supplementary incomes for large numbers of rural families and the main source of income for many others. Carpenters and builders are active throughout the rural areas as are barbers, *dukuns*, midwives and other service activities of various kinds.... The rural based transport network is also very labour intensive".[39]

A paper documenting recent trends in migration flows to core regions within 46 Third World nations found that several centrally planned economies do not have the continued concentration of production and urban population that is evident in most nations with market or mixed economies, at least up to 1980.[40] The case of China's de-urbanization between 1961 and 1976 and the case of Cuba in Latin America have already been noted. In North Korea, the population in P'Yongyang Metropolitan area (the capital) has also been carefully controlled.[41] In Vietnam too, comparing the statistics for 1960 with those for 1982 suggests very slow urbanization, but this hides a complex sequence of rapid urban changes caused by wars and complicated political changes. For instance, Hanoi had grown to nearly 120,000 inhabitants by the early 1940s, then lost population during the period of guerilla fighting and French bombardment, then grew rapidly during the 1950s to reach over 900,000 by 1961, then shrank with the bombing, then grew in 1968 when the bombing stopped, then shrank when the bombing resumed in 1972. Saigon (now Ho Chi Minh City) and other urban centres in Vietnam also have complex histories over the last forty years linked to the wars and to settlement programmes and, more recently, to the government's de-urbanization programme in the south, "shifting population into the food-producing suburbs, developing small towns and planning development of the more remote New Economic Zones".[42]

Africa

Africa has long been the least urbanized of the world's continents despite a rich and varied (if poorly documented and often ill-understood) urban history which stretches back centuries in many nations and millenia in some. As in other continents, there is great diversity in levels of urbanization and urban growth trends. By 1985, according to UN estimates, no urban agglomeration had reached 10 million inhabitants although other sources suggest that by then Cairo had more than 10 million inhabitants.[43] The urban agglomeration in and around metropolitan Lagos is probably the second largest in Africa and estimates suggest more than 5 million inhabitants lived there by 1985.[44]

While, in 1980, most sub-Saharan African nations had three-quarters or more of their population still living in rural areas and most of their economically active population working in agriculture, it is in sub-Saharan Africa that some of the most spectacular examples of increases in the population of cities have been evident in the last four decades. For instance, the population of cities such as Khartoum (the Sudan), Nairobi (Kenya), Abidjan (Ivory Coast) and Dar es Salaam (Tanzania) increased more than sixfold between 1950 and the mid 1980s while that of Lagos (Nigeria) increased more than sixteenfold.[45] Estimates suggest that the population of Nouakchott (Mauritania) has increased more than fortyfold since 1965.[46] Examples of very rapid population growth in other sub-Saharan African nations' largest city could be given. For most of these, net in-migration contributed more than natural increase to their population growth in the 1950s, 1960s and 1970s – despite the fact that many sub-Saharan African nations have among the world's highest rates of natural increase.

For the 1960s and 1970s, it was not uncommon for sub-Saharan African nations to experience rapid growth in their level of urbanization and relatively slow (or no) growth in their economies. Indeed, for nations such as Chad, Zaire, Central African Republic or Ghana, economic indicators suggest little change during these two decades. But their levels of urbanization grew substantially between 1960 and 1982: from 7 to 19 per cent in Chad, from 16 to 38 per cent in Zaire;

from 23 to 37 per cent in Central African Republic and from 23 to 37 percent in Ghana. If these estimates accurately reflect what was happening in these nations, they contrast with trends in Latin America and Asia where in recent decades, a combination of slow economic change and rapid urbanization has been rare.

Part of the explanation for the rapid growth in the level of urbanization in many sub-Saharan African nations is simply that they began from relatively small urban bases in 1960. When a nation has a low level of urbanization, a relatively small proportion of rural people moving to urban centres produces a much larger increase in the level of urbanization than the same proportion moving to urban centres in an already highly urbanized nation. However, part of the explanation also lies in their political history over the last 40 years, with most making the transition to independence. When they gained political independence, most sub-Saharan African nations had very small urban populations, largely as a result of restrictions imposed by colonial powers on African's right to live in urban centres. Many had virtually no industrial base; in many this had been suppressed or discouraged under colonial rule. The newly independent nations also lacked most of the institutions which are part of a modern nation-state – national government departments and ministries, judiciaries, armed forces, city and municipal governments with the personnel and resources to meet urban needs, the professionals and technicians that a modern state needs, the universities and other higher education institutes required for their training. The capitals of what were now independent governments lacked basic infrastructure. Embassies and other institutions associated with capital cities had to be developed. Many governments gave a high priority to developing industries to lessen their dependence on imports and symbolically to rid themselves of another colonial legacy. The development of these and other aspects of independent nation-states helped underpin rapid urbanization since independence, even when national economies have not grown rapidly.

The case of Tanzania can serve as an example of the impact of lifting colonial restrictions on population movements. In 1952, 27 per cent of the inhabitants of the colonial capital, Dar es Salaam, were non-African and among the African population, there were 1.5 men to every woman. An important part of the migration from rural to urban areas during the 1950s and 1960s was the movement of women and children to join their spouses. Under colonial policies in previous decades, women and children had been strongly discouraged from living with their husbands in urban centres. Between 1951 and 1967, a period of rapid growth in urban population (with net rural-to-urban migration contributing more than natural increase), it was generally the urban centres with the highest proportion of men to women which grew most rapidly. Women made up a higher proportion of the migrants than men, as the much less imbalanced urban sex ratio in 1967 attests. By then, there were 1.2 men to every woman in Dar es Salaam. Other urban centres also experienced large reductions in the imbalance of their sex ratios.[47] We suspect that processes such as these plus the consolidation of the institutional base of independent governments, the general enthusiasm among newly independent governments for promoting import substitution industry and the low priority given to agriculture, have been the main factors behind the rapid urbanization that many sub-Saharan African nations have experienced over the last four decades.

South Africa stands out as an exception in that relatively rapid economic growth between 1960 and 1982 was accompanied by very little change in its level of urbanization. South Africa is the only Third World nation with a market or mixed economy which had relatively effective policies to control migration flows to large cities in these years. There, the apartheid system, which denies to the majority of the country's population basic economic, political and social rights on the basis of race, also denied them the right to free movement in response to, for example, the lack of employment and the poverty in predominantly rural homelands to which many have been forcibly relocated. In North Africa, the relationship between economic change and urbanization is more like that evident in Asia and Latin America. For instance, between 1970 and 1982, Algeria, Tunisia, Libya and Morocco had among the highest growth in GDP and in industrial output in Africa; they also had among the highest increases in urbanization levels.

In terms of population growth rates in different size cities, or population distribution within core regions, the data base is too poor to point to continent wide trends. It is possible that the largest cities within each nation are attracting a lower proportion of new productive investment; it is perhaps surprising to find that the two largest cities in Kenya, Nairobi and Mombasa, had the slowest population growth rates of any of the 16 urban centres with more than 20,000 inhabitants in 1979 during the last inter-censal period, 1969–79.[48] Recent reports suggest that population growth in Cairo has slowed considerably in recent years.[49] The population growth rate of one city close to metropolitan Lagos was recently estimated to have been more rapid than that of metropolitan Lagos itself.[50] But it would be unwise to consider these to be pointers to trends towards decentralization of urban development from all or even most of the cities in Africa.

The underpinnings of urban change

To understand urban change, one needs an understanding of its economic, social, physical and political causes; as noted earlier, population growth alone rarely has much impact on a nation's or region's level of urbanization.[51] While certain regularities in urban changes for certain nations or groups of nations have long been recognized, perhaps insufficient attention has been given to the differences, which are often more significant.

Today, the most important influences on urban change in Third World nations are changes in their economic and employment base. In most nations – especially those with weaker economies – population movements are essentially responses to where employment (or, on occasion, education opportunities) are concentrated. The cities and metropolitan areas listed in Box 8.1 grew rapidly because they contained such a high proportion of non-agricultural jobs, income earning opportunities and educational opportunities.

However, often, the movement of people to those cities which attract large numbers of migrants is because their survival is more certain there. We know of no rapidly growing cities with declining economies – except some cities which provide refuge for people fleeing wars or natural disasters. But here too, survival is more certain because there are international agencies helping to provide food, water, clothing, health care and some shelter. This is in sharp contrast to richer western nations where for a substantial proportion of the population, individual and household choice as to where they want to live has become an important influence on urban change.

Economic changes usually mean changes in income distribution, in the demand for different goods and services, and changes in where urban growth takes place. Economic changes never benefit all income groups equally, so income distribution changes, which in turn means changes in the mix of goods and services demanded by those with money to spend. In turn, this changes the spatial pattern of demand for goods and services as (say) one city's economy expands rapidly and brings higher incomes to a proportion of its inhabitants, while another declines. Inevitably, this is a powerful influence on urban change. The highly unequal distribution of income within many nations shows up within cities in the large contrasts between the quality of housing enjoyed by the richest and the poorest groups. Unequal income or asset distribution also shows up in national or regional urban systems. For instance, many predominantly rural Third World regions have had little or no growth in their level of urbanization in recent decades, because there has been no increase in demand for the goods or services normally supplied by urban based enterprises. Poorly-paid landless labourers or farmers with small, largely subsistence-oriented plots have little or nothing to spend.[52]

Similarly, inequitable land-owning structures or crop pricing and marketing structures can keep down such demand and minimize local urban development even in areas with highly productive commercial farming.[53] Conversely, there are a few regions where rapid growth in agricultural production and relatively equal distribution of land ownership have been the main factors in supporting rapid urban development (see pp. 274–82). A more even spread of urban centres of different sizes across the national territory of most First World nations reflects both higher average incomes and a more equal income distribution.

Changes in political structure – as in the case of nations gaining political independence or of nations where governments committed to central planning come to power – are also important influences on urban change; examples in Tanzania and Cuba have been given already. But the extent of government influence on urban change varies enormously from nation to nation and from government to government within each nation. Perhaps surprisingly, the slower growth experienced by many of the world's largest cities in recent decades seems to owe relatively little to explicit government policies to slow their growth.

In centrally planned economies, the role of government is usually more explicit. A desire to lessen regional differences in industrial development and strategic military thinking have often influenced the location of productive investment. For instance, in China, a dispersed pattern of industrial development, and initiatives to develop the interior, have been much influenced by the government's desire, until recent years, to reduce the concentration of industry on its vulnerable eastern seaboard.[54] The government of North Korea has also sought to reduce the concentration of productive activities close to its southern border for comparable reasons.[55] But even in market or mixed economies, public investments in infrastructure and services, public expenditures and incentives or controls to encourage or discourage investments in certain regions or cities are an important influence on urban change. Just as the US Government's expenditures in defence and the space programme helped underpin the redistribution of population and productive activities towards the south and west, so too comparable expenditures by the Indian Federal Government (and by the former colonial government) have helped to underpin Bangalore metropolitan centre's rapid growth.[56] South Korea, like North Korea, has sought to reduce population and industrial concentration close to the border which divides them.

What may be more significant influences on urban change (although certainly less well understood), are government's macro-economic policies, tax systems, interventions in setting prices for certain goods or services, and the distribution of power and resources between national, regional and local governments. Within many Third World nations, the spatial effects of these have helped to encourage a high concentration of productive activities in a few cities (or core regions).[57] This happens when such policies explicitly or implicitly favour the better-off inhabitants of larger urban centres and the more powerful industrial, commercial and financial interests which are also generally concentrated there. This is not urban bias since it is only certain groups in certain urban centres which benefit – most urban centres and most urban citizens receive no benefits from this bias (see p. 308).

There is also the influence of the world market on the economies of all nations. All nations have been affected by the unprecedented transformation of the world's economy and political structure over the last 150 years or so. Rapid population growth in and around Sao Paulo, Seoul or Bangkok in recent decades is intimately linked to the increasing role within world markets of enterprises located there – just as London's rapid population growth during much of the nineteenth century and, in part, its loss of population since the 1940s, is linked to the growth and then decline in the relative importance within the world market of businesses located there.

Take the example of the growing importance within the world economy of nations around the Pacific rim; this can be viewed as a region (including California and Japan) which challenges the dominance of the North Atlantic as the core of the world's economy.[58] In many Pacific nations, the form and pace of urban change is intimately tied to developments in the integrated network of production, trade, communications, and producer services which has developed there.[59] Cities such as Bangkok, Hong Kong, and Singapore serve as major centres for banking and other financial services and as administrative headquarters for multinational corporations; many other cities also have significant concentrations of offices of foreign companies. Some of these cities have developed as major centres for foreign (principally US and Japanese) investment in manufacturing or as centres for international tourism (or both). These in turn support a whole range of new service enterprises such as "financial services from banking to broking, insurance underwriting, advertising, management consultancy, real estate consultancy, legal services and executive search" as well as "all kinds of consumer oriented firms such as business hotels and retailing chains".[60]

It is hardly surprising that the cities and city-regions in Asia which have been most successful in becoming what are sometimes termed "world cities" (i.e. cities which are major centres of organization and control for world production and markets) have experienced among the most rapid and sustained economic growth. This in turn supports rapid population growth, except in Singapore where immigration is strictly controlled and where there is virtually no rural population left to migrate to the booming city region. Given the significant proportion of world production, trade and services controlled by multinationals, the urban future of many cities will be much influenced by the extent to which they can attract multinational investments and offices. This in turn has implications for the form of the city since a rapid growth in multinational investment can greatly increase prices – perhaps most notably land-prices – which in turn greatly increase housing problems.[61]

Certain governments have insulated their economies from world market forces; examples include the Chinese government for much of the 1950s, 1960s and early part of the 1970s, or the Burmese Government in recent decades. Groups or blocs of nations have also sought to do so – for instance COMECON (especially during the 1950s) or, in the West, the EEC (particularly in the case of agriculture). But no economy is completely impervious. With the present debt crisis facing so many nations, the changes in government spending and social orientation which many are obliged to make will have a critical impact on urban change. So too will a continuing trend towards protectionism in the First World; a Third

World city whose economic growth has been dependent on exports will have its economic structure and population growth rate considerably influenced if the market for enterprises located there is suddenly restricted. The decline in the availability of concessional multilateral aid may inhibit the construction or improvement of infrastructure to support urban development in many Third World nations. These are given as examples to show the complexity of the mix of factors which underpin urban change within any nation or region.

The urban future?

Urban change may be too sensitive to economic, social, political and physical change to justify predictions more than one or two decades into the future. Certainly, many examples can be cited to caution against long-range projections based on extrapolating past trends into the future. Extrapolating trends in urban population growth in China from 1949 to 1960 to give a guide as to what would happen in the next 40 years would make China's population 100 per cent urban before the year 2000, and could hardly provide a useful indicator of future trends after 1960, since the proportion of China's population in urban areas declined between 1961 and 1976.[62] Extrapolating population growth in Sao Paulo from its growth from 48,000 inhabitants in 1886 to 484,000 in 1916 would have given it a population of some 48 million in 1976,[63] more than three times its actual population by that date. Less than 14 years ago, specialists projected that Calcutta would have 40–50 million inhabitants by the year 2000.[64] The projection was based on extrapolating Calcutta's rapid population growth for the 1930s, 1940s and 1950s far into the future. Such rapid rates of growth in these decades were largely due to an influx of refugees from what was formerly East Pakistan (now Bangladesh) after the partition of India in 1947[65] and to population figures for 1941 being exaggerated for political reasons.[66] The most recent projections made by Calcutta's Metropolitan Development Authority suggest a population of 14.7 million by 2001 in the metropolitan district; this district covers 1,450 square kilometres and includes not only Calcutta urban agglomeration but also outlying rural areas.[67]

The projections for a Calcutta of 40–50 million people by the year 2000 were made with no consideration as to the economic or political changes needed to make Calcutta grow to this size. These were considered by other authors from that period; for instance a study of Calcutta published in 1974 pointed to a whole series of reasons why Calcutta would not continue to grow rapidly: the damage to its economy from the loss of its industries' main markets, and its major source of raw materials and food, when the partition of India removed its main hinterland to become a separate state of East Pakistan (later Bangladesh); the image of the city as the centre of British capital which meant it was not favoured by independent governments; and the political differences since independence between most federal governments and the state governments, which ruled in West Bengal, within which Calcutta is located.[68]

These may seem extreme examples to use in questioning the value of future projections – but United Nations projections published in 1980 for cities such as Dar es Salaam (Tanzania), Nairobi (Kenya) and various Nigerian cities seem just as unreal. Even someone with a relatively unsophisticated knowledge of Tanzania's economy and potential for urban development would find it hard to imagine sufficient economic change to sustain a city of 4.6 million people in Dar es Salaam by the year 2000.[69] The obvious question is – on what will they live and how will they be fed? People will not move to Dar es Salaam if there is no chance of an income or of food. For comparable reasons, suggestions that Nairobi will grow from under one million inhabitants to 18.9 million inhabitants between 1980 and 2025, as projected by the United Nations in 1982, must be treated with a measure of disbelief. This would mean that in less than 40 years, Nairobi would have three times the population currently living in Greater London.

There is also a certain measure of unreality in the fact that projections some 40 years in the future can be made for cities for which there has been no reliable population data for more than 20 years. Population projections for the year 2025 are confidently given for certain Nigerian cities like Lagos or Ado Ekiti when there has been no reliable census in Nigeria since 1963. Ado Ekiti, a relatively unknown Nigerian city even appears as the worlds twenty-fifth largest urban agglomeration in projections for 2025, with 15.4 million inhabitants in UN estimates published in 1982. A few years earlier, another relatively unimportant Nigerian city (Jos) had been listed as the twenty-fifth largest city in the world by the year 2000.[70]

Towards new forecasting techniques?

A parallel can be drawn between current techniques for forecasting cities' future populations and techniques used for forecasting energy demand in the early 1970s. At that time, it was assumed that energy demand in the West would simply continue to rise in line with past trends, just as urban trends in the immediate past are still assumed to be a guide to urban change in the future. The 1973 oil price rise led to energy demand forecasts being revised downwards a bit, but there was no fundamental change in the way forecasts were made.

Forecasts for future urban and city growth in the Third World may be at this stage now, with projections made 5, 10 or 15 years ago being scaled down, because of the recession. Successive United Nations reports in the last 15 years have generally given lower figures for the projected population for the year 2000. Table 8.2 lists the eight largest Third World urban agglomerations in the year 2000 according to the 1973–5 assessment of the United Nations Population Division, and how the projections for the year 2000 have changed in subsequent assessments.

Table 8.2: Examples of changing projections for city populations by the year 2000 (Figures in millions of inhabitants)

Urban *Agglomerations*	*UN projections for populations in the year 2000 from*				
	1973–5	*1978*	*1980*	*1982*	*1984–5*
Mexico City	31.6	31.0	27.6	26.3	25.8
Sao Paulo	26.0	25.8	21.5	24.0	24.0
Calcutta	19.7	16.4	15.9	16.6	16.5
Rio de Janeiro	19.4	19.0	14.2	13.3	13.3
Shanghai	19.2	23.7	25.9	13.5	14.3
Bombay	19.1	16.8	16.3	16.0	16.0
Peking/Beijing	19.1	20.9	22.8	10.8	11.2
Seoul	18.7	13.7	13.7	13.5	13.8

Source: See note 71.

Mexico City's projected population for 2000 was 31.6 million in the Population Division's 1973–5 assessment, but down to 25.8 million in the 1984–5 assessment. Projections for the population of Rio de Janeiro by 2000 were 19.4 million in the 1973–5 assessment and only 13.3 million in the 1984–5 assessment. Perhaps more significantly, the 1984–5 assessment no longer talks of a world population being half urban by the year 2000 but of more than 50 per cent of the world's population "projected to live in urban areas" before 2010. The date when half the Third World's population becomes urban is put off until 2016.

Although the techniques used by the United Nations Population Division to make projections have changed – for instance to reflect the fact that the rate at which a nation urbanizes is likely to slow as its population becomes increasingly urban – there is still an assumption that urbanization will continue and that large urban centres will continue to grow. Even some of the most recent UN projections seem questionable, especially for sub-Saharan Africa. For instance, Maputo in Mozambique is projected to have a population of 2.7 million by the year 2000; in the 1980 census it had some 740,000. Given long standing problems of economic destabilization and disruption from the South African-backed guerillas and the enormous economic hardships facing the nation, it is difficult to imagine how Maputo's economy could develop to the point to allow its population to more than triple between 1980 and 2000. Only through massive camps for displaced persons developing in Maputo as a result of war and famine could such a prediction be realized.

Similarly, UN projections may understate the future growth of certain cities which substantially increase their role in the world economy within the next two or three decades. For instance, certain South-East Asian cities may continue to grow very rapidly, if this region remains one of the most dynamic parts of the world economy. But even here, the rapid growth of cities is not certain since many of the new or expanding enterprises may locate outside the main city or metropolitan area – so again, core regions consolidate while populations within them decentralize.

To return to the comparison with projecting energy demand into the future; it needed rigorous studies of the economic and social changes which would underpin changes in energy demand to show that past trends were not a reliable guide to future demand. Projecting past trends, even making some adjustments, does not take into account the economic and social changes which underpin changes in energy demand. In most Western nations, there is a very slow growth in population, a slow growth in the number of households, a declining importance for energy intensive industries and a growing importance for economic activities, with very low energy inputs per unit of value added. Clearly such factors have a major influence of how energy demand changes. If realistic projections for Third World cities' populations are to be produced, then these too must be based on comparable understandings of social and economic change for each city and nation and not on a set of equations applied in the same way to all nations.

Specialists looking at urban change in the West may have stronger grounds for claiming that there are urban trends which are comparable between nations and comparable factors under-pinning such trends. Recent censuses there suggest urban change is best character-ized as counter-urbanization in many nations or regions, and thus in the opposite direction to the steady progression to megalopolis which little more than ten years ago was widely projected as the urban future. The fact that there are comparable trends in terms of population redistribution at regional level within metropolitan centres and between metropolitan centres, non-metropolitan centres and rural areas gives more scope for a study as to whether comparable factors underlie such trends.

There may also be the beginnings of some counter-urbanization in certain Third World regions. If this is so, some will be in the richest, most urbanized areas, with economic structures and levels of wealth which do compare to those in Western nations also experiencing counter-urbanization. But there may also be counter-urbanization in many poorer nations or regions of the Third World for very different reasons. In some cities in the poorer nations or nations facing serious economic decline, counter-urbanization may be taking place because of people moving from cities to rural areas to improve their chances of obtaining sufficient food to survive. This is hardly comparable to the First World where counter-urbanization reflects the ability of people to live or work in rural areas but maintain ways of life which are more urban than rural, due largely to enormous advances in transport and communications technology, and higher incomes.

The real danger of the UN making projections far into the future of urban and city populations is their widespread mis-use and mis-interpretation. When a UN Population Division publication pro-duced in 1980 suggests a Mexico City with 31 million inhabitants by 2000, it makes explicit the assumptions on which this projec-tion is made. When UN figures are quoted by other sources, these qualifications are rarely repeated and what was a projection becomes a certainty. This figure of 31 million inhabitants is still quoted in books published in 1986, despite three revisions published since 1980 which give lower projections.[72] United Nations projections have been widely used by other institutions to focus governments' attention on city population growth as the problem. But this is misleading. First, enormous numbers of urban centres have not grown rapidly and yet have major problems with regard to poverty and environmental degradation. Second, most of the really serious problems of poverty, very poor housing conditions and environmental destruction in and around major cities need not have arisen if per capita incomes were higher and more equally distributed, and if city governments had the power, resources and personnel to cope with rapid growth. The evidence presented in this and in previous chapters suggests that the issue of how fast or slow a city is growing is of secondary importance.

Three other issues are of central importance. The first is whether economic change is increasing the proportion of people with adequate livelihoods. The second is whether government agencies at national, regional and local level are increasing the proportion of people protected against preventable diseases who also have access to safe and sufficient supplies of water, secure housing, education, health care and (where needed) provision for the hygienic disposal of household and human wastes. The third is whether governments are raising the funds needed to protect the environment and to provide basic infastructure and services from the individuals, companies and corporations who derive most benefits from the city and its population. In most cities, it is the evident failure or limited achievement of most governments on the second issue of social provision and the third issue of recapturing costs which is far more to blame for city-problems than the rate at which cities have grown. This has far more to do with inappropriate institutional and legal structures at national, city and local government level (in many countries a hang-over from colonial rule) and the low priority these have received from both governments and aid agencies.

Peter Hall has suggested an alternative to the vision of the urban future dominated by large cities. He suggests that there is a general model for urban growth and change which can be applied to nations, as their urban systems go from those dominated by a primate city, through decentralization of urban development away from city cores to suburban rings, and finally to urban growth concentrating in non-metropolitan areas.[73] Thus, in time, regions or nations in the Third World will also arrive at counter-urbanization. This almost implies that Third World governments need not worry about the growth of their largest cities since in time urban developments will become decentralized. This model receives some support from recent changes which have become apparent in or close to some of the Third World's largest urban centres, as described earlier.

But this model assumes that economic, social and political changes in all Third World nations will be comparable to those apparent in much of the West. For these are the underlying causes of urban change. But there are two reasons which make Peter Hall's vision of the future as unlikely as that of the United Nations. The first is the enormous diversity within the Third World; a common model for urban change will only be apparent if nations experience similar patterns of economic, social and political change, and this is impossible. As more research on urban change and its causes is undertaken by groups within each Third World city, we suspect that this will show an ever greater diversity in the rate of urban growth and the form it takes. The second is the fact that there are so many Third World nations which, without a major modification to the world economic system, have no hope of developing prosperous and stable economic bases. As such, they can hardly be expected to develop along an urban model which depends on very large capital investments, major economic changes and a very considerable level of prosperity. Most of their citizens are never likely to have the luxury of being able to choose where to live, based on anything but a search for an adequate economic base for their lives.

Thus, there is a need to go beyond broad and often inaccurate generalizations about urban change in the Third World. New classifications other than rural and urban are needed in analyses of the form, content and spatial distribution of non-agricultural population and production.[74] The concept that there is urban bias in development expenditures must be tested on a nation by nation basis; certainly in many nations, it is not evident that poorer groups in large cities or smaller urban centres are benefiting more than the rural poor. In urban issues, studies of urban change must build from the bottom up, from detailed city and sub-city studies.

At present, there are relatively few mega-cities of 5 million or more inhabitants in the Third World. In 1990, they are likely to house less than 5 per cent of the Third World's population with less than 2.5 per cent in agglomerations of 10 million or more inhabitants, although verification of this will have to await the results of the censuses taken in the late 1980s and early 1990s. If our concern is to improve the performance of governments and aid agencies in providing basic services, in reducing poverty and in controlling environmental degradation, the priority is to know to whom special attention should be paid; the question of where they live is dependent on this. To do this, more attention must be given to understanding the "what", "how" and "why" of change within individual cities and nations, and perhaps rather less to overviews of change in the Third World, like this chapter.

Postscript – the ruralization of cities?

Research undertaken by Third World based researchers and non-government research groups has long pointed to complex processes at work within particular cities which do not conform to the Western idea of a city. For instance, a recent study by the Mazingira Institute (a Kenyan NGO), pointed to the importance for most households in Nairobi of food they grow or produce themselves; under such circumstances, access to land on which crops can be grown and some livestock raised becomes of great importance to most households.[75] This is hardly a conventional view of a nation's capital city. In Lusaka, Zambia's capital and largest city, more than half of all households in some low income areas grew a proportion of their own food, either on plots next to their shelters or on plots elsewhere cultivated during the rainy season; for many families in Lusaka, the food they grow themselves provides a vital food supplement, although insufficient information is available to gauge its importance.[76] In Dar es Salaam, the largest city in Tanzania, many families grow a significant proportion of their own food on plots within the city and/or cultivate larger plots in rural areas; again the scale of such activities and their contribution to the food supplies of different income groups is not known. Discussions with researchers from other African and Asian cities suggest that we may be underestimating the proportion of people in other cities who depend on food they grow themselves, within or outside the city, or on complex reciprocal arrangements with extended families or friends who have access to cultivable land. If an assured, adequate diet now demands access to cultivable land or some non-monetary transaction for a substantial proportion of city dwellers in Africa (and perhaps elsewhere), this has major implications for the urban future. It means urban forms very different to Western concepts of urban development. It also implies constraints on the development of large urban agglomerations. Richard Stren writes of the "ruralization" of African cities:

... as African cities continue to grow under conditions of economic stagnation, or even absolute deterioration, they take on more of the qualities of their rural hinterlands. Some of the evidence for this ... includes the increasing importance of urban agriculture, the weakening of effective land-use controls and the more diverse utilization of urban space, the spread of "spontaneous" settlements and of petty commodity production, the deterioration of formerly high standards of urban infrastructure and services and the maintenance (perhaps even the strengthening) of rural economic links and regional cultural identities on the part of the urban migrants. As the institutions of urban management respond – albeit haltingly and incrementally – to the inevitability of these profound changes, the special qualities of the African city become institutionalized and its distance from the colonial past becomes more pronounced. In the years ahead, a primary task for African researchers will be to study both the changes themselves, and the adaptation of formal institutions to the new reality.[77]

9. Outside the Large Cities

Most books, articles and research reports about urban issues in the Third World are about capital cities or large cities. Most of the concern expressed about urban problems is for large cities.

However, only a small proportion of the Third World's population live in large cities. Most live in rural areas, and the latest UN projections suggest that it will be 2016 before there are more urban than rural dwellers in the Third World.[1] In fact, far more people depend on what we term small and intermediate urban centres than on large cities for shops, markets and services. Either they live in small and intermediate sized urban centres, or they live in rural areas but use these urban centres' shops, markets and services.

This chapter will consider the importance of small and intermediate urban centres both for their inhabitants and for their surrounding rural populations. It will discuss the proportion of people living in them and how and why they developed. It will also discuss how governments can best devise a special programme for such centres and the links that must be forged with rural and agricultural development. The biases against smaller urban centres in government's macro-economic and pricing policies will also be described as will the costs of improving basic service provision. So too will the possible role of small and intermediate urban centres in helping to control the growth of large cities. First, we will consider how to distinguish a "small and intermediate urban centre" from a "large urban centre".

The problem of definition

The simplest way to define small, intermediate and large urban centres would be by population size. All urban centres with more than 250,000 inhabitants could be considered large while all those with 20,000 to 250,000 would be intermediate and those with less than 20,000 (but still considered urban by their government) would be small. However, this introduces certain problems. A city of 250,000 inhabitants may be a large urban centre in one nation, but a relatively small urban centre in another. For instance, Port Moresby is the capital and much the largest city in Papua New Guinea, so it could not be a small or intermediate urban centre within its national context. The same is true for Kathmandu in Nepal, also with less than 250,000 inhabitants, but also the capital and the largest city. In nations such as India, Pakistan, Brazil or Mexico, many urban centres are much bigger than Port Moresby or Kathmandu but cannot be regarded as large urban centres within their national context. Our interest in small or intermediate urban centres is in understanding their function within their national economies and societies. This is also the main interest of governments wanting to develop policies for such centres. Thus, small and intermediate urban centres are best defined in ways which are appropriate to their own national context. Although much of the literature on small and intermediate urban centres gives standard definitions used in all nations, we think that this is misleading.

A further problem with defining urban centres according to their populations is that an urban centre's population does not tell one much about the urban centre itself. Two urban centres with (say) around 40,000 inhabitants can have completely different economic bases; one a booming and rapidly growing urban centre, with a lot of heavy industry, which is developing close to a major metropolitan centre, the other an isolated administrative centre in a poor, predominantly rural region.

In this chapter, the term small and intermediate urban centre will be used to include all urban centres except national capitals and other urban centres which have concentrations of economic activities which are of national importance. This rather loose definition is chosen deliberately, in order to stress the importance of considering urban centres within their national context.

Background

Table 9.1 gives examples of the proportions of national populations and national urban populations living in small and intermediate urban centres. It shows how a lot of urban citizens do not live in large cities – even if the trend in most nations has been towards such increased concentration, at least until recent years.[2] India provides an interesting example. When referring to India's urban problems, it is almost always urban problems in Calcutta and Bombay which are described. But these two cities contain little more than 10 per cent of India's urban population. Even taking India's twelve largest urban centres each with more than a million inhabitants, in 1981 these contained only one-quarter of India's total urban population. In 1981, Havana (Cuba's capital) contained just 30 per cent of Cuba's urban population. In 1985, Colombia's capital (Bogota) contained only 20 per cent of its urban population while Bogota plus the next three largest urban centres contained just 43 per cent of total urban population. These and other examples in table 9.1 suggest that there is a very large urban population which lives outside large cities.

Table 9.1: Proportions of national and urban population in small and intermediate urban centres

country	% of national population		% of urban population	
	small and intermediate urban centres	large urban centres	small and intermediate urban centres	large urban centres
Kenya (1979)	7.5	7.7	49.5	50.5
The Sudan (1973)	12.3	5.3	69.0	30.1
Tanzania (1978)	8.7	4.6	65.9	34.0
India (1981)	16.8	5.8	75.5	24.5
Pakistan (1981)	17.4	10.9	61.5	38.5
Colombia (1985)	40.5	30.7	56.9	43.1
Cuba (1981)	46.3	19.8	70.0	30.0
Ecuador (1982)	23.7	25.6	47.9	52.0

Note: Cross-country comparisons are invalid since the choice as to which urban centres are large is made within the urban context for each country.[3]

The uniqueness of each centre

Governments and aid agencies have become more interested in small and intermediate urban centres. This is usually because they hope that these centres will take some of the pressure off the large cities. There are many special government programmes for small and intermediate urban centres: their success will depend largely on whether they help develop untapped potential or under-utilized resources within these centres. There is no point in encouraging the development of tourism or industry in urban centres which have little potential to attract either.

It is not easy to identify the urban centres with potential and ascertain the government actions needed to release this potential. Each urban centre is unique – so a government programme to develop one urban centre may be totally inappropriate for others. Historical studies show the extremely diverse reasons for the development of different urban centres.

Many urban centres first developed because they were chosen as centres for provincial or state government, or centres of military control. Others developed because new businesses developed there, linked to prosperous commercial agriculture nearby, or to the demand for goods and services generated by those earning an income in agriculture. Some urban centres developed as road or rail transport centres; others because they became the constituency of a prominent politician who steered public investments and public enterprises there; and others because enterprises there successfully exploited one specialized niche in a regional, national or international market – for instance tourism, mining or timber. Others developed because they were located close to a metropolitan centre and became favoured locations for new industrial, commercial or recreational enterprises linked to that metropolitan centre. Some developed because their location was judged to be the right place to develop defence industries. Some examples of the factors underlying the development of different urban centres are given in Box 9.1. Ismailia in Egypt would not have developed into an urban centre of more than 200,000 inhabitants if the Suez Canal had not been built. The concentration of industry in Rae Bareli in India owes more to the fact that it was in the parliamentary constituency of the late Mrs Gandhi when she was Prime Minister than it does to any inherent advantage the urban centre offers to industries. Pereira's development was much helped by the expenditures and investments of prosperous farmers living nearby. Owerri would be far smaller and less prominent if it had not been chosen as capital of a new state in 1976.

The histories of different small and intermediate urban centres reveal the complex mix of local and regional factors – and often national and international factors – which influence their development. There

Box 9.1: Examples of influences on the development of some urban centres

ISMAILIA (Egypt): With around 175,000 inhabitants in 1975, it had been established some 100 years earlier as the headquarters for the Suez Canal Authorities when Egypt was under British rule. The Suez Canal Authority remains the largest employer while small scale shipbuilding, light manufacturing and service industries also provide employment.

OWERRI (Imo State, southeast Nigeria): with some 9,331 inhabitants in 1953 and 90,000 in the late 1970s, the modern urban centre dates from 1901 when the colonial (British) government established a small military/administrative headquarters there. Much of its early development related to the location of public services and facilities – a native court, government station, barracks, prison, school. It became a provincial headquarters in 1914 but was bypassed by the railway; other urban centres nearby developed stronger economic bases. The residency and consulate of the Province moved to Port Harcourt in 1927. But with the creation of Imo State in 1976, many civil servants, professionals and traders came to Owerri since it was chosen as the new state capital. It became the centre for numerous state and Federal government departments, parastatal organizations and corporations.

PEREIRA (Colombia): With 328,000 inhabitants in 1985, it was founded by a group of entrepreneurs in the mid-19th century in what was then an inhospitable jungle. At that time, forests in the region around it were being cleared by thousands of settlers and with rich volcanic soil, cocoa, sugar cane and coffee became the dominant crops. As coffee became the dominant export of Colombia, the region around Pereira grew rich. Pereira shared this prosperity with booming commerce as local businesses re-invested their profits in such industries as textiles, clothing, electrical equipment and agro-industry. A further boost to its development was its choice as capital of a newly designated province in the mid-1960s. These and the fact that it was on the crossroads for the highways linking the region to Colombia's three largest urban centres explain its growth to become the region's largest urban centre. In 1951, it had 76,262 inhabitants, but by 1985 there were 328,000, including nearly 96,000 in Dos Quebradas, a separate municipality which developed next to Pereira, across the Otun river.

RAE BARELI (India): With over 90,000 inhabitants by 1981, this has become an important industrial centre and a commercial and service centre for its region. It owed its early development to selection as a district headquarters and a centre for the colonial army under British rule in the mid-nineteenth century. It was a station on one of the earlier railway lines. But it remained a relatively poor, small urban centre, reflecting the poverty of most farmers in its region. With just under 17,000 inhabitants in 1901, it grew very slowly and still had under 30,000 inhabitants by 1961. But during the 1970s, it attracted some large government-owned industries which meant an unprecedented expansion and diversification of its economy. The main reason why government-owned industries set up there was that it was the main urban centre within the parliamentary constituency of the late Mrs Gandhi, who at that time was the Prime Minister of India.

Sources: Forbes Davidson, "Ismailia: from masterplan to implementation", *Third World Planning Review*, vol. 3, no. 2, May 1981; Geoffrey I. Nwaka, "Owerri, development of a Nigerian state capital", *Third World Planning Review*, vol. 2, no. 2, Autumn 1980; Julio D. Davila, "City profile: Pereira-Dos Quebradas" in *Cities*, vol. 5, no. 1, February 1988; Harikesh Misra, "Rae Bareli, Sultanpur and Pratapgarh Districts, Uttar Pradesh", Jorge E. Hardoy and David Satterthwaite (eds), *Small and Intermediate Urban Centres: Their Role in Regional and National Development in the Third World*, Hodder and Stoughton (UK) and Westview Press (USA) 1986.

are examples of small settlements which suddenly develop into relatively important centres. Puerto Stroessner in Paraguay provides a good example. Its growth was initially boosted by being a service centre and labour camp for the construction of the Itiapu dam, and of a bridge linking it to Brazil. It has developed to serve newly settled farmers and is a major market centre. It has rapidly become the nation's second largest urban centre and much of its recent growth is due to the free flow of goods from Brazil and Argentina into Paraguay and the sale of goods imported illegally from Europe, Japan and North America.

However, in regions with long histories of settled population and of commercial agriculture, urban centres usually have long histories.

For example, India has always been a predominantly rural nation and yet most of its urban centres have long histories. While India's urban population increased more than 500 per cent between 1901 and 1981, the number of urban centres increased by only 77 per cent; since very few urban centres decline to the point where they lose their status as urban centres, this suggests that most existing urban centres in India were also urban centres in 1901.[4] In fact, in many regions of India, a very high proportion of urban centres are centuries old.[5]

In most nations, there is often a surprising degree of similarity between a list of today's urban centres and a list of administrative centres founded many decades or even centuries ago; Box 9.2 give some examples.

Box 9.2: Similarities between contemporary urban centres and old administrative centres

LATIN AMERICA: Most national and provincial capitals were founded under colonial rule – including all ten of today's largest cities/metropolitan centres, all of which were founded by the year 1580 (Mexico City, Sao Paulo, Rio de Janeiro, Buenos Aires, Bogota, Lima, Santiago, Caracas, Guadalajara, Monterrey). All national capitals in the 20 Latin American nations and in Jamaica and Trinidad and Tobago are colonial foundations with the exception of the capital of Brazil. Thirteen were founded in the sixteenth century (although Mexico City had an indigenous precedent), two in the seventeenth century, five in the eighteenth century and one in the twentieth century. With two exceptions (Brasilia and Quito), they are their nations' largest urban centres. All national capitals which were founded during the colonial period were important administrative centres under colonial rule as sites of viceroyalties (Mexico City, Lima, Buenos Aires and Bogota) in the sixteenth to the eighteenth century and/or sites of regional legal courts (*audiencias*) and headquarters of universities.

NORTH AFRICA: The basic outline of current urban patterns was established during the colonial period. The colonial extractive economies, which were well established in the nineteenth century, tended to concentrate urban development in port cities – reviving old ports like Algiers, Tunis and Alexandria, and creating new ones like Casablanca, Ismailia and Port Said. The urban centres that developed in the interior were essentially centres for military control, or served the mining of a resource or gradually expanding European agriculture.

EAST AFRICA: Virtually every urban centre which had 20,000 or more inhabitants by the mid-1970s had been an established colonial administrative station by 1910. The size, location and distribution of urban centres in East Africa today is almost entirely the product of British and German decision-making prior to the First World War. In Tanzania, 17 of the 18 urban centres with 20,000 or more inhabitants were originally colonial townships; 12 of them were on the railway lines developed under colonial rule to transport cash crops to ports for export.

INDIA: In three districts in Karnataka state which have urbanized rapidly in the last 70 years (Bangalore, Mysore and Mandya), nearly all urban centres had been the administrative centres set up by the British colonial government in the mid-nineteenth century. The two most important administrative centres established by the British at that time are much the largest urban centres today. In three districts in Uttar Pradesh state which have not urbanized rapidly (Rae Bareli, Sultanpur and Pratapgarh), the three largest urban centres today were the only military cantonments, the only district headquarters and the first municipalities under colonial rule in the nineteenth century. Most other urban centres are also sub-district headquarters designated as such in the nineteenth century.

Sources: Janet Abu-Lughod, "Urbanization in North Africa" in B.L.J. Berry (ed.), *Patterns of Urbanization and Counter-urbanization*, Sage Publications, 1975; Jorge E. Hardoy, "Two thousand years of Latin American urbanization" in Jorge E. Hardoy (ed.), *Urbanization in Latin America: Approaches and Issues*, Anchor Books, New York, 1975; H.N. Misra "Rae Bareli, Sultanpur and Pratapgarh Districts" and B.S. Bhooshan, "Bangalore, Mysore and Mandya Districts" in Jorge E. Hardoy and David Satterthwaite (eds), *Small and Intermediate Urban Centres: Their Role in Regional and National Development in the Third World*, Hodder and Stoughton (UK), Westview (USA), 1986.

Of course, there are many new urban centres in regions being settled for the first time. Many regions have been settled in the last 40–50

years which were previously either uninhabited or sparsely populated; the search for new farmland and pasture, timber and minerals
has usually been the reason. Many governments have sponsored such
colonizations, but there is usually an additional spontaneous and
uncontrolled colonization movement which may be larger than official programmes. Examples of settlement in previously uninhabited
or sparsely inhabited regions are evident in the eastern regions of
Peru, Bolivia and Ecuador, in Amazonia and in southern Nepal (in
the Terai region), and in many parts of Indonesia and Malaysia.
Some of the most rapidly growing cities over the last 30–40 years
are those which grew as administrative, service or processing centres
in these newly settled areas.

Although so much of the literature on Third World cities talks
about rapid urban growth, in fact a considerable proportion of the
Third World's urban centres are not growing rapidly; many have
hardly grown at all in recent decades and some have actually had
declining populations. A growth in employment opportunities (or
the possibilities for survival) usually fuels the growth of an urban
centre.[6] A stagnating or declining economy will usually mean slower
population growth or even no growth or population decline. Urban
centres in any region or nation can be likened to businesses and each
of them competes with each other for investments and expenditures.
Their economic growth (and their population growth) is linked to
their success or failure in this competition. The literature on urban
centres in the Third World concentrates too much on the ones which
grow rapidly.

There are hundreds of urban centres which have stagnated with
little or no population growth or even population decline in the last
40 years. There are also dozens of urban centres which were once
cities of great importance in their nation but then declined as other
urban centres grew more rapidly; Box 9.3 gives some examples.

**Box 9.3: Examples of cities whose importance in their
national economies has declined**

NORTH AFRICA: Many of the great historical cities of the
Islamic period (ninth–fifteenth century) were inland, reflect-

ing the importance of land trading routes – Meknes, Fez, Tlemcen, Constantine, Kairouan, Marrakesh being examples. These generally had little role in the colonial economies, which were largely based on mineral and agricultural export. Such illustrious cities as Tlemcen, Kairouan and Fez found their economic bases of handicraft production and trade systematically undermined by the new commercial firms in the ports which grew to serve the colonial economy. Certain cities in sub-Saharan Africa such as Timbuktu and Kano also had greater importance within their region in previous centuries; both these cities were important centres of Islamic culture, with strong trade links with cities in North Africa.

BRAZIL: Under Portuguese colonial rule, in the sixteenth and seventeenth centuries, urban centres developed to serve the sugar plantations producing for export in the north-east. By 1600, Salvador/Bahia was the most important and prosperous urban centre and the national (colonial) capital. With Brazil's economy firmly based on the export of sugar, cotton, hides, and fine woods from the north-east, Sao Paulo, today Brazil's largest city, was only a small frontier town. The gradual decline in the European sugar market during the second half of the seventeenth century shifted the economic centre south. Rio de Janeiro grew as the port serving the gold mines in what is now Minas Gerais state and it became the national capital in 1762. As gold deposits became exhausted, coffee exports became the main commerical activity and the coffee boom helped develop the urban economy in the south-east with the expansion of railroads increasing the importance of certain centres, notably Santos (a major port), and Sao Paulo.

HAMADAN (IRAN): Hamadan, with around 150,000 inhabitants in 1978, became famous as one of the cities on the silk route during the eleventh and twelfth centuries, but collapsed when invading armies over-ran it in the early thirteenth century. Its role as a major commercial centre was restored in the second half of the nineteenth century with the flow of goods between Britain and British controlled India through Baghdad, Hamadan and Tehran. It has long been famous as a centre for leather goods and carpets. But as Iran became an independent nation-state with its economy based on oil export and industrial development, so Hamadan lost its role as an important transport and manufacturing centre. It was by-passed by the new inter-regional rail and road systems built during the 1930s and 1940s. By 1976, its role as a sub-national administrative centre (it became a provincial capital in 1966), and a centre for public services, had become more important than its traditional commercial and manufacturing activities.

POTOSI (BOLIVIA): Around 1640, Potosi was the largest city in both North and South America with some 140,000 inhabitants, and its rich silver deposits were a symbol of wealth around the world. During its peak years, silver mining there stimulated the economies in other regions, with mule raising in central Argentina (the mules were crucial for transporting minerals and people and they were sold in the markets of Tucuman and Salta), mercury (quicksilver) production in Huancavelica (Peru), wines from Central Chile and Western Argentina, and food from the lower and warmer valleys around Sucre and Cochabamba (Bolivia). Potosi was never an important religious, administrative or educational centre but was an important stop on the old land route connecting Lima-Callao (Peru) with Buenos Aires (Argentina) via Huamanga (Ayacucho), Cusco, Puno, La Paz, Oruro and Potosi and then Jujuy, Salta, Tucuman, Cordoba and Buenos Aires. As silver became increasingly difficult, and more costly, to mine, Potosi's population declined. So too did the regional economies it had stimulated. It experienced a brief revival in the late eighteenth century with the advent of improved imported extraction technologies, but then it declined to 26,000 inhabitants in 1854 and 21,000 in 1900. Today it has around 45,000 inhabitants, and mining is still the main economic base.

Sources: Janet Abu-Lughod, "Urbanization in North Africa" in B.L.J. Berry (ed.), *Patterns of Urbanization and Counter-urbanization*, Sage Publications, 1975; Jorge E. Hardoy, "Two thousand years of Latin American urbanization" in Jorge E. Hardoy (ed.), *Urbanization in Latin America: Approaches and Issues*, Anchor Books, New York, 1975; and Hiromasa Kano, "City development and occupational change in Iran: a case study of Hamadan", *The Developing Economies*, vol. 16, no. 3, September 1978.

Many inaccurate generalizations have been made about 'urban centres' or specifically about 'small and intermediate urban centres'. Several authors have generalized about the social and economic functions of small and intermediate urban centres. Drawing on these, advice is then given to governments on how to develop special programmes for these centres.[7]

Urban centres are so diverse that few generalizations are accurate. Some do have enormous untapped economic potential while others have little or no potential. The potential sometimes has little to do with the size of the urban centre. And an urban centre's potential can change; for instance, when coffee prices are high in the world market, many urban centres in coffee growing areas have more potential to expand and diversify than if coffee prices are low.

There are hundreds of industrial estates in small and intermediate urban centres around the Third World which lie empty or only partially-used; these estates were often built at great expense. They were built without careful evaluations of the potential of each centre to attract and sustain industrial development. There are dozens of factories in small urban centres – located or pushed there by governments trying to decentralize – which have either closed down or are currently producing very expensive goods, because the location was chosen for political reasons. Developing tourist facilities in small urban centres now seems more common than developing industrial estates. In this, the public sector usually has less role since most hotels, shops and service-enterprises come from private investments. But significant public sector investment may take place in the infrastructure and services that tourist resorts need – roads, drains, sewers, water supplies, telephones, electricity. Some of the fastest growing small urban centres in Latin America are ones where tourism has developed rapidly, for instance Pinamar and Villa Gessell in Argentina, Salinas in Ecuador, Viña del Mar in Chile and Cancun, Zihuatanejo and Puerto Vallarta in Mexico. Government investments to support tourism and government incentives to encourage private investment in tourist resorts must also be based on careful evaluations of the real potential of each centre to attract expenditures from tourists. Small urban centres can be tourist attractions but with little benefit to the local economy if tourists simply visit an old church or some other attraction and spend little or no money there. A lot of tourism is also seasonal with all the problems this can bring for local people who only find employment for the tourist season.

Certain authors have also claimed that generalizations can be made about the rates at which small or intermediate urban centres grow.[8] But this too does not stand up to detailed examination. An analysis of population growth rates for small and intermediate urban centres for two or more inter-census periods in Mexico, Peru, Ecuador, Tanzania, the Sudan, Kenya, Colombia and Pakistan and for several inter-census periods in regions in Argentina, North and South India and the Sudan found no valid generalizations either for such centres within nations or for international comparisons.

In conclusion, many small and intermediate urban centres had comparable historical roles under colonial rule and often under post-colonial rule as administrative or military centres. Many such centres have strong links with commercial agriculture. Many have considerable potential to develop larger and more diversified economies. But the extent of such common influences and their importance relative to other influences varies enormously. If governments want to develop these urban centres, they must design policies which meet each urban centre's own unique needs and potentials. Each urban centre will have its own resources, development potential, skills, constraints and links with its surrounds and with the wider regional and national economies.

The role of local government

If the possibilities and constraints on development are so specific to each urban centre (and region), this implies the need for local input in designing any nation-wide or region-wide government programme for small and intermediate urban centres. Without local input, how can the government understand local needs, make best use of local resources, and tackle local constraints?

Local input implies the need for decentralization of power and resources. If assessments of development possibilities are unique to each centre, it is local governments, (mostly located in small and intermediate urban centres), not national governments based in the capital, which should articulate local needs and influence resource allocations at higher levels. This is a fundamental part of participatory government. Only through representative local governments is such an articulation of local needs likely to take place. No national ministry or agency can know the specific needs of each locality and the preferences of its population.

To return to an issue first raised in Chapter 2, local assessments of available skills and resources and the monitoring of changes over time require strong, competent and representative local government. This is probably the most essential element of a national programme for small and intermediate urban centres and it brings with it many developmental advantages. As a review of the experiences with decentralization noted,

> A ministry of agriculture that applies crop production quotas to all areas of the country without taking regional variations in soil and climate conditions into account . . . hinders production and wastes resources. When central planners design rural development projects in the national capital without thoroughly understanding local social, economic, physical and organization conditions, they often generate opposition among local groups or encounter such apathy that the projects are doomed to failure at the outset. Overworked and cautious central finance officers, who typically are responsible for approving even petty expenditures for local development projects, often release funds for agricultural projects so late in the fiscal year that optimal planting times are missed. Central administrators cannot know the complex variety of factors that affects the success of projects in local communities throughout the country. In their attempt to cope with this uncertainty, they create highly centralized and standardized procedures; or through fear of making mistakes, they do nothing about urgent decisions that are essential for implementing local projects and programs.[9]

Competent and representative local governments can mobilize local resources more effectively than higher levels of government. But they are more likely to do so if they receive a share of this rather than simply acting as tax or revenue collectors for higher levels of government.

Building a stronger and more effective local government demands the reversal of policies apparent in many nations in the last 20–30 years. It must reverse the tendency for national government to impose severe limits on local government's revenue raising powers and to take for itself the more lucrative and easily collected taxes. And, as stated by United Nations recommendations on small and intermediate urban centres, it also demands a clear definition of the constitutional and legal status of local governments (which is often still lacking) and the establishment of clear lines of authority and responsibility.[10] As suggested in the current debate in Latin America on decentralization and democratization, this also implies a more representative local government with the ability to generate considerable concensus on local development initiatives.[11]

Again, there are no general recipes on how to increase local government revenues. The fact that the employment base and economic trends can differ greatly even for urban centres within the same region suggests a need for considerable flexibility, as national governments revise their definition of the activities local governments can use to generate revenue. For instance, a small urban centre with a prosperous (and growing) agricultural market could use market fees or bus-park charges to raise funds to improve services and facilities in the market. A centre with a developing tourist trade could utilize a "bed tax" for hostels, hotels and boarding houses. Local taxes on beer, liquor and tobacco have proved important sources of revenue in many instances[12] and have the additional advantage of raising prices for goods whose over-consumption produces serious health problems. Broad-based sales taxes can provide substantial revenues for local governments, but few national governments allow their use[13]; however, care must be taken not to tax basic commodities since this would fall very heavily on poorer groups. A property tax can fit much better both with ability to pay and extent to which public infrastructure and services are used. While relatively complex to collect, it has the advantage that many local governments already have the power to use it and already derive some income from it. Support from national government may be needed to increase the tax-yield, not least because local property-owners will oppose this. Cadastral surveys and tax assessments are often out-of-date and the revenues collected are far below potential yields. Up-to-date cadastral surveys also help in physical and land-use planning.

It is not only local governments which deserve support from higher levels of government. In many nations, local associations or co-operatives can implement certain development initiatives. For example, an association or co-operative of farmers might become responsible for local road or bridge upkeep, or electricity supply, while local parents and teachers associations might help raise funds to maintain the school and supply it with books or equipment. Perhaps the possibility of government support for such groups has been given too little consideration – especially where local government is particularly weak. It is usually a short-term measure; richer governments often try to exploit private groups like parent teachers associations by demanding that they meet certain costs formerly met by government. But it may provide a valuable stop-gap.

Thus, one of the main justifications for a government programme on small and intermediate urban centres is not related to these urban centres in themselves. It is about how local levels of government can respond to local needs and the ways in which these needs can be met. It is also about mobilizing local resources for national and regional development. To achieve this requires a long-term programme by national government to help build institutional capacity, revenue base and skilled personnel at local level. Clearly, this must be backed by better censuses and surveys to provide the information for local development plans so these are more geared to local needs, resources and potentials than the "standard packages" for all smaller urban centres so often proposed and implemented by national governments.

Given the scarcity of resources and the time needed to build stronger and more competent local governments, national governments could try out innovative approaches in selected urban centres and their surrounds. This can allow their effectiveness to be assessed before a commitment is made to a national programme. One possibility could be for local government to offer financial incentives and technical assistance to community or neighbourhood organizations in undertaking work to upgrade their own settlements.

National government might also support local government schemes to generate employment in slack agricultural periods of the year. Public works with substantial long-term paybacks, but which are unattractive for private investors, could be especially important. For instance, activities such as rural feeder-road construction or maintenance, bus-park surfacing or maintenance, reforestation plus watershed management, installation of water pipes, construction or maintenance of flood control or irrigation channels all can provide seasonal employment and much needed income supplements to many lower income households. Important social and economic benefits could be achieved at relatively low costs.

In most instances, national government will have to work out revenue-sharing arrangements with local governments. One relatively simple way to transfer resources from central to local levels is an annual block grant to each small or intermediate urban centre (or each local government area) based, perhaps, on population size and an assessment of need. The use to which the grant is put would be decided locally (within broad guidelines) for projects relating to social and economic development. This has been done for many years in Indonesia, although we have never found an evaluation of the programme and the extent to which local populations felt that their needs were being addressed.

Pools of skilled personnel and specialized equipment could be shared by groups of local governments or local associations; this could lower the cost to each of purchasing and maintaining equipment and paying professional salaries. Groups of local governments could also share accountants, engineers and road construction equipment. Governments in smaller urban centres can also borrow equipment or seek professional advice from governments in larger urban centres nearby; there are examples where this has been done.[14]

Such suggestions are of central importance to the promotion of social and economic development within and around small and intermediate urban centres. They are also of central importance in increasing the attraction of such centres to productive investment. As Johannes Linn notes:

> The quality of management by the urban authorities may have an
> important effect on whether and how a city grows. . . Among the
> elements of urban management at issue here are: the provision
> of adequate public utilities for industry and commerce; the exist-
> ence of a well functioning urban transport system for the speedy
> distribution of goods and services; availability of developed
> land for new industrial developments; adequate public marketing
> facilities, both wholesale and retail; a good communications
> system (telephones and postal); and a public administration that
> minimises efficiency losses and compliance costs for regulations
> and taxes.[15]

The links between agricultural and urban development

Few governments appear to appreciate that productive, intensive agriculture can support both a prosperous rural population and rapid growth and diversification in the economies of small and intermediate urban centres. Increases in the value of agricultural production can go hand in hand with rising prosperity for most of the local population and rapid urban development within or close to the main farming areas (see Box 9.4). This increase in agricultural production can also go hand in hand with rapid impoverishment for most of the local population so many move out of the area to fuel the growth of large cities (see Box 9.5).

Box 9.4: Positive links between agriculture, rural and urban development

The Upper Valley of Rio Negro and Neuquen in Argentina is a 700 square kilometre fertile river-valley, where the total population has grown from around 5,000 inhabitants in 1900 to over 300,000 in 1981. Although growth and diversification of agricultural production have been the main engine of growth, more than 80 per cent of the Upper Valley's population live in urban centres with 5,000 or more inhabitants.

One hundred years ago, the first colonists had just begun to grow crops; the establishment of a military fort there in 1879 provided the nucleus for the first town and provided much of the demand for food and fodder. But the Upper Valley's prosperity began to grow when a railway linked it to Buenos Aires in 1899 and gave local farmers access both to the national and the international market, and when government investment in a dam and flood control/irrigation system encouraged intensive agriculture.

For the first quarter of the twentieth century, there was very rapid in-migration to the region, including many immigrants. Initially, alfalfa was the main crop but this was gradually replaced by fruit trees – especially apples and pears. The land-owning structure was relatively equitable; most of the land came to be farmed by farm-owners with sufficient capital to invest in intensive production. Relatively small farms producing a good income were the norm.

The growing number of prosperous farmers provided a considerable stimulus to local urban development. Despite its small area of only 700 square kilometres, no single, dominant urban centre emerged. A chain of urban centres developed around railway stations, running along the river valley. Each had shops and businesses selling to farmers in their immediate vicinity, while they shared specialized businesses and government offices which served the whole valley's population.

Growing agricultural production also stimulated many urban-based enterprises. First, cold storage plants were built. As fruit crops usually ripen within a relatively short period of time, this brings enormous demands on the transport system over a small portion of the year. Cold storage plants allowed the packaging and transporting of fruit to be spread over a longer period. In addition, industries developed to produce packing material and boxes for the fruit and to produce cider, apple juice, jams, and dried or tinned fruits. Industries also grew to support the farmers including a large agricultural chemicals factory and a factory producing machines for preparing land and picking fruit.

In 1957, the two national territories in which the Upper Valley was located became provinces. This meant a considerable increase in the power and resources available to the provincial government, and one of the Upper Valley's urban centres was a provincial capital. This in turn also stimulated and supported urban development as the administrative machinery grew to cope with its increased responsibility – although this stimulus was largely confined to the provincial capital.

In recent years, the Upper Valley has experienced economic problems. Perhaps the most notable was in the second half of the 1970s, when the economic management of the (then) military government made the Argentine currency strong against the currencies of countries which bought Argentine farm exports, and thus greatly reduced farmers' returns. But the Valley does illustrate how rapid growth in agricultural production can be accompanied by rapid growth in employment linked to agriculture, and rapid growth in urban population.

Source: Mabel Manzanal and Cesar A. Vapnarsky, "The development of the Upper Valley of Rio Negro and its Periphery within the Comahue Region, Argentina" in Jorge E. Hardoy and David Satterthwaite (eds), *Small and Intermediate Urban Centres; Their Role in National and Regional Development in the Third World*, Hodder and Stoughton (UK) and Westview Press (USA) 1986.

At least four factors are critical in determining the balance between the extremes of prosperity and impoverishment, and the extent to which growing agricultural production helps stimulate urban development within the same area: the structure of land ownership, the type of crop or livestock raised, the use to which profits are put, and government's policy on the price of crops.

For example, if there are many farmers making a good living by intensive farming on relatively small farms (as in Box 9.4) with relatively equitable land ownership, this provides a very strong stimulus to local urban centres, as businesses there meet these farmers' needs. If a few farmers or absentee landowners own most of the land and there is a rural labour surplus (which is usually the case), then land owners can keep wages very low for agricultural labourers. This lessens these labourers' level of consumption and thus level of support for local shops and services. This is the case in many plantations where agricultural production is highly profitable for the owners yet relatively few local people receive reasonable incomes and there is little support for businesses in urban centres nearby. Large landowners may increasingly push small, subsistence farmers off their land as in the case in Box 9.5.

Box 9.5: Growth in agricultural production, rural poverty and out-migration: the case of Cruz Das Almas

In Cruz das Almas, in the Reconcavo de Bahia region of north-east Brazil, most farmers cultivate cassava (the main subsistence food crop) and citrus fruits or tobacco as cash crops for sale. Small amounts of other food crops are grown for family consumption.

Traditionally, farmers choose their mix of crops to match the availability of family labour; hiring labour is too expensive for small farmers. Those with the smallest holdings usually grow tobacco; although low prices from an exploitative marketing system ensure a low return for the work put into cultivating it, tobacco produced the highest income per hectare – which is more important than the highest return on labour, if you only have a small plot. On small holdings with free family labour, maximizing income-per-hectare guides the choice of crop mix. But it is common for one or more members of the family to migrate to a city, as family size grows too large for the farm's income. Cash sent to those on the farm from family members in cities is important for many households. But as family members do move away from the farm, so too the mix of crops is adjusted as less family labour is available.

The government encouraged citrus production in the region and, supported by favourable prices, this has grown at the expense of cassava and tobacco production. But citrus production requires less labour and more capital than cassava and tobacco. As citrus cultivation expands, the demand for labour declines and small farms are absorbed by larger farms. This has meant a sharp increase in migration out of the area. Between 1960 and 1975, there was a rapid drop in the number of tenants and sharecroppers which suggests that these were forced out as part of the process of land concentration.

In this instance, government policies to encourage a growth in agricultural production encouraged increasing concentration of land-ownership and increasing migration out of the area, most of it to large cities. In effect, such policies have encouraged an increase in wealth for a few and impoverishment for many. The example shows how government policies to stimulate agricultural development may increase rather than decrease people's migration to cities – although the stated objective of many agricultural development policies is to slow such migration.

Source: William S. Saint and William D. Goldsmith, "Cropping systems, structural change and rural-urban migration in Brazil", *World Development*, vol. 8 (1980), pp. 259–272.

Many studies of the impact of the Green Revolution in rural areas in Asia, and of the development of commercial farming in Latin America, have shown that increasing agricultural production and productivity can mean impoverishment for many rural dwellers. Inequitable land owning structures are usually the principal cause.

The type of crop or animal raised also influences the number of jobs and the incomes they generate. The amount of labour needed per hectare of land can vary by a factor of 100 or more for different agricultural products raised under different circumstances. At one extreme, pastoralists may need 100–200 hectares or more of land per person to generate enough income to survive. At the other extreme, an intensively cultivated farm of only one or two hectares provides a reasonable living for entire families in many parts of the world.[16] There are also cases of families surviving on what they produce on land holdings as small as one-tenth of a hectare.[17]

Cattle ranching in Uruguay illustrates how extensive agricultural production and inequitable land ownership can minimize employment generation in rural areas and small market towns. The concentration on cattle ranching for export in the late nineteenth and early twentieth century is one reason why Uruguay is among the world's most urbanized nations, with so much of its urban population concentrated in the national capital, Montevideo. Cattle ranching often goes with an inequitable land owning structure since it produces good returns on capital but very low returns per hectare. In Uruguay, a combination of cattle ranching and an inequitable land owning structures meant that only a tiny proportion of the rural population earned a good living.

Cattle ranching requires far less labour than crop cultivation; one family with one or two agricultural workers can look after cattle on several thousand hectares. Rather than having one or two households making a good income from agriculture every 5–10 hectares (as intensive crop production) there are one or two households making a very high income every 500–1000 hectares. This means little stimulus for small urban centres, since there are too few rural dwellers nearby with incomes to spend, save or invest in such urban centres' shops and services. And businesses in these urban centres also receive little of the business from rich cattle ranchers who usually deal directly with banks, export houses and industrial and transport enterprises in Montevideo. Shops and firms in small urban centres close to the cattle ranches cannot provide the range of goods and services that the relatively few, rich families want.[18] Farming in the Upper Valley (Box 9.4) was completely different because lots of small, relatively well-off farmers bought goods and services from local enterprises and stimulated local urban development.

Intensive crop cultivation may also bring considerable potential for the development of agro-industries within certain smaller urban centres. As noted in Box 9.4, the development of apple and pear production in the Upper Valley of the Rio Negro stimulated the development of industries producing packing material and boxes for the fruit and also the production of cider, apple juice, jams and dried and tinned fruits. The development of such industries also meant the development of infrastructure and services that industries need and this in turn helped attract other industries to the region which were not linked to local agricultural production.

Another example of the influence of land-owning structure and crop-type is provided by the north-east of Brazil. The north-east has long been a region associated with great poverty (especially in rural areas, many of which are prone to regular droughts). The flight of poor people from this region has done much to fuel the rapid growth of large cities in the south-east of Brazil and the settlement of Amazonia. But the root cause of poverty in the north-east is not a lack of land. A World Bank study shows that there are nearly a million farms or sharecropped plots in the north-east which provide an acceptable standard of living for farmers. This states that there are also "nearly 30 million hectares of under-utilized land of similar if not superior quality on the estates" on which "nearly another million families could achieve comparable living standards".[19] Most of this land is unused or under-utilized land but it is the property of large landowners; just 4 per cent of landowners own more than half the agricultural land and only one in four families dependent on agriculture owns the land they work.

If this land was transferred to those with no land or too little land, this would provide adequate incomes for perhaps another million families. The smallest farmers in the region

> employ 25 times more labour per hectare on their land than do the largest farms and obtain vastly higher productivity levels. The smaller farms (less than 50 hectares) cover only 10 per cent of the agricultural land, produce over 25 per cent of the region's sugar, cotton and rice and 40 per cent of the beans, corn and manioc. Yet two million agriculturally dependent families own no land at all while an area of land the size of France is un- or under-utilized.[20]

Once again, this shows the importance of agricultural land-owning structures to small and intermediate urban centres. If unutilized and under-utilized land was transferred to those lacking land with farm sizes sufficient to allow a good living, this would bring a major stimulus not only to agricultural production (which would help feed city populations) but also to small urban centres.

Ironically, the north-east of Brazil has one of the longest-running and best known government initiatives to develop a backward area. During the 1960s and early 1970s, special incentives attracted hundreds of new factories to the north-east while many existing factories expanded their operations. But this did little or nothing for the rural poor. Most of the new jobs were in the largest cities within the richest states. One analysis of this programme (and other government programmes that had preceded it) suggested that groups outside the north-east were always the main beneficiaries, and those that did benefit within the north-east were not among the poor and did not need government help.[21] The cost to government of steering industry into this region was also enormous – the equivalent of US$15,000 for every job created.[22] Consider what might have been achieved if this same sum was spent on purchasing unutilized and under-utilized land and allocating it to those with no land or inadequate land. Indeed, such a programme would probably have proved far cheaper, as those who received the land paid back part of the cost as their farms began to generate a good income.

The stimulus from a growth in agricultural production to local urban centres can also be removed by profits being steered elsewhere. This might simply be the result of absentee land-owners or foreign owners of cash crop plantations. One example was the vast Gezira scheme developed by the Anglo-Egyptian condominium government in the Sudan, to produce good quality cotton for Lancashire Mills and to lessen the cost to the British government of maintaining the colonial government. Between 1925 and 1950, the company managing the scheme and the government received good returns. But the tenant farmers received a very low return for the crops they produced and so had little or no income to spend. This meant little stimulus for trade, commerce and industry in local urban centres.[23]

The potential stimulus from agricultural production to local urban centres can also be removed by government influence on prices for crops. A study of agricultural pricing in Thailand, Egypt, Argentina and Pakistan found that government intervention in setting prices for crops had the effect of taxing farmers and transfering income to urban areas.[24] In Pakistan, low urban food prices have helped maintain low wages in industry which, combined with low prices paid for cotton and other raw materials, helped maintain export industries' competitive position in the world market.[25] Studies in the late 1970s showed that farmers in many sub-Saharan African nations were receiving less than half the world market value of their crops from government crop purchasing agencies. For example, one of the main reasons for the rapid decline in cocoa production in Ghana was the heavy tax imposed on farmers by the government through the Cocoa Marketing Board's pricing policies; obviously this too has an impact on rural incomes and thus on the development of urban centres in or close to the cocoa growing areas.[26]

Ironically, most of the advice given to Third World governments on how to develop their smaller urban centres (so often by Western consultants) says little or nothing about the influence of different types of crop- and land-owning structures on these centres. Indeed, many consultants see the problem of backward regions stemming from a lack of small urban centres. Their solution is the creation of "articulated hierarchies" of settlements (including small urban centres). But this is muddling cause and effect. Small urban centres with buoyant economies develop because there are sufficient people and businesses, with incomes to spend and capital to invest in their shops and businesses. If government builds some small urban centres because no such centres exist in a backward region, this does not provide these urban centres' shops and businesses with customers. As United Nations Recommendations on this subject commented,

> there is no obvious economic or social rationale behind the often recommended policy for governments to create an articulated hierarchy of small and intermediate centres in backward areas.[27]

Creating or imposing an articulated hierarchy of urban centres does little or nothing to deal with the most fundamental causes of poverty and lack of development in so many regions – poor or depleted soil, inequitable land-owning structures (including perhaps many absentee land-owners) or lack of investment in flood control, irrigation and other essential infrastructure. If governments can support growing agricultural production, intensification and diversification and full use of good quality land, while at the same time preventing inequitable land ownership structures, and encouraging the development of agro-industries to increase the value of local produce, where viable, they will do far more to stimulate the economies of many small urban centres than any explicit policy for these centres.

Social and spatial biases in government priorities

Virtually every government policy, action or expenditure has some influence on the spatial distribution of investments and jobs – and through this on the spatial distribution of population (both rural and urban). Some of the most powerful influences on the spatial distribution of investments and jobs come from government policies which have no explicit urban or rural goals – for example, policies aimed at reducing deficits in balance of payments or at keeping inflation in check. Many "non-spatial" policies such as macro-economic and pricing policies, transport tariffs and taxation systems, and factors such as the relative strength of national, sub-national and local levels of government, are important influences on which urban centres develop rapidly and which do not. It is important to understand how these influence the spatial distribution of jobs and investments because of the conflict between non-spatial and spatial policies. It may be that a government's economic and fiscal policies are indirectly a major cause of the rapid growth of the capital city yet at the same time, another ministry or department in the government is trying to slow this rapid growth.

The extent to which government policies and actions can help concentrate population in capital cities is illustrated by the case of Lima in Peru (Box 9.6). With 4.4 million inhabitants in its metropolitan area in 1981, it was ten times the size of Peru's next largest city, Arequipa.

Box 9.6: Capital city bias: the case of Lima, Peru

Lima has received a disproportionately high share of infrastructure and public investments, a response to the more vocal political pressures in the capital and greater awareness of the extent of public service lags in Lima than elsewhere. Utilities such as water and domestic electricity have been subsidized more heavily in Lima. In an attempt to rationalize the invasion of land by squatters seeking to build their own housing, the government has supplied free lots in many peripheral areas to migrant households; mortgage finance has been heavily subsidized with most of the loans made in Lima. Until very recently, gasoline was priced far below the world price, again benefiting Lima because two-thirds of the country's motor vehicles are concentrated there. Food prices have also been subsidized, shifting the internal terms of trade against the rural areas and resulting in heavy government support for the food import bills for urban consumers. The persistent over-valuation of the currency harmed the agricultural areas and natural resource regions (i.e. the periphery) by eroding their export potential and subsidizing the main focus of import demand, Lima itself.

Source: Harry W. Richardson, "Planning strategies and policies for Metropolitan Lima", *Third World Planning Review*, vol. 6, no. 2, May 1984.

Governments' import substitution policies have often helped concentrate industries in large cities. Many governments supported the development of industries in their own nations to substitute for goods previously imported. This usually has had the effect of subsidizing industrial investment in the largest cities. One reason for the growth of many of Latin America's largest cities (also now among the world's largest cities) was the support given by governments to import substitution after 1930. In Brazil, the states of Sao Paulo and Rio de Janeiro (with Brazil's two largest metropolitan centres) have benefited most from government incentives to promote import substitution while some of the poorest, most rural states benefited least.[28] In Nigeria, in recent decades, indirect subsidies from national trade policies have favoured enterprises in Lagos (with more than 5 million people in the conurbation) and the region around it.[29] In Thailand, it is enterprises in Bangkok, much the largest city, which have received the benefit of import substitution policies. By the end of the 1960s, protected industries were given full duty exemption on capital goods and raw materials, most of this protected industry being located in Bangkok.[30]

For countries which export agricultural crops, the exchange rate of their national currency against those of nations to which they export affects farmers' incomes. An over-valued national currency (perhaps kept that way by the Ministry of Finance to cheapen imports) reduces returns for farmers producing export crops. One reason for rural-urban migration in Nigeria during the 1970s was the fact that oil exports kept the exchange rate of the Nigerian naira high against the currencies of nations which had previously been major markets for its agricultural exports. This led to extremely unattractive prices for export crops and lowered the costs of imports, including imported basic foodstuffs. Rural incomes suffered and so too did the economies of small and intermediate urban centres which had served as markets and centres for goods and services for the rural population. Some urban consumers benefited.[31] Similarly, the fact that during the second half of the 1970s, the Argentine peso became increasingly strong against the US dollar and the currencies of other nations to which Argentina exported, seriously affected the income of farmers producing export crops.[32]

A study of spatial development in Mexico[33] illustrates how various government policies helped ensure that Mexico City Metropolitan Area remained the main focus for rural-urban migration throughout the 1950s and 1960s. The Federal District (the central part of the metropolitan area) received the highest share of public investment in transport, water and power, a "disproportionately large share"[34] of total outlays on education and subsidies for water, corn, electric power, diesel fuel and public transport. Furthermore, railroad freight rates "were structured to favour routes to and from Mexico City" while property in the Federal District "was relatively undervalued for tax purposes and other states were taxed at relatively high rates".[35] Mexico City or the wider metropolitan area also received many of the new industries encouraged by the Federal Government's import substitution policy.

Thus, many government policies and expenditures whose objectives are social, economic or political have strong spatial effects. Many have helped to cause very rapid growth rates in the largest city (or cities) in recent decades. Changes to these policies could help promote the development of small and intermediate urban centres. As Andrew Hamer stresses, "eliminating sectoral distortions may do more for decentralized development than all the myriad spatial efforts conventionally proposed by Third World policy makers".[36]

However, the fact that social or economic policies do have strong spatial influences is not in itself the issue; the issue is whether such spatial influences are judged to contribute to, or work against, other social and economic goals. If governments want to stimulate urban development away from their large cities, they must include considerations as to how non-spatial policies contribute to, or conflict with, this goal.

Basic service provision

Government expenditures on low cost housing, urban infrastructure and services have usually been concentrated in the largest city or in a few large urban centres – although in recent years, several governments have steered more investment to smaller urban centres.[37] Many such initiatives have been partially funded by international aid agencies and these have also been concentrated in the largest cities, even if in recent years certain aid agencies have consciously sought to fund more projects in small and intermediate urban centres.[38] Certainly, only a small proportion of the inhabitants of small and intermediate urban centres have water piped to their house and provision for the hygienic removal of household and human wastes. In most nations, only a small proportion of houses are served by paved roads and storm drains. Few of the neighbourhoods within small and intermediate urban centres have within them first aid posts, dispensaries or other services to provide their inhabitants with primary health care. Most small urban centres have very inadequate or no public provision for emergency life saving services.

Public provision for water supply and for the removal of household and human wastes does not necessarily cost more in small urban centres, compared to large urban centres. This was highlighted in the recommendations given to governments by the United Nations:

> The economies of scale in providing such physical services as
> protected water supplies and hygienic disposal of household
> and human wastes have been much over-stated in development
> literature. If the appropriate technology is chosen, and a suitable
> organization is set up for operation and maintenance, per capita
> costs in small and intermediate urban centres can be lower than
> in large urban centres. Many options are available to match
> the wide range of physical conditions, social preferences and
> economic resources found in different settlements.[39]

In regard to public transport, governments have perhaps under-estimated the extent to which appropriately designed and managed systems can be largely self-financing. But with these and other public services and facilities, the possibilities for improvement largely depend on a level of skilled personnel and resources at local government level which is rarely apparent.

There is also the need to improve service provision to rural inhabitants, and small and intermediate urban centres are the best locations for many services. For governments intent on reaching a higher proportion of rural citizens with health care, health education and preventive health coverage, and more options for education and training, an increase in services and facilities within many small and intermediate urban centres will be needed. While primary health care units often need to be located in villages, small or intermediate urban centres will usually be the best location for hospitals (where health problems which health care units cannot deal with are referred to) and for co-ordinating and managing local schools and health care centres. Similarly, primary schools for rural citizens may be best located in rural settlements, but as education at secondary and higher levels expand, many of the schools and colleges will be best located in small and intermediate urban centres.

In education, there is an evident need to lessen the centralization of school curricula. School programmes are often uniform for entire nations; rarely do they make allowances for local and regional needs and resources. Skill-training appropriate to local development possibilities is even rarer. As Max Neef notes, vocational training, as traditionally practiced in most countries of Latin America

> discriminates in the sense that it tends to benefit the large metropolitan areas more than the small cities, towns and villages. Furthermore . . . the orientation and content of any vocational training curricula has to be determined by – and adapted to – regional and local characteristics, and not by the extrapolation of national and global trends.[40]

One example of an alternative approach is provided by the Tiradentes project in Brazil. This was based on locally-articulated needs and local skills and resources. Tiradentes municipality has some 10,000 inhabitants, divided into two urban districts and a rural area of poor soils. In recent decades, its economy stagnated after a period of splendour when gold was mined nearby. The Tiradentes project sought to build on old traditions of craft skills and to allow the older generation, skilled in crafts, to pass on their knowledge to younger apprentices. The project had many other aspects such as the preparation of an exhibition on 100 years of photographs of Tiradentes, and the formation of a Guild of the Artisans. The relevance of this project to other urban centres is not so much in what was done but on how its plans were based on the resources of that particular municipality and on the needs of its inhabitants.

One important but rarely discussed aspect of small and intermediate urban centres is the role of such centres as a focus for social life and social contacts in their area. In a review of some 400 papers and articles on small and intermediate urban centres in the Third World,[41] few considered this aspect. But in many nations or regions, there are likely to be friendship, kinship and family links between many rural inhabitants and those in small and intermediate urban centres. Such centres may be the place where young people in the area socialize and where there are opportunities for sport, recreation, and attending religious services and festivals. It is within many such centres that the culture of the area has its most concentrated expression. And simply because such aspects are less tangible and less researched than the potential for increasing agricultural production, it should not mean that their role in making smaller urban centres desirable places to live and work should be under-estimated.

Small urban centres – and controlling the growth of large cities

Many Third World governments have adopted special programmes for small and intermediate urban centres in the last 15 years; we have details of such programmes from more than 30 nations and this is certainly not a complete list. These programmes go under many names – for instance special programmes for "secondary" cities, "intermediate" cities, "medium size" cities, "growth centres", and "migrant interceptors". Some government programmes for small and intermediate urban centres serve national political goals – for instance consolidating population on a border area. In others, they are seen as supporting local or regional development, or serving a new land colonization programme or the exploitation of some natural resource. But most have a primary or secondary goal of diverting growth away from the largest city (or cities).

One of the most ambitious plans to control the growth of large cities was launched in Egypt in the second half of the 1970s. Cairo was declared over-congested. So, too, was the city of Giza nearby (which is part of Metropolitan Cairo) and Port Said. These cities were to have their population *reduced* by the year 2000. Various other urban centres and areas were declared saturated and were to have no more population growth. Meanwhile, most of the growth in population between 1978 and 2000 was to be in various satellite cities around Cairo and Alexandria, in the zone beside the Suez Canal and the so called "virgin areas" (including the Red Sea Coast, the New Valley to the south, the Sinai and the area around Mirsa Matruh on the Mediterranean coast). These four virgin areas were to have 14 million people by the year 2000.

At first sight, such an ambitious plan has considerable appeal. Cairo is very congested and its growth is taking place over valuable fertile land; since only 4 per cent of Egypt is fertile land, the loss is particularly serious. But the cost of implementing even a part of this plan would be prohibitively expensive. To get 14 million people to live in the virgin areas, the Egyptian government would have to develop them to the point where these millions of people chose to move there. This means that hundreds of thousands of jobs would have to be created there – so tens of thousands of businesses would have to be persuaded to set up. But most businesses would never set up in these virgin areas because they need the labour force, the infrastructure, the goods and services and the contacts with government agencies which can only be found in or close to Cairo or Alexandria. There is already evidence of reluctance on the part of businesses to move to the large new satellite cities around Cairo. But a more worrying implication of such a plan would be that it would starve all other cities, municipalities and rural areas of investment funds; while relatively few people were being persuaded to move to virgin areas at great expense, conditions elsewhere – where most of Egypt's population lives – would deteriorate.

Many Third World governments are investing considerable sums of money in developing small and intermediate urban centres to try to slow the growth of their largest cities. But if governments are concerned about slowing down the growth of large cities or stimulating the development of smaller urban centres, they must look at why the large cities are growing rapidly and many small urban centres are growing slowly. As noted earlier, governments' macro-economic and pricing policies, their sectoral priorities and the fact that local government remains weak and ineffective may be the real reasons. Investing large sums in developing some 'small urban centres' will not achieve much, if these more fundamental causes are not addressed.

Box 9.7 lists some reasons why modern industries and service enterprises become concentrated in one large city.

Box 9.7: Factors which create or consolidate the primacy of one large city

Below are listed some historical and contemporary factors which help explain why one city or metropolitan area dominates the economy of many Third World nations; in most such nations, many of the factors listed below work together.

Historical factors

Initial creation of a nation-wide administrative hierarchy with power highly centralized in primate capital city

Initial development of a commercial economy based on the export of mineral or agricultural products which focused development on ports (which were also usually capitals). If profits were steered out of the nation (e.g. foreign owned plantations or mines) the low incomes of the labour force meant

---

little demand to support urban enterprises in the producing
areas

For many nations in Africa and some in Asia, the colonial
legacy created the necessity for centralized government control (and thus primacy of the national capital) because the
nation-state boundaries defined by the colonial powers brought
together in one "nation" different ethnic or religious groups
or regional-based economic interests – which meant a fragile
national unity at independence

Concentration by independent Third World governments in
the twentieth century on industrialization and on achieving
sectoral planning targets; again the existing primate city was
often the only one with the infrastructure and services and
pivotal position on national and international transport routes

The dominance, in nations achieving independence, of one
political party with a strong support from urban union and
labour interests with headquarters or constituencies based in
the capital city

Current factors

Businesses in the primate city not being charged the full cost of
the publicly provided infrastructure and services they use and
the costs they generate – including not having to pay for the
disposal of wastes or the control of air and water pollution

Centralization of power and resources within national government with government bureaucracy heavily concentrated in
the national capital. Governments in other cities lack power
and resources to be able to compete with primate city for new
investments since they cannot provide the infrastructure and
services that new businesses need. Government centralization
exacerbated by weak or unstable economy and the social unrest
that economic instability encourages

Investments in infrastructure (e.g., roads, railways, power,
water supply, ports, airports. . .) favouring primate city – and
its region

Concentration of richer income groups in or near primate city – so this remains the major consumer market. Part of this may be due to the unwillingness of executives, professionals and skilled labourers to move away from the primate city because only here is there the quality of services and facilities that they desire

The government's macro-economic and pricing policies having net effect of subsidizing certain investments and certain consumers in the primate city

An industrial and service sector not having developed to the point where decentralization of some activities (e.g., branch plants, routine administration, research, distribution) can take place spontaneously

Necessity for major enterprises to have close contact with government agencies (e.g., to acquire licenses for imports or government contracts). If most government agencies are in the primate city, enterprises will also locate there or at least have offices there

A national economy strongly integrated into the world market which will focus attention on major port cities – which for historical reasons also developed as primate cities

Nations which remain dependent on cash crop or mineral exports so primate city dominated urban system imposed by colonial rule remains the one which best serves the economic model and export crop dominated inter-regional transport system

National capitals have to have various institutions and activities associated with being the centre of government for a nation state e.g., government ministry head offices, offices of public agencies, national legislative, executive and judicial institutions, foreign embassies and all the higher order goods and services which all these require. Few if any of these can be located away from the national capital. In predominantly rural nations, these alone can create a primate city. In addition, in relatively rural nations, demand for higher order services such as insurance, international banks and travel agents can be so

small with demand for them so concentrated in the national
capital that they also help reinforce primacy

Note: This is not a complete list and the extent to which some
or all of these are relevant to one particular nation will vary
greatly, as will their relative importance.

In relatively poor and un-industrialized nations, it can damage the
economy if a government spends large sums of money trying to
steer industries to locations which will not suit them. Many of their
industries will need to be in or close to the largest city. If they are
producing consumer goods, costs are often greatly reduced by being
close to the largest consumer market. Since most nations' largest city
is also their port, costs are also cut if they import machinery or inputs
or they export some of their output. Large cities also have a greater
variety of skilled people and specialized services. Perhaps they are
the only cities with sufficient water and reliable electricity supplies.
As Bertrand Renaud points out, only in relatively large cities can
many specialized enterprises exist – for instance specialized business
services, shippers and jobbers, financial offices, legal offices, trade
unions, repairs, specialized printing, consulting firms, equipment
leasing firms, laboratories and professional schools. For many businesses, these are more important than cheap labour.[42]

A lot of research has tried to establish the optimum size for a
city – the size at which it would have all the specialized enterprises
noted above but none of the disadvantages of very large cities. Some
researchers have claimed that cities with 140,000 inhabitants are the
optimum size while another has claimed that the optimum size is
between 1 and 2 million inhabitants.[43] But such figures make no
sense because each city has its own unique advantages and disadvantages, and many do not relate to its size but its location and to the costs
of drawing on certain resources nearby. Take the question of getting
a water supply. The cost of obtaining water varies enormously from
place to place; for some cities of (say) 1 million, the cost of doubling
the water supply to allow heavy industry to expand is not so great;
they are close to a major river or have large ground water reserves
which can be tapped without depleting them. Doubling water supply in other cities of 1 million inhabitants could be very expensive,
because there is no water source nearby.

However, one very important reason for an over-concentration of industries and commercial and financial businesses in large cities is that they are not charged for the costs they generate there. The discussion about the optimum size for a city forgets that most of the benefits of large city size go to businesses while most of the costs are dumped on poorer citizens. Major industries and commercial or financial businesses often get all the advantages. They get the water they need, the telephone service, electricity and solid waste collection – usually from government utilities. In their areas, the roads are paved and are served with storm drains – paid for by government. And in most cases, they pay little or nothing to dispose of their wastes – so industries pollute the air and dump untreated wastes into nearby water bodies or into the sewage or drainage system. Their professionals and senior management usually live in neighbourhoods which also receive water, telephones, electricity, roads and garbage collection.

Meanwhile, the poor live in areas which have few or none of these public investments and services. They often live in areas which suffer most from air and water pollution. They suffer most from traffic congestion, because they live in the worst located areas. If governments charged the rich the full cost of all the public investments from which they benefit, their revenues would increase enormously. If governments charged industries for the full cost of the roads they use and air and water pollution they generated, again, government revenues would increase and pollution levels would fall. If governments charged businesses for part of the cost of supplying the residential areas of their workforce with basic services, this combined with extra revenues from full cost recovery from the rich would pay for improving conditions for poorer groups. But, more importantly for the focus of this chapter, the increased cost for major businesses in large cities would also encourage them to consider whether certain smaller urban centres might not be cheaper and better places for their factories or offices. We suspect that governments' failure to fully charge large businesses in the major cities for the costs they generate and the costs of servicing them, is one of the most important reasons why these businesses remain so concentrated in large cities.

Thus, the best long-term strategy to slow the growth of the largest cities and to stimulate the development of small and intermediate urban centres is a combination of four elements. The first is stronger, more competent, more representative local government. With more funds, more trained personnel and more realistic local development plans, local governments can attract and support more new businesses and improve the quality and quantity of basic services. The second is more productive and diversified agriculture, with plans also to tackle problems of un- or under-utilized land held by large land-owners and of poorer groups' access to land. The third is adjustments to macro-economic and pricing policies so these do not have the effect of taxing the poor and those outside the largest cities and subsidizing the rich within the larger cities. The fourth is the point noted above – making middle and upper income groups and businesses in large cities pay for the costs they generate, and the infrastructure and services they use.

In many of the richer and more urbanized Third World nations, there are greater possibilities for a more decentralized pattern of urban development. Trends in the First World may provide some pointers. In most First World nations, there are strong counter-urbanization trends as an increasing proportion of people and businesses develop outside large cities – in small urban centres or "greenfield sites" outside any urban centre. There is some evidence of this also taking place in parts of Brazil, Argentina, South Korea and Mexico – usually in and around the richest and most urbanized regions. Box 9.8 lists some of the reasons why this happens. This decentralized pattern of urban development would be greatly encouraged by the strategy sketched in the previous paragraph.

Box 9.8: Factors which can encourage a more decentralized pattern of urban development

Strong and efficient local government for urban centres other than primate ones, and a good data base to inform prospective investors about local climate/water availability/resources

Business support services like banking, development credit agencies, technical assistance facilities, etc. in urban centres other than primate city (to help in the birth and development of local firms) and good cultural/entertainment/recreation facilities for managers, executives, professionals and skilled labour plus good schools for their children

Businesses and middle and upper income groups in large cities being charged the full cost of the publicly provided infrastructure and services they use – and also businesses not being allowed to dump solid and liquid wastes (including toxic wastes) and pollute the air

Relatively high per capita incomes and equitable income distribution nationally – so in areas other than that around the primate city, demand for goods and services encourages businesses to locate there

Good inter-regional transport and communications systems (e.g., telephone and telex systems, radio, television)

Industrial and retail/wholesale/service sector within a nation with size, diversity and concentration of units within single enterprises to allow the decentralization of branch units outside large cities to lower production costs or better tap markets there

Cheaper labour, cheap and plentiful land and basic infrastructure in urban centres other than primate city

High level of literacy and education among the inhabitants of urban centres other than the primate city including higher education located there – plus active regional/local business communities

Strong tourist sector related to natural sites (beaches, parks, lakes, rivers. . .)

No need for businesses to have long negotiations with bureaucrats, government agencies, located in primate city

Influential labour movements developing in existing industrially developed areas which businesses can avoid if they set up elsewhere

Advanced systems of management and control linked to sophisticated communications' systems allowing spatial dispersion of large enterprises' activities (each seeking location best suited to its operation) with no loss of management/control of whole enterprise from head office

Note: Many of these factors have contributed to a decline in population in many large cities or metropolitan areas in the First World and many seem to be acting in some of the Third World's most urbanized and industrially advanced regions within nations.

In most nations there are many small and intermediate urban centres where there is little or no possibility that strategic public investments or supports will stimulate development. Some have too poor or depleted a resource base. Others have stagnant or declining economies because enterprises there no longer sell goods or services at a competitive price or because demand for them has declined and there is little practical possibility of finding more buoyant alternatives. The appropriate public response to such problems needs to be place-specific and case-specific. But the widely used policy of steering some public enterprises to small and intermediate urban centres, only for them to struggle to survive because of inappropriate locations and poor supporting infrastructure and services, or the policy of giving a large subsidy to private enterprises to move there, are unlikely to tackle the causes of such centres' problems. Indeed, in many instances, they may have little or no effect on alleviating the poverty of such centres' inhabitants, despite the high cost to the government.

Take the case of La Rioja, one of the smaller provincial capitals in Argentina with 66,000 inhabitants in the 1980 census and close to 95,000 by 1988. One reason for its rapid growth has been the development of an industrial park as part of a central government policy to develop industries in certain provincial capitals. Enterprises locating there also receive substantial tax benefits for a certain number of years from both federal and provincial governments and subsidized electricity. Most industries are branch plants of enterprises based elsewhere and are no more than assembly lines with components brought in and finished products shipped out. In other instances, enterprises simply import industrial products which are then sold outside the province. These new enterprises have brought little stimulus to local businesses. A calculation of the total cost to government – the revenues lost to government through the subsidies and tax benefits and the development of the industrial estate – may show this to be a very expensive way to generate jobs. In addition, when the enterprises' tax exempt status runs out, they may well close down their operation in La Rioja.

In considering the problems of large cities or of small urban centres, one must not forget that it is people's needs, not urban centres' needs, which are the real concern. It is easy to muddle the two. As Charles Gore states in an analysis of regional problems, it is very common for social problems located in cities and regions to be muddled with the problems of those cities and regions or a confusion of "place prosperity with people prosperity".[44] This confusion is evident in much of the advice given by small and intermediate urban centre specialists to governments.

It is also evident in government policies. Many of the goals of such policies are explicitly spatial – for example to reduce the concentration of urban population in the capital city. If the proportion of urban citizens living in the capital city fell, this could be counted as a success. But this success might be associated with increasing poverty and economic stagnation. Certainly in Argentina, the decline in recent years in the proportion of urban citizens living in Buenos Aires has been partially the result of a decline in national output, an increase in social inequality and a decline in the capacity of the metropolitan centre to generate new jobs.[45]

The reason for inappropriate spatial goals is not simply ignorance. Many businesses would face large increases in costs, if they were charged realistic prices for the public infrastructure and services they use and were prohibited from dumping untreated wastes. Many special government programmes on small and intermediate urban centres are merely cosmetic operations to give the impression of government activity and concern. Indeed, some seem no more than attempts to disguise the increasing centralization of power in national government with the decline in the power and resources available to local government.[46]

Conclusions

The whole subject of human settlements, which brings in metropolitan centres, large cities, small and intermediate urban centres and rural settlements, is very poorly understood outside a narrow group of specialists and researchers. Such people talk of urban systems[47] since it is only possible to make sense of an urban centre, if its role in relation to other urban centres is understood. Thus, a nation's urban system is all its urban centres and the movements between them of goods, people, information and capital. The critical connections between urban centres include roads, railways and sometimes aircraft, and also all forms of telecommunications.

Since people, resources and economic activities are distributed in space around a region or nation, it is through the urban system that they are connected. This urban system and its connections with rural settlements provides the backbone on which all development projects or programmes are planned. Yet governments and aid agencies still tend to treat urban development or wider human settlements issues as if these were a sector in their own right – with their own ministry or division. Human settlements are viewed as being a convenient, discrete component of development so that, like agriculture or industry, responsibility for planning and implementing projects or programmes can be left to one agency. This hardly aids the needed co-ordination between investments in infrastructure and investments in agricultural or industrial projects. It ensures that human settlements receive a low priority since investments in them produce less visible and measurable results than investments in agriculture or industry. Meanwhile, the understanding that each nation's human settlements and their many complex inter-linkages, are the physical context within which all investments are made, is rarely reflected in national plans and government structures.

We have tried to show how it is only through the urban system and its links with smaller settlements that farmers can be reached with agricultural extension services, inputs, credit, storage, marketing and processing. Similarly, only through an urban system and its links with smaller settlements can governments increase the proportion of the population reached with health care, education, postal and telephone services, emergency life saving services and so on. It is through the urban system that both agricultural and non-agricultural enterprises have access to inter-regional and intra-regional transport and communications systems. Finally, we have argued that it is through the different levels of local government (most located in small and intermediate urban centres) that local needs and resources are best assessed, most development initiatives efficiently implemented and most multi-sectoral development programmes co-ordinated.

The role of small and intermediate urban centres within national and regional urban systems and national production is usually given scant attention. Obviously the development roles of such centres cannot be considered in isolation from those of larger urban centres or those of the rural economy. Small and intermediate urban centres (however one chooses to define them) are merely part of a range of different size settlements within any nation or region. An understanding of trends in population or in economic structure within such centres can only be achieved through an understanding of the role of each particular centre within the wider system.

Special government programmes for small and intermediate urban centres must be based on the understanding that each centre will have its own unique mix of resources, development potential, skills, constraints and links with the surrounds and the wider regional and national economy. Of course, the potential for development – or constraints on development – change over time; among the reasons for such change might be changes in the national economy or government's macro-economic policies or the world market. Governments cannot afford to view too narrowly their small and intermediate urban centres. Nor can they afford to ignore contributions that people, citizens, businesses and local governments based in such centres may make to more realistic local development plans, to the mobilization and better use of resources, and to agricultural development.

Epilogue

The failure of government

This book has sought to document how governments are failing in four of their most fundamental tasks within urban centres: to provide the legislative and regulatory system to protect citizens from exploitation by landlords and employers; to ensure all citizens can find adequate accommodation and access to basic services; to protect the human environment from contamination with pathogens and pollutants; and to allocate the costs of implementing these three tasks to those who benefit from urban locations, urban labour forces and government provided infrastructure and services.

Virtually all governments in the Third World – national, provincial/state and local – are failing in these four tasks. The result is an enormous burden of ill health, disablement and premature death; of poverty and of pollution. There are also important but less tangible burdens arising from these – of exhaustion, frustration and aggression among those most affected. Most could be removed if existing public resources were used in different ways. As has been documented elsewhere, governments' failures in rural areas are comparable; this book has emphasized the failures in urban areas.

Of course, governments' failures or inadequacies usually go much further than this: the failure to create the pre-conditions for democratic representation and to ensure all citizens have legal rights, security, jobs (or the means to provide their own subsistence) and education.

Governments fail to provide basic services or to ensure that other organizations or businesses do so. In addition, most governments' legal and regulatory systems for planning and managing urban areas inhibit and repress the efforts of their citizens to meet their own basic needs with their own resources and organizations. Most of the new housing that such citizens build and many other aspects of their daily lives are deemed "illegal". Yet the same legal and regulatory systems fail to protect these citizens from exploitative landlords and employers. While the poorest groups are strongly penalized in their search for shelter and a source of income, major companies and institutions (both public and private) ignore or circumvent legislation on health and safety at work, on social security, on air pollution and on the disposal of liquid and solid wastes.

Such failures on the part of government contribute much to the large mismatch between the number of urban citizens and the possibilities open to them for finding adequate jobs, homes and public services. Cities have become centres where vast numbers of people compete for the most basic elements of life: for a room within reach of employment with an affordable rent, or vacant land on which a shelter can be erected without fear of eviction; for places in schools; for medical treatment for health problems or injuries, or a bed in a hospital; for access to clean drinking water; for a place on a bus or train; for a corner on a pavement or square to sell some goods – quite apart from the enormous competition for jobs. In the majority of cases, governments have the power and resources to increase the supply and reduce the cost of many of these.

The Third World may be much less urbanized than the First and Second World but it has a much larger urban population – because of a much larger total population. The latest United Nations projections suggest that there are some 1.3 billion people in the Third World living in urban centres and that its urban population is growing by 50 million each year.[1] Although we suggest that the Third World is urbanizing more slowly than most other authors have proposed (see Chapter 8), the Third World's urban population is still growing rapidly. Within the next 20 years, it is likely to reach 2 billion and to make up two thirds of the entire world's urban population.

If present trends continue, we can expect to find tens of millions more households living in squatter settlements or in very poor quality and overcrowded rented accommodation owned by highly exploitative landlords. Tens of millions more households will be forcibly evicted from their homes. Hundreds of millions more people will build shelters on dangerous sites and with no alternative but to work in illegal or unstable jobs. The quality of many basic services (water, sanitation, garbage disposal, health care) will deteriorate still further and there will be a rise in the number of diseases related to poor and contaminated living environments including those resulting from air pollution and toxic wastes.

Government actions and institutions are not only the dominant influence on the conditions under which most of their urban citizens live but they also strongly shape future society, culture and environment. A failure today to invest in water, sanitation and health care condemns hundreds of millions of citizens to ill health – and tens of millions to premature death. A failure today to guarantee each neighbourhood sufficient public space is likely to ensure that not only current but also future inhabitants of that neighbourhood lack space for recreation and leisure, and children will not have the possibility of play and development away from dangerous streets. Once an area is built up, it is very difficult to remedy deficiencies in public space. A failure today to develop competent, representative local government also has damaging long-term consequences since the habit of democracy and participation become lost and must be relearnt. These cities are ruled from above, where the poor majority are segregated in unserviced squatter settlements or deteriorated and overcrowded rented accommodation and where many of the actions which are part of their daily life are "illegal". They are no basis for a stable society today or in the future.

Third World cities are developing some common characteristics. Beset by comparable problems – demographic pressures, land markets dominated by speculative interests, class structures, inadequate administrations and insufficient public investments – cities come to present an increasingly similar picture. Among the illegal settlements, neither climate nor building materials, nor cultural and ecological differences are sufficient to allow an observer to distinguish one settlement from another. Only the historical centres and the old districts retain the characteristics which distinguished the Islamic city from the Hispano-American city, a Portuguese-American city from an Eastern city. Today the poverty of most inhabitants is the common denominator and is seen in the urban landscape of recently established neighbourhoods where much of the housing is self-built, and in the districts of lower-income workers. In some illegal settlements – perhaps more so in the older, more consolidated ones – there is evidence of design, site lay-out and the use of materials which are more appropriate reflections of the nation's culture. However, poverty combined with the indifference or repression of government does not allow those to develop and does not permit the full use of these people's knowledge and skills.

Meanwhile technological uniformity pervades the residential districts of the rich, the commercial and financial centres, and the architecture of government buildings and government housing projects. International fashions cross international borders rapidly (whether in homes or offices) and can be seen almost as a denial of the culture and history of the city which they transform.

Two parallel urban histories, closely interconnected but visually very different, are emerging. One is the official history, represented by the explicit concerns of government and major building firms about the construction and management of the city. This official history is reflected in official statistics about the number of housing starts, the number of new factories or offices, or lengths of paved roads or water mains laid. The other history, that of the low income urban groups, has rarely been written about. It is fragmented and ill-recorded, inevitably different from the official version. It is the daily experience of millions of anonymous protagonists who must find immediate solutions to ensure their survival, with little possibility of long-term perspectives. But this unofficial history is the more accurate portrayal of city development in the late twentieth century.

Cities grow and deteriorate while governments do little or nothing to respond to the social and environmental costs which are part of urban change. The historical moment in which Third World cities are now forming themselves is very critical. The transformation and "globalization" of the world economy underlies an increasingly urbanized world population and an increasing homogenization of culture. Developments in most major cities are much influenced by the role that local enterprises has in the world market.

Governments have not come to terms with this transformation. Their approach to the problems which accompany it is rooted in outdated institutional structures combined with inappropriate and often irrelevant foreign models and precedents. In the last decade of the twentieth century, Third World city problems cannot be tackled with weak, ineffective and unrepresentative forms of urban government; nor can they be tackled with a legal system and an institutional structure little changed from late nineteenth- or early twentieth-century precedents, most of which were imported from alien cultures and originally applied under very different economic circumstances and political structures.

Conflicts of interest within any society are concentrated within the city and further magnified within one that is rapidly growing. Such conflicts can be seen in who gets to use the best located land and the use to which that land is put. They are also reflected in who receives the benefits of government investment in infrastructure and services.

The individual citizen's right to vote, and so to influence new developments in their own city (and neighbourhood), is perhaps the only effective check against the exclusion of their needs in government decisions. Unrepresentative forms of government rarely include much consideration of poor citizens' needs and where they do, government provision is usually ill-matched with the poorer groups' needs and priorities.

If current trends in the deterioration of conditions are to be slowed, halted and then reversed, some basic questions have to be addressed – principally, what measures should governments adopt to establish the preconditions for a more equitable, efficient and citizen-directed urban development which also responds to a shortage of capital and (for most nations) a serious economic recession.

Reviewing the past 30 years, the evidence does not suggest a diminution of the role of government (as has been suggested by many) but that that role should be different: more activist, more developmental, more decentralized, more representative and more supportive of citizen efforts. Without doubt, the first step for governments is to inform their citizens about their plans and the real possibilities for their implementation. This might appear politically dangerous, given the scarce public resources invested in cities and the criticisms which such announcements might provoke. But more open and participatory forms of government are an essential part of addressing the fundamental problems of Third World cities. These require a frankness and honesty which have hardly characterized the actions of most governments in the past. To elude the open dissemination of information concerning real possibilities for urban change is not only dangerous but also reinforces governments' present isolation.

Third World cities have to be built with the resources available to each nation and its people. This means a recognition of the resources to hand and what their best possible use might be. Inevitably, one turns to the knowledge, resources and capacities of the tens of millions of people who are already the most active city builders: the individual citizens and the organizations they form. At present, their efforts are the major influence on how cities actually develop. Governments' failure to support and help to co-ordinate such efforts represents an enormous and unnecessary loss both to themselves and to these citizens. Co-ordination on the location of new infrastructure and services, on their design and the timing for their installation can save both governments and citizens large sums of money.

The work undertaken by informal community or neighbourhood organizations in providing basic services and site improvements for themselves (when official agencies refuse to do so) is a rich though poorly documented source of examples from which governments can learn much. Some have been noted in earlier chapters: the co-ordinating committee in San Martin (Buenos Aires), the residents' association in Brasilia Teimosa (Recife), the residents' organizations in Jabra (Khartoum) and Ganeshnagar (Pune), the low income women who organize the *barrio*-level committee in Indo Guayas in Guayaquil (Eduador), and the development by the people of Villa El Salvador in Lima of their own municipal government. We also noted many positive examples of non-government organizations or groups of professionals who work with such community groups as in the case of FUNDASAL in El Salvador, SPARC in Bombay with their work with women pavement dwellers, and the Orangi Pilot Project and their community-organized sewer construction and maintenance programme.

There are also the experiences of various governments – some positive, some negative – which have tried new approaches to city management, construction or service provision: for instance, the Million Houses Programme in Sri Lanka, the Presidential Commission on Urban Poverty in the Philippines, the Community Development Department in Hyderabad (India), the Mexican Government's national fund for popular housing (FONHAPO) and the land-sharing projects in Bangkok. While it would be a mistake to assume that project designs or technologies are transferable from one city to another, successful projects or programmes often contain within them principles and precedents which have relevance to other social and cultural settings.

Even when added together, the more innovative actions implemented in the last 20 years in quantitative terms have had little impact on the living conditions on the poor and even less on their employment problems. If all those who had ben-efited from these kinds of initiatives were added together, they would represent a tiny proportion of those in need, perhaps the equivalent of the population of a few mid-sized metropolitan areas. But these innovative actions point to the need for new government attitudes to legalize countless settlements and neighbourhoods, thus changing what has hindered better relations between government and civil societies. These initiatives give substance to the idea that there are more effective and cost effective ways in which governments can work with low-income groups and their community organizations. The minimum conditions which governments must guarantee to citizens are coherent action and a connection between what they promise and what they carry out. At the same time, grassroots or neighbourhood groups want more open, wide ranging participation in the development of their own housing and neighbourhoods without hindrance from government. This would allow governments to learn from the most active builders and designers of Third World cities.

The role of aid agencies

This kind of approach – called "the Popular Approach" in Chapter 5 – means a recognition that aid cannot provide the solution. The solution is for governments to begin and then consolidate a process by which the initiatives of citizens and community organizations are encouraged, supported and built upon. The government also has to remove certain constraints (most often by providing land in a suitable location and access to finance) and ensure that investments in basic infrastructure and services are made.

This cannot be done "project by project", even if this is how many governments and most aid agencies operate. Successful projects usually owe much to the fact that they removed the constraints on the actions and initiatives of citizens and their community organizations but these constraints are only removed "within the project". Nothing is done outside the project boundaries to remove the constraints on the vast majority of people who were not part of the "successful" project.

Aid is never likely to provide more than a small proportion of the capital needed for investment in the delivery of basic services. It cannot and should not take the lead role in making the institutional changes; indeed, some aid agencies have promoted new institutional "solutions" which fail because they are so inappropriate to local culture and institutional arrangements. Even if the agencies multiplied the volume of aid going to basic service provision many times over, it would still provide only a small proportion of the needed investment. At best, aid can provide some help in funding basic-needs projects. It has a more important role in supporting national governments in their task of building the capacity and competence of urban government (and of national agencies which work with urban government) to make basic investments, increase locally-generated revenue and manage and maintain urban areas. Aid agencies have some role in helping to start and consolidate the process already mentioned: the year-by-year building up of the capacity of local governments to respond to citizens' needs and work with them to ensure these are met. A handful of governments and aid agencies have recognized the necessity for such changes but these are the exceptions rather than the rule.

If such a change in direction is not considered "viable", then it would be better for governments and aid agencies to simply forget about our cities and wait until the degradation and injustices provoke reactions which would be totally justified. The "patchwork" approach – a project here, a project there – which prevails in official attitudes in the construction and management of cities, is no solution.

The search for new approaches, promoted by the economic crisis, might be turned to positive use. For example, governments' recognition of their impotence in dealing with the causes and effects of rapid urban growth would suggest the possibility of an end to "big" government, at least in relation to the established methods of urban construction and management being replaced by the permanent participation of neighbourhood associations in local government. This would respect the role the people want (and could) play in development. It could also mean less emphasis on big urban projects and resources being more widely distributed to smaller kinds of projects and programmes, giving priority in different areas. Of course, there are large projects which are necessary and will inevitably involve extensive government intervention. These include flood control and other measures to improve the environmental quality of already-occupied sites, and the preparation of sites for new districts and the installation of infrastructure and services.

However, multilateral and bilateral aid agencies who insist on big projects simply because their progress is easier to oversee and the loan or grant application easier and quicker per dollar to process, seem to be misallocating scarce resources. More representative and decentralized forms of government provide the appropriate context for decisions about the use of scarce resources. In this way, the discussion about whether to favour large-scale or community-based projects, about whether it is convenient to reduce or increase density in metropolitan areas, and about many other aspects related to the construction and management of cities will also acquire a measure of reality and connection to everyday urban life.

Urban bias, large-city bias or rich-person bias?

Since we are proposing that *more* rather than *less* attention is given to urban problems, we must consider the criticism that urban centres are already privileged in the attentions they receive both from governments and aid agencies.

Much of the literature about development in the last fifteen years assumes that there is an "urban bias" in the policies and expenditures of governments and aid agencies. This was the view suggested by Michael Lipton (in *Why Poor People Stay Poor: Urban Bias in World Development* first published in 1976)[2] and this has been accepted as conventional wisdom by most people.[3] With the discovery in the early 1970s that rapid economic growth was not necessarily lessening poverty – and in some instances, seemed to contribute to more poverty – explanations were sought and urban bias seemed to be a valid one. If there is urban bias in most government policies, it greatly weakens the argument in this book, since it implies that governments and aid agencies already favour people living in urban centres over those living in rural centres.

It is worth considering the evidence presented in this book. Do urban dwellers or urban governments receive more national government resources, programmes and subsidized goods and services than rural dwellers?

As Chapter 9 shows, there is little or no evidence that the inhabitants of most small and intermediate sized urban centres benefit from any bias in their favour. Indeed, most seem to have been as starved of public investments and as ignored in public programmes as the rural areas. In the majority of cases, their local governments have been progressively weakened. Very few small urban centres have benefited greatly from the public provision of basic services; indeed, their inhabitants' access to safe and sufficient water supplies, schools and health clinics usually seems as inadequate as that of most of the rural population. Many governments do depress the price that farmers receive for their crops, either to provide tax revenues or to keep food prices low in urban areas, but so many people in small and intermediate urban centres depend on the rural demand for goods and services that low crop prices lower their incomes.

Although we lack sufficient information to know precisely the extent to which the populations of small and intermediate urban centres have or have not benefited from government expenditures and policies, at least there is sufficient evidence to cast doubt on the idea that their populations benefit from urban bias. It is also worth recalling that a very considerable proportion of the Third World's population lives in small and intermediate urban centres and that a relatively small proportion live in large cities. Although there are no exact figures, estimates for 1980 suggest more than 82 per cent of the Third World's population lived outside urban centres with 100,000 or more inhabitants.[4] However, the complex interactions between rural economies and the economies of many urban centres, and the arbitrary way in which "rural" and "urban" are distinguished, severely limit the validity of any rural – urban comparisons.

Perhaps the concept of "urban bias" should be amended to become "large city bias" or "capital city bias". Certainly, Chapters 7, 8 and 9 note how many government policies directly or indirectly subsidize consumers or businesses in capital cities or other large cities. Most of the evidence presented by those who write about urban bias is drawn from a comparison of rural areas with capital cities or large cities. But the key question is does all, most or some of the population in large cities benefit from this bias? The (limited) statistics that we found on health problems among lower income groups in large cities implies that they are not healthier than rural populations; in some instances they had substantially higher rates of infant mortality or infection from serious disease. Perhaps in some nations, the poorest households in large cities have worse health problems than the poorest households in rural areas. This suggests that in spatial terms, the bias favours certain districts within certain large urban centres.

Large cities do appear to have benefited from many more public services. For instance, the concentration in them of investments in hospitals, water supplies, sewers and drains. But what proportion of the population in each city actually benefits from these investments? In many large cities, a considerable proportion of all households receive no such benefits. Large hospitals, doctors and other medical specialists may be concentrated in big cities but this does not mean that they provide medical care for poorer households. The less wealthy household paying water vendors 10–20 times the price paid by middle income groups for a litre of water, is unlikely to be benefiting from "bias".

City-dwellers may have access to subsidized food. But for those living in illegal settlements, it may be impossible to obtain the ration card needed to buy cheap food because to acquire such a card, the person would have to be resident at an official, legal address. In the large cities of many countries, heavily subsidized public housing or serviced site schemes have been built but the evidence presented earlier suggests that a small section of middle or upper income households are usually the main beneficiaries. Subsidized credit is often provided for house construction or purchase but again, poorer groups rarely meet the criteria which govern who is eligible for such credit. Many industries and businesses in large cities are indirectly heavily subsidized in that the government does not enforce regulations to ensure they protect their workers from unsafe conditions and over-long working hours, and does not enforce pollution controls. But again, poorer households receive no benefit from this and many bear a heavy health cost from such a "bias". Subsidies on health care and education may favour urban over rural citizens but does this bias favour *all* urban citizens?

We suspect that the bias in public policies, investments and services is largely only in favour of the better-off inhabitants and more powerful industrial, commercial and financial concerns. Even if some poorer urban households do benefit from some subsidies – for instance cheap food – the benefit might be nullified as their employers lower wage levels because food is cheaper.

If, within a nation, the better off inhabitants and the more powerful industrial, commercial and financial concerns are concentrated in or close to large cities, this will appear to be large city bias unless consideration is given to who benefits. It may also be that in certain (especially the largest) urban centres in certain countries, workers' organizations and associations of community leaders from illegal settlements have successfully organized and received some concessions from government. As such they are beneficiaries of some bias, but we suspect that this is unusual and that the concessions made to these groups are rarely sufficient to compensate for the biases against them in other areas of public policy.

If there is no urban or large city bias but only one favouring the more important businesses and the upper and some of the middle income households in larger cities (too few studies exist to determine whether or not this is so) the case against government investment in urban areas is greatly weakened. But the case for more investment rests on meeting the needs of poorer groups in urban areas and in building the government capacity to do this. In fact, much of what we suggest in regard to agriculture and small urban centres (see Chapter 9) echoes the demands of authors writing about "urban bias", that is the need for rural policy to concentrate on more equitable land-owning structures and more attention to the needs of small farmers. One returns to the point that prosperous intensive agriculture where land-ownership patterns are relatively equitable can prove a most powerful stimulus to urban development and economic diversification within small urban centres.

Perhaps the most poorly tapped potential sources of revenue to finance such operations are the people and businesses who are the main beneficiaries of government investment, services and subsidies. Those enterprises and households fortunate enough to have piped water supplies and services that remove household and human wastes should pay the real cost of providing and maintaining such services – and help to provide the capital needed to extend such services to others. Mechanisms must be established that recapture the increments in land value that land-owners currently receive as a result of government-funded infrastructure. This should be re-invested in public services. There must also be mechanisms that will make businesses located in large cities contribute towards the cost of the roads, transport services, water supplies, waste services and so on from which they benefit. The businesses which benefit from a labour force whose health and education is largely the result of government investments and services should contribute towards those costs.

New interpretations

It constantly strikes us how narrowly the problems of Third World cities are presented. Far more material about Third World cities and their problems is written and published by people in Europe and North America than by people in the Third World. Much of this generalizes on what cannot be generalized; it reduces all Third World cities and the cultures of which they are part to "rapidly growing cities of slums". Authors often assume that what they have studied in one city is relevant to all others because they are all part of "Third World".

Researchers in the Third World are coming up with fresh interpretations of the city and its problems, aided by the experience of the individuals and community organizations with whom they work. These help to locate urban problems within a real understanding of local economies and power structures. In this book, we have drawn on such work in order to highlight the diversity of Third World city life and to avoid inaccurate generalizations. At the same time, we have tried to extract unifying or comparable themes.

Many governments claim to be ignorant about the magnitude of the crisis in their citizens' habitat and are reluctant to admit that there are other ways to approach and seek to ameliorate the social impacts of such a crisis. Degraded human environments will always exist if there is poverty. Poverty is rooted in the way that society is organized and wealth distributed, both within nations and internationally. Poverty cannot be eliminated without a redistribution of power and resources. As such, it cannot be eliminated through international aid as provided in its current form; so much aid is oriented to supporting the survival of friendly governments in nations for which the donor has a strategic interest. Even a substantial increase in such aid will not address the problems of poverty because it does not address the redistribution of power and resources. Like so many world problems which are the result of an uneven distribution of power and wealth, the solution to poverty should be accepted as a collective responsibility. Just as in many Western nations, cheap or free health care and a minimum income to the unemployed or disabled is accepted as a collective responsibility, so too must the world community accept a comparable collective responsibility for the world's poor nations and poor groups.

In discussions about Third World cities, too little attention is given to the potential contributions of free people and democratic institutions. The improvement of human habitats requires the involvement of the "users" of those habitats. One difficulty is that even with the spread of community movements evident in so many squatter settlements and illegal urban developments in cities, their organization requires time. Years or even decades of government repression or indifference have hindered their development in many nations. And the rate of formation of new illegal settlements is much faster than the current capacity of existing groups to train themselves and to develop their capacity to receive and work with professional assistance. Much as we dislike throwing on the shoulders of the poor, the unskilled and the poorly fed, the responsibility also for building their own habitats, a total reversal of this cannot be accomplished unless there is a sharp reversal in income distribution, both nationally and globally. The catastrophe predicted in many world models published during the 1970s and the threats posed by climatic change noted more recently may not impinge much, as yet, on the daily lives of those in the West. But another catastrophe is a daily reality for a large part of the world's population. If city construction and the question of who receives an adequate house, income and access to basic services is to become oriented to social need and not determined by profit, a sharp reversal of present trends could be accomplished.

But within Third World nations, much could be achieved in terms of direct improvements to living conditions in urban areas if governments no longer chained and repressed but supported a vast range of activities at present invisible to them – individuals, households and communities building or extending their homes and creating a living for themselves. This great range of activities where people are working with small amounts of capital and with both individual and collective efforts could be supported and co-ordinated to provide certain services, to mobilize production and to improve human habitats. Of course, this is insufficient to solve more fundamental problems, as we have already stressed. Of course, it demands complementary safeguards to protect individuals from exploitation by employers, landlords and land-owners. But these and strategies by which governments support the efforts of the true builders of their cities, adapted to each culture and society, would help initiate more effective and appropriate responses to contemporary problems in Third World cities.

Notes and References

Chapter 1
This and Chapter 2 draw from two previous published works: "The legal and the illegal city" in Lloyd Rodwin (ed.), *Shelter, Settlement and Development*, Allen and Unwin, Boston and London, 1987, pp. 306–338; and "The legal and the reasonable" in *Development: Seeds of Change*, issue 4, 1986, pp. 61–72. An earlier draft of these two chapters was also published as *La Ciudad Legal y la Ciudad Ilegal*, Ediciones IIED-AL/GEL, Buenos Aires, 1987.

1. This study is published in Spanish and is available from CEUR, Piso 7, Cuerpo A, Corrientes 2835, (1193) Buenos Aires, Argentina. A condensed version is published in English as a chapter in Sandy Cairncross, Jorge E. Hardoy and David Satterthwaite (eds), *The Poor Die Young: Housing and Health in the Urban Third World*, Earthscan Publications, London, forthcoming.

2. McAuslan, Patrick, "Legislation, regulation and shelter", *Cities*, vol. 4, no. 1, February 1987.

3. Oliver, Paul, *Dwellings: The House across the World*, University of Texas Press, 1987.

4. Soja, E.W. and C.E. Weaver, "Urbanization and underdevelopment in East Africa" in Brian L.J. Berry (ed.), *Patterns of Urbanization and Counterurbanization*, Sage Publications, Beverly Hills, 1976.

5. Douglass, Mike, "The future of cities on the Pacific Rim", *Discussion Paper no. 3*, Department of Urban and Regional Planning, University of Hawaii, July 1987.

6. Aradeon, David, Tade Akin Aina and Joe Umo, "South-West Nigeria" in Jorge E. Hardoy and David Satterthwaite (eds), *Small and Intermediate Urban Centres: Their Role in Regional and National Development in the Third World*, Hodder and Stoughton (UK) and Westview (USA), 1986.

7. Lawless, Richard I., "Social and economic change in North Africa's Medinas" in John I. Clark and Howard Bowen Jones (eds), *Change and Development in the Middle East*, Methuen, London, 1981.

8. King, Anthony D., *Colonial Urban Development: Culture, Social Power and Environment*, Routledge and Kegan Paul, London, 1976.

9. Simons, H.J., "Zambia's urban situation" in B. Turok (ed.), *Development in Zambia*, Zed Press, London, 1979, pp. 1–25. Quoted in Rakodi 1986, see note 10.

10. Rakodi, Carole, "Colonial urban policy and planning in Northern Rhodesia and its legacy", *Third World Planning Review*, vol. 8, no. 3, August 1986, pp. 193–217.

11. Amis, Philip, "Squatters or tenants: the commercialization of unauthorized housing in Nairobi", *World Development*, vol. 12, no. 4, 1984, pp. 87–96. See also Andreasen, Jorgen, *Urban Development and Housing in Kenya* (background paper no. 1 for "Rented rooms and rural relations – housing in Thika, Kenya, 1969–85"), Royal Danish Academy of Fine Arts, Copenhagen, 1987.

12. Doyal, Lesley with Imogen Pennell, *The Political Economy of Health*, Pluto Press, London, 1981.

13. See Alexander, Linda, "European planning ideology in Tanzania", *Habitat International*, vol. 7, no. 1/2 1983, pp. 17–36, for a detailed case study of this.

14. Rakodi 1986 p. 213, see note 10.

15. Moser, Caroline O.N., "Women, human settlements and housing: a conceptual framework for analysis and policy-making" in Caroline O.N. Moser and Linda Peake, *Women, Housing and Human Settlements*, Tavistock Publications, London and New York, 1987, pp. 12–32.

16. Moser 1987, see note 15.

17. McAuslan, Patrick, *Urban Land and Shelter for the Poor*, Earthscan Publications, London, 1984 (a new revised edition of this is now in press). A Spanish edition is also available from the Human Settlements Programme, IIED, 3 Endsleigh Street, London WC1H ODD, while a French edition was published by Editions L'Harmattan under the title *Les Mal Loges du Tiers Monde*, 1986.

18. Bhooshan, B.S., "Bangalore, Mandya and Mysore Districts", in Hardoy and Satterthwaite 1986, see note 6.

19. Theunynck, S., and M. Dia, "The young and the less young in infra-urban areas in Mauritania" in *African Environment*, vol. 14/15/16, ENDA, Dakar, 1981.

20. Moser, Caroline O.N., "A home of one's own: squatter housing strategies in Guayaquil, Ecuador" in Alan Gilbert, Jorge E. Hardoy and Ronaldo Ramirez (eds), *Urbanization in Contemporary Latin America*, John Wiley and Sons, Chichester (UK), 1982.

21. Harth Deneke, A. and M. Silva, "Mutual help and progressive housing development: for what purpose? Notes on the Salvadorean experience" in Peter Ward (ed.), *Self Help Housing: A Critique*, Mansell, London, 1982.

22. Soliman, Mounir, "Informal land acquisition and the urban poor in Alexandria", *Third World Planning Review*, vol. 9, no. 1, February 1987 pp. 21–40.

23. Schteingart, Martha, "The role of informal sector in providing urban employment and housing in Mexico", paper presented at the International Workshop on "Improving Urban Management Policies", East–West Center, Hawaii, January 1989.

24. Soliman 1987, see note 22.

25. Aina, Tade Akin, *Health, Habitat and Underdevelopment – the case of a Low Income Settlement in Metropolitan Lagos*, IIED Technical Report, 1989, available from IIED, 3 Endsleigh Street, London WC1H ODD.

26. Cohen, Monique, *The Urban Street Foods Trade: Implications for Policy*, Equity Policy Center, Washington DC, 1984.

27. Bugnicourt, J., "Which urban alternative for Africa", *African Environment*, vol. 2, no. 3, 1976; and Caroline O.N. Moser, "Informal sector or petty commodity production: dualism or dependence in urban development", *World Development*, vol. 6, no. 9/10, September/October 1978.

28. McAuslan 1984, see note 17.

Chapter 2
1. Harpham, Trudy, Patrick Vaughan and Susan Rifkin, *Health and the Urban Poor in Developing Countries; a Review and Selected Annotated Bibliography*, EPC Publications no. 5, London School of Hygiene and Tropical Medicine, 1985.

2. Riddell, Roger C., *Foreign Aid Reconsidered*, The John Hopkins University Press (Baltimore) and James Currey (London), 1987.

3. In 1954, at a meeting of British and foreign officials concerned with African housing problems in Cambridge University, UK, there seemed to be almost complete agreement on the need to tear down "slums" without regard for housing need or for housing shortage. But the agreed definition of a slum based on age, obsolescence and lack of amenities would have meant that King's College Cambridge, in which the delegates were housed, should also be torn down. Charles Abrams, *Man's Struggle for Shelter in an Urbanizing World*, MIT Press, Cambridge, USA, 1964.

4. Stren, Richard E., "Administration of urban services" in Richard E. Stren and Rodney R. White (eds), *African Cities in Crisis*, Westview Press, USA, 1989. Drawing from Dieng, Isidore, M'Baye, *Relogement de Bidonvillois à la Peripherie Urbaine*, ENDA, Dakar, 1977; Richard E. Stren, "Urban policy" in Joel D. Barkan (ed.), *Politics and public policy in Kenya and Tanzania*, Praeger, New York, 1984; and Heather Joshi, Harold Lubell and Jean Mouly, *Abidjan: Urban Development and Employment in the Ivory Coast*, International Labour Office, Geneva, 1976.

5. Sources for Box 2.2.
Evictions in Latin America:
Drakakis Smith, David, *Urbanization, Housing and the Development Process*, Croom Helm, London, 1981.
Dwyer, D.J., *People and Housing in Third World Cities*, Longman, London, 1975.
Portes, Alejandro, "Housing policy, urban poverty and the state: the *favelas* of Rio de Janeiro", *Latin American Research Review*, no. 14, Summer 1979, pp. 3–24; and *Revista Interamericana de Planificacion*, no. 13, March 1979, pp. 103–124.
Schütz, Eike, "Para festejar el día actualmente son desaslojadas miles de familias en Santo Domingo", *Medio Ambiente y Urbanización*, no. 25, year

7, December 1988, pp. 78–81.

Turner, John F.C., *Housing By People – Towards Autonomy in Building Environments, Ideas in Progress*, Marion Boyars, London, 1976.

Evictions in Africa:

Abrams, Charles, *Man's Struggle for Shelter in an Urbanizing World*, MIT Press, Cambridge, USA, 1964.

Aina, Tade Akin, *Health, Habitat and Underdevelopment – the Case of a Low Income Settlement in Metropolitan Lagos*, IIED Technical Report, London 1989.

Marris, Peter, "The meaning of slums and patterns of change", *International Journal of Urban and Regional Research*, vol. 3, no. 3, 1979.

Stren 1989, see note 4.

Evictions in Asia:

Angel, Shlomo and Somsook Boonyabancha, "Land sharing as an alternative to eviction: the Bangkok experience", *Third World Planning Review*, vol. 10, no. 2, May 1988.

Anzorena, E.J. , "Niwara Hakk Suraksha Samiti – Organization for Protection of the Homeless Rights", *SELAVIP Newsletter* (Latin American and Asian Low Income Housing Service), March 1988.

Asian Coalition for Housing Rights, "Evictions in Seoul, South Korea", *Environment and Urbanization*, vol. 1, no. 1, Human Settlements Programme, IIED, April 1989.

Asian Coalition for Housing Rights, *Eviction in Seoul – 1988*, Mimeo of Fact Finding Team's Report, Seoul, 1988.

Boonyabancha, Somsook, "The causes and effects of slum eviction in Bangkok" in Shlomo Angel, Raymon W. Archer, Sidhijai Tanphiphat and Emiel A. Wegelin (eds), *Land for Housing the Poor*, Select Books, Singapore, 1983, pp. 98–103.

Centre for Science and Environment, *The State of India's Environment 1982: a Citizen's Report*, New Delhi, 1982.

ESCAP, *Study and Review of the Human Settlements Situation in Asia and the Pacific Volume 2*, United Nations, Bangkok, 1986.

Jeong Ku, Paul and J.V. Daly, "Three villages near Seoul, Korea", *SELAVIP Newsletter* (Latin American and Asian Low Income Housing Service), E.J. Anzorena, Japan, September 1985.

Juppenlatz, Morris, *Cities in Transformation – The Urban Squatter Problem of the Developing World*, University of Queensland Press, 1970.

Ruland, Jurgen, "Squatter relocation in the Philippines: the case of Metro Manila", Institute of Philippine Culture, Ateneo de Manila University, July 1982 – reprinted in Concerned Citizens for the Urban Poor, *No Room in the Inn*, Metropolitan Manila (no date).

Shrivastav, P.P., "City for the citizen or citizen for the city: the search for an appropriate strategy for slums and housing the urban poor in developing countries – the case of Delhi", *Habitat International*, vol. 6, no. 1/2, 1982, pp. 197–207.

6. Abrams 1964, see note 3.

7. Lomnitz, Larissa Adler, *Networks and Marginality – Life in a Mexican Shantytown*, Studies in Anthropology, Academic Press, New York, 1977.

8. Moser, Caroline O.N., "Residential struggle and consciousness: the experience of poor women in Guayaquil, Ecuador", *Gender and Planning Working Paper No. 1*, Development Planning Unit, University College London, 1985; and Caroline O.N. Moser, "Mobilization is women's work: struggles for infrastructure in Guayaquil, Ecuador" in Caroline O.N. Moser and Linda Peake, *Women, Housing and Human Settlements*, Tavistock Publications, London and New York, 1987 pp. 166–194.

9. Juppenlatz 1970, see note 5.

10. Ruland 1982 and Drakakis-Smith 1981, see note 5.

11. Makil, Perla Q., "Slums and squatter settlements in the Philippines", *Concerned Citizens of the Urban Poor*, series no. 3, Manila, 1982.

12. Urban Poor Institute, *Information Packet on the Urban Poor of Korea*, Seoul, South Korea, 1988 (mimeo) and Asian Coalition for Housing Rights 1989, see note 5.

13. Juppenlatz 1970, Shrivastav 1982 and Centre for Science and Environment 1982, see note 5.

14. Gilbert, Alan , "The housing of the urban poor" in Alan Gilbert and Josef Gugler, *Cities, Poverty and Development: Urbanization in the Third World*, Oxford University Press, 1982 – quoting Richard E. Stren, "Urban policy and performance in Kenya and Tanzania", *Journal of Modern African Studies*, vol. 13, 1975, pp. 267–294.

15. Portes 1979, see note 5.

16. Concerned Citizens for the Urban Poor, *Wretched of the Earth*, series no. 2, Manila, 1982.

17. Aiken, S. Robert, "Squatters and squatter settlements in Kuala Lumpur", mimeo, 1977.

18. Aina, Tade Akin, *Health, Habitat and Underdevelopment – the case of a low income settlement in Metropolitan Lagos*, IIED Technical Report, London, 1989.

19. Portes 1979, see note 5.

20. Bapat, Meera, "Resisting eviction disguised as 'rehabilitation'; the case of a struggle by squatters in Poona, India", paper presented to the World Sociology Congress, New Delhi, August 1986.

21. Personal communication with Asian Coalition for Housing Rights, Bangkok, February 1989, after the Fact Finding Tour they organized in 1988.

22. Portes 1979, see note 5.

23. Angel and Boonyabancha 1988 and Boonyabancha 1983, see note 5.

24. Urban Poor Institute in Seoul, see note 12 and Concerned Citizens for the Urban Poor, see note 16.

25. Stren 1989, see note 4.

26. Stren 1989, see note 4.

27. Concerned Citizens for the Urban Poor 1982, see note 16.

28. Drakakis Smith 1981, see note 5.

29. For details of the de-urbanization programme in China see R.J.R.

Kirkby, *Urbanisation in China: Town and Country in a Developing Economy 1949–2000 AD*, Croom Helm, London and Sydney, 1985.

30. Quoted in Moser, Caroline O.N. and David Satterthwaite, "The characteristics and sociology of poor urban communities", paper presented to the workshop on Community Health and the Urban Poor, Oxford, July 1985, which in turn was quoted in Trudy Harpham, Tim Lusty and Patrick Vaughan (eds), *In the Shadow of the City: Community Health and the Urban Poor*, Oxford University Press, 1988.

31. Koenigsberger, Otto, "The absorption of newcomers in the cities of the Third World", *ODI Review No. 1*, 1976.

32. Cochrane, Glynn, *Policies for Strengthening Local Government in Developing Countries*, World Bank Staff Working Paper no. 582, Washington DC, 1983, p. 5.

33. Cochrane 1983, see note 32.

34. Bird, Richard, *Inter-Governmental Fiscal Relations in Developing Countries*, World Bank Staff Working Paper no. 304, Washington DC, October 1978, pp. 68–69.

35. Rondinelli, Dennis A., John R. Nellis and Shabbir G. Cheema, *Decentralization in Developing Countries – a Review of Recent Experiences*, World Bank Staff Working Paper no. 581, Washington DC, 1984, pp. 3–4.

36. Cochrane 1983, see note 32.

37. Cochrane 1983, see note 32.

38. This is a subject which Chapter 9 will treat in more detail; see also Gilbert, Alan G. and David E. Goodman, "Regional income disparities and economic development: a critique" in Alan Gilbert (ed.), *Development Planning and Spatial Structure*, John Wiley and Sons, Chichester and New York, 1978, pp. 113–142; and Alan Gilbert, "Urban and regional systems: suitable case for treatment" in Alan Gilbert and Josef Gugler (eds), *Cities, Poverty and Development: Urbanization in the Third World*, Oxford University Press, 1981, pp. 162–197.

39. See Harris, Nigel, "Spatial planning and economic development", *Habitat International*, vol. 7, no. 5/6, 1983; and Hardoy, Jorge E. and David Satterthwaite, "Government policies and small and intermediate urban centres" in Jorge E. Hardoy and David Satterthwaite (eds), *Small and Intermediate Urban Centres: their role in Regional and National Development in the Third World*, Hodder and Stoughton (UK) and Westview (USA), 1986.

40. For further discussion of this, see Kanyeihamba, G.W., "The impact of received law on planning and development in anglophonic Africa", *International Journal of Urban and Regional Research*, vol. 4, no. 2, June 1980, pp. 239–266.

41. Kalbermatten, J.M., DeAnne S. Julius and C.G. Gunnerson, *Appropriate Technology for Water Supply and Sanitation: A Review of the Technical and Economic Options*, World Bank, Washington DC, 1980.

42. UNCHS (Habitat), Chapter on "Infrastructure" in *Global Report on Human Settlements, 1986*, Oxford University Press, 1987; and Gehan Sinnatamby, "Low cost sanitation" in Sandy Cairncross, Jorge E. Hardoy

and David Satterthwaite (eds), *The Poor Die Young: Housing and Health in the Third World*, Earthscan Publications, London, forthcoming.

43. Gakenheimer, Ralph and C.H.J. Brando "Infrastructure Standards" in Lloyd Rodwin (ed.), *Shelter, Settlement and Development*, Allen and Unwin, Boston and London, 1987, pp. 133–150.

Chapter 3

Chapters 3, 4 and 5 draw on an unpublished briefing document prepared for the World Commission on Environment and Development at the request of its Secretariat in 1984. A condensed version of this document was published in *Habitat International*, vol. 10, no. 3, 1986.

1. Sobreira de Moura, Alexandrina, "Brasilia Teimosa – the organization of a low income settlement in Recife, Brazil", *Development Dialogue*, no. 1, 1987, pp. 152–169; see Box 1.3, p. 32 for more details.

2. Cuenya, Beatriz, H. Almada, D. Armus, J. Castells, M. di Loreto and S. Penalva, *Habitat and Health Conditions for Popular Sectors: a Pilot Project of Participative Investigation in the San Martin Settlement, Greater Buenos Aires*, CEUR, Buenos Aires, 1984.

3. The Society for Promotion of Area Resource Centres (SPARC), *We, the Invisible* (a census of pavement dwellers), Bombay, 1985; and other documents produced by SPARC, 52 Miami Apartments, Bhulabhai Desai Road, Bombay 400 026, India.

4. Hardoy, Jorge E. and Mario dos Santos, *Impacto de la Urbanizacion en los Centros Historicos Latinamicanos*, PNUD/UNESCO, Lima, 1983. For a description of the development of different kinds of tenement, some sub-divided from older housing, some custom built, and the problems facing their inhabitants, see Mario Padron and Julio C. Calderon, "Some contradictions about the Tugurios; two case studies of the development and eradication of two slums in Lima, Peru" in Eugen Bruno, Arnold Korte and Kosta Mathey (eds), *Development of Urban Low-Income Neighbourhoods in the Third World*, Archimed-Verlag, Darmstadt, 1984.

5. Connolly, Priscilla , "Uncontrolled settlements and selfbuild: what kind of solution? The Mexico City case", in Peter Ward (ed.), *Self Help Housing: A Critique*, Mansell, London, 1982.

6. Rodell, M.J. , "Colombo, Sri Lanka" in Mahdu Sahrin (ed.), *Policies Towards Urban Slums*, ESCAP, Bangkok, 1980, pp. 22–43.

7. Drakakis Smith, David, *Urbanization, Housing and the Development Process*, Croom Helm, London, 1981.

8. Das, S.K., "Bombay" in Sahrin 1980, see note 6.

9. UNCHS (Habitat), *Upgrading of Inner City Slums*, Nairobi, Kenya, 1984.

10. Okoye, T.O., "Urban planning in Nigeria and the problem of slums", *Third World Planning Review*, vol. 1, no. 1, 1979, pp. 71–85.

11. Drakakis Smith 1981, see note 7.

12. Asian Coalition for Housing Rights, "Evictions in Seoul, South Korea", *Environment and Urbanization*, vol. 1, no. 1, IIED-London, April 1989, pp. 89–94.

13. Furedy, Christine, "Whose responsibility? Dilemmas of Calcutta's bustee policy in the nineteenth century", *South Asia*, vol. 5, no. 2, 1982, pp. 24 – 46.

14. Roy, Dilip K., "The supply of land for the slums of Calcutta" in Shlomo Angel, Raymon W. Archer, Sidhijai Tanphiphat and Emiel A. Wegelin (eds), *Land for Housing the Poor*, Select Publications, Singapore, 1983, pp. 98–108.

15. References for Bangkok: Somsook Boonyabancha, "The causes and effects of slum eviction in Bangkok", in Angel *et al.* (eds) 1983, pp. 254 –283, see note 14; C. Nitaya and U. Ochareon, "Bangkok, Thailand" in Sahrin (ed.) 1980, pp. 78–93, see note 6; and E.A. Wegelin and C. Chanond, "Home improvement, housing finance and security of tenure in Bangkok slums" in Angel *et al.* (eds) 1983, pp. 75–97, see note 14.

Delhi: P.P. Shrivastav, "City for the citizen or citizen for the city: the search for an appropriate strategy for slums and housing the urban poor in developing countries – the case of Delhi", *Habitat International*, vol. 6, no. 1/2, 1982, pp. 197–207.

Guayaquil: Moser, Caroline O.N., "A home of one's own: squatter housing strategies in Guayaquil, Ecuador" in Alan Gilbert, Jorge E. Hardoy and Ronaldo Ramirez (eds), *Urbanization in Contemporary Latin America*, John Wiley and Sons, Chichester, 1982.

Lima: Sanchez Leon, Abelardo and R. Guerrero, J. Calderon and L. Olivera, *Tugurizacion en Lima Metropolitana*, Ediciones DESCO, Lima, 1979.

Manila: Keyes, William J., "Metro Manila – the Philippines" in Sahrin 1980, pp. 44–61, see note 6.

Mexico City: Connolly 1982, see note 5.

Nairobi: Amis, Philip, "Squatters or tenants: the commercialization of unauthorized housing in Nairobi", *World Development*, vol. 12, no. 1, 1984; D. Kabagambe and C. Moughtin, "Housing the Poor: a Case Study in Nairobi", *Third World Planning Review*, vol. 5, no. 3, August, 1983; and G. Njau, "Human Settlements in the 1980s: Nairobi's Experience", in Papers and Proceedings of Habitat Forum Conference, mimeo, 1982.

Nouakchott: Theunynck, S., and M. Dia, "The young and the less young in infra-urban areas in Mauritania", *African Environment*, vol. 14/15/16, ENDA, Dakar, 1981.

16. UNCHS 1984, see note 9.

17. See Payne, Geoffrey K., *Informal Housing and Land-subdivisions in Third World Cities – A Review of the Literature*, CENDEP, Oxford Polytechnic (for ODA), 1989.

18. Baross, Paul, "The articulation of land supply for popular settlements in Third World cities", in Angel *et al.* 1983, see note 14.

19. Carroll, Alan, *Pirate Subdivisions and the Market for Residental Lots in Bogota*, World Bank Staff Working Paper no. 435, Washington DC, 1980.

20. Gilbert, Alan, "Pirates and invaders; land acquisition in urban Colombia and Venezuela" *World Development*, vol. 9, 1981, pp. 657–678.

21. Carroll 1980, see note 19.

22. Connolly 1982, see note 5.

23. "Ejido" land is land granted to peasant communities under the agrarian reform; it cannot be sold or rented, legally, to outsiders.

24. Connolly 1982, see note 5.

25. Shrivastav 1982, see note 15.

26. Bonduke, N.G. and R. Rolnik, "Loteo clandestino – jardin flor da primavera", *Medio Ambiente y Urbanizacion*, Year 3, no. 9, IIED-America Latina, Buenos Aires, 1984.

27. Sachs, Celine, "The growth of squatter settlements in Sao Paulo: a study of the perverse effects of the State Housing Policies", *Man and his Environment*, Social Science Information 22, 4/5, 1983.

28. Law 13517 passed in 1961 declared that the remodelling, improvement and legalization of what it termed "marginal barrios" (which included squatter settlements) was "of necessity, public utility and in the national interest". This allowed for the legalization of previously illegal settlements and for government agencies to provide them with services. The law also tried to prohibit the development of new "marginal barrios" although with little success. Between 1968 and 1975, under the presidency of General Juan Velasco Alvarado, considerable support was given to the legalization and development of illegal settlements, now renamed *pueblos jovenes* ("young communities"). Information drawn from a case study of Villa El Salvador by Lisa Peattie - mimeo, 1982.

29. Schlyter, Anne, "Commercialization of housing in upgraded squatter areas: a preliminary presentation of the case of George, Lusaka", paper presented in the International Research Conference on Housing Policy, Sweden, June, 1986. See also Schlyter, Ann and Thomas Schlyter, *George – the Development of a Squatter Settlement in Lusaka, Zambia*, The Swedish Council for Building Research, Stockholm, 1980.

30. El Agraa, Omer M.A. and M.Y. Shaddad, *Housing Rentals in the Sudanese Capital*, Sudanese Group for Assessment of Human Settlements, Khartoum University Press, 1988.

31. Aina, Tade Akin, *Health, Habitat and Underdevelopment – the Case of a Low Income Settlement in Metropolitan Lagos*, IIED Technical Report, London, 1989.

32. El Agraa and Shaddad 1988, see note 30.

33. Wahab, E.A., *The Tenant Market of Baldia Township*, Urban Research Working Paper no. 3, Amsterdam Free University, 1984.

34. Connolly 1982, see note 5.

35. Urban Poor Institute, *Information Packet on the Urban Poor of Korea*, mimeo, 1988.

36. Statistics for 1985 released by the Economic Planning Board and the Ministry of Construction quoted in Urban Poor Institute 1988, see note 35.

37. *SELAVIP Newsletter* (Latin American and Asian Low Income Housing Service), Tokyo, September 1988; and Lim, Gill-Chin, James Follain and Bertrand Renaud, "Determinants of homeownership in a developing

economy: the case of Korea", *Urban Studies*, 17, 1980, pp. 13–22.

38. Asian Coalition for Housing Rights 1989, see note 12.

39. Edwards, Michael, "Cities of tenants: renting among the urban poor in Latin America", in Alan Gilbert, Jorge E. Hardoy and Ronaldo Ramirez (eds) *Urbanization in Contemporary Latin America*, John Wiley and Sons, Chichester, 1982.

40. Leeds, Anthony, "Housing-settlement types, arrangements for living, proletarianization and the social structure of the city" in F.M. Trueblood and W.A. Cornelius (eds), *Latin American Urban Research*, Sage Publications, Beverley Hills, USA, 1974.

41. Payne 1989, see note 17.

42. Angel, Shlomo, "Land tenure for the urban poor" in Angel *et al.* (eds) 1983, see note 14.

43. Wegelin and Chanond 1983, see note 15.

44. Payne, Geoffrey, "Self help housing: a critique of the Gecekondus of Ankara" in Ward 1982, see note 5.

45. Angel 1983, see note 42.

46. Peil, Margaret, "Africa squatter settlements: a comparative study", *Urban Studies*, 13, 1976, pp. 155–166.

47. Sachs 1982, see note 27.

48. Perez Perdomo, Rogelio and Pedro Nicken (with the assistance of Elizabeth Fassano and Marcos Vilera) "The law and home ownership in the barrios of Caracas", in Gilbert *et al.* 1982, see note 39.

49. Hardoy and dos Santos 1983, see note 4; and Jorge E. Hardoy, "The inhabitants of historic centres", *Habitat International*, vol. 7, no. 5/6, 1983, pp. 151–162.

50. Middleton, John, "Home town: a study of an urban center in Southern Ghana", in Aidan Southall (ed.), *Small Urban Centers in Rural Development in Africa*, African Studies Program, University of Wisconsin-Madison, 1979, pp. 356–370.

Chapter 4

1. For example see Moser, Caroline O.N. "Mobilization is women's work: struggles for infrastructure in Guayaquil, Ecuador" in Caroline O.N. Moser and Linda Peake (ed.), *Women, Human Settlements and Housing*, Tavistock Publications, London, 1987, pp. 166–194; and Caroline O.N. Moser, "A home of one's own: squatter housing strategies in Guayaquil, Ecuador" in Alan Gilbert, Jorge E. Hardoy and Ronaldo Ramirez (eds), *Urbanization in Contemporary Latin America*, John Wiley and Sons, Chichester, 1982.

2. Perez Perdomo, Rogelio and Pedro Nicken (with the assistance of Elizabeth Fassano and Marcos Vilera), "The law and home ownership in the barrios of Caracas" in Alan Gilbert, Jorge E. Hardoy and Ronaldo Ramirez (eds) *Urbanization in Contemporary Latin America*, John Wiley and Sons, Chichester, 1982.

3. Misra, Harikesh, "Housing and health problems in three squatter settlements in Allahabad, India" in Sandy Cairncross, Jorge E. Hardoy and David

Satterthwaite (eds), *The Poor Die Young: Housing and Health in the Urban Third World*, Earthscan Publications, London, forthcoming.

4. The Urban Poor Institute, *Information Packet on the Urban Poor of Korea*, Seoul, South Korea, 1988 (mimeo).

5. Sahrin, Mahdu , "The rich, the poor and the land question" in Shlomo Angel, Raymon W. Archer, Sidhijai Tanphiphat and Emiel A. Wegelin (eds), *Land for Housing the Poor*, Select Publications, Singapore, 1983, pp. 237–253.

6. Bolaffi, G., lecture given at the Institute of Development Studies, Sussex, March 1977.

7. van der Linden, Jan, "Squatting by organized invasion – a new reply to a failing housing policy?", *Third World Planning Review*, vol. 4, no. 4, November 1982.

8. McAuslan, Patrick, *Urban Land and Shelter for the Poor*, Earthscan Publications, London, 1984 (this edition is out of print; a new updated edition is being published by Earthscan in 1990).

9. Hardoy, Jorge E., "Teorias y practicas urbanisticas en Europa entre 1850 y 1930; su traslado a America Latina" in Jorge E. Hardoy and Richard Morse (compilers), *Repensando la Ciudad de America Latina*, Grupo Editor Latinoamericano (GEL), Buenos Aires, 1988, pp. 97–126.

10. Hardoy 1988, see note 9.

11. Hardoy, Jorge E. and David Satterthwaite, *Shelter: Need and Response; Housing, Land and Settlement Policies in Seventeen Third World Nations*, John Wiley and Sons, Chichester, 1981.

12. Unless otherwise stated, statistics on public housing programmes in the text are drawn from Hardoy and Satterthwaite 1981, see note 11.

13. Blitzer, Silvia, Jorge E. Hardoy and David Satterthwaite, "The sectoral and spatial distribution of multilateral aid for human settlements", *Habitat International*, vol. 7, no. 1/2, 1983, pp. 103–127.

14. Bangladesh: Chogill, C.L., *Problems in Providing Low-Income Urban Housing in Bangladesh*, Centre for Development Planning Studies, University of Sheffield DPS 2, June, 1987.

Egypt: Ministry of Housing and Reconstruction, Joint Housing and Community Upgrading Team and Office of Housing, US AID, *Housing and Community Upgrading for Low Income Egyptians*, 1977; and Soliman, Mounir, "Informal land acquisition and the urban poor in Alexandria", *Third World Planning Review*, vol. 9, no. 1, February 1987, pp. 21–40.

Kenya: Kenya, Republic of, *Development Plan 1979-1983*, vol. 1, 1979, p. 50.

Nigeria: Okoye, T.O., "Housing the urban poor in Nigeria: current trends and problems", paper presented at the International African Institute seminar on "Housing the urban poor in Africa" (mimeo, undated); and Stephen Ekpenyong, "Housing, the state and the poor in Port Harcourt", *Cities*, vol. 6, no. 1, February 1989.

Pakistan: Kalim, Syed Iqbal, "Incorporating slum dwellers into redevelopment schemes: the Jacob Lines Project in Karachi", in Shlomo Angel,

Raymon W. Archer, Sidhijai Tanphiphat and Emiel A. Wegelin (eds) *Land for Housing the Poor*, Select Publications, Singapore, 1983, pp. 461–472.
Philippines: ESCAP, *Study and Review of the Human Settlements Situation in Asia and the Pacific*, vol. 2, United Nations, Bangkok, 1986.

15. Kalim 1983, see note 14.

16. Linn, J.F., *Policies for Efficient and Equitable Growth of Cities in Developing Countries*, World Bank Staff Working Paper, Washington DC, 1979.

17. Batley, Richard , "National housing banks in India and Brazil", *Third World Planning Review*, vol. 10, no. 2, May 1988.

18. Cortijo, R. "Os 11 anos de fracasos do BNH", *Opinao*, 1 August 1975, p. 8.

19. Ekpenyong 1989, see note 14.

20. Chogill 1987, see note 14.

21. Moser, Caroline O.N., "Women, human settlements and housing: a conceptual framework for analysis and policy making" in Moser and Peake 1987, see note 1.

22. Moser 1987, see note 21.

23. Hardoy and Satterthwaite 1981, see note 11.

24. Egypt, Arab Republic of, *National Report* Interim Version, Report to the UN Conference on Human Settlements, 1975.

25. Chander, R., H. Karunanayake, J. de Vera and Stephen H.K. Yeh, "Housing conditions and housing needs", chapter 2 in Stephen H.K. Yeh and A.A. Laquian (eds), *Housing Asia's Millions*, IDRC, Ottawa, 1979.

26. DANE, *Boletin Mensual de Estadistica*, nos 262–3, Bogota, June 1973, p. 88.

27. Micro-brigades were formed by groups of workers who instead of working in their factory or other workplace, constructed housing for themselves and their colleagues. Those who remained in the workplace were meant to maintain production without those working in micro-brigades. The micro-brigades sought to reduce over-staffing in factories and other enterprises and address Cuba's housing problems at the same time. During the 1970s, micro-brigades produced around two-thirds of the public housing units constructed but after 1980, they were no longer organized on a large scale. See E. Bjorklund, "Shelter policies – the Cuban experience"; and Patrick Castex, "Les contradictions de la production du logement à Cuba, 1959-85", papers presented at a seminar on "Shelter Policies in Socialist Third World Nations" in Kleve, 1985.

28. Bjorklund 1985 and Castex 1985, see note 27.

29. Kirkby, Richard, *Urbanization in China: Town and Country in a Developing Economy 1949-2000 AD*, Croom Helm, London, 1985, p. 170.

30. Kirkby 1985, see note 29.

31. Cain, Allan, "Barrio upgrading in Luanda's Musseques", *Development Workshop*, Toronto and Luanda, 1986.

32. Cain 1986 p. 6, see note 31.

Chapter 5

1. Matos Mar, Jose "Migracion y urbanizacion – las barriadas Limenas: un case de integracion a la vida urbana" in Philip Hauser (ed.), *La urbanizacion en America Latina*, UNESCO, 1962.

2. Carlson, Eric, "Evaluation of housing projects and programmes: a case report from Venezuela", *Town Planning Review*, vol. 31, 1960-61, pp. 187–209.

3. See for instance Turner, John F.C., *Uncontrolled Urban Settlements: Problems and Policies*, report for the United Nations seminar on Urbanization, Pittsburg, 1966; and William Mangin, "Latin American squatter settlements; a problem and a solution", *Latin American Research Review*, vol. 2, no. 3, Summer 1967.

4. Devas, N., "Financing urban land development for low-income housing: an analysis with particular reference to Jakarta", *Third World Planning Review*, vol. 5, no. 3, August 1983; and Johan Silas, "Spatial structure, housing delivery, land tenure and the urban poor in Surabaya, Indonesia" in Shlomo Angel, Raymon W. Archer, Sidhijai Tanphiphat and Emiel A. Wegelin (eds), *Land for Housing the Poor*, Select Publications, Singapore, 1983.

5. Kulaba, Saitiel, "Local government and the management of urban services in Tanzania" in Richard E. Stren and Rodney R. White (eds), *African Cities in Crisis*, Westview Press, USA, 1989; and S.S. Sadashiva, "Financial management of the national sites and services and squatter upgrading project in Tanzania", paper presented at the International Conference on the management of sites and services and squatter upgrading housing areas, Centre for Housing Studies, Ardhi Institute, Dar es Salaam, 1985.

6. Angel, Shlomo and Somsook Boonyabancha, "Land sharing as an alternative to eviction: the Bangkok experience", *Third World Planning Review*, vol. 10, no. 2, May 1988.

7. Carroll, Alan, *Pirate Subdivisions and the Market for Residential Lots in Bogota*, World Bank Staff Working Paper 435, Washington DC, 1980.

8. El Agraa, Omer M.A. and Adil M. Ahmad, *Human Settlements in Arab Nations Volume 1*, Khartoum University Press, the Sudan, 1981.

9. Anzorena, E.J., "The presidential commission for the urban poor", *SELAVIP Newsletter* (Latin American and Asian Low Income Housing Service), Japan, March 1988.

10. Bird, Richard, "Fiscal decentralization in Colombia", background paper for *World Development Report 1988*, World Bank, Washington DC, 1988; and George E. Peterson, "Financing shelter-related infrastructure", paper prepared for UNCHS (Habitat), the Urban Institute, Washington DC, 1988.

11. UNCHS (Habitat), *Global Report on Human Settlements 1986*, Oxford University Press, 1987.

12. UNCHS (Habitat), "Habitat Hyderabad squatter upgrading project, India", project monograph produced for the International Year of Shelter for the Homeless, Nairobi, 1986.

13. UNICEF, *Improving Environment for Child Health and Survival*, Urban Examples no. 15, UNICEF New York, 1988.

14. Duhau, Emilio, "Politica habitacional para los sectores populares en Mexico: la experiencia de FONHAPO", *Medio Ambiente y Urbanizacion*, no. 24, IIED-America Latina, September 1988, pp. 35–45.

15. Stein, Alfredo, "The Tugurios of San Salvador: a place to live, work and struggle", *Environment and Urbanization*, vol. 1, no. 2, IIED-London, October 1989; and Harth Deneke, A. and M. Silva, "Mutual help and progressive housing development: for what purpose? Notes on the Salvadorean experience" in Peter Ward (ed.), *Self Help Housing: A Critique*, Mansell, London, 1982.

16. Jere, Harrington, Marijke Vandersuypen Muyaba and Francis Ndilila, "NGO promotes community development" in Bertha Turner (ed.), *Building Community: A Third World Case Book*, Habitat International Coalition, 1988, pp. 19–24.

17. Connolly, Priscilla, "Guerrero – tenement renters buy and rebuild their Mexico City homes" and Lombera G. Rocio "Rural migrants gain secure housing in Mexico" in Turner (ed.) 1988, see note 16.

18. See for instance the case studies in Turner, Bertha (ed.), *Building Community – A Third World Case Book* from Habitat International Coalition, 1988; and UNCHS (Habitat), *Shelter for the Homeless: the Role of Non-Governmental Organizations*, Nairobi, Kenya, 1987.

19. Harth Deneke and Silva 1982, see note 15.

20. UNCHS (Habitat), *Community Based Finance Institutions*, Nairobi, Kenya, HS/44/84/E, 1984; and UNCHS (Habitat), *Promotion of Non-Conventional Approaches to Housing Finance for Low-Income Groups*, Nairobi, Kenya, HS/62/84/E, 1984.

21. Buckley, Robert M., "Housing finance in developing countries: a transaction cost approach", background paper for the *1989 World Development Report*, World Bank, Washington DC, November 1988.

22. Connolly, Priscilla, lecture given at the Institute for Latin American Studies, London, 11 June 1986.

23. UNCHS (Habitat), *Rehabilitation of Inner City Areas: Feasible Strategies – Bombay (Building Repair and Reconstruction) and Bangkok (Land Sharing)*, Nairobi, Kenya, 1986.

24. Mohandas, S.K., *Ganeshnagar – Organizing for Change*, Centre for Development Studies and Activities, Poona, 1988; and S.K. Mohandas, "Ganeshnagar: renters take over and transform an Indian slum community" in Bertha Turner (ed.) 1988, see note 18.

25. For descriptions of the Sri Lankan Million Houses programme and comments on its orientation, see: *Habitat International*, vol. 10, no. 3, 1986 with several papers devoted to the Sri Lankan Million Houses Programme including: Patrick I. Wakely, "The devolution of housing production: support and management" pp. 53–64; Susil Sirivardana, "Reflections on the implementation of the Million Houses Programme", pp. 91–108; and Disa Weerapana, "Evolution of a support policy for shelter: the experience of Sri Lanka",

pp. 79–90; Pigott, Marni, *The Origin and Implications of the Million Houses Programme*, Sectoral Activities Programme Working Papers, International Labour Office, Basic Industries and Transport branch, Geneva, 1986; Kioe Sheng, Yap, *The Construction and Management of Infrastructure in Low-Income Settlements through Community Participation: an Example from Sri Lanka*, HSD Working Paper, Asian Institute of Technology, Bangkok; and UNCHS (Habitat), *Shelter for Low Income Communities: Sri Lanka Demonstration Project* Case Study Part 1, HS/80/85/E, Nairobi, 1985. The urban component of the Million Houses Programme is too recent for these publications to be able to comment on its implementation. A publication which includes a consideration of this is currently being prepared for publication in late 1989 or 1990: Lalik Lankatilleke, Babar Mumtaz, Susil Sirivardana and Patrick I. Wakely, *The Sri Lankan Million Houses Programme: a Government's Experiment in Support*, Development Planning Unit, University College London.

26. Angel and Boonyabancha 1988, see note 6; and Shlomo Angel and Yap Kioe Sheng, *The Sengki Land Sharing Project: A Preliminary Evaluation*, UNCHS (Habitat), Nairobi, 1988.

27. Jimenez, Rosario D. and Sister Aida Velasquez, "Metropolitan Manila: a framework for its sustained development", *Environment and Urbanization*, vol. 1, no. 1, IIED-London, April 1989, pp. 51–58.

28. Silas 1983, see note 4.

29. Silas, Johan and Eddy Indrayana, "Kampung Banyu Urip" in Turner (ed.) 1988, see note 18.

30. Payne, Geoffrey K., "Introduction" in G.K. Payne (ed.), *Low Income Housing in the Developing World – the role of Sites and Services and Settlement Upgrading*, John Wiley and Sons, Chichester (UK), 1984; and M.J. Rodell, "Sites and services and low-income housing" in R.J. Skinner and M.J. Rodell (eds), *People, Poverty and Shelter*, Methuen, London and New York, 1984.

31. Devas 1983, see note 4.

32. Silas and Indrayana 1988, see note 29.

33. Kulaba 1989, see note 5 and Hardoy, Jorge E. and David Satterthwaite, *Shelter: Need and Response; Housing, Land and Settlement Policies in Seventeen Third World Nations*, John Wiley and Sons, Chichester (UK), 1981.

34. Kulaba 1989, see note 5.

35. ESCAP, *Study and Review of the Human Settlements Situation in Asia and the Pacific Volume 2*, United Nations, Bangkok, 1986.

36. ESCAP 1986, see note 35, page 25.

37. ESCAP 1986, see note 35, page 22.

38. ESCAP 1986, see note 35, page 27.

39. ESCAP 1986, see note 35, page 33.

40. Marroquin, H., "Importancia y limitaciones de financiamento en el mejora nuento de los asentamientos humanos precarios en america latina", vol. 2, (mimeo), Guatemala, August 1984.

41. Marroquin, H., "Importancia y limitaciones del financiamento

internacional en mejoramiento de los asentamientos humanos precarios en America Latina", *Carta Informativa Latinoamericana*, no. 3, June 1985.

42. Payne 1984, see note 30.

43. Payne 1984, see note 30.

44. Hardoy and Satterthwaite 1981, see note 33.

45. Laquian, Aprodicio A. "Sites, services and shelter – an evaluation", *Habitat International*, vol. 7, no. 5/6, 1983, pp. 211–225.

46. El Agraa and Ahmad 1981, see note 8.

47. Carroll 1980, see note 7.

48. Stein, Alfredo, "A critical review of the main approaches to self help housing programmes", Masters thesis, Development Planning Unit, University College London, 1988.

49. Turner, John F.C., *Housing By People – Towards Autonomy in Building Environments*, Ideas in Progress, Marion Boyars, London, 1976; John F.C. Turner, "Issues and conclusions" in Turner (ed.) 1988, see note 17; and UNCHS 1987, see note 11.

50. Stren, Richard E., "Administration of Urban Services", in Richard E. Stren and Rodney R. White (eds), *African Cities in Crisis*, Westview Press, USA, 1989.

51. Abiodun, Y. William Alonso, Donatien Bihute, Priscilla Connolly, S.K. Das, Jorge Hardoy, Louis Menezes, Caroline Moser, Ingrid Munro and David Satterthwaite, *Rethinking the Third World City*, Swedish Ministry of Housing, 1987.

52. One of the first persons to point this out was Gunnar Myrdal, *Asian Drama: an Inquiry into the Poverty of Nations*, Allan Lane/the Penguin Press, 1968.

53. Moser, C.O.N. and S. Chant, *The Role of Women in the Execution of Low-Income Housing Projects*, Training Module, DPU Gender and Planning Working Paper no. 6, 1985.

54. Moser, Caroline O.N., "Community participation in urban projects in the Third World", *Progress in Planning*, vol. 32, no. 2, Pergamon Press, Oxford, 1989.

55. Quoted in Stren, Richard E. "Urban local government" in Stren and White (eds) 1989, see note 50.

56. Abiodun *et al.* 1987, see note 51.

57. Cabannes, Yves, "Human settlements – an overview" in Czech Conroy and Miles Litvinoff (eds), *The Greening of Aid*, Earthscan Publication, London, 1988, pp. 249–259.

58. Hardoy, Jorge E. and David Satterthwaite, "Laying the foundations: NGOs help to house Latin America's poor", *Development Forum*, October (part 1) and November (part 2), New York, 1987; and *The Limuru Declaration*, declaration by representatives of 45 Third World NGOs and 12 international NGOs after a seminar in Limuru in April 1987, printed in Turner (ed.) 1988, pp. 187–190, see note 18.

59. El Agraa, Omer M.A., Adil M. Ahmad, Ian Haywood and O.M. El

Kheir, *Popular Settlements in Greater Khartoum*, Sudanese Group for Assessment of Human Settlements, Khartoum, the Sudan, 1985.
60. For one carefully documented example see Barry Pinsky, "Territorial dilemmas: urban planning and housing in Mozambique" in John Saul (ed.), *Mozambique: Another Road*, MR Press, New York, 1985.
61. Hardoy, Jorge E. and David Satterthwaite, "Housing and health – do architects and planners have a role", *Cities*, vol. 4, no. 3, 1987, pp. 221–235; and World Health Organization, *Urbanization and its Implications for Child Health: Potential for Action*, Geneva, 1988.

Chapter 6

Chapters 6 and 7 draw from Jorge E. Hardoy and David Satterthwaite, "Third World cities and the environment of poverty", *Geoforum*, vol. 15, no. 3, 1984, pp. 307–333. A condensed version of this *Geoforum* paper was published as a chapter in Robert Repetto (ed.), *The Global Possible*, Yale University Press, New Haven, 1985. An earlier draft of these two chapters are published in Spanish under the title *Las Ciudades del Tercer Mundo y el Medio Ambiente de la Pobreza*, IIED-America Latina/GEL, Buenos Aires, 1987.
1. Sources for Box 6.1
For information on Asian cities: Sivaramakrishnan, K.C. and Leslie Green, *Metropolitan Management – The Asian Experience*, Oxford University Press (for the World Bank), 1986.
For additional information on Bangkok: Phantumvanit, Dhira and Wanai Liengcharernsit "Coming to terms with Bangkok's environmental problems", *Environment and Urbanization*, vol. 1, no. 1, IIED, April 1989, pp. 31–39; and United Nations, *Population Growth and Policies in Mega-Cities: Bangkok*, Population Policy Paper no. 10, Department of International Economic and Social Affairs, ST/ESA/SER.R/72, New York, 1987.
For additional information on Karachi: Sahil, "Marine pollution and the Indus Delta", vol. 1 (House journal of National Institute of Oceanography, Karachi, Pakistan), 1988, pp. 57–61; and United Nations, *Population Growth and Policies in Mega-Cities: Karachi*, Population Policy Paper no. 13, Department of International Economic and Social Affairs, ST/ESA/SER.R/77, New York, 1988.
For additional information on Manila: Jimenez, Rosario D. and Sister Aida Velasquez "Metropolitan Manila: a framework for its sustained development", *Environment and Urbanization*, vol. 1, no. 1, IIED-London, April 1989, pp. 51–58.
Information on African cities drawn from chapters in Stren, Richard E. and Rodney R. White (eds), *African Cities in Crisis*, Westview Press, USA, 1989, especially: Thiecouta Ngom, "Appropriate standards for infrastructure in Dakar", pp. 176–202; Kulaba, Saitiel, "Local government and the management of urban services in Tanzania", pp. 203–245; Mohamed O. El Sammani, Mohamed El Hadi Abu Sin, M. Talha, B.M. El Hassan and Ian Haywood, "Management problems of Greater Khartoum", pp.

246–275; and Kankonde Mbuyi, "Kinshasa: problems of land management, infrastructure and food supply", pp. 148–175.

For Sao Paulo: Faria, Vilmar Evangelista, chapter on Sao Paulo in Mattei Dogon and John D. Casada, *The Metropolis Era Volume 2*, Sage Publications, Beverly Hills, London and New Delhi, 1988, pp. 294–309.

2. Cairncross, Sandy "Water supply and the urban poor" in Sandy Cairncross, Jorge E. Hardoy and David Satterthwaite (eds), *The Poor Die Young: Housing and Health in the Third World*, Earthscan Publications, London, forthcoming.

3. Cairncross 1990, see note 2.

4. Cairncross 1990, see note 2.

5. Briscoe, John, "Selected primary health care revisited" in Joseph S. Tulchin (ed.), *Health, Habitat and Development*, Lynne Reinner, Boulder, 1986.

6. Ngom 1989, see note 1.

7. Schteingart, Martha, chapter on Mexico City in Mattei Dogon and John D. Casada (eds), *The Metropolis Era Volume 2*, Sage Publications, Beverly Hills, London and New Delhi, 1988, pp. 268–293.

8. Sinnatamby, Gehan, "Low cost sanitation" in Sandy Cairncross *et al.* 1990, see note 2.

9. Centre for Science and Environment, *The State of India's Environment – a Citizen's Report*, Delhi, India, 1983.

10. Sinnatamby 1990, see note 8.

11. Kulaba 1989, see note 1.

12. Sivaramakhrishnan and Green 1986, see note 1.

13. Schteingart 1986, see note 7.

14. For more details and discussion see Hardoy, Jorge E. and David Satterthwaite, *Shelter: Need and Response; Housing, Land and Settlement Policies in Seventeen Third World Nations*, John Wiley and Sons, Chichester (UK), 1981.

15. Centre for Science and Environment 1983, see note 9.

16. World Health Organization, *Urbanization and its Implications for Child Health: Potential for Action*, Geneva, 1988.

17. Basta, Samir S. "Nutrition and Health in low income urban areas of the Third World", *Ecology of Food and Nutrition*, vol. 6, 1977, pp. 113–124.

18. Basta 1977, see note 17.

19. Basta 1977, see note 17.

20. Phantumvanit and Liengcharernsit 1989, see note 1.

21. See Centre for Science and Environment, *The State of India's Environment: a Second Citizens' Report*, Delhi, India, 1985; and Centre for Science and Environment 1983 (see note 9) for many examples.

22. Centre for Science and Environment 1983, see note 9.

23. Centre for Science and Environment 1983, see note 9.

24. Schteingart 1986, p. 274, see note 7.

25. Connolly, Priscilla, "Uncontrolled settlements and self-build: what kind of solution? The Mexico City case" in Peter Ward (ed.), *Self Help Housing:*

a Critique, Mansell, 1981, pp. 141–174.

26. Lee, James A., *The Environment, Public Health and Human Ecology*, The World Bank, Johns Hopkins University Press, Baltimore and London, 1985.

27. For one example see Izeogu, C.Z., "Urban development and the environment in Port Harcourt", *Environment and Urbanization*, vol. 1, no. 1, IIED-London, April 1989, pp. 59–68.

28. Cairncross, Sandy and Richard G. Feachem, *Environmental Health Engineering in the Tropics – An Introductory Text*, John Wiley and Sons, Chichester (UK), 1983.

29. Sources for Box 6.4: The same as for Box 6.1, see Note 1 and:

Beg, M. Arshad, Ali S. Naeem Mahmood and Sitwat Naeem, "Environmental problems of Pakistan: Part 1, composition of solid wastes of Karachi", *Pakistan Journal of Science, Industry and Resources*, vol. 28, no. 3, June 1985 pp. 157–162.

Castaneda, Fernando Casas, "The risks of environmental degradation in Bogota, Colombia", *Environment and Urbanization*, vol. 1, no. 1, IIED-London, April 1989, pp. 16–21.

30. Hardoy, Jorge E. and David Satterthwaite, "Housing and health in the Third World – do architects and planners have a role?", *Cities*, vol. 4, no. 3, Butterworth Press, August 1987, pp. 221–235.

31. Cairncross 1990, see note 2.

32. Adrianza, B.T. and G.C. Graham, "The high cost of being poor: water", *Architecture and Environmental Health*, no. 28, 1974, pp. 312–315, quoted in Briscoe 1986, see note 5.

33. Cairncross 1990, see note 2.

34. Cairncross 1990, see note 2.

35. Bachmann, Gunter and Max Hammerer, "80 percent of losses come from 20 percent of leaks", *World Water*, October 1984, pp. 48–50.

36-37. Cairncross 1990, see note 2.

38. Sinnatamby 1990, see note 8.

39. For further discussion, see Gakenheimer, Ralph and C.H.J. Brando, "Infrastructure standards" in Lloyd Rodwin (ed.), *Shelter, Settlement and Development*, Allen & Unwin, Boston and London, 1987, pp. 133–150.

40. For further discussion, see Cairncross, Sandy "The private sector and water supply in developing countries: partnership or profiteering?", *Health, Policy and Planning*, vol. 2, no. 2, 1987, pp. 180–184.

41. Lee, Kyu Sik, *Infrastructure Investment and Productivity: the case of Nigerian Manufacturing – a framework for policy study*, discussion paper, Water Supply and Urban Development Division, the World Bank, 1988.

Chapter 7
1. UNIDO, *A Statistical Review of the World Industrial Situation in 1980*, February 1981.
2. Calculated from tables in *World Development Report 1988*, The World Bank, Oxford University Press, 1988.

3. Phantumvanit, Dhira and Wanai Liengcharernsit, "Coming to terms with Bangkok's environmental problems", *Environment and Urbanization*, vol. 1, no. 1, IIED-London, April 1989, pp. 31–39.

4. Smil, Vaclav, *The Bad Earth: Environmental Degradation in China*, M.E. Sharpe, New York and Zed Press, London, 1984.

5. Sani, S., "Urbanization and the atmospheric environment in Southeast Asia" in *Environment, Development, Natural Resource Crisis in Asia and the Pacific*, Sahabat Alam Malaysia, 1987.

6. Anandalingam, G. and Mark Westfall, "Hazardous waste generation and disposal: Options for developing countries", *Natural Resources*, vol. 11, no. 1, February 1987, pp. 37–47.

7. Phantumvanit and Liengcharernsit 1989, see note 3.

8. Ruddle, Kenneth, "Inshore marine pollution in Southeast Asia", *Mazingira*, vol. 7, no. 2, 1983, pp. 32–44.

9. Centre for Science and Environment, *The State of India's Environment – a Citizen's Report*, Delhi, India, 1983.

10. IRENA, *Taller International de Salvamento y Aprovechamiento Integral del Lago de Managua*, vol. 2, no. 2, 1982; and Annie Street, "Nicaraguans cite Pennwalt, US company has poisoned its workers and Lake Managua", *Multinational Monitor*, vol. 2, no. 5, May 1981, pp. 25–26.

11. Hamza, Ahmed, "Management of industrial hazardous wastes in Egypt", *Industry and Environment*, special issue on industrial hazardous waste management, no. 4, UNEP-Paris Office, 1983, pp. 28–32.

12. Lopez, Jose Manuel, "The Caribbean and Gulf of Mexico", *The Siren*, no. 36, April 1988, pp. 30–31.

13. Smil 1984, see note 4.

14. Jimenez, Rosario D. and Sister Aida Velasquez, "Metropolitan Manila: a framework for its sustained development", *Environment and Urbanization*, vol. 1, no. 1, IIED-London, April 1989; and H. Jeffrey Leonard, *Confronting Industrial Pollution in Rapidly Industrializing Countries – Myths, Pitfalls and Opportunities*, Conservation Foundation, October 1984.

15. Centre for Science and Environment 1983, see note 9.

16. Escobar, Jairo, "The south-east Pacific", *The Siren*, no. 36, April 1988, pp. 28–29.

17. UNEP/WHO, *Global Pollution and Health – results of health-related environmental monitoring*, Global Environment Monitoring System, 1987.

18. Leonard 1984, see note 14.

19. Smil 1984, p. 108, see note 4.

20. Smil 1984, see note 4. European standards from Nigel Haigh, *EEC Environmental Policy and Britain – an Essay and a Handbook*, ENDS, London, 1984.

21. Anderson, Ian, "Isotopes from machine imperil Brazilians", *New Scientist*, 15 October 1987, p. 19; and Consumer Information and Documentation Centre, *Consumer Currents*, International Organization of Consumers Unions March, April 1988, pp. 5–6.

22. Consumer Information and Documentation Centre 1988, see note 21.

23. Castleman, B.I., "The export of hazardous factories to developing countries", *International Journal of Health Sciences*, vol. 9, no. 4, 1979, pp. 569–597.

24. Castleman 1979, see note 23; and El-Hinnawi, Essam, "Three environmental issues", *Mazingira*, vol. 5, no. 4, 1981, pp. 26–35.

25. Nishikawa, Jun, "The strategy of Japanese Multinationals and Southeast Asia", *Development and the Environment Crisis – A Malaysian Case*, Consumers Association of Penang, 1982.

26. Irena 1982 and Street 1981, see note 10.

27. Sources for Box 7.2.

Consumer Information and Documentation Centre, *Consumer Currents*, International Organization of Consumers Unions March/April, 1988, p. 3.

Kone, Sidiki, "Stop Africa from becoming the dumping ground of the world", *The Siren*, no. 37, July 1988, pp. 2–3.

MacKenzie, Deborah and James Mpinga, "Africa wages war on dumpers of poisonous waste", *New Scientist*, 23 June 1988, pp. 30–31.

Phantumvanit and Liengcharernsit 1989, see note 3.

Secrett, Charles, "Deadly offer poor countries find hard to refuse", *The Guardian*, 15 July 1988, p. 11.

28. Consumer Information and Documentation Centre, *Consumer Currents*, International Organization of Consumers Unions, August 1988, p. 6.

29. Lee, James A., *The Environment, Public Health and Human Ecology*, The World Bank, Johns Hopkins University Press, Baltimore and London, 1985.

30. Centre for Science and Environment 1983, p. 23, see note 9.

31. Centre for Science and Environment 1983, p. 25, see note 9.

32. Centre for Science and Environment 1983, p. 20, see note 9.

33. Sources for Box 7.4.

Ahmad, Yusuf J, "Saving the pearl", *The Siren*, no. 32, November 1986, pp. 11–14.

Hamza, Ahmed, "An appraisal of environmental consequences of urban development in Alexandria, Egypt", *Environment and Urbanization*, vol. 1, no. 1, April 1989, pp. 22–30.

Castaneda, Fernando Casas, "The risks of environmental degradation in Bogota, Colombia", *Urbanization and Environment*, vol. 1, no. 1, IIED-London, April 1989, pp. 16–21.

Beg, M. Arshad Ali, S. Naeem Mahmood, Sitwat Naeem and A.H.K. Yousufzai, "Land based pollution and the marine environment of the Karachi coast", *Pakistan Journal of Science, Industry and Resources*, vol. 27, no. 4, August 1984, pp. 199–205.

Faria, Vilmar Evangelista, chapter on Sao Paulo in Mattei Dogon and John D. Casada (eds), *The Metropolis Era Volume 2*, Sage Publications, Beverly Hills, London and New Delhi, 1988, pp. 294–309.

Sahabat Alam, *Environmental News Digest*, no. 4, 1986.

Sivaramakrishnan, K.C. and Leslie Green, *Metropolitan Management – The Asian Experience*, Oxford University Press (for the World Bank), 1986.

34. Maheswaran, A., "Water pollution in Malaysia; problems, perspectives and control", *Development and the Environment Crisis – A Malaysian Case*, Consumers Association of Penang, 1982.

35. Schteingart, Martha, "The environmental problems associated with urban development in Mexico City", *Environment and Urbanization*, vol. 1, no. 1, April 1989, pp. 40–49.

36. Toksoz, Sadik, "Impacts of the growth of Mexico City through water supply and waste disposal", UNCHS (Habitat), Nairobi, Kenya, reported in *Habitat News* 5, 1983.

37. Douglass, Mike, "The environmental sustainability of development – coordination, incentives and political will in land use planning for the Jakarta Metropolis", *Third World Planning Review* (forthcoming), 1989.

38. Lee 1985, see note 29.

39-41. Centre for Science and Environment 1983, see note 9.

42. Marco del Ponte, Louis, "El crimen de la contaminacion", Universidad Autonoma Metropolitana-Atzcapotzaldo, Mexico, 1984, quoted in Martha Schteingart, chapter on Mexico City in Mattei Dogon and John D. Casada (eds), *The Metropolis Era Volume 2*, Sage Publications, Beverly Hills, London and New Delhi, 1988.

43. Report in *The Economist*, 18-24 February 1989, p. 69.

44. Smil 1984, see note 4.

45. Murphey, Rhoads, chapter on Shanghai in Mattei Dogon and John D. Casada (eds) *The Metropolis Era Volume 2*, Sage Publications, Beverly Hills, London and New Delhi, 1988, pp. 157–183.

46. Sahabat Alam Malaysia, *Environmental News Digest*, vol. 5, no. 1, 1987.

47. Sahabat Alam Malaysia, *Environmental News Digest*, vol. 4, no. 2, 1986.

48. Sahabat Alam Malaysia, *The State of Malaysian Environment 1983-4 – Towards Greater Environmental Awareness*, 1983.

49. Khalifa, Ahmed M. and Mohamed M. Mohieddin, Chapter on Cairo in Mattei Dogon and John D. Casada (eds), *The Metropolis Era Volume 2*, Sage Publications, Beverly Hills, London and New Delhi, 1988.

50. Sani 1987, see note 5.

51. Murthy, B.S., "India: environmental aspects of motor vehicles", *Industry and Environment*, UNEP-Paris, April-June 1979, pp. 6–7.

52. Achayo Were, P.T., "The development of road transport in Africa and its effect on land use and environment", *Industry and Environment*, UNEP-Paris, April-June 1983, pp. 25–26.

53. Leonard 1984, see note 28.

54. Jimenez, Rosario D. and Sister Aida Velasquez, "Metropolitan Manila: a framework for its sustained development", *Environment and Urbanization*, vol. 1, no. 1, April 1989, pp. 51–58.

55. UNEP/WHO 1987, see note 17.

56. UNEP/WHO 1987, see note 17.

57. Smil 1984, see note 4.

58. Leonard, H. Jeffrey, "Environmental pollution from urban and industrialized development in rapidly changing societies: causes, consequences and public policy choices", mimeo (undated).

59. Lee 1985, see note 29.

60. Lee 1985, see note 29.

61. Phantumvanit and Liengsharernsit 1989, see note 3.

62. Phantumvanit and Liengsharernsit 1989, see note 3.

63. The information on Douala and Yaounde is drawn from papers presented at a national seminar on "La Gestion d l'Environnement", Palais des Congres, Cameroun, November 1983.

64. Jeune Afrique, *Republique Unie de Cameroun*, les Atlas Afrique, Editions j.a., Paris , 1979.

65. United Nations, *Urban, Rural and City Populations 1950-2000, as assessed in 1978*, Population Division, Department of Economic and Social Affairs, ESA/P/WP.66, 1980.

66. World Bank, *World Development Report, 1983*, Washington DC, 1983.

67. Onono, Ondja and A. Mebenga, "Le problème de la pollution au Cameroun", Paper presented at Seminaire National sur la Gestion de l'Environnement, Cameroun, November 1983.

68. Onono and Mebenga, see note 67.

69. Ebwele, P., "Urbanisation et environnement", Paper presented at Seminaire National sur la Gestion de l'Environnement, Cameroon, November 1983.

70. For discussions of this in different Latin American nations, see Maria G. Caputo, Jorge E. Hardoy and Hilda Herzer (compilers), *Desastres Naturales y Sociedad en America Latina*, CLACSO, Buenos Aires, 1985.

71. Bopda, A. "Industrie, urbanisation et pollution", Paper presented at Seminaire National sur la Gestion de l'Environnement, Cameroon, November 1983.

72. Schteingart 1988, see note 42.

73. Jimenez and Velasquez 1989, see note 54.

74. Hardoy, Jorge E. "Natural disasters and the human costs in urban areas of Latin America", mimeo, IIED Human Settlements Programme, London 1988.

75. Centre for Science and Environment 1983, see note 9 and Centre for Science and Environment, *The State of India's Environment 1984-5: The Second Citizens' Report*, Delhi, 1986.

76. Douglass, Mike, "The future of cities on the Pacific Rim", *Discussion Paper No 3*, Department of Urban and Regional Planning, University of Hawaii, July 1987.

77. UNFPA, Presentation at the Conference on Population and the Urban Future, Rome, 1980.

78. Mike Douglass 1989, see note 37.

79. Soto Sierra, Pedro Javier, "Transformacionen el sector urbano", VI Congreso Interamericano de Vivienda, Interhabitat 77, 1977.

80. Kishk, M.A., "Land degradation in the Nile Valley", AMBIO, vol. 15,

no. 4, 1986, pp. 226–230; and Silvia Blitzer, Jorge E. Hardoy and David Satterthwaite, "Shelter: people's needs and government response", *Ekistics*, no. 286, 1981, pp. 4–13.

81. Blitzer *et al.* 1981, see note 80.

82. Chaturvedi, A. "Bricks versus food: Delhi's dilemma", *Earthscan Feature*, London, 1983.

83. Sources for Box 7.8.

Ahmad 1986, see note 33.

Beg, M. Arshad, Ali S. Naeem Mahmood, Sitwat Naeem and A.H.K. Yousufzai, "Land based pollution and the marine environment of the Karachi coast", Pakistan Journal of Science, Industry and Resources, vol. 27, no. 4, August 1984, pp. 199–205.

Escobar 1986, see note 16.

Hamza, Dr Ahmed, "An appraisal of environmental consequences of urban development in Alexandria, Egypt", *Environment and Urbanization*, vol. 1, no. 1, April 1989, pp. 22–30.

Kebe, Moctar, "The West and Central African Action Plan", interview in *The Siren*, no. 37, July 1988, pp. 31–34.

Maheswaran 1982, see note 34.

84. Agarwal, Anil, "The poverty of nature: environment, development, science and technology", *IDRC Report No 12*, no. 3, Ottawa, Canada, 1983, pp. 4–6.

85. Consumers Association of Penang, *Development and the Environment Crisis – A Malaysian Case* and reports in Environmental News Digest, 1982.

86. Hamza 1989, see note 83.

87. Cover Story, *The Siren*, no. 38, UNEP, Nairobi, October 1988.

88. Kebe 1988, see note 83.

89. Sahil, "Marine pollution and the Indus Delta", vol. 1 (house journal of National Institute of Oceanography, Karachi, Pakistan), 1988, pp. 57–61.

90. Jimenez and Velasquez 1989, see note 54.

91. Jimenez and Velasquez 1989, see note 54.

92. Hungspreugs, Manuwadi, "Heavy metals and other non-oil pollutants in Southeast Asia", AMBIO, vol. 17, no. 3, 1988, pp. 178–182, quoting A.A. Jothy, "A regional review of the state of the marine environment in East Asian seas – a Malaysian perspective", paper presented at a meeting of the East Asian Seas Task Team on the Health of the Ocean, May 1986.

93. Gennino, Angela and Tim Shorrock, "South Korea: paying a high price for an 'economic miracle' ", *Not Man Apart*, July 1982, pp. 10–11.

94. Smil 1984, see note 4.

95. Leonard 1984, see note 14.

96. Such a coliform count is a good indicator of water quality since faecal coliform bacteria are found in human and animal wastes. Although coliform bacteria themselves do not cause disease, their presence can indicate the presence of bacteria that cause typhoid, cholera, dysentery and other water-borne bacterial diseases. A faecal coliform bacteria count gives the number

of bacterial colonies per 100 ml of water and a sample with less than 100 is considered safe to drink while a sample with less than 200 is considered safe for swimming.

97. Moreno, Gloria, "Drinking water: black with foam on top", *Earthscan Feature*, London, 1980.

98. USAID, *Bolivia: State of the Environment and Natural Resources – a Field Study*, Washington DC, 1980.

99. Earthscan, *The Gulf: Pollution and Development*, Press Briefing Document, London 1980.

100. Lopez 1988, see note 12.

101. Smil 1984, see note 4.

102. Smil 1984 page 121, see note 4.

103. Gennino and Shorrock 1982, see note 93.

104. Lee 1985, see note 29.

105. Smil 1984, see note 4.

106. Sahabat Alam 1983, see note 48.

107. Centre for Science and Environment 1983 (see note 9) and 1986 (see note 75).

108. Bo Landin, *Air Pollution*, film produced as part of the Television Series "Battle for the Planet", Television Trust for the Environment, 1987.

109. Phantumvanit, Dhira and Suthawan Sathirathai, "Promoting clean technologies in developing countries", *Industry and Environment*, vol. 9, no. 4, October 1986, pp. 12–14.

110. Vimal, O.P., 1982, "Recycling of organic residues – status and trends in India" in UNEP, *Industry and Environment*, April-June 1982, pp. 7–10.

111. Caballero Almeida, Gilberto, "Turning sugar into newspapers", *Earthscan Feature*, 1983.

112. El Ebiary, M.A., "Disilication of black liquors: a new solution for pollution problems using rice straws", *Industry and Environment*, UNEP-Paris, January-March 1983, pp. 5–9.

113. Leonard, H. Jeffrey and David Morell, "Emergence of environmental concern in developing countries: a political perspective", *Stanford Journal of International Law*, vol. 17, no. 2, 1981, pp. 281–313.

114. Lerner, Jaime, "The City and Scale: one turn less of the screw" *Development – Seeds of Change*, no. 2, Rome, 1982.

115. Calculated from tables in World Bank, *World Development Report 1988*, Oxford University Press, 1988.

116. Leonard 1984, see note 14.

117. Leonard and Morell 1981, see note 113.

118. King, Bob, "Taiwan's industrial pollution bills mount", *Financial Times*, 8 November 1988.

119. United States Environmental Protection Agency, *Regulatory Impact Analysis: Protection of Stratospheric Ozone*, Washington DC, 1987.

120. UNCHS (Habitat), "Financial and other assistance provided to and among developing countries on human settlements and on the human settlements activities of the United Nations system", Biennial reports submitted

to the Inter-Governmental Commission on Human Settlements in 1987 and 1989, HS/C/9/6 and HS/C/11/6, Nairobi, Kenya.

Chapter 8

This Chapter draws on several previously published works. It originates from a background paper prepared for the *World Resources Report 1986* published by the International Institute for Environment and Development (IIED) and the World Resources Institute in 1986 which reviewed urban change throughout the world. Part of this paper was published in English as "Urban change in the Third World" in *Habitat International*, vol. 10, no. 3, 1986, and in Spanish under the title "El cambio urbano en el Tercer Mundo. Son las ultimas tendencias un indicador util del futuro urbano?", *Estudios Demograficos y Urbanos*, vol. 3, no. 2, May-August 1988, pp. 209–236. A condensed version of this chapter is to appear in David Cadman and Geoffrey Payne (eds), *Future Cities*, Routledge, Chapman and Hall, 1989.

Statistics for nations' economic performance, changes in the proportion of their economically active population in different sectors and changes in their level of urbanization for the period 1960 to 1982 are drawn from the World Bank's *World Development Report, 1984*. We did not use statistics available for later years (for instance in the *World Development Report 1988*) since most statistics for urbanization levels for later years are based on extrapolations from data from earlier years, not on new census data.

1. Potter, R.B., *Urbanization and Planning in the Third World: Spatial Perceptions and Public Participation*, Croom Helm, London, 1985.

2. Repetto, Robert, *World Enough and Time*, Yale University Press, 1986.

3. Many authors still confuse "growth in urban population" and "growth in a nation's or region's level of urbanization". Virtually all changes in the level of urbanization (i.e., in the proportion of population living in urban centres) are a result of population movements in or out of urban centres. Natural increase in population (i.e., the excess of births over deaths) does not contribute to increases in urbanization levels except where the rate of natural increase in urban centres is higher than that in rural areas. If this is the case, this may be the result of high proportions of migrants from rural to urban areas being of child-bearing age and their movement to urban centres changing urban centres' rate of natural increase. A small part of a change in a nation's level of urbanization may be due to rural settlements growing to the point where they are reclassified as urban (and thus are added to the urban population) and rapid rates of natural increase can increase this contribution. But in general, a nation's level of urbanization is not influenced much by population increases for it is essentially the result of changes in economic structure; increased proportions of national populations in urban centres reflect an increase in the proportion of employment opportunities (or possibilities for survival) concentrated in urban centres.

4. United Nations, *Estimates and Projections of Urban, Rural and City Populations, 1950-2025: the 1982 Assessment*, ST/ESA/SER.R/58, New York, 1985.

5. Aradeon, David, Aina, Tade and Umo, Joe, "South-West Nigeria" in Jorge E. Hardoy and David Satterthwaite (eds), *Small and Intermediate Urban Centres: Their role in national and regional development in the Third World*, Hodder and Stoughton, London and Westview Press, USA, 1986.

6. In most major Third World nations, the definition as to what constitutes an urban centre is based on a stated threshold for the number of inhabitants above which a settlement is "an urban centre". But this threshold may be a few hundred (or less) or up to 50,000 inhabitants. Most fall within the range of 1,500 to 5,000 inhabitants. Two other sets of urban criteria, not based on population thresholds, are widely used to arrive at "national urban population". The first is simply by stating that certain specified settlements are to be regarded as "urban centres"; this is widely used in small-population and in relatively un-urbanized nations with just a few named settlements being the only ones regarded as urban. In some of the smallest nations, just one settlement is regarded as urban. The second is based on the population in settlements which perform government functions; a settlement is "urban" if it is the seat of a certain level of local government. In some nations, local government status and population size are combined – so a settlement is urban if its population exceeds a defined threshold and it is the administrative headquarters of a certain level of local government. More sophisticated criteria may be added to population thresholds or local government status such as the proportion of the labour force working in non-agricultural activities or population density or other characteristics thought to be typical of an "urban centre". In a few nations, the "urban population" are those people living in "townships" or "municipalities", or other forms of administrative area within which most of the population lives in one or more nucleated settlements said to have "urban" characteristics. Research into how different Third World nations obtained the urban criteria they use today might prove interesting; for instance, several former French colonies' urban criteria are similar to that of their former ruler. But this is a question beyond the scope of this Chapter.

The great diversity in the way that national governments arrive at the figures for their nation's level of urbanization greatly limits the validity of international comparisons. This is made most clear with some examples. In 1976, Bolivia's population was 32.2 per cent urban if a population threshold of 20,000 inhabitants was used to define whether a settlement was "urban" or 42.6 per cent urban if the threshold was 2,000 inhabitants. Mexico's population would have been 43.3 per cent urban in 1970 if urban centres are settlements with 20,000 or more inhabitants instead of 59 per cent urban, a figure based on an urban criterion of localities with 2,500 or more inhabitants.

Since the United Nations produces statistics for all nations as to the number of inhabitants in cities of 100,000 or more inhabitants, this should provide a more valid base for international comparisons since the same criterion is used for each nation. But even here, the statistics for certain nations are known to be inaccurate. Many nations have not had a census in recent years. For such nations, UN figures for the population in cities of 100,000 plus inhabitants are based on extrapolations of older data. These extrapolations do not seem to make allowances for cities which are likely to have grown into the 100,000 plus inhabitant category between the last census and recent years. Thus, according to a recently published UN compendium of urban statistics, China had only one city with between 100,000 and 249,999 inhabitants in 1980. This is hardly believable in a nation with more than a billion inhabitants and (whichever way the urban population is calculated) one of the world's largest urban populations.

There also seems to be a considerable time-lag between the point when new national censuses become available and their use in UN statistics. For instance, the figures for the percentages of the urban population in cities of 500,000 plus in 1980 for nations such as Kenya (57 per cent) and Tanzania (50 per cent) are far higher than those suggested by the censuses in Kenya in 1979 and in Tanzania for 1978. Such United Nations figures were still being quoted in material published in 1988 – for instance in the data tables of the *World Development Report, 1988*. Using statistics from these nations' censuses would mean a much lower proportion of the urban population in cities of 500,000 or more inhabitants in 1980; in both nations, it would be of the order of 35 per cent. The extent to which national urban populations are concentrated in cities of 500,000 or more inhabitants may well be over-stated for many other nations. But to list the proportion of nations' urban populations in cities of 500,000 or more inhabitants is in itself misleading, again because of the major differences in the criteria by which national urban populations are calculated.

One final example of United Nations urban statistics which seem open to question is the estimates for the proportion of many small nations' or territories' populations living in cities of 100,000 or more inhabitants. Between 95 and 100 per cent of the urban populations of many of the Third World's nations with small populations are said to be living in cities of 100,000 plus inhabitants in 1950, 1955 and 1960. But these nations or territories had no cities at all which had reached 100,000 inhabitants. Examples include Burundi, Djibouti, Sao Tome and Principe, the Gambia, Antigua, the Seychelles, Gibralter, New Caledonia, Cook Islands, Niue and the Faroe Islands. Indeed, for some of these, their national populations had not reached 100,000 inhabitants by these dates and some still have no urban centre with 100,000 inhabitants.

7. In recent censuses in Peru, "urban centres" are defined as populated centres with 100 or more occupied dwellings. In India, the criteria are more complicated but with relatively few exceptions, urban centres have 5,000 or more inhabitants, a relatively high density and more than three-quarters of the adult male population employed in non-agricultural activities. Most of India's rural population live in villages which have more than 100 occupied dwellings.

8. See, for instance, Manzanal, Mabel and Cesar Vapnarsky, "The development of the Upper Valley of Rio Negro and Neuquen within the Comahue

region, Argentina" in Hardoy and Satterthwaite (eds) 1986, see note 5.

9. UNCHS (Habitat), "Expert group on human settlements statistics: report of the meeting held in Nairobi, Kenya, 12-16 October 1987", forthcoming, Nairobi, Kenya.

10. Hawkins, J.N., "Shanghai: an exploratory report on food for a city", *GeoJournal*, supplementary issue, 1982.

11. Sivaramakrishan K.C. and Leslie Green, *Metropolitan Management – The Asian Experience*, Oxford University Press (for the World Bank), 1986.

12. PADCO, *Philippines Shelter Sector Assessment*, vol. 1, prepared for USAID Office of Housing, Washington DC, 1978.

13. Statistics for Dhaka drawn from United Nations, *Dhaka*, in the series of monographs on "Population Growth and Policies in Mega-Cities", Population Policy Paper no. 5, ST/ESA/SER.R/65, New York, 1986.

14. Hardoy, Jorge E. and David Satterthwaite, "A survey of empirical material on the factors affecting the development of small and intermediate urban centres" in Hardoy and Satterthwaite (eds) 1986, see note 5.

15. Sources for Box 8.2: *Bissau*: Julio D. Davila, *Shelter, Poverty and African Revolutionary Socialism: Human Settlements in Guinea Bissau*, IIED, London, Washington DC and Buenos Aires, 1987. *Dhaka*: World Bank Urban Sector Memorandum quoted in ESCAP 1985, *Study and Review of the Human Settlements Situation in Asia and the Pacific*, vol. 2, Country Monographs, United Nations Bangkok, 1986. *Lagos*: Aradeon, Aina and Umo 1986, see note 5. *Lima*: Harry W. Richardson, "Planning strategies and policies for metropolitan Lima" in *Third World Planning Review*, vol. 6, no. 2, May 1984. *Managua*: MINVAH, "Politica de ordenamiento y desarrollo de los asentamientos intermedios y rurales en Nicaragua", Managua, September 1983. *Manila*: M.S. Apacible and M. Yaxley, "Manila through the eyes of the Malinenos and the Consultant" PTRC Summer Annual Meeting, 1979, and Rosario D. Jimenez and Sister Aida Velasquez, "Metropolitan Manila: a framework for its sustained development", *Environment and Urbanization*, vol. 1, no. 1, IIED-London, April 1989, pp. 51–58. *Mexico City*: Ian Scott, *Urban and Spatial Development in Mexico*, the World Bank, Johns Hopkins University Press, Baltimore and London, 1982. *Nairobi*: Harry W. Richardson, "An urban development strategy for Kenya", *The Journal of Developing Areas*, vol. 15, no. 1, October 1980. *Port au Prince*: USAID, *Haiti Shelter Sector Assessment*, Office of Housing and Urban Development, December 1980. *Rangoon*: John B. Leonard, "Rangoon – city profile" in *Cities*, vol. 2, no. 1, February 1985. *Sao Paulo*: Andrew M. Hamer, *Decentralized Urban Development and Industrial Location Behaviour in Sao Paulo, Brazil: A Synthesis of Research Issues and Conclusions*, Discussion Paper, Water Supply and Urban Development Department, the World Bank, Washington DC, 1984.

16. For further details see United Nations, "Migration, population growth and employment in metropolitan areas of selected developing countries", Dept of International Economic and Social Affairs, ST/ESA/SER.R/57, New York, 1985.

17. UNCHS (Habitat), *Global Report on Human Settlements 1986*, Oxford University Press, 1987.

18. See Townroe, Peter M. and David Keen, "Polarization reversal in the state of Sao Paulo, Brazil" in *Regional Studies*, vol. 18.1, 1984, pp. 45–54 for a discussion as to how this is best measured.

19. Derived from census statistics quoted in Rofman, Alexandro B., "Argentina: a mature urbanization pattern" in *Cities*, vol. 2, no. 1, February 1985.

20. Part of the reason for the decline in population of the Federal District was the former Military Government's destruction of illegal settlements (*villas miserias*), forcing their population to live outside the Federal District.

21. Derived from census statistics presented in fact sheet on Sao Paulo City, 1985, prepared by the Municipal Planning Bureau, City Hall.

22. Townroe and Keen (1984), see note 18.

23. Schteingart, Martha, chapter on Mexico City in Mattei Dogon and John D. Kasarda, *The Metropolis Era Volume 2*, Sage Publications, Beverly Hills and London, 1988, pp. 268–293.

24. Derived from figures from the 1981 census quoted in Harry W. Richardson, "Planning strategies and policies for metropolitan Lima", *Third World Planning Review*, vol. 6, no. 2, May 1984.

25. Scott, Ian, *Urban and Spatial Development in Mexico*, Johns Hopkins University Press, Baltimore and London, 1982.

26. Gugler, J., "A minimum of urbanism and a maximum of ruralism: the Cuban experience" in *International Journal of Urban and Regional Research*, vol. 4, 1980, pp. 516–535 and Jorge E. Hardoy, *Urban and Agrarian Reform in Cuba*, SIAP/IDRC, Ediciones SIAP, 1979, Buenos Aires.

27. Note that Japan is not included in the discussion and in aggregate statistics of East Asia.

28. The reader should note the reservations expressed earlier in the chapter about the validity of the population figure for Shanghai.

29. Harris, Nigel, "Some trends in the evolution of big cities", *Habitat International*, vol. 8, no. 1, 1984.

30. Bhooshan, B.S., "Mysore, Mandya and Bangalore Districts" and H.N. Misra, "Rae Bareli, Sultanpur and Pratapgarh Districts", Chapters 4 and 5 in Hardoy and Satterthwaite (eds) 1986, see note 5.

31. Buch, M.N., *Urbanization Trends in India: the emerging Regional Patterns*, mimeo; and Harris 1984, see note 29.

32. Statistics drawn from United Nations, Calcutta in the series of monographs on "Population growth and policies in mega-cities", Population Policy Paper no. 1, ST/ESA/SER.R/61, New York, 1986.

33. United Nations, *Bombay*, in the series of monographs on "Population Growth and Policies in Mega-Cities", Population Policy Paper no. 6, ST/ESA/SER.R/67, New York, 1986.

34. Kirkby, R.J.R., *Urbanization in China: Town and Country in a Developing Economy, 1949-2000 AD*, Croom Helm, London, 1985.

35. Jones, Gavin W., "Structural change and prospects for urbanization in

Asian countries", papers of the East-West Population Institute, no. 88, East–West Center, Honolulu, August 1983.

36. Jones, Gavin W., "Structural change and prospects for urbanization: South-East and East Asia with special reference to Indonesia", paper prepared for the Conference on Urban Growth and Economic Development in the Pacific Region, Tapei, quoted in Dean Forbes and Nigel Thrift, "International impacts on the urbanization process in the Asian region: a review" in Roland J. Fuchs, Gavin W. Jones and Ernesto M. Pernia (eds), *Urbanization and Urban Policies in Pacific Asia*, Westview Special Studies on East Asia, Boulder and London, 1987.

37. Jones 1983, see note 35.

38. Shand, R.T. and Ariff Hussein Mohd, "Data requirements for a large-scale irrigation project: a case study of the Kemubu irrigation project, Kelantan, Malaysia", Development Studies Centre, Australian National University, Canberra, Australia (forthcoming) quoted in Jones 1983, see note 35.

39. Jones, Gavin W., "Population growth in Java" in R.G. Garnaut and P.T. McCawley (eds), *Indonesia: Dualism, Growth and Poverty*, Research School of Pacific Studies, Australian National University, 1980, quoted in Jones 1983, see note 35.

40. Vining, Daniel R., Jr, "The growth of core regions in the Third World", *Scientific American*, vol. 252, no. 4, April 1985.

41. Vining 1985, see note 40.

42. Forbes, Dean and Nigel Thrift, "International impacts on the urbanization process in the Asian region: a review" in Roland J. Fuchs, Gavin W. Jones and Ernesto M. Pernia (eds), *Urbanization and Urban Policies in Pacific Asia*, Westview Special Studies on East Asia, Boulder and London, 1987, p. 80.

43. Vining 1985, see note 40.

44. Aradeon, Aina and Umo 1986, see note 5.

45. Derived from census data or estimates quoted in Hardoy, Jorge E. and David Satterthwaite, *Shelter: Need and Response; Housing, Land and Settlement Policies in 17 Third World Nations*, John Wiley and Sons, Chichester (UK), 1981.

46. Theunynck, Serge and Mamadou Dia, "Young (and less young) in infra-urban areas in Mauritania", *African Environment*, 14-15-16, ENDA, Dakar, 1981, pp. 206–233.

47. Bryceson, Deborah, *Urbanization and Agrarian Development in Tanzania with Special Reference to Secondary Cities*, IIED internal paper, 1983.

48. Derived from census data quoted in C.M. Kiamba, K. Maingi, N. Ng'ethe and W.M. Senga, "The role of small and intermediate cities in national development: the case study of Thika, Kenya", paper presented at an International Seminar on Small Cities and National Development, New Delhi, January 1983.

49. Vining 1985, see note 40.

50. Aradeon, Aina and Umo 1986, see note 5.

51. See Note 3 for a discussion of this.
52. For examples, see Misra, H.N., "Rae Bareli, Sultanpur and Pratapgarh Districts" in Hardoy and Satterthwaite (eds) 1986, see note 5.
53. El Agraa, Omer M.A. *et al.*, "The Gezira Region, the Sudan", B.S. Bhooshan, "Mysore, Mandya and Bangalore Districts", and Jorge E. Hardoy and David Satterthwaite, "A survey of empirical material on the factors affecting the development of small and intermediate urban centres" in Hardoy and Satterthwaite (eds) 1986, see note 5.
54. Kirkby 1985, see note 34.
55. Vining 1985, see note 40.
56. Bhooshan 1986, see note 53.
57. Renaud, Bertrand, *National Urbanization Policy in Developing Countries*, World Bank, Oxford University Press, 1981; and Jorge E. Hardoy and David Satterthwaite (1986), "Government policies and small and intermediate urban centres" in Hardoy and Satterthwaite (eds) 1986, see note 5.
58. Douglass, Mike, *The Future of Cities on the Pacific Rim*, discussion paper no. 3, Department of Urban and Regional Planning, University of Hawaii, July 1987.
59. Douglass 1987, see note 58 and Forbes and Thrift 1987, see note 42.
60. Forbes and Thrift 1987, p. 84, see note 42. See also Friedmann John and Goetz Wolff, "World city formation: an agenda for research and action", *International Journal of Urban and Regional Research*, vol. 6, no. 3, 1982.
61. Friedmann and Goetz 1982, see note 60.
62. Kirkby 1985, see note 34.
63. Statistics drawn from Di Loreto, Maria and Jorge E. Hardoy "Procesos de urbanizacion en America Latina" in *Boletin de Medio Ambiente y Urbanizacion* Year 3, no. 9, IIED-America Latina/CLACSO, Buenos Aires, 1984.
64. Brown, Lester, *In the Human Interest*, W.W. Norton and Co., New York, 1974.
65. Roy, Dilip K., "The supply of land for the slums of Calcutta" in Shlomo Angel, Raymon W. Archer, Sidhijai Tanphiphat and Emiel A. Wegelin (eds), *Land for Housing the Poor*, Select Books, Singapore, 1983.
66. United Nations, *Calcutta* in the series on "Population growth and policies in mega-cities", Population Policy Paper, ST/ESA/SER.R/61, 1985.
67. United Nations 1985, see note 66.
68. Row, Arthur T., "Metropolitan problems and prospects – a study of Calcutta", Chapter 5 in Leo Jakobson and Ved Prakash (eds), *Metropolitan Growth: Public Policy for South and South East Asia*, Sage Publications, Beverley Hills, 1974.
69. Dar es Salaam is estimated to have 4.6 million people by the year 2000 in United Nations, "Urban, rural and city population, 1950-2000 as assessed in 1978", New York, June 1980.
70. United Nations 1980, see note 69.
71. Pietro Garau has also questioned the validity of these projections and also contrasted projections made by the United Nations in 1980 and in 1982 in

Garau, Pietro, "Big Cities: myths and challenges", *Populi*, vol. 13, no. 1, 1986, pp. 57–63.

The documents from which the projections are drawn are all from the United Nations Population Division, Department of International Economic and Social Affairs, New York.

1973-5: "Trends and prospects in the populations of urban agglomerations, 1950-2000, as assessed in 1973-5", ESA/P/WP.58, 1975.

1978: "Urban, rural and city population, 1950-2000 as assessed in 1978", 1980.

1980: "Estimates and projections of urban, rural and city populations, 1950-2025: the 1980 assessment", ST/ESA/SER.R/45, 1982.

1982: "Estimates and projections of urban, rural and city populations, 1950-2025: the 1982 assessment", ST/ESA/SER.R/58, 1985.

1984-5: "The prospects of world urbanization – revised as of 1984-5", ST/ESA/SER.A/101, 1987.

72. Repetto 1986, see note 2.

73. Hall, Peter, "Cities as dinosaurs: the end of the urban age?", keynote paper presented at the Royal Town Planning Institute Annual Conference, 1983.

74. See for instance the suggestions for new classifications in T.G. McGee, "Urbanisasi or Kotadesasi – the emergence of new regions of economic interaction in Asia", Working Paper, Environment and Policy Institute, East–West Center, Honolulu, April 1987.

75. Mazingira Institute, *Urban Food and Fuel Study*, Nairobi, Kenya, 1987. Available from Mazingira Institute, PO Box 14550, Nairobi, Kenya.

76. Rakodi, Carole, "Self reliance or survival: food production in African cities with particular reference to Zambia", paper presented at Workshop on Urban Food Supplies and Peri-Urban Agriculture, Centre for African Studies, SOAS, University of London, 6 May 1988.

77. Stren, Richard E., *The Ruralization of African Cities: Learning to Live with Poverty*, Project Ecoville working paper no. 34, June 1986, p. 20. This paper is also the introduction to a long annotated bibliography in French and English entitled *Coping with Rapid Urban Growth in Africa*, Centre for Developing-Area Studies, McGill University, Montreal, Canada.

Chapter 9

This chapter draws heavily on the five case studies and review of the literature in Jorge E. Hardoy and David Satterthwaite (eds), *Small and Intermediate Urban Centres: Their Role in Regional and National Development in the Third World*, Hodder and Stoughton, London, and Westview, USA, 1986, and on the authors' work with the United Nations Centre for Human Settlements (UNCHS) in Nairobi in developing material and recommendations for the eighth Meeting of the Intergovernmental Commission on Human Settlements in Jamaica in 1985. It also draws on work for the Development Directorate of the European Economic Commission on the links between food production and secondary cities undertaken with Anthony O'Connor

(University College, London), Deborah Bryceson and Ian Simpson (University of Leeds). A shorter version of this chapter was published under the title "Small and intermediate urban centres: what role for government" in *Third World Planning Review*, vol. 10, no. 1, 1988, pp. 5–26.

1. United Nations, *The Prospects of World Urbanization (revised as of 1984-5)*, Population Studies, no. 101, ST/ESA/SER.A/101, New York, 1987.

2. See Chapter 8 for more details.

3. We chose to give data only on nations for which recent census data was available in a form which allow their disaggregation into the two categories used in the table.

For each nation which appears in Table 9.1, details are given below as to which urban centres are categorized as "large". Since the dividing line between "intermediate" and "large" urban centres is best defined only after a detailed analysis of the functioning of the urban system within each nation, and this is research that we have not had time to undertake, other researchers may disagree with our choice as to which urban centres have developed beyond "intermediate" status. But this table is intended as no more than an illustration of the high proportion of the urban population which lives outside the large and better known cities.

KENYA: Nairobi and Mombasa are classified as "large urban centres"; census data quoted in C.M. Kiamba, K. Maingi, N. Ng'ethe and W.M Senga, "The role of small and intermediate cities in national development; the case study of Thika, Kenya", UN Centre for Regional Development, Nagoya, Japan, 1983.

THE SUDAN: Only the three town capital, Khartoum-Khartoum North-Omdurman (also known as Greater Khartoum) is classified as a large urban centre in 1973. Census data quoted in Ian Simpson, *Secondary Cities and Food Security: the Sudan*, IIED London (Mimeo), 1984.

TANZANIA: Only Dar es Salaam is classified as a large urban centre. Dodoma, the new national capital which has been built for more than a decade, was not included since recent reports suggest that it has not developed into an urban centre with a sufficient concentration of economic activities to be considered a 'large urban centre'. Census data quoted in Deborah Bryceson, *Urbanization and Agrarian Development in Tanzania with Special Reference to Secondary Cities*, IIED London (mimeo), 1984.

INDIA: The 12 urban centres with a million or more inhabitants in 1981 are classified as large urban centres. Census data quoted in Rakesh Mohan, "India: coming to terms with urbanization", *Cities*, vol. 1, no. 1, August 1983, pp. 46–58.

PAKISTAN: The three largest urban centres (Karachi, Lahore and Faisalabad) are classified as large urban centres. Census statistics were quoted in United Nations Economic and Social Commission for Asia and the Pacific, *Study and Review of the Human Settlements Situation in Asia and the Pacific*, vol. 2; Country Monograph on Pakistan, Bangkok, 1986.

COLOMBIA: Only preliminary 1985 census statistics were available. Four urban centres (Bogota DE-Soacha, Medellin-Valle de Aburra, Cali-Yumbo and Barranquilla-Soledad) were classified as large urban centres. Statistics drawn from Julio Davila, Maria Errazuriz, Franciso Londono and Consuelo de Marulanda, "El Rol de las Ciudades Intermedias y Pequenas en el desarrollo nacional y regional", IIED Latin America, Buenos Aires, 1986.

CUBA: Havana is taken as the only large urban centre in Cuba in 1981. Census data from Comite Estatal de Estadisticas, *La poblacion cubana en 1953 y 1981*, Instituto de Demografia y Censos, Havana, February 1984.

ECUADOR: Both Quito (the national capital) and Guayaquil (the largest urban centre) are classified as "large urban centres". Census data quoted in Larrea, Carlos, "Crecimiento urbano y dinamica de las ciudades intermedias en el Ecuador (1950-1982)" in Carrion, Hardoy, Herzer and Garcia (compilers), *Ciudades en Conflicto*, Editorial El Conejo, Quito, 1986.

4. Mohan, Rakesh, "India: coming to terms with urbanization", *Cities*, vol. 1, no. 1, August 1983, pp. 46–58.

5. Bhooshan, B.S., "Bangalore, Mandya and Mysore Districts, Karnataka Southern India", and H.N. Misra, "Rae Bareli, Sultanpur and Pratapgarh Districts, Uttar Pradesh State, North India" in Jorge E. Hardoy and David Satterthwaite (eds), *Small and Intermediate Urban Centres: their Role in National and Regional Development in the Third World*, Hodder and Stoughton, London and Westview, USA, 1986.

6. There are many urban centres which grow rapidly not as a result of a growth in employment opportunities but because of the movement there of people fleeing wars, droughts, famines etc; see Chapter 8.

7. See for instance Mathur, Om Prakash, "The role of small cities in national development" in O.P. Mathur (ed.), *Small Cities and National Development*, United Nations Centre for Regional Development, Nagoya, Japan, 1982 and Dennis A. Rondinelli, "Intermediate cities in developing countries", *Third World Planning Review*, vol. 4, no. 4, November 1982.

8. As in note 7 and Rondinelli, Dennis A. "A comparative analysis of demographic, social and economic characteristics of intermediate cities in developing countries" in O.P. Mathur (ed.), *Small Cities and National Development*, UNCRD, Nagoya, Japan, 1982.

9. Rondinelli, Dennis A., John R. Nellis and G. Shabbir Cheema, *Decentralization in developing countries – a review of recent experience*, World Bank Staff Working Papers, no. 581, 1984, pp. 3–4.

10. UNCHS (Habitat), "Planning and management of human settlements with emphasis on small and intermediate towns and local growth points: report of the Executive Director", paper HS/C/8/3 presented to the Eighth Session of the UN Commission on Human Settlements, February 1985.

11. See the proceedings of the seminar on "Municipalities and local government in Latin America" held in June 1986 in Bogota in *Revista Mexicana de Sociologia*, Autumn 1987.

12. Bahl, Roy, Daniel Holland and Johannes Linn, *Urban Growth and Local Taxes in Less Developed Countries*, papers of the East-West Population Institute, no. 89, Hawaii, September 1983.

13. Bahl, Holland and Linn 1983, see note 12.

14. See for instance Davila, Julio D., Maria Errazuriz, Francisco Londono and Consuelo de Marulanda, *El Rol de las Ciudades Intermedias y Pequenas en el desarrollo Nacional y Regional* – Estudios de caso de Pereira-Dos Quebradas y Santa Rosa de Viterbo, Colombia, IIED Latin America, Buenos Aires, November 1986.

15. Linn, Johannes F., *Cities in the Developing World*, World Bank, Oxford University Press, 1983, pp. 57–58.

16. See energy budgets and land requirements in different farms and crop types in Gerald Leach, *Energy and Food Production*, IPC Science and Technology Press, Guildford, 1976.

17. See energy and land budgets for Chinese smallholders in Leach 1975, see note 16.

18. Collin Delavaud, Anne, *Uruguay; Medium and Small Cities*, Institute des Hautes Etudes de l'Amerique Latine, Laboratoire Associe du Centre National de la Recherche Scientifique, Paris, 1976.

19. Kutcher, Gary P. and Pasquale L. Scandizzo, *The Agricultural Economy of Northeast Brazil*, Johns Hopkins University Press, Baltimore, 1981, p. 216.

20. Kutcher and Scandizzo 1981, p. 218, see note 19.

21. See for instance Dickenson, John "Innovation for regional development in Northeast Brazil, a century of failures", *Third World Planning Review*, vol. 2, no. 1, Spring 1980; Gilbert, Alan and David E. Goodman, "Regional income disparities and economic development: a critique" in Alan Gilbert (ed.) *Development Planning and Spatial Structure*, John Wiley & Sons, Chichester, 1976, pp. 113–142.

22. Hamer, Andrew M., *Decentralized Urban Development and Industrial Location Behaviour in Sao Paulo, Brazil: A Synthesis of Research Issues and Conclusions*, discussion paper, Water Supply and Urban Development Department, the World Bank, Washington DC, 1984.

23. El Agraa, Omer M.A., Ian Haywood, Salih El Arifi, Babiker A. Abdalla, Mohamed O. El Sammani, Ali Mohamed El Hassan and Hassan Mohamed Salih, "The Gezira Region, The Sudan", in Hardoy and Satterthwaite (eds) 1986, see note 5.

24. Bale, Malcolm D. and Ernst Lutz, *Price Distortions in Agriculture and their Effects: an International Comparison*, World Bank Staff Working Paper no. 359, Washington DC, October 1979.

25. Gotsch, Carl and Gilbert Brown, *Prices, Taxes and Subsidies in Pakistan Agriculture 1960-76*, World Bank Staff Working Paper no. 387, Washington DC, April 1980.

26. World Bank, *Accelerated Development in Sub Saharan Africa*, Washington DC, 1981.

27. UNCHS (Habitat) 1985, p. 11, see note 10.

28. Tyler, William G., *The Brazilian Sectoral Incentive System and the Regional Incidence of Non Spatial Incentive Policies*, discussion paper UDD-31, Water Supply and Urban Development Department, World Bank, 1983.

29. Daly, M., *Development Planning in Nigeria*, Planning Studies Programme, University of Ibadan, quoted in Michael Olanrewaju Filani, "Nigeria: the need to modify centre-town development planning" in W. Stohr and D.R.F. Taylor (eds), *Development from Above or Below?*, John Wiley & Sons, Chichester, 1981.

30. Douglass, Mike, "Thailand: territorial dissolution and alternative regional development for the central plains" in W. Stohr and D.R.F. Taylor (eds), *Development from Above or Below?*, John Wiley & Sons, Chichester, 1981.

31. O'Connor, A.M., *Secondary Cities and Food production in Nigeria*, IIED, London, February 1984.

32. Manzanal, Mabel and Cesar A. Vapnarsky, "The development of the upper valley of Rio Negro and its periphery within the Comahue region, Argentina", in Hardoy and Satterthwaite (eds) 1986, see note 5.

33. Scott, Ian *Urban and Spatial Development in Mexico*, Johns Hopkins University Press, Baltimore and London, 1982.

34. Scott 1982, p. 111, see note 33.

35. Scott 1982, p. 118, see note 33.

36. Hamer 1984, see note 22.

37. Hardoy, Jorge E. and David Satterthwaite, "Government policies and small and intermediate urban centres" in Hardoy and Satterthwaite (eds) 1986, see note 5.

38. Analyses undertaken by IIED's Human Settlements Programme during 1988-9; these will be published during 1989/90. Findings from some preliminary analyses were published in Blitzer, Silvia, Jorge E. Hardoy and David Satterthwaite, "The sectoral and spatial distribution of multilateral aid for human settlements", *Habitat International*, vol. 7, no. 1/2, 1983.

39. UNCHS (Habitat), "Planning and management of human settlements with emphasis on small and intermediate towns and local growth points: report of the executive director", paper HS/C/8/3 presented to the Eighth Session of the UN Commission on Human Settlements, February 1985, p. 6 – drawing from information provided in Johannes F. Linn, "The costs of urbanization in developing countries", *Economic Development and Cultural Change*, vol. 30, no. 3, University of Chicago, 1982, pp. 636–637.

40. Max Neef, Manfred, *From the Outside Looking In*, Dag Hammarskjold Foundation, Uppsala, Sweden, 1982, p. 121.

41. Hardoy, Jorge E. and David Satterthwaite, "A survey of empirical material on the factors affecting the development of small and intermediate urban centres" in Hardoy and Satterthwaite (eds) 1986, see note 5.

42. Renaud, Bertrand, *National Urbanization Policy in Developing Countries*, Oxford University Press (for World Bank), Washington DC, 1981.

43. Bairoch, Paul, "Employment and large cities: problems and outlook", *International Labour Review*, vol. 121, no. 5, September-October 1982.

44. Gore, Charles, *Regions in Question: Space, Development Theory and Regional Policy*, Methuen, London and New York, 1984, p. 263. Although this book concentrates on examining the validity of theories on urban,

regional and rural development which are used to justify regional policy in the Third World, it has considerable relevance to the subject of small and intermediate urban centres. Many governments have sought to justify their programmes on small and intermediate urban centres in terms very similar to earlier justifications for regional policies.

45. Manzanal, Mabel, "Changes in Argentina's urban systems and the economic crisis", *Cities*, vol. 5, no. 3, August 1988, pp. 260–267.
46. Harris, Nigel, "Spatial planning and economic development", *Habitat International*, vol. 7, no. 5/6, 1983.
47. Bourne, L.S. and J.W. Simmons, "Introduction" to *Systems of Cities*, Oxford University Press, 1978.

Epilogue

1. Calculated from statistics in United Nations, *The Prospects of World Urbanization – Revised as of 1984-5*, ST/ESA/SER.A/101, New York, 1987.
2. Lipton, Michael, *Why Poor People Stay Poor: Urban Bias in World Development*, Temple Smith, UK, 1976 and Harvard University Press, Cambridge USA, 1977.
3. While most authors writing about development in recent years accept the idea of "urban" or "city" bias, certain authors have also questioned its validity. See, for instance, Richard Sandbrook, *The Politics of Basic Needs – Urban Aspects of Assaulting Poverty in Africa*, Heinemann, London, 1982; and Gavin Kitching, *Development and Underdevelopment in Historical Perspective*, Methuen, London, 1982.
4. Calculated from statistics in United Nations, *Estimates and Projections of Urban, Rural and City Populations 1950-2025: the 1982 Assessment*, ST/ESA/SER.R/58, New York, 1985.

Suggested Further Reading

Below are suggestions for further reading. The intention is to help readers follow up any particular point or subject covered in *Squatter Citizen*; most of the works listed below are ones from which we drew in writing the book. This list also seeks to highlight some of the outstanding works by Third World researchers and non-government organizations which do not receive the circulation they deserve in Europe, North America, Japan and Australasia. It includes works in Spanish and a few in French.

1. General City Problems

UNCHS (Habitat), *Global Report on Human Settlements 1986*, Oxford University Press, 1987. This gives a broad overview and includes details of innovative policies to address urban problems.

Case studies in Africa
Richard E. Stren and Rodney R. White (eds), *African Cities in Crisis*, Westview Press, USA, 1989; especially Mohamed O. El Sammani, Mohamed El Hadi Abu Sin, M. Talha, B.M. El Hassan and Ian Haywood, "Management problems of Greater Khartoum", pp. 246–75; Saitiel Kulaba, "Local government and the management of urban services in Tanzania", pp. 203–45; Kankonde Mbuyi, "Kinshasa: problems of land management, infrastructure and food supply", pp. 148–75; and Thiecouta Ngom, "Appropriate standards for infrastructure in Dakar", pp. 176–202.

Latin America
Perhaps the best coverage of city problems comes from Latin American journals which are listed later (see p. 367). See also the following:
Pensamiento Iberoamericano – Revista de Economia Politica on "El reto de las metropolis", no. 7, January–June 1985, available from ICI, Avenida de los Reyes Catolicos 4, Madrid 28040, Spain.
Kowarick L. and P. Jacobi, "Economic development, urbanization and environment: the case of Sao Paulo", Project Ecoville Working Paper no. 20, 1985; available from Project Ecoville, Institute of Environmental Studies, University of Toronto, Toronto, Ontario, Canada M5S 1A4, Can$5 (there are also other relevant papers in this working paper series;

write to this same address for a list of these).

Roberts, Bryan, *Cities of Peasants – Explorations in Urban Analysis*, Edward Arnold, London, 1978.

Faria, Vilmar Evangelista, chapter on Sao Paulo; and Martha Schteingart, chapter on Mexico City, in Mattei Dogon and John D. Casada (eds), *The Metropolis Era Volume 2*, Sage Publications, Beverly Hills, London and New Delhi, 1988.

Asia

Angel, Shlomo, Raymon W. Archer, Sidhijai Tanphiphat and Emiel A. Wegelin (eds) *Land for Housing the Poor*, Select Books, Singapore, 1983. Available from Select Books, 03-15, Tanglin Shopping Centre, 19, Tanglin Road, Singapore 1024, 556 pages, US$18 paperback.

Sahrin, Mahdu (ed.), *Policies Towards Urban Slums*, ESCAP, Bangkok, 1980; especially: S.K. Das, "Bombay", pp. 101–14; William J. Keyes, "Metro Manila – the Philippines", pp. 44–61; and M.J. Rodell, "Colombo, Sri Lanka", pp. 22–43. For a copy, write to Housing, Building and Planning Section, ESCAP, Rajadamnern Avenue, Bangkok 2, Thailand.

The series of papers from the United Nations Population Division called *Population Growth and Policies in Mega-Cities* contain basic information on Demographic Characteristics, the Economy, Decentralization and Location, Issues and Sectors, Resources and Management and Conclusions. To date, papers have been published in Calcutta, Seoul, Manila, Bombay, Dhaka, Karachi, Delhi, Seoul, Madras and Bangkok, and more are planned. To obtain these, write to Dr Ellen Brennan, Population Division, Dept of Economic and Social Affairs, Room DC II–1938, United Nations, New York, NY 10017, USA. They are free, as long as stocks last.

2. Housing Conditions in Cities

Most of the publications in section 1 above also describe housing conditions – especially chapters in Stren and White (eds), Angel *et al.* (eds) and Sahrin (ed.). See also the following.

Andreasen, Jørgen, *Rented Rooms and Rural Relations: Housing in Thika, Kenya, 1965-1985*, Royal Danish Academy of Fine Arts, 8 Peder Skramsgade, DK 1054 Copenhagen K, Denmark.

Connolly, Priscilla, "Uncontrolled settlements and selfbuild: what kind of solution? The Mexico City Case" and other chapters in Peter Ward (ed.), *Self Help Housing: A Critique*, Mansell, London, 1982, pp. 141–74.

Curuchet, Mirina, *Vivienda y participacion en Nicaragua Sandinista*, Facultad de Arquitectira u Urbanismo de la Universidad Nacional de Cordoba, 1987. Write to the above Faculty at Universidad Nacional de Cordoba, Av. Velez Sarsfield 264, 5000-Cordoba, Argentina.

Davila, Julio D., *Shelter, Poverty and African Revolutionary Socialism – Human Settlements in Guinea Bissau*, IIED Technical Report, 1987, available from IIED, 3 Endsleigh Street, London WC1H 0DD, UK, £6.50 (£4.50 Third World).

El Agraa, Omer M.A., Adil M. Ahmad, Ian Haywood and O.M. El Kheir, *Popular Settlements in Greater Khartoum*, Sudanese Group for Assessment of Human Settlements, Khartoum, the Sudan, 1985; and El Agraa, Omer M.A. and M.Y. Shaddad, *Housing Rentals in the Sudanese Capital*, Sudanese Group for Assessment of Human Settlements, Khartoum University Press, 1988. Write to SGAHS, Dept of Architecture, University of Khartoum, PO Box 321, Khartoum, the Sudan.

Gilbert, Alan and Peter M. Ward, *Housing, the State and the Poor – Policy and Practice in Three Latin American Cities*, Cambridge University Press, 1985.

Sanchez Leon, Abelardo, R. Guerrero, J. Calderon and L. Olivera *Tugurizacion en Lima Metropolitana*, Ediciones DESCO, Lima, 1979. Write to DESCO, Av. Salaverry 1945, Lima 14, Peru.

Stein, Alfredo, "The Tugurios of San Salvador: a place to live, work and struggle" and other papers in special issue of the journal *Environment and Urbanization* on "Beyond the stereotype of slums: how poorer people find shelter in Third World cities" – available from IIED, 3 Endsleigh Street, London WC1H 0DD, UK, £4 for orders from Latin America, Asia and Africa, £7 elsewhere.

See also the special issue of *Revue Tiers Monde*, vol. 29, no. 116, October-December 1988 which is on "Le logement des pauvres dans les grandes villes du Tiers Monde".

3. The Illegal City

Case studies of illegal settlements

Aina, Tade Akin, *Health, Habitat and Underdevelopment – the Case of a Low Income Settlement in Metropolitan Lagos*, IIED Technical Report, London, 1989. Available from Human Settlements Programme, IIED, 3 Endsleigh Street, London WC1H 0DD, UK, £4.50 orders from Latin America, Asia and Africa; £6.50 from elsewhere.

Amis, Philip, "Squatters or tenants: the commercialization of unauthorized housing in Nairobi", *World Development*, vol. 12, no. 1, 1984.

Moser, Caroline, "A home of one's own: squatter housing strategies in Guayaquil, Ecuador", in Alan Gilbert, Jorge E. Hardoy and Ronaldo Ramirez (eds) *Urbanization in Contemporary Latin America*, John Wiley & Sons, Chichester, 1982.

Schlyter, Ann and Thomas Schlyter, *George – the Development of a Squatter Settlement in Lusaka, Zambia*, The Swedish Council for Building Research, Sankt Goransgatan 66, S-112 30 Stockholm, Sweden, 1980.

Sobreira de Moura, Alexandrina, "Brasilia Teimosa – the organization of a low income settlement in Recife, Brazil", *Development Dialogue*, no. 1, 1987, pp. 152–69.

van der Linden, Jan, "Squatting by organized invasion – a new reply to a failing housing policy?", *Third World Planning Review*, vol. 4, no. 4, November 1982.

See also special issue of *Medio Ambiente y Urbanizacion* on "Habitat Popular en America Latina", Year 3, no. 9, December 1984. Available for US$5.00 from IIED-AL, Piso 6, Cuerpo A, Corrientes 2835, (1193) Buenos Aires, Argentina.

Land markets and other aspects

Cohen, Monique, *The Urban Street Foods Trade: Implications for Policy*, Equity Policy Center, Washington DC, 1984. Write to EPC, 2001 S Street NW, Suite 420, Washington DC 20009, USA.

Durand-Lasserve, Alain, *L'exclusion des pauvres dans les villes de Tiers-Monde*, L'Harmattan, Paris, 1986 – write to Editions L'Harmattan, 5-7, rue l'Ecole Polytechnique, 75005 Paris, France.

Marris, Peter, "The meaning of slums and patterns of change", *International Journal of Urban and Regional Research*, vol. 3, no. 3, 1979.

McAuslan, Patrick, *Urban Land and Shelter for the Poor*, Earthscan Publications, London (forthcoming). This is an expanded and updated version of the book published under the same title in 1984. This is also available in Spanish under the title *Tierra Urbana y Vivienda – Las Opciones de los Pobres* from Human Settlements Programme, IIED, 3 Endsleigh Street, London WC1H 0DD, UK, £4.50; and in French as *Les Mal Loges du Tiers Monde*, L'Harmattan/Earthscan, Paris, 1986 from Editions L'Harmattan, 5-7, rue l'Ecole Polytechnique, 75005 Paris, France.

Payne, Geoffrey K., *Informal Housing and Land Sub-divisions in Third World Cities – A Review of the Literature*, CENDEP, Oxford Polytechnic, Oxford OX3 0BP, £9.50.

Perez Perdomo, Rogelio and Pedro Nicken (with the assistance of Elizabeth Fassano and Marcos Vilera), "The law and home ownership in the barrios of Caracas", in Alan Gilbert, Jorge E. Hardoy and Ronaldo Ramirez (eds), *Urbanization in Contemporary Latin America*, John Wiley & Sons, Chichester, 1982.

Soliman, Mounir, "Informal land acquisition and the urban poor in Alexandria", *Third World Planning Review*, vol. 9, no. 1, February 1987, pp. 21–40.

See also various chapters in Angel *et al.* (eds), *Land for Housing the Poor* listed in section 1, especially Shlomo Angel, "Land tenure for the urban poor", pp. 110–43; Paul Baross, "The articulation of land supply for popular settlements in Third World cities", pp. 180–210; Dilip Roy, "The supply of land for the slums in Calcutta", pp. 98–109; and Mahdu Sahrin, "The rich, the poor and the land question", pp. 237–53.

Also a series of *Urban Research Working Papers* published by the Department of Sociology of Development/Institute of Cultural Anthropology, Free University, PO Box 7161, 1007 MC Amsterdam, the Netherlands which include many (English language) case studies of illegal settlements, their economies, the social structures, tenant markets and other aspects; these cost between $2.50 and $4.00 per paper.

4. Housing and Evictions

Asian Coalition for Housing Rights (ACHR), "Evictions in Seoul, South Korea", *Environment and Urbanization*, vol. 1, no. 1, IIED, April 1989. Offprints available from ACHR, PO Box 24-74, Klongchan, Bangkapi, Bangkok 10240, Thailand or from IIED, 3 Endsleigh Street, London WC1H 0DD, UK.

Boonyabancha, Somsook, "The causes and effects of slum eviction in Bangkok", in Shlomo Angel, Raymon W. Archer, Sidhijai Tanphiphat and Emiel A. Wegelin (eds), *Land for Housing the Poor*, Select Publications, Singapore, 1983, pp. 254–83.

Jeong Ku, Paul and J.V. Daly, "Three villages near Seoul, Korea", *SELAVIP Newsletter* (Latin American and Asian Low Income Housing Service), Japan, September, 1985.

Portes, Alejandro, "Housing policy, urban poverty and the state: the favelas of Rio de Janeiro", *Latin American Research Review*, no. 14, Summer 1979, pp. 3–24; and in Spanish in *Revista Interamericana de Planificacion*, no. 13, March 1979, pp. 103–24.

Ruland, Jurgen, "Squatter relocation in the Philippines: the case of Metro Manila", Institute of Philippine Culture, Ateneo de Manila University July, 1982.

Schutz, Eike, "Para festejar el dia – actualmente son desaslojados miles de familias en Santo Domingo", *Medio Ambiente y Urbanizacion* Year 7, no. 25, December 1988. Available from IIED-AL, Piso 6, Cuerpo A, Corrientes 2835, (1193) Buenos Aires, Argentina.

Urban Poor Institute, *Information Packet on the Urban Poor of Korea*, Seoul, South Korea, 1988, available from ACHR, see above.

5. Health Problems of Poorer Groups and Links with their Housing

Aina, Tade Akin, 1989, see under section 3.

Basta, Samir S., "Nutrition and health in low income urban areas of the Third World", *Ecology of Food and Nutrition*, vol. 6, 1977, pp. 113–24.

Bisharat, Leila and Magdy Tewfig, "Housing the poor in Amman – can upgrading improve health?", *Third World Planning Review*, no. 7 (1), 1985.

Hardoy, Jorge E. and David Satterthwaite, "Housing and health in the Third World – do architects and planners have a role?", *Cities*, vol. 4, no. 3, Butterworth Press, August 1987; offprints available from IIED, 3 Endsleigh Street, London WC1H 0DD, UK.

Harpham, Trudy, Patrick Vaughan and Susan Rifkin, *Health and the Urban Poor in Developing Countries; a Review and Selected Annotated Bibliography*, 1985, EPC Publications, no. 5, London School of Hygiene and Tropical Medicine, Keppel Street, London WC1E 7HT.

Rosenfield, P.L., C.G. Widstrand and A.P. Ruderman, "How tropical diseases impede social and economic development of rural communities: a research agenda", *Rural Africana* (8-9), Fall-Winter 1980.

UNICEF, *Improving Environment for Child Health and Survival*, Urban Examples, no. 15, UNICEF New York, 1988. Write to Urban Section, Programme Division, UNICEF HQ Rm H-11-F, 3 United Nations Plaza, New York, NY 10017, USA for a free copy.

World Health Organization, *Urbanization and its Implications for Child Health: Potential for Action*, RUD Programme, Division of Environmental Health, Geneva, 1989. Available from Publications Division, WHO, 1211 Geneva 27, Switzerland or from WHO appointed booksellers (which exist in many Third World nations); price 18 Swiss francs (First World orders); 9 Swiss francs (Third World).

A quarterly newsletter *RUD Network* is published by the World Health Organization's programme on "Environmental health in rural and urban development in housing". This includes articles and gives details of new projects and publications in this field. Available free, write to Robert Novick at the RUD Programme, Division of Environmental Health, WHO, 1211 Geneva 27, Switzerland.

ENDA-Third World have a series of publications on Environment and Health. One of the editions of their bulletin *Lettre Urbaine* was on habitat and health (no. 15, 1988). Write to ENDA, BP 3370, Dakar, Senegal for details.

Case studies

Sandy Cairncross *et al.* (eds), *The Poor Die Young: Housing and Health in the Urban Third World*, Earthscan Publications, London. Available from 3 Endsleigh Street, London WC1H 0DD, forthcoming. See the following chapters:

Beatriz Cuenya, H. Almada, H.D. Armus, J. Castells, M. di Loreto and S. Penalva "Housing and health problems in Buenos Aires – the case of Barrio San Martin"; Harikesh Misra, "Housing and health problems in three squatter settlements in Allahabad, India"; and Tade Akin Aina, "Housing and health problems in Olalaye-Iproni Village, Lagos, Nigeria".

See also under section 9.

6. NGOs and Housing

Cabannes, Yves, "Human settlements – an overview", and case studies in Czech Conroy and Miles Litvinoff (eds), *The Greening of Aid*, Earthscan Publications, London, 1988.

Hardoy, Jorge E. and David Satterthwaite, "Laying the foundations: NGOs help to house Latin America's poor", *Development Forum*, October (part 1) and November (part 2), New York, 1987.

Turner, Bertha (ed.), *Building Community: A Third World Case Book*, Habitat International Coalition, 1988, available from BCB, PO Box

28, Dumfries DG2 ONS, Scotland, £10 for Third World orders; £14 for others.

UNCHS (Habitat), *Shelter for the Homeless: the Role of Non Governmental Organizations*, Nairobi, 1987 – available from Publications Division, UNCHS, PO Box 30030, Nairobi, Kenya.

UNCHS (Habitat), *Community Based Finance Institutions*, Nairobi, Kenya, HS/44/84/E, 1984. Available from Publications Division, see above.

Latin America

See certain issues of the quarterly journal *Medio Ambiente y Urbanizacion* – "Los asentamientos populares y el papel de los ONGs en America Latina", special issue of case studies, year 5, no. 18, 1987; and "Los asentamientos populares y el papel de los ONGs en America Latina", special supplement to issue no. 16, September 1986. Available from IIED-AL, Piso 6, Cuerpo A, Corrientes 2835, (1193) Buenos Aires, Argentina.

Africa

See special dossier of case studies compiled by Mazingira Institute, PO Box 14550, Nairobi, Kenya.

More information on case studies

Anzorena, E.J., "SPARC – society for promotion of area resource centres", *SELAVIP Newsletter* (Latin American and Asian Low Income Housing Service), March 1988.

Harth Deneke, A. and M. Silva, "Mutual help and progressive housing development: for what purpose? Notes on the Salvadorean experience", in Peter Ward (ed.), *Self Help Housing: A Critique*, Mansell, London, 1982.

Hasan, Arif, "Orangi Pilot Project: a low cost sewer system by low income Pakistanis"; and Harrington Jere, Marijke Vandersuypen Muyaba and Francis Ndilila, "NGO promotes community development", in Bertha Turner (ed.), see above.

7. Historical/Colonial Case Studies

Alexander, Linda, "European planning ideology in Tanzania", *Habitat International*, vol. 7, no. 1/2, 1983, pp. 17–36.

Furedy, Christine, "Whose responsibility? Dilemmas of Calcutta's bustee policy in the nineteenth century", *South Asia*, vol. 5, no. 2, 1982, pp. 24–46.

Juppenlatz, Morris, *Cities in Transformation – The Urban Squatter Problem of the Developing World*, University of Queensland Press, 1970.

King, Anthony D., *Colonial Urban Development: Culture, Social Power and Environment*, Routledge and Kegan Paul, 1976.

Rakodi, Carole, "Colonial urban policy and planning in Northern Rhodesia and its legacy", *Third World Planning Review*, vol. 8, no. 3, August 1986, pp. 193–217.

8. New Approaches to Understanding and Addressing Urban Problems

Abiodun, Y., William Alonso, Donatien Bihute, Priscilla Connolly, S.K. Das, Jorge Hardoy, Louis Menezes, Caroline Moser, Ingrid Munro and David Satterthwaite, *Rethinking the Third World City*, the Swedish Ministry of Housing, 1987. Available from Human Settlements Programme, IIED, 3 Endsleigh Street, London WC1H 0DD. Also published in Spanish as *Repensando la Ciudad del Tercer Mundo*, IIED-AL/Ediciones GEL, available from IIED-AL, Piso 6, Cuerpo A, Corrientes 2835, 1193 Buenos Aires, Argentina, $8.00.

Angel, Shlomo and Somsook Boonyabancha, "Land sharing as an alternative to eviction: the Bangkok experience", *Third World Planning Review*, vol. 10, no. 2, May 1988.

Anzorena, E.J., "The incremental development scheme of Hyderabad", *SELAVIP Newsletter* (Latin American and Asian Low Income Housing Service), Tokyo, March, 1988.

Cain, Allan, "Bairro upgrading in Luanda's musseques", Development Workshop, Toronto and Luanda, 1986. Write to Development Workshop, Box 133, 238 Davenport Road, Toronto, Ontario, Canada M5R 1J6.

Maskrey, Andrew, "Villa El Salvador – low income Peruvians build a new township", in Bertha Turner (ed.) *Building Community: A Third World Case Book*, Habitat International Coalition, 1988. Available from BCB, PO Box 28, Dumfries DG2 0NS, Scotland, £10 for Third World orders; £14 for others.

McCallum, Douglas and Stan Benjamin, "Low income urban housing in the Third World: broadening the economic perspective", *Urban Studies*, no. 22, 1985, pp. 277–87.

Morse, Richard and Jorge E. Hardoy (compilers), *Repensando la ciudad de America Latina*, Ediciones GEL, available from IIED-AL, Piso 6, Cuerpo A, Corrientes 2835, 1193 Buenos Aires, Argentina, $15.00.

Moser, Caroline O.N. "Women, human settlements and housing: a conceptual framework for analysis and policy-making"; and Caroline O.N. Moser and Linda Peake, "Postscript: what hope for the future?", in Moser and Peake (eds), *Women, Housing and Human Settlements*, Tavistock Publications, London and New York, 1987, pp. 195–201. This book also contains seven case studies, each illustrating aspects of "gender-blindness". Available from International Thompson Publishing Services, North Way, Andover, Hants SP10 5BE, (UK) £12.05 (including postage and packing).

Moser, Caroline O.N., "Community participation in urban projects in the Third World", *Progress in Planning*, vol. 32, no. 2, Pergamon Press, Oxford, 1989.

Sadashiva, S.S., "Financial management of the national sites and services and squatter upgrading project in Tanzania" and other papers presented at the International Conference on the Management of Sites and Services and Squatter Upgraded Housing Areas, edited by Pat Crooke, available from Centre for Housing Studies, PO Box 35124, Dar es Salaam, Tanzania.

Silas, Johan and Eddy Indrayana, "Kampung Banyu Urip", in Bertha Turner (ed.) *Building Community: A Third World Case Book*, Habitat International Coalition, 1988, available from BCB, PO Box 28, Dumfries DG2 0NS, Scotland, £10 for Third World orders; £14 for others.

UNCHS (Habitat), *Rehabilitation of Inner City Areas: Feasible Strategies* – Bombay (Building Repair and Reconstruction) and Bangkok (land sharing), Nairobi, Kenya, 1986, available from Publications Division, UNCHS, PO Box 30030, Nairobi, Kenya.

UNCHS (Habitat), *Upgrading of Inner City Slums*, Nairobi, Kenya, 1984 (available from same address as above).

9. Water and Sanitation

Cairncross, Sandy and Richard Feachem, *Environmental Health Engineering in the Tropics: an Introductory Text*, John Wiley & Sons, Chichester, 1983.

Kalbermatten, John M., DeAnne S. Julius and Charles Gunnerson, *Appropriate Technology for Water Supply and Sanitation: a Summary of Technical and Economic Options*, World Bank, 1981. Available from Publications Division, the World Bank, 1818 H Street NW, Washington DC, 20433, USA or regional offices of the World Bank. Since the World Bank, the United Nations Development Programme and the World Health Organization have collaborated in reviewing a very large range of different options for water supply, sanitation and garbage disposal – and there are over 50 different publications in this area – ask for a complete publication list from this same address.

There are many relevant publications produced by *UNCHS (Habitat)* in Nairobi which are free; many are available in French and Spanish as well as English. For a list, write to Publications Division, UNCHS (Habitat), PO Box 30030, Nairobi, Kenya. Among those of special interest are *Delivery of Basic Infrastructure to Low Income Settlements: Issues and Options*, HS/101/86/E, 1986; and *A Review of Technologies for the Provision of Basic Infrastructure in Low Income Settlements*, HS/40/84/E, 1984.

10. Environment

Problems in cities

Environment and Urbanization, vol. 1, no. 1, has papers on environmental problems in Indian cities, Bogota, Alexandria, Bangkok, Manila, Mexico City, Port Harcourt and Montevideo. This is available from Human Settlements Programme, IIED, 3 Endsleigh Street, London WC1H 0DD, £4 for orders from Latin America, Asia and Africa; £7 for orders from elsewhere.

For a broad overview of environmental problems, see James A. Lee, *The Environment, Public Health and Human Ecology* published for the World Bank by Johns Hopkins University Press, Baltimore and London, 1985.

India
See the two citizens reports on *The State of India's Environment* produced
by the Centre for Science and Environment. Each report has separate
sections on Land, Water, Forests, Dams, Atmosphere, Habitat, People, Health, Energy, and Resources. The first Report also has sections on Wildlife and Government while the second has additional sections on Living Resources, Agents of Change (which includes Government, NGOs and Legislation) and the Politics of Environment. The
first report is some 200,000 words; the second, close to 400,000.
There is very little overlap between the two. To order these reports,
write to CSE, 807 Vishal Bhawan, 95 Nehru Place, New Delhi 11
00 19, India; send international money order or bankers draft made
out to CSE US$21 for either of the Reports ($25 if you want it sent
airmail).

China
See Smil, Vaclav, *The Bad Earth: Environmental Degradation in China*, M.E.
Sharpe, New York and Zed Press, London, 1984.

Malaysia
See Consumers' Association of Penang, *Development and the Environmental
Crisis: a Malaysian Case*, 1982. Available from CAP, 87 Jalan Canton-
ment, Pulau Penang 10250, Malaysia.
Environment, Development, Natural Resource Crisis in Asia and the Pacific
Meenakshi Raman, $16 surface mail, $30 airmail, Sahabet Alam.
Different editions of the *State of the Malaysian Environment* report and other
publications produced by Sahabat Alam Malaysia, 43 Salween Road,
10050 Pulau Pinang, Malaysia.

Three international newsletters are also worth noting:

Environmental News Digest, published four times a year by Sahabat Alam
Malaysia. Annual subscription is $25 surface mail, $30 airmail to address
given above.
Consumer Currents published 10 times a year by the International Organiza-
tion of Consumer Unions; write to IOCU, PO Box 1045, 10830 Penang,
Malaysia. One-year subscription US$10 for non profit groups and individ-
uals in the Third World, $20 for non-profit groups and individuals in the
First World and $50 for others.
Industry and Environment, Paris office of the United Nations Environment
Programme published four times a year. Available from the Industry and
Environment Office, UNEP, Tour Mirabeau, 39-43 quai André-Citroën,
75739 Paris Cedex 15, France.

Other environmental issues
Anandalingam, G. and Mark Westfall, "Hazardous waste generation and

disposal: options for developing countries", *Natural Resources*, vol. 11, no. 1, February 1987, pp. 37–47.

Castleman, B.I., "The export of hazardous factories to developing countries", *International Journal of Health Sciences*, vol. 9, no. 4, 1979, pp. 569–97.

Douglass, Mike, "The environmental sustainability of development – coordination, incentives and political will in land use planning for the Jakarta Metropolis", *Third World Planning Review* (forthcoming), 1989.

Leonard, H. Jeffrey and David Morell, "Emergence of environmental concern in developing countries: a political perspective", *Stanford Journal of International Law*, vol. 17, no. 2, 1981, pp. 281–313.

Leonard, H. Jeffrey, *Confronting Industrial Pollution in Rapidly Industrializing Countries – Myths, Pitfalls and Opportunities*, Conservation Foundation, 1250 Twenty-Fourth Street NW, Washington DC 20037, USA, October 1984.

The Regional Seas Programme of the United Nations Environmental Programme publish *The Siren*, a free quarterly newsletter. This often contains detailed information about environmental problems in rivers, estuaries and coastal waters caused by sewage and industrial effluents from cities. This is available from OCA/PAC, UNEP, PO Box 30552, Nairobi, Kenya.

11. Urban Change

Douglass, Mike, "The future of cities on the Pacific Rim", Discussion Paper no. 3, Department of Urban and Regional Planning (University of Hawaii, Honolulu 96848, USA), July 1987.

Harris, Nigel, "Some trends in the evolution of big cities: studies of the USA and India", *Habitat International*, vol. 8, no. 1, 1984, pp. 7–28.

Kirkby, Richard, *Urbanization in China: Town and Country in a Developing Economy 1949–2000 AD*, Croom Helm, London, 1985.

Renaud, Bertrand, *National Urbanization Policies in Developing Countries*, Oxford University Press, 1981.

Vining Jr, Daniel R., "The growth of core regions in the Third World", *Scientific American*, vol. 252, no. 4, 1985.

12. Local Government

Herzer, Hilda and Pedro Pirez, *Gobierno de la ciudad y crisis en la Argentina*, Ediciones GEL, available from IIED-AL, Piso 6, Cuerpo A, Corrientes 2835, 1193 Buenos Aires, Argentina, $15.00.

Rondinelli, Dennis A., John R. Nellis and Shabbir G. Cheema, *Decentralization in Developing Countries – A Review of Recent Experiences*, World Bank Staff Working Paper No. 581 Washington DC, 1984, and other working papers on local government. Write to Publications Division, the World Bank, 1818 H Street NW, Washington DC 20433, USA.

Stohr, Walter B. and D.R.F. Taylor, "Introduction", and other chapters in *Development from Above or Below*, John Wiley & Sons, Chichester, 1981.

Stren, Richard E., "Urban local government", and "Administration of urban services", Chapters 2 and 3 in Richard E. Stren and Rodney R. White (eds), *African Cities in Crisis*, Westview Press, USA, 1989.

13. Small and Intermediate Urban Centres

Carrion, Diego *et al.*, *Ciudades en Conflicto – poder local, participacion popular y planificacion en las ciudades intermedias de America Latina*, Edial El Conejo, available from CIUDAD, Casilla Postal 8311, Quito, Ecuador.

An annotated bibliography by Silvia Blitzer *et al.*, *Outside the Large Cities*, contains long annotations of works and a guide to the literature on this subject. Available from IIED's Human Settlements Programme, 3 Endsleigh Street, London WC1H 0DD, UK, £6.50 orders from Latin America, Africa and Asia, £9.50 orders from elsewhere.

UNCHS (Habitat), *The Role of Small and Intermediate Settlements in National Development*, Nairobi, 1985, HS/OP/85-19, available free from the Publications Division, UNCHS, PO Box 30030, Nairobi, Kenya.

For case studies of how urban centres develop within regions, see the following chapters in Jorge E. Hardoy and David Satterthwaite (eds), *Small and Intermediate Urban Centres; their role in Regional and and National Development in the Third World*, Hodder and Stoughton, UK, and Westview, USA, £15, available from IIED, 3 Endsleigh Street, London WC1H 0DD.

El Agraa, Omer M.A., Ian Haywood, Salih El Arifi, Babiker A. Abdalla, Mohamed O. El Sammani, Ali Mohamed El Hassan, Hassan Mohamed Salih. "The Gezira Region: the Sudan".

Manzanal, Mabel and Cesar Vapnarsky, "The development of the Upper Valley of Rio Negro and its periphery within the Comahue Region, Argentina".

Misra, H.N., "Rae Bareli, Sultanpur and Pratapgarh Districts, Uttar Pradesh, North India".

Aradeon, David, Tade Akin Aina and Joe Umo, "South West Nigeria".

Bhooshan, B.S., "Bangalore, Mandya and Mysore Districts, Karnataka, India".

Case studies in Africa
See many of the papers in Aidan Southall (ed.), *Small Urban Centres in Rural Development in Africa*, African Studies Program, University of Wisconsin-Madison, 1979. Write to African Studies Program, University of Wisconsin, Madison, Wisconsin 53706, USA.

14. General Works and Key Third World Journals

Sandbrook, Richard, *The Politics of Basic Needs: Urban Aspects of Assaulting Poverty in Africa*, Heinemann, London, 1982.
Wisner, Ben, *Power and Need in Africa: Basic Human Needs and Development Policies*, Earthscan Publications, London, 1988.

Latin America
There are many good journals dealing with issues like the ones covered in this book. They include:

Cahiers de l'Amerique Latine, Institute des Hautes Etudes de l'Amerique Latine, Université de la Sorbonne Nouvelle, Paris.
Estudios Demograficos y Urbanos, El Colegio de Mexico, Departmento de Publicaciones, Camino al Ajusco, no. 20, CP 10740, Mexico DF, Mexico.
Estudios Sociales Centroamericanos, Secretaria General del CSUCA, Apartado Postal 37, Ciudad Universitaria Rodruigo Facio, San Jose, Costa Rica.
Hechos Urbanos, SUR, Casilla 323-V, Correo 21, Santiago de Chile.
Revista Foro, Foro Nacional por Colombia, AA 10141, Bogota, Colombia.
Ambiente y Desarrollo, CIPMA, Casilla 16362, Santiago, Chile.
El Trimestre Economico, Fondo de Cultura Economica, Av Universidad 975, Mexico 12 DF, Mexico.
Revista Paraguaya de Sociologia, Centre Paraguayo de Estudios Sociologicos, Elijio Ayala 973, Asuncion, Paraguay.
Revista Mexicana de Sociologia, Institute of Social Research of the University of Mexico, Torre de Humanidades no. 2, 7 Piso, Ciudad Universitaria, Mexico 20 DF, Mexico.
Estudios Urbanos y Regionales (EURE), CIDU (Comite Interdisciplinario de Desarrollo Urbano), Universidad Catolica de Chile, Santiago, Chile.
Medio Ambiente y Urbanizacion, IIED-America Latina, Piso 6, Cuerpo A, Corrientes 2835, (1193) Buenos Aires, Argentina.

Asia and Africa

We know far fewer journals dealing with urban issues published in Asia and Africa.

Settlements Information Network Africa, newsletter, comes out three times a year and has news from its many members, of conferences, publications, and courses. Also some case studies. Write to Mazingira Institute, PO Box 14550, Nairobi, Kenya, $25 per year but free to members in Africa who do not have access to foreign exchange.
ENDA-Tiers Monde (Environment and Development in the Third World) produce a series of publications from its office in Dakar, Senegal, including the periodical *African Environment* published in English and French. It also publishes *Lettre Urbaine* in collaboration with the Chilean NGO

SUR (which is also published in Spanish) which is a bulletin which reports on action research and human settlements management in Asia, Africa and Latin America. Write to ENDA, BP 3370, Dakar, Senegal for the French version and SUR, Casilla 323-V, Correo 21, Santiago, Chile for the Spanish version.

African Urban Quarterly, c/o Dr Obudho, PO Box 74165, Nairobi, Kenya.

Lokayan Bulletin produced by the NGO of the same name (which means literally "dialogue with the people") includes many articles and discussions relating to housing and housing rights. Write to Lokayan, 13 Alipur Road, Delhi 110 054, India.

Index

acid rain, 212
Abidjan, 242
Ado Ekiti, 250
Africa
  colonial legacy in, 19–22, 243
  illegal settlements, government attitude to, 91–2
  ruralization, 256–7
  slum clearance, 42
  tenement development, 73
  urban centres, 264–5, 266–7
    change, 242–5
agricultural
  development, urban development and, 127, 274–82
  land loss, 208–9
aid agencies
  conservatism and, 61
  role, 107, 144, 298, 306–7, 312
air pollution, 179–80, 194–9, 201–3, 211–12, 293
  control, 214–15
airports
  land ownership by, 102
  settlements near, 200, 203–4
Alexandria
  illegal settlements, 25, 26
  public housing, 108
  water pollution, 192
Allahabad
  health problems, 155
  squatter settlements, 100
Ankara, squatter settlements in, 83, 89
apartheid, 244
  in colonial era, 20
Aquino, Corazon, 122
Argentina
  agricultural and urban development links, 275–6
  government change in attitude in, 125–6
  slum clearance, 42
armed forces, land ownership by, 102, 202
arsenic toxicity, 182
asbestos
  manufacture, 186
  toxicity, 183
Asia
  economic changes and population movements, 247–8
  slum clearance, 42–3

  tenement development, 73–4
  urban change, 237–42
Asian Coalition for Housing Rights, 48

bagasse use, 214
Baldia, illegal settlements in, 87
Bangalore
  air pollution in, 199
  early development, 24
  rapid growth, 238, 247
Bangkok
  illegal settlements, 95
    government attitude to, 89
  inner-city population change, 78
  industry, 180, 284
  land sharing, 119–21, 124–5
  noise pollution, 200
  sanitation problems, 147–8
  slum clearance, 43, 50
  toxic waste disposal, 187
  waste collection, 161
  water problems, 147–8
    supplies, 194
Bangladesh
  land acquisition problems, 129
  public housing, 109, 110
barracos, 47
barriadas, 76
barrios, 12–15, 106
Baross, Paul, 79
Basta, S.S., 156
beach pollution, 209–10
beehive buildings, 73
Beijing population growth projections, 251
Benin, toxic waste disposal in, 187
benzene toxicity, 183
beryllium toxicity, 183
Bhopal, 181, 202
Bissau, 230
black economy, 30
Bogota
  illegal settlements, 82, 95
  river pollution, 191, 211
  sub-division development, 82, 132
  waste collection, 160
  water pollution, 191
Bolivia, sanitation in, 152
Bombay
  air pollution, 195–6
  colonial origin, 24

illegal settlements, 76, 95
inner-city population change, 78
primacy, 230
water supply, 164
squatter settlements, 83–5
loans, government-supported, 104, 123
local government
co-ordination problems, 135–6
national policies and, 57–8
policies, 54–7, 171–8, 293–4, 304
role in urban centres, 270–74
weakness, 37, 54–7
Linn, Johannes, 274
Lipton, Michael, 308
Los Angeles growth, 53
Luanda, public provision in, 115–16
low-income groups
bias against, 202–3, 212, 310
contribution to community projects, 138–9
government changing attitude to, 118
health problems, 154–7
housing availability for, 66–7, 68–71
living in polluted areas, 202–4
pollution effects on, 212
pressure on government by, 140–41
public housing availability to, 109–10
rented accommodation for, 68–9
Lusaka
colonial development, 21, 22
food production, 256
illegal settlement legalization, 119
rental, 87

Madras
colonial development, 24
water and sanitation problems, 149–50
maintenance problems in public housing, 111
Malaysia
air pollution, 198
pollution control, 217–18
water pollution, 193
malnutrition, 155, 156
Managua
primacy, 230
toxic waste disposal, 186–7
Mangin, William, 119
Manila
air pollution, 199, 203
colonial origin, 19
government change in attitude in, 122, 125
illegal settlements, 76–7, 95
infant mortality, 156
population statistics, 227–8
primacy, 230–31
slum and squatter clearance, 43, 44–6, 51
sub-division development, 132
water and sanitation problems, 149–50
maps, city planning, 39
Maputo, population growth projections in, 252
market forces, 132–6

Marrakesh, 20, 267
Matos Mar, 118
Mazingira Institute, 256
Max Neef, M., 287
McAuslan, Patrick, 35
Medellin, 160
mercury toxicity, 183, 184, 186–7
Mexico City
air pollution, 180, 196, 199, 202–3
economic policy bias serving, 284–5
housing conditions, 77
illegal settlements, 77, 82, 95
rental, 88
polluted housing sites, 159–60
population, 53, 236–7
growth projections, 251, 253
primacy, 231
public housing 106, 111–12
sanitation, 152
tenements, 72
water resources, 151, 193
migration to cities, 51–3, 62–66, 229
control of, 51
model copying, inappropriate, 22–3, 38–40, 61, 164–5
mohallas, 73
Mombasa, 244
Montevideo
population concentration, 279
population growth, 72, 233
tenements, 72
illegal settlements, 74
mortality, infant, see infant mortality
Moser, Caroline, 23
musseques, 116

Nairobi
colonial origin, 21
evictions, 42, 46
illegal settlements, 77–8
primacy, 231
landlordism, 86–7
population growth, 242, 244
population projections, 250
racial discrimination, 21
ruralization, 256
natural disasters, 203
population movements and, 226–7
Nigeria
import substitution, 284
population figures, 224
projections, 250
public housing, 107, 108, 110
slum clearance, 42, 46
tenements, 73
toxic waste import, 188
nitrogen oxides toxicity, 195
noise pollution, 199–200
non-government organizations
as intermediaries, 119, 122–3, 141, 143–5, 305
pollution and, 181, 217–18